Cracking the Emerging Markets Enigma

FINANCIAL MANAGEMENT ASSOCIATION
Survey and Synthesis Series

Asset Management: A Systematic Approach to Factor Investing
Andrew Ang

Asset Pricing and Portfolio Choice Theory
Kerry E. Back

Beyond Greed and Fear: Understanding Behavioral Finance and the Psychology of Investing
Hersh Shefrin

Beyond the Random Walk: A Guide to Stock Market Anomalies and Low-Risk Investing
Vijay Singal

Consumer Credit and the American Economy
Thomas A. Durkin, Gregory Elliehausen, Michael E. Staten, and Todd J. Zywicki

Debt Management: A Practitioner's Guide
John D. Finnerty and Douglas R. Emery

Dividend Policy: Its Impact on Firm Value
Ronald C. Lease, Kose John, Avner Kalay, Uri Loewenstein, and Oded H. Sarig

Efficient Asset Management: A Practical Guide to Stock Portfolio Optimization and Asset Allocation, 2nd Edition
Richard O. Michaud and Robert O. Michaud

Last Rights: Liquidating a Company
Dr. Ben S. Branch, Hugh M. Ray, and Robin Russell

Managing Pension and Retirement Plans: A Guide for Employers, Administrators, and Other Fiduciaries
August J. Baker, Dennis E. Logue, and Jack S. Rader

Managing Pension Plans: A Comprehensive Guide to Improving Plan Performance
Dennis E. Logue and Jack S. Rader

Mortgage Valuation Models: Embedded Options, Risk, and Uncertainty
Andrew Davidson and Alex Levin

Real Estate Investment Trusts: Structure, Performance, and Investment Opportunities
Su Han Chan, John Erickson, and Ko Wang

Real Options: Managing Strategic Investment in an Uncertain World
Martha Amram and Nalin Kulatilaka

Real Options in Theory and Practice
Graeme Guthrie

Slapped by the Invisible Hand: The Panic of 2007
Gary B. Gorton

Survey Research in Corporate Finance: Bridging the Gap between Theory and Practice
H. Kent Baker, J. Clay Singleton, and E. Theodore Veit

The Financial Crisis of Our Time
Robert W. Kolb

The Search for Value: Measuring the Company's Cost of Capital
Michael C. Ehrhardt

Too Much Is Not Enough: Incentives in Executive Compensation
Robert W. Kolb

Trading and Exchanges: Market Microstructure for Practitioners
Larry Harris

Truth in Lending: Theory, History, and a Way Forward
Thomas A. Durkin and Gregory Elliehausen

Value Based Management with Corporate Social Responsibility, 2nd Edition
John D. Martin, J. William Petty, and James S. Wallace

Valuing the Closely Held Firm
Michael S. Long and Thomas A. Bryant

Working Capital Management
Lorenzo Preve and Virginia Sarria-Allende

Cracking the Emerging Markets Enigma

G. Andrew Karolyi

OXFORD
UNIVERSITY PRESS

OXFORD

UNIVERSITY PRESS

Oxford University Press is a department of the University of
Oxford. It furthers the University's objective of excellence in research,
scholarship, and education by publishing worldwide.

Oxford   New York
Auckland   Cape Town   Dar es Salaam   Hong Kong   Karachi
Kuala Lumpur   Madrid   Melbourne   Mexico City   Nairobi
New Delhi   Shanghai   Taipei   Toronto

With offices in
Argentina   Austria   Brazil   Chile   Czech Republic   France   Greece
Guatemala   Hungary   Italy   Japan   Poland   Portugal   Singapore
South Korea   Switzerland   Thailand   Turkey   Ukraine   Vietnam

Oxford is a registered trademark of Oxford University Press
in the UK and certain other countries.

Published in the United States of America by
Oxford University Press
198 Madison Avenue, New York, NY 10016

© Oxford University Press 2015

Library of Congress Cataloging-in-Publication Data
Karolyi, G. Andrew.
Cracking the emerging markets enigma / G. Andrew Karolyi.
pages cm.—
(Financial Management Association survey and synthesis series)
Includes bibliographical references and index.
ISBN 978–0–19–933662–3 (alk. paper)
1. Investments, Foreign—Developing countries.   2. Investments—Developing countries.
I. Title.
HG5993.K37 2015
332.67′3091724—dc23
2014046283

1 3 5 7 9 8 6 4 2
Printed in the United States of America
on acid-free paper

{ CONTENTS }

{ PREFACE }

During World War II, the British Government Code and Cypher School at Bletchley Park built up an extensive cryptanalysis team designed to read substantial amounts of secret Morse-coded radio communications of the Axis powers that had been enciphered using so-called Enigma machines. This massive effort over a five-year period yielded military intelligence that was considered by western Supreme Allied Commander Dwight Eisenhower to have been decisive to the Allied victory. The Enigma machines were portable, plug board-equipped cipher machines with rotor scramblers, which made the ciphers virtually unbreakable as long as good operating and proper enforcement procedures were followed. Alan Turing, a Cambridge University mathematician and widely considered the father of computer science and artificial science, provided much of the analytical thinking that led to the design of the Bombe machines—precursors of the modern-day computer—that eventually broke the Enigma code.

Much has been written and told about Bletchley Park, Turing, and the Enigma codebreaking, including a serious treatise by Frederick William Winterbotham published in 1974 by Orion Books titled *The Ultra Secret: The Inside Story of Operation Ultra, Bletchley Park, and Enigma*. The "Ultra" in Winterbotham's title was the designation adopted by British military intelligence for the wartime signals intelligence obtained by breaking encrypted enemy communications. This serious book inspired, in turn, the 1986 London play by Hugh Whitemore, *Breaking the Code*, which focused on Alan Turing himself; another wonderful fictional thriller by Robert Harris titled *Enigma* (1995, Arrow Books), and the 2001 film by the same name starring Kate Winslet and Dougray Scott (Jagged Films). The 2014 Black Bear Pictures release of *The Imitation Game*, the newest installment, will undoubtedly draw even more attention. Bletchley Park is today a heritage site where visitors can see the original code-breaking huts and blocks.

While I would love to envision myself as a modern-day Enigma code-breaker tasked with devising an understanding of the risks associated with investing in emerging markets, I know I am not worthy of the comparison. But this is the goal of my book. And I would be remiss in failing to give due credit to the men and women of Bletchley Park who inspired my title for the project. I am fascinated by their story and feel lucky to have visited the site, seen the actual German Navy 4-rotor Enigma machines, and even pulled the start levers of one of Turing's rebuilt Bombes that cracked the code.

What Is This Book About?

This book develops a rigorous, comprehensive, and practical framework in which to evaluate the opportunities—and, more importantly, the risks—of investing in emerging markets. It is *rigorous* in that it is built on a foundation of sound academic research on foreign direct and portfolio capital flows and the principles underlying international finance and economics. The framework is *comprehensive* in that it incorporates in an empirically coherent framework multiple dimensions of the potential risks that a prospective corporation or investor faces walking into those markets. These dimensions of risk reflect the uneven quality and fragility of the various institutions designed to assure integrity in the functioning of the country's capital markets. Finally, the framework is *practical*, as it distills these various dimensions of risk into an internally consistent scoring system that ranks emerging markets by each dimension of risk and overall across all dimensions.

Philosophically, this book posits that what fundamentally characterizes emerging markets are not the high rates of actual economic growth, but the even higher rates of potential economic growth that are hampered by the underdeveloped capital markets needed to finance them. The limited capacity of the financial markets in those countries, mandates active engagement of multinational corporations and foreign investors to help fund the shortfall. But these capital flows are stunted in turn by operational inefficiencies, restrictions on foreign participation, problems of poor governance and transparency rules, weak legal protections for investors, and political instability. These are the six dimensions of risk that comprise the scoring system around which the book is built and that will constitute its main chapters.

To enable its practical use, the book will also feature recent case studies of corporations and investors that have done deals in many of the emerging markets that embody my risk scoring system. The case studies focus on recent financial decisions involving corporations from emerging markets issuing securities to fund their businesses, global corporations seeking acquisition opportunities in emerging markets, cross-border asset sales, joint public-private project financing of infrastructure investments, and many other situations. They are relatively recent events, and have been used as teaching cases in my course on emerging markets at Cornell University. A case study will be seamlessly integrated into the chapter associated with the dimension of risk it is designed to showcase.

The primary force behind this book project was my consulting engagement with Dimensional Fund Advisors, a major US-based asset management firm with over $325 billion in assets under management (as of early 2014). In 2005, they hired me for a multiyear project to help determine objective criteria by which they should judge the countries into which they were deploying their investment strategies and client monies—and, more importantly, those into which they did not. Like so many managers with global mandates, and especially in emerging markets, the firm was concerned with market capacity constraints, operational inefficiencies, foreign investability restrictions, and the quality of legal protections for minority investors, corporate governance, and disclosure issues. For Dimensional, it was important that these criteria be well grounded in sound academic research on international markets. Fortunately, much of my own research program during the preceding 20 years had been focused on one or the other of these various dimensions of risk toward understanding their consequences for investors or corporations. I am glad that Dimensional gave me the green light to build on, extend, and update the core elements of the original consultative white paper from 2006 for this book today.

How Is the Book Organized?

The book has four parts. The first part, which involves three separate chapters, sets the stage. The opening chapter is called "Accepting the Challenge" (which is how I responded to Dimensional in 2005), and gives a complete overview of the book. It gives the reader a taste of the six different indicators, how they are built, what the overall findings are across the countries that constitute my emerging market set, and how I try to validate their usefulness. This is my one-stop-shopping chapter; if you read only one, then this is the one to pick. The other two chapters justify the set of emerging market countries I will study ("The Emerging Market Landscape," Chapter 2) and describe in detail the multivariate statistical methodology I used to distill the data into a single index for each risk indicator. Some readers may want to skip "A Primer on Methodology" (Chapter 3) to get straight to the results, but I strongly recommend that they do not. The methods define the outcomes and I make strategic choices that deserve scrutiny.

Part II builds the emerging market risk indicators one by one, with chapters corresponding to each of the six risk indicators. They follow the same methodical structure of defining the category, highlighting the extensive research that lies at its core, describing the data sources that I integrate into the statistical analysis, and exhibiting the resulting scores. I always wrap the analysis in each chapter around one of the case studies to bring the key concepts alive.

In order to validate the risk indicators I turn to the penultimate Part III of the book, in which I put some tough tests before them. Specifically, I obtain data on foreign portfolio holdings and net foreign portfolio flows by global investors into emerging markets, to see if one can reconcile how they might choose to do so with the risk indicators that I built. Chapter 10 offers up evidence that they work quite well.

In an unexpected twist of fate, the year 2013 turns out to have delivered a wonderful experiment in which to test out my indicators, which are built using data as of the end of 2012. During 2013, the US Federal Reserve had hinted that it would taper its quantitative-easing bond-buying program by year's end, and this turns out to have created anxiety among many global investors in emerging markets leading them to exit quickly. In May of 2013, when Fed Chairman Ben Bernanke hinted before Congress that the taper might begin by December (which it did, in fact), foreign portfolio outflows from the emerging markets spiked to over $35 billion, by some estimates. The outflows were concentrated in some emerging markets, while others escaped the investor flight altogether. I show in Chapter 11 ("Making Sense of the Emerging Market Swoon of 2013") that my risk indicators can explain a good fraction of the cross-country variation in those outflows.

Part IV closes out the book. I give an overview and add a number of cautions and warnings. The closing matter of the book includes some valuable appendices of the data and their sources, in case any of my readers have the inclination to build their own using my methods.

Who Should Read This Book?

My book is primarily written for the trade publications marketplace. The scoring system and the rigorous and comprehensive framework for measuring the risk of doing deals in emerging markets will be of practical benefit to global asset managers and even corporate financial managers domiciled in developed markets pursuing opportunities in emerging markets. Those investors domiciled in emerging markets considering opportunities in other emerging markets will also find the framework useful.

The book could also serve as a tool in the classroom. It may be ideal for an elective course on emerging markets finance—of which there are relatively few today in business schools in North America, but which will certainly grow in number over time. It could also anchor a nondegree executive education short-form course for managers with new responsibilities in emerging markets. Business education, like the deals themselves, is growing rapidly outside North America and especially in many emerging markets in Latin America, Asia, Eastern Europe, the Middle East, and Africa. Educators in these markets crave new teaching materials of relevance to their regions. The case studies in these chapters are currently unpublished teaching materials that I make available from the Emerging Markets Institute at the Johnson Graduate School of Management at Cornell University.

{ ACKNOWLEDGMENTS }

This book is the culmination of 20 years of research on international financial markets. Needless to say, I have been inspired by many colleagues and collaborators, students and clients along the way.

This book would not have been written without a long-standing relationship with Dimensional Fund Advisors. The genesis of a risk-scoring system for emerging markets to guide global investors comes from their firm's management and thought leadership. I am grateful to co-CEOs David Booth and Eduardo Repetto for their ongoing support, and to my former professors from the University of Chicago's Booth School, Eugene Fama and Ken French (Ken is now at Dartmouth University), who are leading figures at Dimensional. I have benefited from many useful discussions with Dimensional's Bob Deere, Karen Umland, Andrew Cain, Jacobo Rodriguez, Jim Davis, Sam Adams, and David Swanick, among others. The views and opinions in this book as well as any errors are my own and are not endorsed or recommended by Dimensional.

Many coauthors and collaborators have shaped my thinking through the projects on which we have worked together. Among them, three stand out: René Stulz, Craig Doidge, and Louis Gagnon, who have worked with me regularly over the last decade or so, and for that I am grateful. I know they are ready for me to get back to work on our other projects now that the book is finished.

Much of this book was written during my sabbatical leave in 2013. I served as a visiting fellow at the Judge Business School at the University of Cambridge and Pembroke College. They gave me all the resources to get the job done, and all the distractions of the beautiful English countryside to make it hard to do so. Raghu Rau was a great host and I thank him. During the fall of 2013, I visited the Research Department of the International Monetary Fund. I thank my hosts, Olivier Blanchard and Ayhan Kose, for sharing the resources of their group.

Two individuals were mission-critical toward the completion of the project in 2013: Elizabeth Cai, who worked for me as a research assistant, and Alan Kwan, a current PhD student at the Johnson School. Both collected and vetted massive quantities of data for the risk indicators. Alan read drafts of the chapters along the way, commenting on exposition and content. I am lucky to have had their assistance, but I do not implicate them in any way if there are remaining errors in the analysis. Those are mine, and mine alone. Students in my course NBA 5510 on Emerging Market Finance read drafts and commented on some of the chapters. They, of course, are the primary motivators for the case studies that are featured in the book. The coauthors on those specific case studies I choose are named in the respective chapters in which they appear. I thank them for their hard work and dedication to the study of emerging markets.

Oxford University Press is fortunate to have Scott Parris as one of their editors. He has been a positive and constructive force in the development of this project. I am also grateful to Cathryn Vaulman, an editorial assistant, who worked tirelessly in keeping me on task. Discussions with Terry Vaughn and Valerie Ashton, previous editors at OUP, helped shape the project in its earliest stages of development. A number of anonymous outside reviewers gave constructive advice on the manuscript for which I am grateful.

Last, but certainly not least, I thank my family. Anne, my wife of 30 years, has stood by my side through this book writing effort. She is not an economist by training, but she pushed her way through each chapter to help me find my voice, and to point out my arcane jargon. Thank goodness! My children continue to inspire me. Stephen Karolyi, his wife Meghan, Paul Karolyi and Megan Arellano were always willing to engage in impromptu conversations about the book when we were together and when there were undoubtedly better things to talk about. Their love means everything.

{ PART I }

Understanding the Risks in Emerging Markets

Accepting the Challenge

Emerging markets are distinctly different from developed markets in that they represent underfunded growth opportunities with problems. These problems impede their ability to secure the very funding they need and are what really set them apart. What exactly are these problems? Read on.

Bharti Airtel Dials into Africa

A "staggering deal," the *Economic Times of India* called it. On March 30, 2010, Bharti Airtel, India's largest and the world's third-largest cellular service provider, with more than 131 million subscribers, announced that it had entered into a legally binding definitive agreement with Kuwait's Zain Group to acquire Zain Africa for $10.7 billion. The deal would become the largest-ever telecom takeover by an Indian firm, and would also be the largest deal to date in emerging markets.[1] With the acquisition Bharti would grow its customer base to 179 million subscribers, gaining Zain Africa's presence in 15 countries with over 42 million customers in tow. Chairman, managing director, and founder Sunil Bharti Mittal declared the agreement a "landmark for the global telecom industry and a game changer for Bharti," and described the acquisition as "a pioneering step toward South-South cooperation and strengthening of ties between India and Africa."[2]

The market did not receive the news at all well. In the two weeks after both Bharti and Zain confirmed that they were in exclusive discussions, Bharti's stock tumbled over 14%, and it did not recover much on the formal announcement.

Yet all the fundamentals appeared to be in place for a successful transaction. Bharti Airtel's mobile telecom business had been built up to a market-leading position in providing India, Sri Lanka, and Bangladesh with second- and third-generation voice and data, fixed line, broadband, and wireless media services. It also served as the largest carrier in India for national and international long-distance communications. It was recognized as the first mobile phone company in the world to outsource everything except marketing and sales. Mittal himself was a charismatic leader who had overcome great odds to build Bharti into a leader in the Indian telecom market. *Fortune magazine* hailed Mittal as Asia's Businessman of the Year in 2006. NDTV, an Indian commercial broadcasting network, awarded him the title of "Transforming India Leader in 2008."[3]

From a start-up cellular company in 1995, Bharti grew rapidly into a full-service provider with 25,000 employees; revenues of $7.25 billion in fiscal year 2009, including over $1.7 billion in foreign equity; a Bombay stock exchange listing; and partnerships with Britain's Vodafone and Singapore-based SingTel, Asia's largest operator. Bharti was admired for two advantages. The first was its so-called minute factory business model based on the outsourced network planning and information technology (IT) backbone.[4] The second was the firm's knack for successfully acquiring and integrating new geographic circles to its operations when it gained cellular licenses, a crucial driver for its rapid growth trajectory.

Bharti Airtel considered corporate transparency to be of utmost importance in building its reputation in domestic—and especially in international financial markets—as it sought to attract foreign equity capital to fund its growth. In a poll of 300 investors and analysts across Asia, Bharti was recognized as India's second-best company in investor relations (after Infosys), second-best in corporate governance, and the second-best managed public company in India.[5]

The Indian cellular market had grown at an annual rate of 7% since 1997, reaching 400 million subscriptions by 2009. But there were serious headwinds. Though Indian mobile operators faced significantly lower average revenues per user (ARPUs) than their European and US counterparts, they typically posted higher profit margins compared to Western peers through cost-optimization methods, like network and IT outsourcing, as well as low subscriber acquisition and retention costs. Upcoming government auctions for licenses to bring third-generation speeds would likely induce a bidding war, putting additional pressure on margins. Competition was eroding voice-line revenues. Going abroad seemed to be the next logical step for expansion.

Zain was the pioneer of mobile telecommunications in the Middle East. It had started off operations in Kuwait in 1983, but expanded to 23 countries with 13,000 employees and 72 million customers. At $20 billion in market capitalization in March 2010, it was the largest publicly traded company on the Kuwait Stock Exchange. Zain's corporate strategy in Africa was launched through its Celtel subsidiary and was coined ACE, for *accelerate* growth in Africa, *consolidate* existing assets, and *expand* into adjacent markets.[6] By 2009, Zain Africa had reached market leader positions in the Democratic Republic of Congo, Zambia, Niger, Congo, Chad, Gabon, and Kenya, and near-leadership positions in a number of other sub-Saharan countries. But its cash positions became strained with the rapid expansion. Foreign suitors, including Vodafone and the French media conglomerate Vivendi, came calling. So did Bharti.

Was Zain Africa really worth the $10.7 billion price tag? What would be the potential adverse consequences for Bharti's investors if it was not? Expansion into Africa appeared to offer significant opportunities for Bharti, including a large population base, significant growth potential, and still relatively low mobile market penetration. But there were challenges, big challenges. To fund the deal, Bharti formed two special purpose vehicles (SPVs), one in the Netherlands and one in Singapore. The SPVs incurred $8.3 billion in loans from a syndicate involving Standard Chartered Bank, Barclay's Bank, HSBC, Bank of Tokyo-Mitsubishi UFJ, and Bank of America Merrill Lynch, among others. Terms were dear at around 175 basis points above LIBOR. Standard and Poor's and Crisil, S&P's local Indian arm, placed Bharti Airtel on its watch list for a potential downgrade, given the enormous debt load the company would need to support.[7] Equity analysts expressed grave concerns over the opaqueness of the SPVs as a financing vehicle. In addition to the usual integration issues associated with acquisitions, regulatory approvals were also needed—and, in fact, separate ones in each of the African countries in which Zain Africa had a footprint.[8] All were early indications that these hurdles were real.

The deal closed on June 7 of that year to great fanfare. "Largest ever deal in emerging markets," declared the *Economic Times* of India. But almost immediately on the heels of the celebration, S&P/Crisil lowered Bharti's debt rating to BB+. The stock price rallied 5% on the day, but this remained well below its price when the merger talks were announced, and the price continued to trail off for the next year. Bharti posted profit declines in 2011 and beyond. Cash flow drained with major investment programs that were announced in Ghana, Niger, and Kenya for needed expansion of the IT networking capacity. Cost overruns continued. Foreign exchange losses and interest carrying costs impeded profit growth. Regulatory headaches continued.

The Key to Understanding the Risks in Emerging Markets

Were the risks Bharti faced in entering the African market by way of the Zain Africa acquisitions knowable? If knowable, were they quantifiable? If all this were so, why then were the outside stakeholders, including shareholders, caught off guard by the deal's announcement and its aftermath? The local market capacity constraints in India mandated that Bharti seek a broad syndicate deal with global banks to secure financing of such a large deal. Restrictions on foreign investor participation may have impeded Bharti's access to external capital. The integrity of the governance and disclosure systems of which Bharti was so proud seemed to be called into question by the intricacy of the deal. So too were the overriding goals of the management team, which was entrenched as one of the controlling shareholders. And the regulatory hassles of entering the African mobile market no doubt revealed the binding political and legal constraints that typically impact cross-border activity in many emerging markets.

The goal of this book is to develop a rigorous, comprehensive, and practical framework in which to understand these very risks associated with investing in emerging markets. It is *rigorous* in that it is built on a foundation of sound academic research by a large number of scholars of foreign direct and portfolio investment flows over the past two decades. The framework is *comprehensive* in that it incorporates in an empirically coherent framework multiple dimensions of the potential risks that a prospective corporation or investor faces walking into those markets. These dimensions of risk reflect the uneven quality, or fragility, of the various institutions designed to assure integrity in the functioning of the country's capital markets. Finally, the framework is *practical*, as it distills these various dimensions of risk into an internally consistent scoring system that ranks emerging markets by each dimension of risk, and overall across all dimensions. To enable its practical use, the book will feature recent case studies of corporations, like that of Bharti Airtel, and investors that have done deals in many of the emerging markets that embody the scoring system.

Philosophically, this book posits that what fundamentally characterize emerging markets are not the high rates of realized economic growth that have been realized, but rather the even higher rates of *potential* economic growth that are unrealized by the underdeveloped capital markets needed to finance them. Underfunded growth opportunities with problems, I call them. This is the very thesis statement with which I launched this chapter. What "problems" do I mean? Basically, they represent various forms of market fragility. The fragility is revealed in the weaknesses of institutions that are crucial to make capital markets work. The limited capacity of the financial markets in those countries is a core problem. Capacity constraints necessitate active engagement of multinational corporations and of foreign portfolio investors to help fund the shortfalls that exist for companies at home. But the free flow of capital to these emerging markets is stunted by operational inefficiencies and restrictions on foreign participation, as well as problems of poor governance and transparency rules, weak legal protections for dispute resolution, and political instability that deter the potential direct and portfolio investors.

These are the six dimensions of risk that comprise the scoring system around which the book is built, and their constructs will constitute its main chapters in Part II. What elements go into the six different fundamental risk indicators? They are:

1. *Market capacity constraints.* This measures the scope and breadth of the equity, debt, and bank capital markets, and the extent of their overall trading activity and vibrancy for capital formation measured relative to the economic size of the country in which the markets are

located. I use measures of market turnover, market capitalization relative to the GDP of a country, and the number of listed firms relative to the population base, among others.

2. *Operational inefficiency.* Even with greater capacity of a market to fund economic growth, capital formation can be impeded by the mechanical and technological inefficiencies of the trading systems, poorly performing settlement, clearing and transfer facilities, risks embodied in the central securities depositories, and the high costs of transacting in the markets. I look at the length of settlement cycles, different settlement methods, the average transfer fees, commissions paid by investors to brokers, a whole host of proxies for market-impact costs, and restrictions on short-sale transactions.

3. *Foreign accessibility restrictions.* Limited capacity to fund growth locally can be overcome by drawing on external sources of capital. But this can happen only if there are no penalizing restrictions imposed on foreign portfolio investors with regards to ownership, currency convertibility limits, repatriation, and other barriers to free flow of capital. To this end, I collect data on withholding taxes, double-taxation treaties, and extra securities taxes for foreign investors, and several measures of the degree of openness by overseas listing and trading of securities.

4. *Corporate opacity.* A well-functioning market is a more transparent one in which there is fair access to information for all market participants. Transparency is effected through mandated disclosure requirements and voluntary reporting by public companies on changes to the nature of the business, acquisitions and disposals of assets, dividends, the appointment and dismissal of managers and directors, and significant shareholders and their holdings. I incorporate indices of accounting standards, the extent of analyst coverage for publicly traded stocks in a country, and the presence of large family or management blockholder interests.

5. *Limits to legal protections.* Markets flourish with the backbone of a strong and impartial legal system. A healthy legal climate must exist for investors—both minority shareowner and creditors' rights alike—including foreign investors. Many indices of anti-director rights, anti-self-dealing, and judicial efficiency are employed, as well as measures of the scope of supervisory powers, enforcement procedures, time, and costs that abound.

6. *Political instability.* Political constraints are linked to the free flow of capital. Tougher constraints limit autocracy, and result in better progress toward development of basic democratic institutions and principles such as civil liberties, freedoms, and limitations on corruption, government inefficiency, and regulatory burdens, all of which

should stimulate capital formation. I use data on the number of independent branches of government, their preferences and status quo policies, how concentrated are seats held by governing and opposition parties in respective legislatures, results of surveys on perceived levels of corruption, government effectiveness, and violent threats to or changes in government, including terrorism.

Empirically, I construct scaled, standardized indices using dozens of individual economic, political, or institutional indices and data, like those listed above, that have been shown in existing academic research to have consequences for actual outcomes (investments, acquisitions, asset sales) in emerging markets. Many of these country-level indices have been developed by corporations and government agencies, such as the World Bank, Standard & Poor's, the Heritage Foundation, and Transparency International. Often, the country-level data are drawn from academic studies that have focused on one particular aspect of emerging markets and that have constructed measures to capture that aspect. Examples include the liquidity of trading in underlying equities in a given market, the extent to which corporations manage their earnings volatility, or the intensity of political constraints on policy development. In some cases, in which there are no measures available, I build new index components from primary source data that are readily available in the public domain.

A unique feature of these risk indicators is that I use a well-known multivariate statistical technique called principal components analysis (PCA) to objectively assign weights to the variables. By design, this statistical procedure ensures that the linear combination of the component scores maximizes the explanatory power of the data across variables and countries. I build the indicators for 33 emerging and 24 developed markets by year for the decade of the 2000s. These scores alert investors or corporations to the indicators—or components of a given indicator—of a particular source of institutional fragility in a given emerging market country. Because I employ both emerging and developed markets in the empirical analysis, the rankings and scores are directly comparable across those groups, and not just within them. This is an important feature of the rankings. It is reassuring when long-recognized developed markets reveal elements of institutional fragility that are not too different from those of many commercially designated emerging markets.

The technique has its strengths and its weaknesses, as any technique does. One weakness is that it is not purely objective, as I claim above. In fact, I have a discretionary role in deciding which component scores drawn from original source data or from existing academic research studies feature in the statistical analysis. I offer up my arguments, but I also know that the reader will judge the integrity of those choices. Another weakness of the PCA procedure for the data reduction exercise is the objective function that is built into it: namely, to maximize the variability of the component scores. The logic behind this choice stems from the fact that I want to give these risk indicator scores the best chance possible to explain other economic and financial outcomes, such as how global investors size up different emerging markets. The less variation one observes in the scores, the lower their potential explanatory power. But of course, greater variation could just as easily stem from greater noise that has been built into the scores, which only adversely impacts their potential explanatory power.

So it is in Part III of the book in which these strengths and weaknesses come out in the wash. I proceed to validate the various risk indicator scores by evaluating how well they explain recent data on actual cross-country equity holdings of global institutional investors for the emerging market universe. It turns out that the scores I develop do a reasonably good job. One can only wonder if these investors had my risk indicator scores at their disposal at the time, whether they would have made different choices.

IT'S NOT JUST ABOUT THE UPSIDE GROWTH POTENTIAL OF EMERGING MARKETS!

The emerging markets growth story is well told. According to the 2012 *World Economic Outlook* (WEO) published by the International Monetary Fund (IMF), the median GDP growth rate (in current US dollars) of what they call the advanced economies (most prominently the United States, European countries, and Japan) averaged 3.3% between 1995 and 2004, and ranged from an annual high of 3.9% in 2007 to a low of –3.7% in 2009.[9] Projections out to 2018 are for 2.2% per year. By contrast, the median emerging market and developing economy grew at an annual rate of 4.2% between 1995 and 2004, reached a peak of 6.2% in 2007, and only dipped to a positive 1.7% in 2009. Emerging market growth forecasts to 2018 were more than double that of the typical advanced economy at 4.5%. However, accompanying these dazzling prospects are the cautions of many emerging markets research teams that often revolve around cyclical "headwinds" like volatile commodity prices, fiscal imbalances, household debt burdens, and even spillovers from monetary conditions in advanced economies. These are all valid and worthy concerns.

But this book is different. The focus on building risk indicators for multinationals and investors seeking opportunities in emerging markets is not because the opportunities are not there. Indeed, they are! The ultimate goal here is to balance them with appropriate caution against other dimensions that matter.

Jim O'Neill, former chairman at Goldman Sachs Asset Management (GSAM) and the first to use the term "BRICs" (in reference to Brazil, Russia, India, and China), eloquently makes the case for growth in his 2011 treatise *The Growth Map: Economic Opportunity in the BRICs and Beyond*.[10] He makes the point that the global economy back in 2001—when he wrote his seminal research paper in the Goldman Sachs' Global Economics white paper series— would be propelled forward by the growth of the four populous countries of the BRIC. The growth conditions in those countries were defined not only by population and the power of demographics, but by their export-orientation, the rise of commodity prices, labor productivity, sound government debt and deficit positions, and economic mobility for the rising consumer class. O'Neill and his team at GSAM followed up the BRIC designation in another paper in 2005 with the "Next Eleven" or N-11, which included Bangladesh, Egypt, Indonesia, Iran, South Korea, Mexico, Nigeria, Pakistan, the Philippines, Turkey, and Vietnam.

To be fair, the GSAM team always offered a balanced perspective on a given emerging market's growth potential against its actual chances of realizing it by developing their own so-called growth environment scores (the GES Index). Their GES scores are, by design, proprietary. O'Neill's book points to 13 variables that are weighted and averaged out, including macroeconomic ones (inflation, government deficit, investment spending, external debt, degree of openness) and microeconomic ones (use of mobile telephones, use of the Internet, use of computers, life expectancy, education, rule of law, corruption, and stability of government).[11] There is clearly an overlap of these variables with those that constitute my own risk indicator scores. The key difference is that mine are drawn directly from the large body of existing academic research on the subject.

Though they may not distill them into index scores like mine or like those of GSAM, I have to acknowledge that other asset management firms and consultancy firms have also built screening criteria for investing in emerging markets for their clients that have common elements with the risk indicator scores I showcase in this book.[12] And there are many other books that have been written on emerging markets that feature the growth opportunities and that also discuss the challenges of doing business or investing there. Most prominent among these are *Emerging Markets Rule: Growth Strategies of the New Global Giants* by Mauro Guillen and Esteban Garcia-Canal (McGraw-Hill, 2012), *Winning in Emerging Markets: A Road Map for Strategy and Execution* by Tarun Khanna and Krishna Palepu (Harvard University Press, 2010), and *Emerging Markets: Resilience and Growth amid Global Turmoil* by Ayhan Kose and my own Cornell University colleague Eswar Prasad (Brookings Institution Press, 2010).[13]

While contributing to this formidable body of research constitutes a tall order, my book attempts to take the next step by emphasizing rigor and comprehensiveness by means of the practical framework I adopt.

THE MAIN FINDINGS

Which of the emerging markets score well on the risk indicators? Which score poorly? Are the markets that score well on market capacity constraints (fewer constraints) the same as those that score well on foreign accessibility restrictions (weaker restrictions)? Do emerging markets in which investors face greater political instability the very same as those with the lowest quality of legal protections in place?

Details obviously will follow, but an early preview is worthwhile. To start, consider Figure 1.1. This is what researchers call a radar chart (sometimes also known, for obvious reasons, as a spider or cobweb diagram). A radar chart is a graphical method of displaying multivariate data in the form of a two-dimensional chart of three or more quantitative variables represented on axes starting from the same point. In this figure, I offer up the median scores for each of the six risk indicators across the emerging markets that constitute the sample of countries that will be part of the analysis in this book. For now, remember that the next chapter will discuss in detail how the sample is determined.

These median scores are plotted with diamond markers connected by lines to make the inner hexagon (admittedly, a wobbly hexagon). The square markers connected by the outer hexagon are the equivalent median scores across the developed markets that are also part of the sample of countries that I study. Let me repeat from earlier in the chapter an important element of the analysis in the book: though the focus is on emerging markets, each of the risk index scores are constructed almost seamlessly using a sample of 57 emerging *and* developed markets around the world. This figure illustrates the stark contrast between the two sets of countries.

The scores for each indicator are scaled and standardized to lie on a standard normal scale, mostly between –2 and +2.[14] The figure is restricted to the

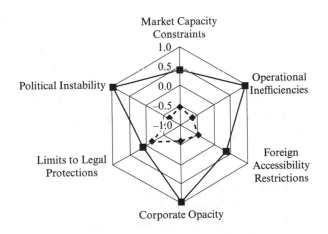

- ◆ - Emerging Markets —■— Developed Markets

FIGURE 1.1 *Benchmarking Emerging Market Risk Indicators in 2012.*

Note: The six risk indicators are each computed on a standardized basis using a standard normal scale for the continuous index values. Negative (positive) values imply worse (better) scores, reflecting greater (lesser) risk. All scores are measured using data up to 2012.

range from –1 to +1 for ease of interpretation. Low, negative scores imply worse values, or higher risk; high, positive scores are better. For the market capacity constraints indicator, a low, negative score is associated with a country that has more limited financial market capacity or vibrancy relative to its economic size. The actual values do not have any specific economic meaning. For example, the fact that the median emerging market has a score around –0.59 on the corporate opacity indicator does not specifically tell you in any interpretable way how well corporations in those countries govern themselves in terms of management discipline, transparency, accountability, or about their reporting practices. But scores are well below the median score of 0.97 for developed markets, and inform the final composite risk score for each country. Also, it is important to remember that this is a simple comparison of the median scores. This means that it is possible—and, in fact, quite likely—that some countries in the emerging market class may achieve scores on corporate opacity that are higher than some countries among the developed markets. I will delve into that in Chapter 7, when I discuss the construction of the corporate opacity risk measure in detail.

One important takeaway from this figure is the clear fact that the median emerging market score is negative regardless of which risk indicator is considered. And the median developed market score is positive. This is not an artificially engineered outcome, but is an organic one that arises from the multivariate statistical (PCA) analysis I applied to many dozens of indicators. A second takeaway comes from comparing the median scores across the six indicators. The spread between the median emerging and developed market scores for the corporate opacity indicator appears to be quite wide compared to that for the indicator on the limits to legal protections (ranging between –0.25 for emerging markets and 0.36 for developed markets) or even foreign accessibility restrictions, suggesting that corporate opacity may be a dimension of risk that is particularly wide-ranging across countries.

Though the scales are standardized, the magnitudes of the spreads still have meaning. The construction of the principal components on foreign accessibility restrictions implies smaller differences in those restrictions between the sets of emerging and developed markets. One adverse consequence of this compressed range of scores may be that an understanding of differences in foreign accessibility restrictions—at least, the way I have measured them—may have a harder time explaining how investors allocate their investments to and across different emerging markets. While I may worry about the explanatory power of the foreign accessibility risk indicator, I am less concerned about prospects for the risk indicators associated with political instability (range of –0.68 to 0.98) and market operational inefficiencies (range of –0.64 to 0.95), which have spreads between emerging and developed markets at least as large as that for corporate opacity.

Figure 1.2 exhibits a simple bar chart of the overall risk indicator score in 2012 for each of the individual emerging markets in my sample. To compute the overall risk indicator score, I average the six component risk indicator scores for each country. Truth be told, I am hesitant to compute this overall average because of the concern about destroying the very valuable information I seek to uncover in sorting out the different types of risks prospective investors might face. But I recognize the convenience of a simple summary measure, and it is not completely unreasonable given that each indicator score is standardized on the same scale. To facilitate comparisons with Figure 1.1, I also add the median overall developed market risk indicator score, which can be seen to be positive (index value of 0.64).

Some striking things jump out from the figure. First, most of the 33 emerging market countries in my sample have a negative overall risk indicator score. But not all of them do. There are six countries that have positive scores, including

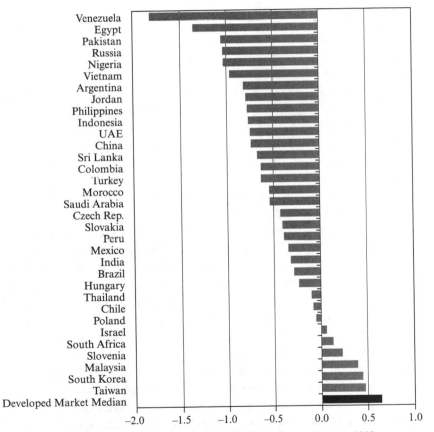

FIGURE 1.2 *Ranking Emerging Markets by Overall Risk Indicator Score in 2012.*

Note: The risk indicators are each computed on a standardized basis using a standard normal scale for the continuous index values. Negative (positive) values imply worse (better) scores, reflecting greater (lesser) risk. The overall risk indicator is an average of the six component risk indicator scores. All scores are measured using data up to 2012.

Taiwan (0.47), South Korea (0.44), Malaysia (0.38), Slovenia (0.21), South Africa (0.12), and Israel (0.06).[15] Indeed, exactly half of the developed markets in the sample have overall index values below 0.64, with a good number of them lying below those for South Korea, Malaysia, and Taiwan.

Second, there are some intriguing threshold jumps or discontinuities across the country scores. These principal component scores around which the standardized scores are built have meaning, so the distances between ranks of countries matter as much as the rankings themselves. The first jump is one already detected above between South Korea, Malaysia, and Taiwan and the next set of countries with positive scores starting with Slovenia. A second jump occurs between the Czech Republic (−0.43), Saudi Arabia (−0.54), and then Morocco (−0.64). A third series of jumps arise at the lowest end of the averaged risk indicator scores between the Argentina (−0.82) and Vietnam (−0.97), between Pakistan (−1.06) and Egypt (−1.35), and finally a big one between Egypt and Venezuela (−1.82). More noteworthy jumps in scores will arise for the individual risk indicators in later chapters. Why these jumps and discontinuities occur is interesting in that they hint at the possibility of natural clusters or tiers of countries by relevant attributes that matter to investors.

Figure 1.3 lowers the microscope on several key individual countries to showcase another advantage of the risk indicators I build. In this figure, a radar chart similar to that in Figure 1.1 is constructed separately for Brazil, Russia, India, and China, the BRIC countries. The range of the axis is reset from the original figure to accommodate a greater range of scores, but it is preserved to be the same across the four countries to facilitate comparisons. Several patterns emerge. First, the shapes of the hexagon of scores are quite different. Remember from Figure 1.2 that Brazil has a higher average score than Russia, so it is not surprising that the size of the hexagon—the area inside it, say—is much greater for Brazil than Russia. Russia's figure is not really a hexagon, but more of a triangle. It is not on every dimension that Brazil dominates Russia. Note how both countries score similarly on the market capacity constraint and limits to legal protections risk indicators. Where Russia loses ground in the overall risk indicator scores is detectable from the differences in the political instability, operational inefficiencies, and especially the corporate opacity risk indicators. Visually, it is harder to distinguish the size of the hexagon of Brazil from India, which makes sense given how close the overall scores are in Figure 1.2.

Comparing the radar diagrams between Brazil and China is made more complex by the unusually skewed shape of the hexagon of scores for China, which is the second interesting pattern. Some of the shapes are oblong, like those for India. India scores reasonably well in terms of the operational inefficiencies and limits to legal protections they afford investors, but the risk indicator scores for foreign accessibility restrictions and for political instability hold India back in the overall score. China's overall score is boosted by its relatively

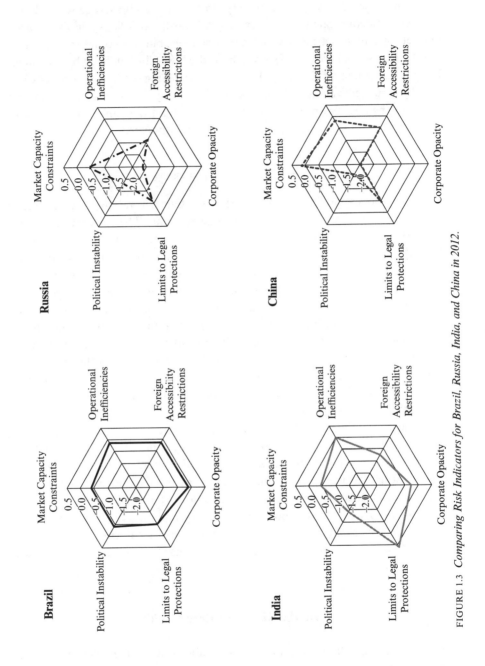

FIGURE 1.3 *Comparing Risk Indicators for Brazil, Russia, India, and China in 2012.*

strong risk indicator scores on market capacity constraints, operational inefficiencies, and limits to legal protections, but the low scores on political instability and especially corporate opacity brings its overall average score down. The score on corporate opacity appears awkwardly to collapse on the axis for market capacity constraints, which seems strange, but this comes from the fact that China's score here (−1.98) lies right at the lower limit defined by the figure. It is just an artifact of the range I chose for displaying the figure. Some readers may be surprised by some of these scores, but I urge you to reserve judgments about their integrity until more of the details about the component data and their weights in the respective risk indicators are discussed.

A CAUTIONARY NOTE: THE PASSAGE OF TIME

I offer another cautionary note out of the gate. One natural question one might ask is how these risk indicator scores change over time. The answer is that some risk indicators are more accommodating of changes over time than others. Recall, for example, that some of the scores distill output variables from academic research, which are studies that can often represent a snapshot analysis. This inhibits a measure of time variation in the scores. Other variables from research papers do embed a time series of these output variables, which helps mitigate the problem, but not necessarily for the sample period of interest of the 2000s through 2012. As a result, there is some uncomfortable mixing of data across different time periods, which is a problem if some of the institutions are changing in a dramatic way over the decade. It is almost certainly the case that the research studies will not be fully updated to 2012, which will leave some readers even more uncomfortable.

Some of the data that I obtain from corporations and government agencies, such as the World Bank, Standard & Poor's, the Heritage Foundation, and Transparency International, are updated with annual (perhaps higher) frequency, which affords a more timely analysis of the risk indicator scores. The risk indicator scores that are easily adaptable to time-series analysis are for market capacity constraints, political instability, and, to a lesser extent, foreign accessibility restrictions. In later chapters, I will provide information about how the risk indicator scores and the rankings change over time where it makes sense to do so.

Do the Risk Indicators Work?

Notwithstanding all of the cautions I issue about the data challenges in making these risk indicators sensible and useable, the real proof is in the pudding. How well can they explain important economic and financial outcomes across these countries? Part III of the book conducts a simple validation exercise.

I test whether the different risk indicator indices have any explanatory power for the actual foreign portfolio holdings of investors. Do global investors tilt their portfolio holdings toward emerging markets with relatively better (more positive) scores on operational inefficiencies? Do they underweight their holdings of bonds or stocks in markets with relatively poorer (more negative) scores on foreign investability restrictions, or political instability?

To this end, I obtain two datasets. The first is from regular surveys of US residents by the Board of Governors of the Federal Reserve System, the Federal Reserve Bank of New York, and the US Treasury Department. The Treasury International Capital (TIC) surveys are done at the individual security level through the largest US custodians, a relatively small group of institutions (about 200) that collectively report on the vast majority of total US holdings. They are conducted under the authority of the International Investment and Trade in Services Survey Act, so it is a reasonably accurate depiction of foreign equity and debt holdings by US residents. As of the end of 2012, the sum total of these foreign holdings exceeded $7.9 trillion. I compute the percentage of total foreign equity or debt holdings in each market relative to all foreign holdings in the survey and perform a regression analysis for each of my risk indicators. I control for the percentage of total foreign equity or bond market capitalization in each market—which I will present in Chapter 2—so that my scores for each indicator needs to explain the foreign bias, or the deviations in actual holding of US investors relative to the world market portfolio as a natural benchmark. This approach to measuring the home bias and the foreign bias is well rooted in theory and well established as a standard practice in the academic finance literature.

I use a second dataset because I want to make sure that the relevance of these risk indicators for emerging markets goes beyond just understanding how US investors allocate their investments. I obtain stock holdings data from the FactSet (formerly called Lionshares) Ownership database, which is a leading information source for global institutional ownership. Institutions, which are defined as professional money managers with discretionary control over assets like mutual funds, pension funds, bank trusts, and insurance companies, are frequently required to disclose publicly their holdings in many countries around the world. In the United States, FactSet secures data on institutional holdings from the mandatory quarterly 13F filings with the Securities and Exchange Commission (SEC), as well as by rolling up the holdings by individual mutual funds (N–30D filings with the SEC) managed by a particular fund management company. Outside the United States, FactSet collects holdings data from sources such as national regulatory agencies, stock exchange announcements, local and offshore mutual funds, mutual fund directories, and company proxies and annual reports. It is the most comprehensive source available outside the United States.

FactSet data represent a nice complement to the TIC data from the United States, even though it is only for equities and not bond holdings and even

though it is only for institutional holdings, not households or individual investors. The data runs through 2012, with holdings data for over 5,000 different
institutions in over 35,000 stocks worldwide, representing a total market value
of $19 trillion as of December 2012. I perform similar regression analysis with
the risk indicators as explanatory variables for the foreign bias in emerging and
developed markets computed with FactSet holdings data.

The regression analysis affirms that there is integrity to the emerging market
risk indicators. Some offer better explanatory power of the foreign portfolio
holdings than others. The risk indicators are differentially effective in capturing
the foreign portfolio holdings of US investors from the TIC data than those of
global institutions investors using the FactSet data.

Figure 1.4 gives a graphical illustration of the explanatory power of the
risk indicators. It uses the FactSet data in 2012, and not the TIC data, so these
results are conservative. The first step is to compute the actual excess holdings
for each emerging market. To do so, I first determine the fraction of total world
equity market capitalization represented by that for each market as of 2011.

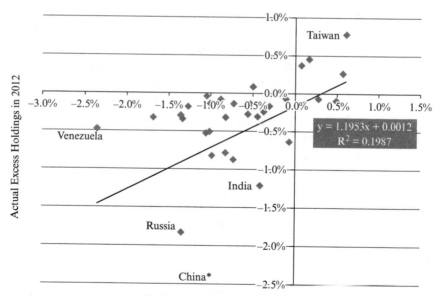

Predicted Excess Equity Holdings in 2012

FIGURE 1.4 *Predicting Excess Holdings for Emerging Markets in 2012 Using*
Risk Indicators.

Note: The excess holdings for emerging markets are computed from FactSet (Lionshares) data. To compute the actual
excess holdings, the fraction of total world equity market capitalization for 2011 for each market is subtracted from
the fraction of total foreign holdings by institutional investors around the world, which, in turn, is aggregated by
country and computed as a fraction of the total. The predicted excess equity holdings are generated as fitted values
from a univariate regression model on the overall risk indicator score.*

Indicates that China's actual fraction of foreign equity holdings is –8.87% below that implied by its weight in the total
world equity market capitalization, which is off the scale on the chart. The equation in the box in the figure shows
that the slope coefficient is 1.1953, the intercept coefficient is 0.12%, and the overall explanatory power of the risk
indicator scores (denoted by the coefficient of determination, or R^2) is 19.87%.

I will discuss the source of this data in the next chapter. This is the benchmark relative to which it is judged whether the actual holdings are in excess of what they should be (both positive and negative, in fact). From FactSet, I aggregate across all stock holdings and all institutions in each country in which those are deployed outside their country of domicile. Call these foreign equity holdings. I sort these by target country, and then aggregate across all source countries the foreign equity holdings that target the given emerging market country of interest. I then determine the percentage of all foreign equity holdings from around the world that target each given emerging market. I subtract from this number for each country its own fraction of the world equity market capitalization to get the excess measure. Think of it as a gauge of how much institutions around the world tend to overweight or underweight a given market relative to a sensible benchmark, its relative market capitalization.

I perform regression analysis in which the object I am trying to explain is the actual excess holdings of global institutional investors in 2012, and the explanatory variable is the overall risk indicator score (from Figure 1.2). Regression analysis tries to find an intercept and a slope coefficient that defines the equation of a line in a scatterplot of the actual excess holdings against the risk indicators in order to minimize the squared deviations of the line from the actual holdings. The figure plots the actual excess holdings relative to the predicted holdings that are computed from the equation of the best-fitting line.[16] Ideally, a perfect prediction would have the individual observations line up along a 45° line in the scatter, implying a one-to-one relationship. You can see that this is not so. In fact, there is an actual line displayed that proves it is not so. The box inside the figure tells us that the resulting slope of the line is 1.1953, higher than 1, which would imply the one-to-one relationship I seek. Overall, the coefficient of determination from the regression—called the R^2—is 19.87%, which means that more than 80% of the variation in the actual excess holdings across countries is left unexplained. The cup is 20% full and 80% empty. I focus on the cup 20% full, and take it as a good sign of the integrity of the risk indicators. You have every right to ask what is missing to leave 80% unexplained.

There are certain countries that are influencing the scatter of observations to have an actual slope that is higher than optimal. Russia, for example, has negative excess holdings of almost −1.75%, implying that the global investors in 2012 hold a much smaller fraction of Russian equities than would be justified by their relative market capitalization in the world. Worse, the overall risk indicator scores do not sufficiently capture why Russia is so severely underweighted by investors. India is also adversely affecting the predictive power of the relationship, for the same reasons. Venezuela is underweight, but it is much less so than is justified by its poor overall score on the risk indicators, so it actually represents a countervailing force to Russia and India in the prediction model. Taiwan, by contrast, is overweight relative to its market capitalization (0.77%), and more importantly in a way that exceeds its relative favorable score on the risk indicators (recall its positive value in Figure 1.2). As a result Taiwan, like Russia and India, is adversely impacting the predictive power of the risk indicator scores forcing the slope of the line to be higher than 1-to-1, but for the opposite reason from Russia and India.

I need to make one final observation that will be repeated regularly in Part III of the book. At the bottom of the figure, there is a label for China with an asterisk. The asterisk means that I have tricked you visually by suppressing another large outlier from the regression line and the scatterplot. China is such a major underweight in terms of actual foreign equity holdings that it is off the edge of the figure (hence the asterisk). The actual fraction of foreign equity holdings is 2.27%, but China's market capitalization of $3.3 trillion in 2011 constitutes an 11.1% fraction of the world market capitalization pie. As a result, its underweight is –8.86% (the vertical scale on the figure stops at –2.5%), though the predicted weight implied by its risk indicator score is only –0.82%. China is clearly an influential observation that impedes the predictive power of the risk indicator scores (helping the cup to be 80% empty, to torture the earlier metaphor a bit more).

The Plan Going Forward

You now have a good sense of the central thesis in this book, as well as its main findings. You might be tempted not to read the rest, though I hope you do. The devil is, after all, in the details.

In the next chapter, I outline the emerging market landscape on which I focus. This is not a trivial exercise, as the definitions of what countries represent emerging markets vary widely. I will offer my own guidance on the representative set of markets, but understand that my goal is not to create my own acronym for some intriguing subset, like BRIC, CIVETS (Colombia, Indonesia, Vietnam, Egypt, South Africa), MIST (Mexico, Indonesia, South Korea, Turkey), TIMP (Turkey, Indonesia, Mexico, the Philippines), or CAPPT (Chile, Argentina, Peru, the Philippines, Thailand). Each of these acronyms has received some investor interest in the financial press; you can tell by the very goal of this book that I am not fond of them. In the third and final chapter of the first part of the book, I will outline the empirical methodology of principal-components analysis (PCA) in considerable detail.

As already discussed above, Part II of the book will devote a chapter to each of the risk indicators with considerable discussion focused on the component data and the academic literature from which much of the component data is drawn. The validation exercise continues in Part III in much more detail than what I offered above. I have coauthored these case studies with my graduate students at the Johnson Graduate School of Management at Cornell University, and they are the basis on which I build my course on emerging market finance for which this book is a marker.

The Emerging Market Landscape

Antoine van Agtmael elegantly articulates his motives for coining the term "emerging market" back in 1981. In the introduction to his insightful 2007 retrospective book, titled *The Emerging Market Century: How a New Breed of World-Class Companies Is Overtaking the World*, he points out how important it was to overcome the stigma associated with the preexisting term "Third World." His objective was to gain the trust and investment dollars of a group of leading investment managers to which he was pitching the idea of a new fund focused on these markets.[1] Somehow the name "Third World Equity Fund" did not cut it with that crowd, even though the idea seemed to have legs. A weekend of brainstorming with van Agtmael's colleagues at the International Finance Corporation (IFC), the private-sector arm of the World Bank, inspired the more appealing designation of "emerging markets," which suggested "progress, uplift, and dynamism."[2]

What compelled van Agtmael to pitch the idea of a fund was the culmination of his efforts with the help of one of his consultants (and one who has inspired me in my own research in this area), Professor Vihang Errunza at McGill University, to develop a new database for the IFC of the stock market performance of leading firms in a number of developing economies. When they put the database together, they discovered very intriguing returns performance. The new IFC database came to be known as the Emerging Market Database, which in turn evolved into a staple research tool for many of us who have dedicated our efforts to the study of international capital markets. The IFC Emerging Market Index constructed from that very database has also become a key benchmark for many institutional and retail funds to be subsequently launched.[3]

Defining the Emerging Market Universe

Throughout this book, I will adopt the definition of emerging markets provided by the IFC. Not strictly *adopt* per se, but I lean quite heavily on it for guidance. Chalk it up to the inspiration I get from van Agtmael, Errunza, and the IFC

team of the 1980s. The IFC defines an emerging market as one that is "in transition, or increasing in size, activity, or level of sophistication."[4] Specifically, it
defines an emerging market as one that meets one of at least two criteria: it is
located in a low- or middle-income economy, as defined by the World Bank,
and its investible market capitalization is low relative to its most recent gross
domestic product (GDP). Emerging market economies then are those that have
not reached a minimum gross national product (GNP) per capita typically
associated with high-income or developed economies.

Comparisons in more detail will follow later in the chapter, but consider,
for contrast, the International Monetary Fund (IMF)'s country classification.[5]
The IMF's annual *World Economic Outlook* divides the world into two major
groups—advanced economies and emerging market and developing economies—but it is not based on strict criteria, economic or otherwise, and they
acknowledge that their rubric evolves over time. They state that it is a way of
"facilitating analysis by providing a reasonably meaningful method of organiz-
ing data."[6] Their key table provides an overview of the country classification
but offers up some key indicators of relative size, like GDP, population, and
other economic aggregates.

My thesis statement in the opening chapter is unapologetic about the focus
I have on emerging markets from an investor's perspective. To capture the IFC
emerging market universe—and, more importantly, to understand the constraints implied by their definition—I obtain information on 127 different stock
exchanges from the World Federation of Exchanges (WFE) as of 2012.[7] The
WFE divides stock markets into three categories: member exchanges; alternative markets and small- to medium-sized enterprise markets, which are secondary
exchanges in a country usually affiliated with member exchanges; and correspondent markets, which are not WFE members but participate in WFE activities,
such as conferences and roundtables, and offer up data for their survey reports.

Table 2.1 presents 2012 statistics sorted by major exchange on the stock
market capitalization (in millions of US dollars), of the number of stocks
listed, on the bond market capitalization (also in millions of US dollars), and
the number of bonds issued. The exchanges are sorted alphabetically with each
WFE region: the Americas, the Asia-Pacific, and Europe-Middle-East-Africa.
There are 62 member exchanges reporting to WFE. They represent 55 different
countries, but there is not a one-to-one matching of market to country. Two
of the markets are multiple-country consortia, like NYSE Euronext (Europe)
(which includes Belgium, France, Netherlands, and Portugal) and Nasdaq
OMX Nordic (Denmark, Estonia, Finland, Iceland, Lithuania, and Sweden).
Five countries have multiple member exchanges (United States, China, India,
Japan, Taiwan, and Russia).

There are many interesting features of the data from this cross-section of
exchanges. The two exchanges in the United States—Nasdaq OMX (US) and
NYSE Euronext (US)—together constitute the largest single-country combined
market capitalization of major markets, with over $15.5 trillion as of the end of

TABLE 2.1 The Major Markets of the World Federation of Exchanges in 2012

Exchange	Country of Domicile	Stock Market Capitalization (US$ millions)	Number of Stocks Listed (total)	Bond Market Capitalization (US$ millions)	Number of Bond Issuers (total)
Panel A—Americas					
Buenos Aires SE	Argentina	43,579.8	105	106,021.9	1390
Bermuda SE	Bermuda	1,232.3	40	4,552.0	.
BM&F Bovespa	Brazil	1,228,936.2	373	65,434.7	.
TMX Group	Canada	1,912,121.9	3945	14,907.2	206
Santiago SE	Chile	270,289.1	267	305,920.0	.
Colombia SE	Colombia	201,295.5	83	.	625
Mexican Exchange	Mexico	408,689.8	476	71,423.5	569
Lima SE	Peru	81,878.2	254	17,523.9	530
NASDAQ OMX	U.S.	3,845,131.6	2680	.	.
NYSE Euronext (US)	U.S.	11,795,575.5	2308	.	.
Panel B—Asia Pacific					
Australian SE	Australia	1,198,187.4	2079	.	.
Shanghai SE	China	2,357,423.3	931	900,588.7	630
Shenzhen SE	China	1,054,685.0	1411	16,106.7	321
Hong Kong Exchanges	Hong Kong	2,258,035.2	1496	75,821.6	.
Bombay SE	India	1,007,182.9	5112	56,491.9	.
National SE India	India	985,269.4	1640	782,888.7	5128
Indonesia SE	Indonesia	390,106.9	440	96,010.4	.
Osaka SE	Japan	215,296.8	1229	8,685,236.5	303
Tokyo SE Group	Japan	3,325,387.8	2291	8,695,621.7	323
Bursa Malaysia	Malaysia	395,623.8	940	1,273.8	.
Philippine SE	Philippines	165,066.4	253	.	.
Singapore Exchange	Singapore	598,272.7	773	.	.
Korea Exchange	South Korea	996,139.9	1816	1,044,260.7	.
Colombo SE	Sri Lanka	19,437.0	272	23.9	181
Gretai SE	Taiwan	46,798.1	608	224,095.6	1240
Taiwan SE	Taiwan	635,505.8	824	153,769.9	.
Thailand SE	Thailand	268,488.8	545	153,961.0	633
Panel C—Europe—Middle East—Africa					
NASDAQ OMX (Nordic)	Multiple[1]	842,100.9	773	.	.
NYSE Euronext (Eur.)	Multiple[2]	2,446,767.5	1112	.	4485
Wiener Börse	Austria	85,269.5	105	428,400.6	3635
Cyprus SE	Cyprus	2,853.3	106	9,706.9	63
Egyptian Exchange	Egypt	48,682.2	233	40,435.9	151
Deutsche Börse	Germany	1,184,500.2	746	26,685,570.0	22463
Athens Exchange	Greece	33,778.9	272	302,245.1	67
Budapest SE	Hungary	18,773.0	54	44,043.0	158
Irish SE	Ireland	108,393.2	55	95,384.7	21095

TABLE 2.1 Continued

Exchange	Country of Domicile	Stock Market Capitalization (US$ millions)	Number of Stocks Listed (total)	Bond Market Capitalization (US$ millions)	Number of Bond Issuers (total)
Tel Aviv SE	Israel	156,938.6	593	192,823.6	718
İMKB	Istanbul	197,074.5	264	.	.
Amman SE	Jordan	27,183.0	247	11,901.3	148
London SE Group	London	3,266,418.1	2886	.	18419
Luxembourg SE	Luxembourg	67,627.4	298	8,090,442.2	29243
Malta SE	Malta	3,428.9	21	7,144.7	113
Mauritius SE	Mauritius	7,845.1	64	1.0	2
Casablanca SE	Morocco	60,087.9	76	1,622.9	48
Oslo Børs	Norway	220,936.4	238	144,583.6	1211
Warsaw SE	Poland	138,244.2	777	154,801.4	246
MICEX	Russian Fed.	770,609.0	284	223,225.4	812
RTS Stock Exchange	Russian Fed.	783,554.8	252	0.0	0
Saudi SE Tadawul	Saudi Arabia	338,873.3	150	481.3	8
Ljubljana SE	Slovenia	6,325.9	66	18,770.9	70
Johannesburg SE	South Africa	789,037.1	395	163,252.2	.
BME Spanish SE	Spain	1,030,987.6	3276	1,984,565.8	.
SIX Swiss Exchange	Switzerland	1,089,519.4	280	618,618.3	1498

[1] Includes Denmark, Estonia, Finland, Iceland, Lithuania, and Sweden.
[2] Includes Belgium, France, Netherlands, and Portugal.

Note: These data are obtained in 2013 and are reported as of the end of 2011 for all markets in the World Federation of Exchanges universe.

2012. Of course, the total market capitalization of the United States includes that associated with listings on the various over-the-counter markets, like the OTC Markets Group, which are not captured by WFE.[8] The combination of the Tokyo and Osaka exchanges in Japan follows distantly in second place at $3.5 trillion market capitalization with the London Stock Exchange and the combination of China's two exchanges—Shanghai and Shenzhen—close on Japan's heels.[9]

An intriguing feature of these exchanges is that the number of stocks listed does not necessarily line up with the stock market capitalization. In fact, the combined listing count for the United States of almost 5,000 stocks is well exceeded by the listing count on the Bombay Stock Exchange alone (5,112) even without the boost from the National Stock Exchange of India, which adds another 1,640 to the overall count for India. The other noteworthy reported listing counts arise for the TMX Group in Canada; this number includes that for the Toronto Stock Exchange (TSX) as well as its Venture Exchange (TSXV), which I will reprise again later in discussing alternative and secondary exchanges. In relative terms, the $3.13 billion average market capitalization for the typical listing on the major US exchanges (computed from dividing the total market capitalization by the number of listed stocks) is actually trumped by the average firm market capitalization on the Switzerland's SIX Exchange ($3.89 billion) and that on the BM&F Bovespa in Brazil ($3.29 billion). To qualify for the next stage of analysis in this book a country will require a sufficiently vibrant equity market, and I will pay special attention to both the number of listings as well as the market capitalization.

One thing to note is that there may be potential unevenness of reporting standards to the WFE among its members, mandating caution on my part as I interpret these count and market capitalization data. They are inevitable given the confusion about what constitutes a stock around the world (such as whether foreign or just domestic listed are included; whether preferred stocks are excluded; or whether multiple share classes, unit trusts, or investment trusts are excluded).

Another set of data from WFE that I present in Table 2.1 is on the bond market capitalization and the number of bond issuers associated with a given securities exchange in a market. WFE is very specific about what it defines to be a bond by type of issuer (domestic versus foreign, private versus public), and it is important to remember that most bonds are not listed for trading on major exchanges in many countries around the world, but are instead traded over-the-counter.[10] This point is made most obvious by the fact that there is no WFE data of the capitalization of the bond market or the number of listings on the NYSE Euronext or Nasdaq OMX markets in the United States, although the United States constitutes the largest bond market in the world.[11] Among those that are reporting, the most notable markets are the Deutsche Börse in Germany ($26.7 trillion, more than 22,000 listed bonds), the Osaka/Tokyo exchanges ($17.3 trillion, despite only 600 bond listings), and the Luxembourg exchange ($8.1 trillion, with over 29,000 listings). The London Stock Exchange reports over 18,000 bonds listed for trading, but quotes no market capitalization associated with those listings.

The important takeaway from this first set of WFE data is that almost all of the countries with major stock and bond exchanges that are members of WFE are likely to qualify for my analysis to follow. Data availability will likely constrain my ability to retain all. The smaller markets—most notably Cyprus, Malta, and Mauritius—are poised to fall off my radar screen.

The Alternative, Small/Medium Enterprise, and Correspondent Exchanges

The need for well-organized and innovative mechanisms to facilitate capital-raising by small- and medium-sized companies (SMEs) has been a priority for many capital market regulators and participants around the world, including in many emerging markets. How best to stimulate that capital-raising has been a huge challenge. One solution adopted by many markets is to bring investment capital to the firms by listing them on some kind of alternative dedicated exchange for SMEs. The qualification criteria for these listings vary widely around the world and, as a group, are as often subject to criticism for being too stringent as they are for being too lax.[12]

The WFE tracks the number and size of alternative, SME-focused markets around the world. Table 2.2 lists their names, their respective countries of domicile, and some statistics on stock market capitalization and number of listings. Most of the alternative markets are affiliated with one of the major markets surveyed earlier. I mentioned the TSX Venture Exchange and its integration with the TMX Group in Canada. Like the TSX Venture, the count of the number of listings is substantial in absolute terms (2,444 listings) and in relative terms (compared to 3,945 total listings for the TMX Group). A similar comparison can be made for South Korea's KOSDAQ market (1,030 listings), Russia's RTS Board (1,036 listings), and Japan's JASDAQ (964 listings). The relative market capitalizations of these SMEs are distinctly smaller than their major market counterparts.

A noteworthy member of this list is the ChiNext of the Shenzhen Stock Exchange. The 281 listings and the $118 billion market capitalization are remarkable statistics, because it was inaugurated only as recently as October 2009. The launch followed ten years of delay after the approval of a high-technology exchange in 1999 by the Communist Party of China's Central Committee and the State Council.[13]

However, given that most alternative and SME exchanges are affiliated with an exchange in a major market, their existence does not fundamentally add to or subtract from the set of countries that I will survey in the remainder of the book. Moreover, the modest size of the SME exchanges (by market capitalization or even by listing count) does not alter my inclination to exclude countries—such as Cyprus, Malta, and Mauritius—from the analysis.

Table 2.3 lists a set of affiliated and correspondent markets of the WFE. Beyond its list of member exchanges, which must meet qualifying criteria, the WFE establishes other categories of relationship with exchanges: affiliate and correspondent. They are interesting to us as affiliates and correspondents because they are located mainly in emerging and frontier markets. In general, however, they do not yet comply with the WFE membership criteria, and unlike members they are not subject to peer review or vote by the WFE's General Assembly to obtain the status of affiliate or correspondent.

This last point is important because one of the key criteria on which full membership is based is the significance of the market for the economy in which it is domiciled.[14] Recall that a key element of my central thesis is that an emerging market's growth potential is dependent on the vitality of its capital markets, if not to promote the formation of domestic capital to fund the growth, then at least to facilitate global capital through foreign portfolio and direct flows. If a country's capital market falls below a reasonable threshold of importance for

TABLE 2.2 The Alternative and Small/Medium Enterprise Markets of the World
Federation of Exchanges in 2012

Exchange	Market Name	Country of Domicile	Stock Market Capitalization (US$ millions)	Number of Stocks Listed (total)
Panel A—Americas				
Buenos Aires SE	Pyme Board	Argentina	27.9	2
BM&F Bovespa	Organized OTC market	Brazil	29,766.4	99
TMX Group	TSX Venture	Canada	48,115.5	2444
Panel B—Asia—Pacific				
Shenzhen SE	ChiNext	China	118,109.2	281
Hong Kong Exchanges	Growth Enterprise	Hong Kong	10,891.4	170
Osaka Securities Exchange	JASDAQ	Japan	110,298.6	964
Tokyo SE Group	Mothers	Japan	15,844.8	178
Bursa Malaysia	ACE Market	Malaysia	2,023.8	119
Philippine SE	SME Board	Philippines	16.3	2
Singapore Exchange	SGX Catalist	Singapore	4,123.7	136
Korea Exchange	Kosdaq	South Korea	92,008.3	1030
Thailand SE	Alternative Investments	Thailand	2,354.3	73
Panel C—Europe—Middle East—Africa				
Wiener Börse	Second Regulated Market & Third Market	Austria	1,268.7	30
NYSE Euronext (Europe)	NYSE Alternext	Multiple[2]	7,163.0	180
Cyprus SE	Emerging Companies	Cyprus	663.0	9
NASDAQ OMX Nordic	First North	Multiple[1]	2,972.3	134
Egyptian Exchange	NILEX	Egypt	167.5	19
Deutsche Börse	Entry Standard	Germany	15,007.0	111
Athens Exchange	Alternative Market	Greece	213.8	14
Irish SE	Enterprise Securities	Ireland	49,217.9	25
Borsa Italiana	AIM Italia	Italy	452.8	14
Borsa Italiana	Mercato Alternativo del Capitale (MAC)	Italy	340.2	10
Luxembourg SE	Euro MTF	Luxembourg	418.9	232
Malta SE	Alternative Companies List	Malta	6.6	1
Mauritius SE	Development & Enterprise	Mauritius	1,178.2	49
Oslo Børs	Oslo Axess	Norway	1,905.2	38
Warsaw SE	NewConnect	Poland	2,475.7	351
RTS Stock Exchange	RTS Board	Russia	134,466.7	1036
Johannesburg SE	Alternative Exchange	South Africa	1,416.5	66
Johannesburg SE	Development Capital	South Africa	7.3	3
Johannesburg SE	Venture Capital Market	South Africa	12.6	3
BME Spanish Exchanges	MAB Expansion	Spain	552.7	17
İMKB 1	Second National Market	Turkey	4,405.4	61
London SE Group	Alternative Investment	United Kingdom	101,690.1	1143

[1] Includes Denmark, Estonia, Finland, Iceland, Lithuania, and Sweden.
[2] Includes Belgium, France, Netherlands, and Portugal.

Note: These data are obtained in 2013 and are reported as of the end of 2011 for all markets in the World Federation of Exchanges universe.

TABLE 2.3 The Correspondent Markets of the World Federation of Exchanges in 2012

Exchange	Country of Domicile	Stock Market Capitalization (US$ millions)	Number of Stocks Listed (total)
Panel A—Americas			
Barbados SE	Barbados	4,567.5	24
Canadian National SE	Canada	1,127.7	142
Cayman Islands SE	Cayman Islands	2,818.0	6
Costa Rica SE	Costa Rica	1,498.4	9
Jamaica SE	Jamaica	5,008.9	53
Panama SE	Panama	10,681.7	37
Panel B—Asia—Pacific			
Chittagong SE	Bangladesh	23,888.6	201
Karachi SE	Pakistan	32,567.9	621
Port Moresby SE	Papua New Guinea	40,118.0	20
Hanoi SE	Vietnam	3,980.4	393
Ho Chi Minh SE	Vietnam	21,455.5	301
Panel C—Europe—Middle East—Africa			
Bahrain Bourse	Bahrain	16,589.9	49
BRVM	Multiple[1]	6,287.6	39
Banja Luka SE	Bosnia & Herzegovina	2,263.9	791
Bulgarian SE	Bulgaria	8,253.3	393
Zagreb SE	Croatia	22,558.4	233
Dubai Financial Market	Dubai	.	.
Ghana SE	Ghana	.	.
Kazakhstan SE	Kazakhstan	22,537.3	67
Nairobi SE	Kenya	10,202.6	58
Beirut SE	Lebanon	9,047.1	10
Libyan Stock Market	Libya	3,104.0	12
Montenegro SE	Montenegro	3,551.9	347
Namibian SE	Namibia	1,152.4	32
Nigerian SE	Nigeria	39,027.5	194
Muscat Securities Market	Oman	18,246.2	114
Palestine Exchange	Palestine	2,782.5	46
Qatar Exchange	Qatar	125,775.8	42
Bucharest SE	Romania	14,023.9	79
Belgrade SE	Serbia	1,791.7	8
Bratislava SE	Slovakia	4,736.5	81
Tunis SE	Tunisia	9,662.0	57
PFTS SE	Ukraine	16,689.2	462
Ukrainian Exchange	Ukraine	25,558.3	195
Abu Dhabi SE	U.A.E.	71,324.9	67
Lusaka SE	Zambia	3,184.5	21

[1] Includes Benin, Burkina Faso, Guinea Bissau, Ivory Coast, Mali, Niger, Senegal, and Togo.

Note: These data are obtained in 2013 and are reported as of the end of 2011 for all markets in the World Federation of Exchanges universe.

the economy, it is unlikely to make the mark in my analysis. This, of course, comes at my own risk of omission. Countries that should be included may be missing from my analysis.

The table lists a large number of exchanges in countries that were not featured above. The most notable by size is the Qatar exchange with a stock market capitalization over $125 billion, a number that exceeds a good number of those listed among member exchanges on Table 2.1. Notwithstanding this size, Qatar will not make my list of countries for construction of the emerging market risk indicators. Problems arise from the lack of academic research on Qatar, as well as the absence of other key input data that I include as components of those indicators. By contrast, the Dubai Financial Market and the Abu Dhabi exchanges that are integral to the capital markets of the United Arab Emirates (UAE) will allow the UAE to qualify for my analysis, though neither is a major market by the WFE definitions. Though neither the market capitalization nor listing counts for Pakistan's Karachi Stock Exchange ($32.5 billion, 621 listings) or for Slovakia's Bratislava Stock Exchange ($4.7 billion, 81 listings) is noteworthy on this list of correspondent exchanges, I will retain these countries in my analysis.[15]

Comparing Emerging and Developed Market Classifications

The IFC's designation of an emerging market is perhaps best known, and I have already acknowledged that it is my primary guide. But it is not the only one. Armed with the universe of markets from the WFE, I can now tackle the critical decisions about which emerging and developing countries I will carry forward in the risk indicator analysis.

Table 2.4 compares emerging and developed market classifications as of 2012. The first panel of the large table is for just the emerging markets, which are listed in alphabetic order; the second panel is similar for the developed markets. There are 57 countries that make the final cut, 33 of them emerging and 24 developed. In the two panels, I include appropriate designations from six different sources, including the S&P/IFC classifications. To help guide the logic I also include recent data on GDP, population, GDP per capita, and stock and bond market capitalization, all obtained from the World Bank's World Development Indicators database. I offer fair warning that the data are organized by country and *not* by securities exchange, as in the previous tables built from the WFE. These data are also (for the most part) computed for 2012, unlike much of the WFE data, which is for 2011. The logic for including the World Bank data is that the IFC designation depends importantly on thresholds for GDP per capita and market capitalization relative to the size of economy, below which a country will be classified as emerging. These are *at least* two criteria used to capture a market's size, activity, or level of sophistication.

TABLE 2.4 Comparing Emerging and Developed Market Classifications in 2012

Country	S&P / IFC	MSCI	FTSE	JPMorgan GBI—EM Index[1]	International Monetary Fund[2]	GDP (US $millions)	Population (millions)	GDP Per Capita (US$)	Stock Market Capitalization (US$ millions)	Bond Market Capitalization (US$ millions)[*]
Argentina	Frontier	Frontier	Frontier		Emerging	475,501.7	41.1	11,573.1	34,240.7	55,004.6
Brazil	Emerging	Emerging	Emerging§	Narrow	Emerging	2,252,664.1	198.7	11,339.5	1,229,849.7	1,522,932.8
Chile	Emerging	Emerging	Emerging	Narrow	Emerging	269,869.3	17.5	15,452.2	313,325.3	84,332.4
China	Emerging	Emerging	Emerging	Broad	Emerging	8,227,102.6	1,350.7	6,091.0	3,697,376.0	3,332,787.4
Colombia	Frontier	Emerging	Emerging	Narrow	Emerging	369,606.3	47.7	7,747.8	262,101.3	78,831.9
Czech Republic	Emerging	Emerging	Emerging§		Advanced	196,446.2	10.5	18,682.8	37,163.3	82,632.5
Egypt	Emerging	Emerging	Emerging		Emerging	262,831.9	80.7	3,256.0	58,008.0	.
Hungary	Emerging	Emerging	Emerging§	Narrow	Emerging	124,600.5	9.9	12,530.5	21,080.4	68,686.2
India	Emerging	Emerging	Emerging	Broad	Emerging	1,841,709.8	1,236.7	1,489.2	1,263,335.5	646,618.2
Indonesia	Emerging	Emerging	Emerging		Emerging	878,043.0	246.9	3,556.8	396,772.1	103,233.9
Israel	Developed	Developed	Developed		Advanced	242,928.7*	7.9	31,281.5*	148,436.2	.
Jordan	Frontier	Frontier	Frontier		Emerging	31,015.2	6.3	4,909.0	26,998.0	.
South Korea	Emerging	Emerging	Developed		Advanced	1,129,598.3	50.0	22,590.2	1,180,473.4	1,159,812.6
Malaysia	Emerging	Emerging	Emerging§	Narrow	Emerging	305,032.7	29.2	10,432.1	476,340.0	322,795.9
Mexico	Emerging	Emerging	Emerging§	Narrow	Emerging	1,178,126.2	120.8	9,748.9	525,056.7	437,706.2
Morocco	Emerging	Emerging	Emerging		Emerging	95,981.6	32.5	2,902.3	52,633.7	.
Nigeria	Frontier	Frontier	Frontier	Narrow	Emerging	262,597.4	168.8	1,555.4	56,389.3	.
Pakistan	Frontier	Frontier	Emerging		Emerging	225,143.3	179.2	1,256.7	43,676.3	64,701.0
Peru	Emerging	Emerging	Emerging	Narrow	Emerging	203,790.3	30.0	6,795.8	96,850.1	25,916.2
Philippines	Emerging	Emerging	Emerging	Narrow	Emerging	250,182.0	96.7	2,587.0	264,142.9	67,492.4
Poland	Emerging	Emerging	Emerging§	Narrow	Emerging	489,795.5	38.5	12,707.9	177,730.0	202,373.8
Russia	Emerging	Emerging	Emerging	Narrow	Emerging	2,014,774.9	143.5	14,037.0	874,659.5	81,092.1
Saudi Arabia	Emerging	Frontier			Emerging	711,049.6	28.3	25,136.2	373,379.7	.

Country	Class 1	Class 2	Class 3	Class 4	IMF					
Slovakia	Frontier	Frontier	Frontier	Frontier	Advanced	91,148.7	5.4	16,847.4	4,610.6	32,870.5
Slovenia	Frontier	Frontier	Frontier	Frontier	Advanced	45,279.5	2.1	22,000.1	6,474.9	8,977.7
South Africa	Emerging	Narrow	Emerging§	Emerging	Emerging	384,312.7	51.2	7,507.7	612,308.4	201,667.3
Sri Lanka	Frontier	Frontier	Frontier	Frontier	Emerging	59,423.0	20.3	2,923.2	17,046.0	·
Taiwan*	Emerging	Narrow	Emerging§	Emerging	Advanced	464,009.0	23.1	20,111.5	634,826.0	70,318.2
Thailand	Emerging	Emerging	Emerging	Emerging	Emerging	365,965.8	66.8	5,479.8	382,999.1	216,090.4
Turkey	Emerging	Narrow	Emerging§	Emerging	Emerging	789,257.5	74.0	10,666.1	308,774.6	202,241.1
U.A.E.	Frontier	Frontier	Frontier	Frontier	Emerging	360,245.1*	9.2	40,363.2*	67,950.5	·
Venezuela	Frontier	Frontier		Frontier	Emerging	381,286.2	30.0	12,728.7	25,301.2	·
Vietnam	Frontier	Frontier	Frontier	Frontier	Emerging	155,820.0	88.8	1,755.2	32,933.1	
Mean						761,670.9	137.7	11,455.8	415,249.8	394,309.4
Median						360,245.1	41.1	10,432.1	177,730.0	84,332.4
Australia	Developed	Developed	Developed	Developed	Advanced	1,532,407.9	22.7	67,555.8	1,286,437.8	1,094,501.0
Austria	Developed	Developed	Developed	Developed	Advanced	394,707.9	8.5	46,642.3	106,036.8	341,544.2
Belgium	Developed	Developed	Developed	Developed	Advanced	483,261.8	11.1	43,372.4	300,058.2	581,960.1
Canada	Developed	Developed	Developed	Developed	Advanced	1,821,424.1	34.9	52,219.0	2,016,117.0	1,594,702.6
Denmark	Developed	Developed	Developed	Developed	Advanced	314,887.4	5.6	56,325.7	224,856.4	735,754.3
Finland	Developed	Developed	Developed	Developed	Advanced	247,545.6	5.4	45,720.8	158,686.7	88,630.1
France	Developed	Developed	Developed	Developed	Advanced	2,612,878.4	65.7	39,771.8	1,823,339.3	3,317,523.2
Germany	Developed	Developed	Developed	Developed	Advanced	3,428,130.6	81.9	41,862.7	1,486,314.8	2,667,137.3
Greece	Developed	Developed³	Developed	Developed	Advanced	249,098.7	11.3	22,082.9	44,584.1	252,982.6
Hong Kong	Developed	Developed	Developed	Developed	Advanced	263,259.4	7.2	36,795.8	1,108,127.3	127,592.7
Ireland	Developed	Developed	Developed	Developed	Advanced	210,771.4	4.6	45,931.7	109,014.0	315,520.6
Italy	Developed	Developed	Developed	Developed	Advanced	2,014,669.6	60.9	33,071.8	480,452.6	2,827,089.9
Japan	Developed	Developed	Developed	Developed	Advanced	5,959,718.3	127.6	46,720.4	3,680,982.1	15,098,250.3

TABLE 2.4 Continued

Country	S&P/IFC	MSCI	FTSE	JPMorgan GBI—EM Index[1]	International Monetary Fund[2]	GDP (US$millions)	Population (millions)	GDP Per Capita (US$)	Stock Market Capitalization (US$ millions)	Bond Market Capitalization (US$ millions)*
Luxembourg	Developed	Developed	Developed		Advanced	55,178.5	0.5	103,828.0	70,338.8	1,913.2
Netherlands	Developed	Developed	Developed		Advanced	770,555.4	16.8	45,954.7	651,004.5	1,001,096.4
New Zealand	Developed	Developed	Developed		Advanced	167,347.1	4.4	37,749.4	79,802.1	.
Norway	Developed	Developed	Developed		Advanced	499,667.2	5.0	99,557.7	252,949.9	254,155.2
Portugal	Developed	Developed	Developed		Advanced	212,274.0	10.5	20,165.3	65,529.6	280,886.1
Singapore	Developed	Developed	Developed		Advanced	274,701.3	5.3	51,709.5	414,125.8	135,764.8
Spain	Developed	Developed	Developed		Advanced	1,322,964.8	46.2	28,624.5	995,094.8	1,472,943.0
Sweden	Developed	Developed	Developed		Advanced	523,805.6	9.5	55,041.2	560,526.0	437,040.2
Switzerland	Developed	Developed	Developed		Advanced	631,173.0	8.0	78,924.7	1,079,022.0	334,424.3
United Kingdom	Developed	Developed	Developed		Advanced	2,471,783.6	63.2	39,093.5	3,019,467.1	1,734,621.9
United States	Developed	Developed	Developed		Advanced	16,244,600.0	313.9	51,748.6	18,668,333.2	26,149,796.8
Mean						1,779,450.5	38.8	49,602.9	1,611,716.7	2,645,470.9
Median						511,736.4	10.8	45,943.2	520,489.3	581,960.1

[1] The JP Morgan GBI EM Broad is the all-encompassing index with all eligible countries included regardless of capital controls, taxes, or replicability issues that limit inclusion for the Narrow.

[2] International Monetary Fund actually defines Emerging and Developing Countries as one classification in their World Economic Outlook (October 2013).

[3] Greece was downgraded in 2013 to emerging market status by MSCI.

* Denotes select data available only for 2011.

§ FTSE International denotes these markets as advanced emerging as distinct from secondary emerging.

The S&P/IFC designation is developed, emerging, or "frontier," which S&P defines as small and illiquid markets that have not yet reached emerging market status.[16] Column 1 lists the 2012 status of each country. My developed market set is fully consistent with that of S&P/IFC. We disagree in the emerging market set on 13 counts out of the 33 countries listed. Nine of those 13 disagreements are not really disagreements at all, but the fact that S&P/IFC demotes Argentina, Colombia, Jordan, Nigeria, Pakistan, Slovakia, Slovenia, Sri Lanka, UAE, and Vietnam to the frontier market set. The other three disagreements stem from Israel's promotion from emerging to developed market status in September 2010. This occurred relatively recently. I retain Israel in the emerging market set, however, since its status is intact for most of the period that the capital market research on which I draw has been done. The other two markets I include in the emerging market set are Saudi Arabia and Venezuela. Venezuela was demoted from the S&P/IFC indices in 2001, and Saudi Arabia has never made the cut. However, while it is important that I provide commentary for understanding, truth be told I worry less about whether I have appropriately classified a country as an emerging market or developed market than whether I have excluded a country that should have qualified for the analysis. The fact that all of the risk indicators are computed with developed and emerging market countries together makes the former distinction less critical.

Before I offer some comparisons with the similar designations by other index providers, it is informative to see how these S&P/IFC assignments line up with the GDP per capita and market capitalization data. The median developed has a GDP per capita of $45,943, and that of the median emerging market country is $10,432. The designation has integrity. Of course, both samples are skewed positively by right-tail outliers, since the means are both above their respective medians ($49,602 for developed, $11,455 for emerging, respectively). The fact is that the right-tail outcomes among the developed market set arise from the low base in the denominator; Luxembourg leads with $103,828 in 2012 with its population of 0.5 million, followed closely by Norway ($99,557) and its 5 million people. Among the emerging market set, the outliers are also notable in Israel ($31,281), which I have duly acknowledged to have graduated to developed market status, and in the UAE ($40,363). The relatively modest market capitalization ($67 billion) for the size of the economy in the UAE ($360 billion) appears to be one binding constraint limiting its status as a frontier market. It seems that regardless of the blurred distinctions between the two sets of countries, the differences empirically can be stark. Only Israel and the UAE present GDP per capita numbers in 2012 that lie above the cutoff for the bottom decile of developed market countries, which is $29,958 per capita. In fact, the cutoff for the *top decile* of the 33 emerging market countries is only $22,472.

I mentioned the IMF's designation of emerging and advanced economies and their own criteria for doing so at the start of this chapter. How consistent the IMF's classification scheme is with the S&P/IFC classification can be seen by comparing the first and fifth columns. There is 100% agreement among the developed countries. Notably, both include Israel on this list. South Korea remains an emerging market in the S&P/IFC, while it is among the advanced in the IMF set. The most noteworthy exceptions are the upgrades by the IMF of the Czech Republic, Slovenia, Slovakia, and Taiwan.[17] This is not an uncomfortable disagreement, as these countries have GDP per capita statistics in the top decile of emerging market countries listed in that panel of the table.

Morgan Stanley Capital International (MSCI) is one of the leading providers of investor support tools, including index construction and portfolio analytics. They provide a comprehensive framework for country classification that emphasizes economic development, liquidity and size factors, and foreign accessibility criteria.[18] Among the developed set of countries, they have reclassified Greece to emerging market status as of 2013—perhaps following the notorious fiscal problems the country has faced—but the list is otherwise consistent with the IMF and S&P/IFC designations. They also place Israel in the developed set. What is intriguing in Column 2 of the table is *not* that Argentina, Jordan, Nigeria, Pakistan, Slovenia, Sri Lanka, Vietnam, and the UAE are in the set of frontier markets for MSCI. Rather, it is that they explicitly classify Saudi Arabia in the set and do not designate at all either Slovakia or Venezuela as such, but instead as emerging markets.

FTSE International is another global leader in indexing and analytical solutions, and another classification scheme against which to calibrate my emerging market universe. They employ a number of criteria and actively update the list for promotions and demotions. An intriguing feature of their country assignments is that they distinguish not only between emerging and frontier markets, but also between "advanced" and "secondary" emerging markets.[19] I flag these in Column 3 of Table 2.4. The advanced emerging set includes the Czech Republic and Taiwan, which fell into the IMF's advanced market bucket, as well as Brazil, Hungary, Malaysia, Mexico, Poland, South Africa, and Turkey. The FTSE frontier market list includes Argentina, Jordan, Nigeria, Slovenia, Sri Lanka, and Vietnam, which accords well with the MSCI and S&P/IFC lists. While neither Venezuela nor Slovakia makes the frontier list, a number of countries are also included there that I do not include in my table. Those countries with relatively large weights in the FTSE International index that I am missing include Qatar (a lingering concern, as discussed above), Kenya, Oman, and Romania.

I have until now focused almost exclusively on equity market indices related to developed, emerging, and frontier markets. JP Morgan Securities has developed a GBI Emerging Market Bond Index that tracks local currency bonds issued by emerging market governments.[20] The "broad" index is the all-encompassing index, while the "global" index is the investible benchmark that includes only those countries that are accessible by most global investors. A "narrow" set further limits inclusion to only those countries that are readily accessible where no impediments exist. The impediments they focus on include regulatory or tax conditions that make direct, onshore investment costly. As with all debt instruments, the qualification criteria are not trivial. They focus on regularly traded, liquid, fixed-rate, domestic-currency government bonds and exclude short-maturity (less than 13 months), callable, puttable, convertible bonds. Column 5 illustrates that even together the broad and narrow sets that qualify (16 markets, in total) are a distinct subset of all 33 emerging markets listed in Table 2.4. The constraints for foreign investor accessibility appear to bind most strictly for government bond markets in China and India.

Next Steps

So, I now have my set of 57 countries to carry forward into the analysis. These are the ones that have viable markets with enough data to do the analysis I plan to do. Some of my choices are worthy of further debate and discussion, but for the most part they accord well with the classifications of the major commercial vendors of investment indices. The next step is to outline the empirical methodology that I will employ to construct the risk indicators. I use principal components analysis (PCA) technology to perform the data-reduction of the disparate sources of information that feed into the six indicator scores. I am unapologetic about the approach I use, but I also understand that the technical aspects may not be of interest to all readers. However I still encourage readers to push through to appreciate the details.

A Primer on Empirical Methodology

What is the best way to aggregate and sort through all the disparate sources of information available in order to build my risk indicators for emerging markets? It is not a small challenge. Nor are the choices obvious. One approach that is common practice is to select arbitrary weights with selected variables that are intuitively sound. Good judgment can guide those weighting schemes. But let's recognize it for what it is: subjective intuition. One may perceive great importance associated with, for example, withholding tax rates on dividend or interest income as a gauge for the market's accessibility for foreign investors, while another may assign little weight to this particular feature of global investing. How important the clearance and settlement procedures are for securities trading may seem to matter less for some investors than others when scoring how operationally inefficient a market may be.

My approach in this book is different. I will let the data tell us the appropriate weights. Specifically, I use principal components analysis (PCA), which assesses the underlying structure of the data to assign the weights to the variables associated with each risk indicator. The procedure uses a transformation to convert a set of observations of possibly correlated variables into values of linear, uncorrelated variables, referred to as "principal components." The goal of the transformation is to build principal components that can account for as much of the overall variability in the data as possible. Each successive component has the highest variance possible under the (by design) constraint that it is orthogonal to (or uncorrelated with) the preceding components. These principal components will become the risk indicator scores in my scheme.

Of course, PCA does not eliminate all intuitive judgment. After all, I have a discretionary role in defining the six indicators as general classes of risk, as well as in identifying the component variables that will be built into each of those risk indicators. I will also have to come up with a decision rule as to how many principal components will be needed to capture enough of the overall variability in the data to be confident that the data reduction makes sense. As you will see, there are lots of other choices for the econometrician. My overarching goal is to be as transparent about these choices as possible. Readers should also be aware that PCA is a popular statistical technique used for data reduction—and, more specifically, index construction—so I should readily acknowledge out of the gate that my methodology is definitely not original. However, that should lend the reader some comfort that the use of this technology certainly has precedent.

In the next section of this chapter, I will give a short history of PCA and describe it with more technical language from multivariate statistics. It is important to be thorough and correct, but the real takeaway here will be to develop a basic understanding of the output from the analysis. I will offer a brief digression on how I deal with a real problem I face: namely, the unbalanced nature of the available data I have across countries. This lack of balance arises when a given input variable for a risk indicator occasionally lacks coverage for a particular country. The solution is called the expectations-maximization (EM) algorithm, which is an iterative estimation strategy devised for PCA. These techniques are readily available in many statistical packages. To close out this chapter, I will discuss some other relevant studies in economics and finance that have employed PCA methods, so I can calibrate my choices against those of others. I also describe a recent case study of the World Bank's Doing Business Indicators and the 2013 controversy that arose from their construction and methodology. Indeed, the choices we researchers make are not always benign.

What Exactly Is Principal Components Analysis?

PCA is credited to the original work of Karl Pearson (1901). In his original article, "On Lines and Planes of Closest Fit to Systems of Points in Space," he never used the term "principal component," but he stated that "it is desirable to represent a system of points in plane, three or higher dimensional space by the 'best-fitting' straight line or plane."[1] He is clearly seeking a convenient data representation. Harold Hotelling is likely to have been the first to coin the actual term, in 1933.[2] Chapter 11 in T. W. Anderson's *An Introduction to Multivariate Statistical Analysis* (1984) provides one of the most lucid and approachable introductions to PCA I have read. It has served me well enough since graduate school days.

To provide a roadmap, let me describe the final product first. In the end, I deliver a composite score for each country summarizing the information in the variables I collect across my country set. To do this, I simply compute a weighted sum of the variables for each country, where the weights have been determined by my PCA method as being the most important in the sense of explaining variability across the variables and across the countries. So, one starts with a matrix of data, X, with dimensions n and p. This would represent p different variables (columns of X) for one of the risk indicators built for the n countries

(n equals the 57 countries, or rows of X) that comprise my sample. Each variable is supposed to have a cross-country mean of zero. The transformation is from a p-dimensional vector of weights—"loadings" in PCA parlance—$w_{(k)} = (w_1, w_2, w_3, \ldots, w_p)_{(k)}$ that can convert each row vector, $x_{(i)}$, of X for each country i, into a new vector of principal component scores, $t_{(i)}$, where $t_{(i)} = (t_1, t_2, t_3, \ldots, t_p)_{(i)}$. In other words, the procedure searches for values of $w_{(k)}$ on each variable to obtain principal component scores $t_{k,(i)}$ for each country i, where $t_{k,(i)} = x_{(i)} \cdot w_{(k)}$, in such a way that the individual variables of t capture as much of the total variability of x as possible subject to constraints.[3] In technical terms, the variability of x is defined by its "covariance" matrix. One key constraint is that the vector w must be a "unit vector," which means that the sum of the squared values of its components must add up to one. This is important because these loadings will look like "weights," though they are not exactly pure weights.

Mathematically, the first loading vector, $w_{(1)}$, or first principal component, equals $w_{(1)} = argmax_{\|w\|=1} \{\Sigma_i (t_1)^2_{(i)}\}$. The "argmax" function implies that the algorithm searches for the largest, positive value possible of what sits in the brackets, "$\Sigma_i(\ldots)$," which in turn means that the elements for the expression inside the brackets are summed across the elements of i. The "$\|w\|$" is the mathematical expression for the unit vector constraint. The complex expression can be rewritten as $w_{(1)} = argmax_{\|w\|=1} \{\Sigma_i (x_{(i)} \cdot w)^2\}$. The expression $x_{(1)} \cdot w_{(1)}$, associated with the maximum possible value for the *argmax* function, is called the "eigenvalue," and the w associated with this eigenvalue is its corresponding "eigenvector." The first component out of the gate has the largest eigenvalue; it is the first among equals and it will be important for us.

There are many instances, including in my various risk indicators, in which I will decide that the first principal component is sufficient to capture the variation in X. I will talk about the criteria and intuition used to come to such a judgment. But there may be other instances in which it is not sufficient. I may decide to build a second, third, or even more principal components to get to this point of satisfaction. The k-th principal component can be found by subtracting the first k-1 principal components from X—call it now transformed X^*—and then finding the vector of loadings that extracts the maximum variance from the resulting data matrix, X^*. By design, the eigenvalues associated with these subsequent eigenvectors will be smaller than that associated with the first principal component, which means that though their construction looks similar to the principal component scores associated with the first component (similar looking quasi-weights), they will contribute increasingly less toward explaining the overall variance of X as more principal components are selected.[4]

The desirable properties of PCA come through if the data fed into it are multivariate normally distributed. The procedure needs this assumption to estimate the eigenvectors using maximum likelihood methods, by far and away the most conventional practice. How far off this assumption is will undoubtedly be tested at times for my application. Where the potential non-normality of the data could disrupt us is in inference procedures, which I will discuss further below. I will assume that the matrix of variables, X, has all distinct and strictly positive eigenvalues to make the interpretations of my quasi-weights meaningful. PCA is also known to be sensitive to the relative scaling of the component data, so fair warning to all my readers.

The output from the PCA analysis will come in two parts. The first will list the eigenvalues of the covariance matrix, ordered from largest to smallest, and the second part exhibits the corresponding eigenvectors, or my quasi-weights for each variable. Remember that the sum of the squared elements of the eigenvector will add up to one. The eigenvalues add up to the sum of the variances of the variables in the analysis, what I keep calling the "total variability." Because the variables are standardized (I actually analyze a correlation matrix, not a covariance matrix) to have unit variance, the total variance is just the count of the number of principal components chosen. Let's assume I go after six components or variables, for example. The eigenvalues are the variances of the principal components, so the value of the first eigenvalue—let's say it has a value of 3—implies that the first component captures 50% (3 out of 6) of the total variance. If the second eigenvalue is 1.5, it captures another 25% (1.5 out of 6) of the total variance, and I will be able to declare that the first two components together deliver 75% of the total variability, and 25% is left unexplained. I will always report the total fraction explained by the number of components chosen as *Rho*.

As a general rule, I will seek the admittedly arbitrary goal of at least 50% of total variance to declare sufficiency. I want to believe it is a seemingly reasonable cutoff, and it is one that I have seen used in many other research studies. That means that I will choose the number of principal components for a given risk indicator to minimally get me over the 50% threshold. If it takes just one, then I will build the risk indicator scores from just the first principal component. If it takes two to get over the 50% threshold, then so be it: I will construct a risk indicator score by averaging across the resulting scores from the first two components. I will weight them by the relative size of their respective eigenvalues, which gives a sense of their relative importance.

I always choose an option to evaluate whether the eigenvalues are equal to zero, an inference judged by computing their respective standard errors, associated z-statistics, the 90% confidence intervals, and p-values.[5] If the 90% confidence interval for the eigenvalue straddles zero or if the p-value is greater than 10%, then a researcher might hesitate as to whether or not this component is statistically important enough to worry about or include. But this inference relies heavily on the multivariate normality assumption. The output of a typical PCA also delivers standard errors for each of the elements of the eigenvector. This information helps guide me on how much each of the individual variables I offer up for each risk indicator actually contributes statistically.

If the quasi-weights are statistically indistinguishable from zero (90% confidence interval straddles zero, or the p-value of its z-statistic exceeds 10%), then this variable gets little attention in capturing the overall variation for this risk indicator. I do not choose to make an intuitive judgment about its importance; rather, it is conferred on us statistically by the data.

Three additional, somewhat useful tests arise from assuming multivariate normality. One is a likelihood ratio test for the equality of the coefficients. That is, I want to know whether the quasi-weights or elements of the eigenvector are equal to each other. In most applications this will be quite unlikely, so there will be few surprises when I show very large values for the chi-squared test statistic (symbolically, χ^2) and very low p-values implying a rejection of the null hypothesis of equality. That is useful for my exercise as it tells us that some variables are more important than others. A second chi-squared test evaluates the independence of the different components and a third tests for multivariate normality (called "sphericity" in PCA language). I give fair warning that this last test will typically reject the null hypothesis of normality in almost every setting I consider. You might then ask why I use the technique at all, given its core assumption is rejected. The answer is that the technique is not wrong, the estimated loadings are valid, and so are the resulting eigenvalues; only the statistical inferences about the precision of individual variables get wobbly.

Dealing with the Problem of Zero Values

In general settings, variation in the availability of data makes PCA infeasible. This will be a real problem for the exercise in this book, as I want to incorporate as broad a cross-section of variables as possible to encapsulate the key elements of the risk indicators. But some observations for some of the variables will unavoidably be missing. I worked hard to justify a reasonable set of countries in Chapter 2 to mitigate this problem, but the zero values do not go away completely. I inevitably face an unbalanced panel of variables across countries.

Thankfully, there is a workable solution to the problem of zero values. It is a technique called the expectations-maximization, or EM algorithm. It is an iterative estimation strategy developed by Watson and Engle (1983) and Stock and Watson (2002).[6] Truthfully, the EM algorithm was developed to deal with variation in the frequency of data in the time domain (for example, months, quarters, and years). Stock and Watson were seeking an optimal forecast of a single time series—such as one-year-ahead growth rates in industrial production—using a large number of potential predictors and time-series observations. They build a small number of indices from the many predictors using PCA. But some predictors have a quarterly frequency, others a monthly frequency. Some are available for only a short subperiod, others for the whole historical period of analysis.

The EM algorithm uses the information from the complete or balanced panel of variables to make the best possible predictions of the incomplete or unbalanced panel of variables. It works reasonably well if the number of variables is sufficiently large, and it delivers the same desirable statistical properties as PCA. It begins with estimation by PCA on a balanced subset of the data to obtain an initial estimate of the index. In my setting, imagine that complete data exists on all five variables for each of the 57 countries in my sample, except Saudi Arabia and Peru. Assume further that these two countries are only missing observations for the second and third of the five variables. I generate the relevant number of principal components for the 55 countries for which there is complete data. The values for the missing countries are actually set equal to the average across all countries as starting values to get the PCA to run. Data for each of the variables is then projected onto the resulting principal component scores using univariate regression analysis. The principal component is the independent variable in the regression and the variable of interest is the dependent variable. The fitted values from the regression are used to predict the missing or zero values. For Saudi Arabia and Peru, in the example above, the missing values for the second variable will come from the fitted values from the regression. The risk indicator scores are re-estimated by PCA on the combination of actual and, where needed, predicted data. This process continues until the difference in the sum of the squared prediction errors between iterations reaches a desired level of convergence. In my application to come in Part II of the book, it is rare that I see convergence take longer than two iterations.

Stock and Watson's EM algorithm faces limitations. One of them is an underlying assumption of normalization of the data known as "stationarity." Recall that they are working in the time domain (and I work on the cross-section of countries), so there is a concern about the mean and variance of each variable varying over time. In my application, the cross-country nature of the application may be inappropriate if any two given variables of interest across developed, emerging, and frontier markets are fundamentally drawn from different populations with different means and variances. This possibility is real. But a core assumption underlying the exercise is that they are comparable; so I propose that stationarity across groups of countries is a decent working null hypothesis. There are a host of other methods that improve on different potential weaknesses of the EM algorithm of Stock and Watson, none of which I employ for convenience.[7] This statistical technology is ever improving with new research, so I could envision adopting newer variants of the EM algorithm in the future.

A Little Benchmarking Against Some Previous Approaches

There are as many useful examples of research studies in business and economics that employ data-reduction techniques like PCA to build indices for various purposes as there are of those that avoid them and do something more direct and simple. I will feature some of these studies for their actual content in Part II, but here I want to examine their methodological approach against mine.

Consider first the study on corporate transparency and disclosure by Bushman, Piotroski, and Smith (2004).[8] The authors analyze an extensive range of measures of corporate reporting practices around the world, including (1) disclosure intensity, which is related to reporting of segment information, research and development expenditures, capital expenditures, subsidiaries, and overall accounting policy ("Disclosure"); (2) governance disclosures, the number of major shareholders, management information, names of board members, and director/officer remuneration ("Governance"); (3) timeliness of disclosures, including frequency of reporting, consolidation of interim reports, and the number of disclosed items ("Timeliness"); and (4) reporting of consolidation and discretionary reserves ("Measurement"). The authors employ factor analysis because, like PCA, "the goal of factor analysis is to identify commonalities, or factors, underlying my measures of corporate reporting."[9] Factor analysis and PCA have very similar origins.[10] Their factor scores are standardized, scale-free (ranging in value from zero to 100, where large values indicate high transparency), extracted from several variables across 203 firms in 46 countries. Their approach, like mine, necessitates some discretionary choices. For example, they focus on six of the 10 country-level, firm-specific measures in order to maximize sample size and degrees of freedom for their analysis. They also justify the use of two factors based on how they are correlated after the fact with the key transparency and disclosure variables.

A related study by Larcker, Richardson, and Tuna (2007) focuses on corporate governance and emphasizes the importance of methodology. The authors evaluate a sample of 2,106 US firms for which they distill 39 so-called structural measures of corporate governance, including board characteristics, stock ownership, institutional ownership, activist stock ownership, existence of debt-holders, mix of executive compensation, and antitakeover variables, into 14 governance constructs (principal component scores) using PCA.[11] They demonstrate how these constructs are empirically associated with future operating performance, stock return performance, and abnormal accruals in financial statements. But what is intriguing is that their methodology is designed to take direct aim at the preceding effort by Gompers, Ishii, and Metrick (2004).[12] Gompers et al. are best known for their governance index or "G-index," which was constructed from 24 governance rules for 1,500 large US firms during the 1990s. They acknowledge the index construction method in Gompers et al. is straightforward in that they sum up points, each one awarded for every one of the provisions that reduce shareholder rights relative to management power.[13]

The Larcker et al. study argues that previous efforts like the G-index uses only a small set of convenient and easy-to-collect indicators rather than a more comprehensive set of governance variables. They also mention how there is little analysis regarding the measurement properties of the selected indicators; that they can be ill-defined, subject to substantial measurement error, and fail to consider complex interactions among the component indicators. A statistical methodology like PCA aims to resolve some of these problems, though the methodology employed by Gompers et al. of course has its own intuitive appeal.

These debates are interesting and worthwhile. I am aware of them, but do not subscribe to all of the points in favor of a more technical approach. While I have made my choice to pursue a PCA approach, I am aware it has its strengths and its weaknesses.

A Case Study of Controversy over the Methodology of Country Rankings

Since 2004, the Private Sector Group of the World Bank has been constructing and publishing their Doing Business Indicators (DBI), which measure the costs to firms, especially small- and medium-sized ones, of business regulations in almost 200 countries (up through 2012). The data are based on research of laws and regulations with input and verification from more than 3,000 local government officials, lawyers, business consultants, and other professionals who routinely administer or advise on legal and regulatory requirements. Standard template questionnaires have been developed for all topics. The World Bank's website is extensive, detailed, and very accessible.[14] And in fact, I will employ some of the key indicators on getting credit, on protecting investors, and on enforcing contracts in my emerging market risk indicators in Part II.

The DBI is focused on a controversial topic, and there are many critics who have focused on the reliability and objectivity of its measurements. Critics allege that it forces attention on mundane business regulation instead of what they consider more important matters, such as poverty alleviation and economic development. The controversy boiled over during 2012 when Bin Han, China's deputy executive director at the World Bank, stated that the index "used wrong methodologies, failed to reflect facts, misled readers, and added little value to China's improvement of the business environment."[15] One concern was the fact that DBI failed to account for macroeconomic conditions, including readily available statistics on real GDP growth or rising foreign direct investment.[16] Others argued that important indicators related to corruption were not included in the ranking.

The World Bank appointed a panel of economists to look at the potential flaws in the index. The report was published in June 2013, titled *Independent Panel Review of the Doing Business Report*.[17] The report focused on the potential of the scores to be misinterpreted, on the narrow set of information sources, its data collection methodology, and the use of aggregate rankings. Among the

11 individual recommendations, the most intriguing was that which proposed to abolish the aggregate rankings across the countries. Instead, they proposed shifting emphasis to components of the aggregate index: procedures, time, cost, and minimum capital needed to start a business; paying taxes, getting credit, enforcing contracts, and resolving insolvency. The panel questioned the integrity of the exercise of distilling multiple variables drawn from independent sources into a single indicator, which is the heart of the exercise in this book!

Global index rankings are popular, and many scholars have recently focused their attention on the methodology of their construction. Some have proposed that they are misleading not because they are missing information or the indicators are wrong, but because the estimation of the scores ignores inherent uncertainty. Consider the recent study by Bjørn Høyland, Karl Moene, and Fredrik Willumsen, "The Tyranny of International Index Rankings."[18] They remark on the controversy discussed above on DBI (as well as Freedom House's *Freedom in the World* and the United Nations' *Human Development Index*), emphasizing how favorable or unfavorable positions in the rankings are likely to be widely noticed with governments standing to lose by not commenting on them. Høyland et al. use a Bayesian approach to account for large numbers of indicators and the correlations among them to estimate uncertainty bounds in the index scores.[19]

I duly acknowledge these warnings from scholars focused on methodology and the controversies that swirl around the construction of these cross-country indices. Nevertheless, I forge forward.

{ PART II }

Building the Emerging Markets Risk Indicators

Market Capacity Constraints

The scope and breadth of the capital markets, the extent of the trading activity taking place in those markets, and their overall vibrancy toward fostering capital formation for business lays the foundation for economic growth. A central tenet of this book is that the less binding the constraints corporations or investors face in participating in capital markets, the greater is a market's capacity, and the healthier is the capital formation process that takes place.

In emerging markets, the vibrancy of the capital markets can be stoked indirectly by macroeconomic policies explicitly designed to promote real GDP growth directed at inflation, exchange rates, or promotion of the trade sector. It can, however, be more directly connected with financial market reforms aimed at developing the domestic financial system. This can be through deregulation of the banking system or privatizations of formerly state-owned enterprises. More developed financial markets and better financial intermediation can enhance growth by relaxing financial constraints and by improving allocation of capital for business investment. Well-functioning equity and bond markets can promote financial development, in turn. By far, the financial liberalization policies that have greatest consequence are those allowing inward and outward foreign investments, both in portfolio and direct form. In fully liberalized markets, foreign investors can, without restriction, purchase or sell domestic securities and domestic investors can purchase or sell foreign securities.

Much research in financial economics affirms this basic principle: fewer restrictions on market participation and activity mean more vibrant capital markets and greater investment and economic development.[1] But there are other perspectives, too.[2]

The next five chapters focus on the various sorts of restrictions that could impede the free flow of capital, both domestic and foreign, in an emerging market. My opening gambit in this particular chapter focuses on what factors limit the capacity of the capital markets in an emerging market defined relative to its economic size. This is, in a way, the first among equals in the set of risk indicators.

Folli Follie Group and Fosun International:
A Global Partnership

"We believe the strategic partnership between Folli Follie and Fosun is win-win cooperation," pronounced Liang Xingjun, vice chairman and CEO of Fosun on May 19, 2011.[3] Added George Koutsolioutsos, CEO of Folli Follie Group: "We are positive that this partnership will mutually benefit both groups, empowering the Folli Follie Group presence in China and the Fosun Group presence in Greece."[4] The two groups had just signed a memorandum of agreement in which Fosun International, a large China-based holding company with diverse business interests, had agreed to acquire a 9.5% stake in Folli Follie, a Greek luxury jewelry designer and retail group, for €84.58 million. Fosun would acquire newly issued stock through a private investment in public equity (PIPE) placement at €13.30 per share and would, as a result, become one of Folli Follie Group's largest strategic investors. On the day of the announcement, Folli Follie Group's stock price rose a modest 1.6% (from €12.75 to €12.95 per share), which is less than the typical reaction after PIPE deal announcements.[5] Much more disappointingly, Folli Follie's stock price fell to as low as €3.30 per share by June of 2012, one year later—a cumulative decline of almost 75%.

Koutsolioutsos, who founded Folli Follie in Athens in 1982, had been aggressively expanding his firm both geographically and by product segments. The firm now designed, manufactured, and distributed jewelry, watches, and fashion accessories.[6] The group expanded, mostly through franchising, all over Greece and Japan and had a presence in 24 countries with 430 points of sale, including some of the most fashionable streets in London, Paris, and Tokyo. Folli Follie Group's merger with Hellenic Duty Free Shops in June 2010 helped them build a strong presence in the travel retail market in numerous airport duty-free shops around the world.

What had stalled out Koutsolioutsos's expansion plans in the last year had been the global financial crisis and the knock-on effects of the sovereign debt crisis in Greece and southern Europe during 2010. The group's consolidated sales had sunk year-on-year, by 1% to €989.6 million in 2010 after many successive years of double-digit growth. Greece had entered into a severe recession in the second quarter of 2010. The Greek government's deficit was estimated to be 13.6% of GDP—one of the highest in the world—and public debt was projected according to some estimates to hit 120% of GDP during that year.[7] The other countries of the Euro bloc together with the International Monetary Fund (IMF) had agreed to a €110 billion rescue package, including an immediate €45 billion bailout loan, but harsh austerity measures were mandated to help bring the deficit under control. Capital in Greece was scarce. In pursuit of the capital he needed to fund his growth plans, Koutsolioutsos hired Crédit Agricole, one of the largest retail banking groups in France, to help Folli Follie find a strategic partner.

China was a logical place to look for one. Accounting for 20% of the luxury division's sales, China was the most important market for Folli Follie. Koutsolioutsos said that the company intended to open 35 stores in China in 2011, after opening 25 outlets the previous year.[8] Overall, it was estimated that China accounted for 10% of Folli Follie's sales and 17% of group earnings before interest, taxes, depreciation, and amortization. But why partner with Fosun International?

Fosun was established in 1992 by four graduates of Shanghai's Fudan University as a pharmaceuticals business, but then moved into real estate, health care, steel, mining, retail, services, and other strategic business units.[9] It grew by acquiring state-run enterprises transitioning to the private sector. Fosun International, the parent holding company, went public in Hong Kong on July 16, 2007, and grew to be the largest private conglomerate in China by 2010, with revenues of $7 billion and total assets of $21 billion. Global expansion was a major component of Fosun's agenda. Fosun sought to "actively capture investment opportunities benefiting from China's growth momentum" as an important task for building up its main business portfolio.[10] It had invested in overseas-listed companies with a China presence, including Focus Media, Chindex, and Club Med, but in a way that was sensitive to the overseas company's brand strength. "For a Chinese company to take control of a US or European brand, you'll run into problems of trust," says Liang Xinjun, Fosun's CEO and one of the four founders. He added: "When I buy into a brand, I want the company's customers to think that nothing will change to existing investors, we have to appear as a benign shareholder, as their China partner."[11]

Macro trends drove this deal's closing. The People's Republic of China was one of the fastest growing economies in the world, with consistent annual GDP growth rates around 10% over the past 30 years. A rising middle class, with its increased spending power in tow, promoted rapid growth in China's luxury goods market, estimated to be about $9.4 billion by 2009.[12] And Chinese outward foreign direct investment soared to over $68 billion in 2010—a total that was still small compared to the US figure of $329 billion, according to the United Nations, but more than five times its own only five years earlier.[13] Early waves of Chinese investment abroad were led by the purchase of mining and energy companies among Chinese state-owned enterprises, well-funded by more than $2 trillion of accumulated foreign currency reserves. But at increasing frequency private companies, such as Fosun, were becoming part of the mix.[14]

The only remaining questions revolved around the terms of the cross-border PIPE deal. The analysts were all over the place.[15] The market's muted response and the longer-run swoon was likely not what the parties expected, but the relationship survives today.[16] According to S&P Capital IQ (as of December 2012), Fosun International held 9.96% of Folli Follie Group shares and Fosun Capital, a division of the Fosun International holding company, owned another 3.89%.

How to Measure a Market's Capacity

One lesson learned from the Folli Follie Group's PIPE deal with Fosun is about how capital constraints can impede business growth. Local capital markets in Europe during the sovereign debt crisis were fragile. Firms like Folli Follie became dependent on external capital to fund their growth plans. Another lesson is how PIPE deals are an emerging force of change in global markets. But the most important takeaway for this book, I would argue, is that simply classifying a country as an emerging market belies what may really be going on there. By conventional definitions outlined in Chapter 2, China is an emerging market. This is undoubtedly correct. But it is not necessarily so because of the lack of capital, though that is a common feature among emerging markets. In fact, China has become a major global supplier of capital. In this chapter I will demonstrate that China effectively looks more like a developed market in terms of its market capacity constraints. By contrast, Greece is typically listed as a developed market (notwithstanding MSCI's reclassification of Greece in 2013). I will show you that as of 2012, it effectively looks much more like an emerging market in terms of the vibrancy of its capital markets.

How should market capacity constraints be measured? Market capacity is about the size of the capital markets, but size has to be defined relative to economic need. And size, however measured, does not fully account for the functions of the financial system, which may ultimately facilitate economic growth. What I need is a rubric to guide my thinking. Thankfully, there is a huge academic literature on the nexus of financial development and economic growth in development economics that goes as far back as the previous century, including the writings of Walter Bagehot, Joseph Schumpeter, John Maynard Keynes, and Joan Robinson, among many others.

A useful theoretical place to start might be with the seminal work of the state-contingent claim framework of Kenneth Arrow and Gerard Debreu.[17] Their framework would propose that there is no need for a financial system designed to facilitate transactions unless there are costs of acquiring information, creating contracts, and making transactions (say, in researching projects, scrutinizing managers, easing risk management, and settling trades). Financial markets and the institutions that support them ease the information and transactions frictions on the reallocation of funds from agents (say, individuals saving) with an excess of capital, given their investment opportunities toward other agents (say, firms investing) with a shortage of capital given their investment opportunities. Building on this and other studies published since, Ross Levine, a thought leader in development economics, crafted an excellent survey of research in 1997, in which he crisply summarizes five basic functions of the financial system.[18] They include (1) facilitating the trading, hedging, diversifying, and pooling of risk; (2) allocating resources; (3) monitoring managers and exerting corporate control; (4) mobilizing savings; and (5) facilitating the exchange of goods and services. Behind each of these five pillars lie dozens of seminal studies, in turn.

The earliest empirical study linking the functioning of the financial system and economic growth is by Raymond Goldsmith. He studied 35 countries and their economic growth from 1860 to 1963, using the value of financial intermediary assets divided by GNP to gauge financial development. The assumption is that the size of the financial system is correlated with the quality of financial services provided.[19] It did not take other leading scholars too long to establish that additional measures of the level of financial development, beyond just private credit extended by financial institutions, might be needed to get it right.[20] The depth, breadth, scope, and vibrancy of the financial sector all promote its functioning.

I stand on their shoulders to define my set of market capacity indicators for analysis.

The Need for Domestic Credit from Financial Institutions

It is intuitive that the banking system is likely to provide for each of the five financial functions in an economy, and so to measure the capacity of a market one should examine the level of activity of a country's banking system. Domestic credit to the private sector refers to financial resources provided to the private sector by financial institutions and banks, such as through loans, purchases of nonequity securities, trade credit, and other accounts receivable, all of which establish a claim for repayment. In many countries, these claims include credit extended to public enterprises. For comparison across countries, I normalize this number by GDP of each country, making it a unitless ratio. The data come from the World Bank's World Development Indicators.

In addition to Goldsmith, King and Levine build measures of the liabilities of the financial system (currency plus demand and interest-bearing liabilities of banks and nonbank financial intermediaries).[21] As a fraction of GDP, these depth measures are strongly positively correlated with real per capita GDP growth across 80 countries between 1960 and 1989. King and Levine consider the relative importance of the mix of central bank and commercial bank assets and evaluate the credit allocated to private firms, in particular, under the assumption that such systems are more engaged in researching firms, exerting corporate control, providing risk management services, mobilizing savings, and facilitating transactions than those that funnel credit to the government or state-owned enterprises. A key weakness of this measure is that it ignores the broader role of capital markets, beyond just that segment involved in intermediation by financial institutions.

The Capitalization of the Equity Markets

Market capitalization to GDP is the value of listed equity or bond shares divided by GDP. This is also a unitless ratio. These data are from the World Federation of Exchanges and the World Bank's World Development Indicators. I include data on the value of listed shares for all stock exchanges associated with a country including multiple exchanges (e.g., Shanghai and Shenzhen for China), alternative, small- and medium-size enterprise, and correspondent markets (from Chapter 2).

Researchers typically use this ratio as an indicator of financial development, because stock market size is correlated positively with the ability to mobilize capital and diversify risk. Existing firms' past retained earnings and future growth prospects are also presumed to be embodied in the ratio: a higher ratio to GDP implies better growth prospects and a more developed market. Many studies have used this measure for stock market development.[22] The key weakness of the indicator is that a few companies with heightened (or suffering) valuations can give a misleading impression of equity market development (or contraction), even when there has been no change in the size of the market in terms of participation or of equity capital raised.

The Size of the Bond Markets

For bond markets, the most commonly used proxy for size is the outstanding volume of debt securities—both private and public—relative to GDP. The data are obtained from the World Bank's Database on Financial Development and Structure.[23] Demirgüc-Kunt and Maksimovic examine whether the underdevelopment of legal and financial systems prevent firms from investing in potentially profitable growth opportunities. They find the greatest difference in linking firms' financial structures to GDP growth in developed and developing countries is the provision of long-term debt.[24]

The real story here is about the complementarities in stock market, bond market, and banking-sector development on the external financing decisions of firms and firm growth.

Number of Publicly Listed Companies

This count is another measure of a market's capacity. It is another unitless ratio as I normalize by the population (in millions). I count the number of domestically listed companies for all equity markets designated for a given country in Chapter 2. Several studies argue that this measure captures the breadth of the stock market without the risk of being tainted by fluctuations in market valuations that stem from only a few companies.[25] But it can be too slow-moving to fully capture higher-frequency changes in the environment. The measure can also be affected by the process of consolidation and by the industrial structure of markets. I follow La Porta, Lopez-de-Silanes, Shleifer, and Vishny and Rajan and Zingales, who deflate the count by the population in the tens of thousands.[26]

Of course, an important factor in driving the number of listed companies is the number of newly listed initial public offerings (IPOs), which vary from year to year. IPO counts capture the breadth of a stock market and they are empirically linked to capital market and macroeconomic conditions, as well as many of the fundamentals that will be described in the chapters of Part II in the book. Consider the Doidge, Karolyi, and Stulz study, which shows how the number of new listings in each country (and the value of capital raised through IPOs) is influenced by the quality of national institutions, such as the legal protections afforded to minority investors (Chapter 8), and by the extent to which a country has liberalized foreign access (Chapter 6).[27] What the study shows is how globalization has opened up the market for global offerings—IPOs with foreign or combined foreign/domestic tranches for investors—by firms in most countries around the world, including emerging markets, and how this shift, in turn, has mitigated the deterrent of weaker legal, regulatory, or governance-related institutions for newly public issues.

The Vibrancy of a Market: Turnover

Turnover measures the value of total shares traded divided by market capitalization. It is in percentage terms. Turnover is a good measure of market capacity because it reflects the level of trading activity in listed companies. Large price volatility could adversely affect this measure for my purpose, as price increases can increase the value traded even without a change in the number of transactions or a fall in transaction costs. It is not a direct measure of liquidity, but high turnover is expected to signal lower transaction costs. Thus, this variable could fit into the operational efficiency indicator to be discussed in Chapter 5 to follow. Turnover in emerging markets is studied actively as an outcome measure related to financial development.[28]

And the Data Show . . . ?

Table 4.1 presents the statistics for emerging and developed markets for these six measures of market capacity. It is clear that each of the measures of market depth, breadth, and scope are greater for developed than emerging markets. Consider that the ratio of domestic credit from financial institutions to GDP is

TABLE 4.1 Measures of Market Capacity Constraints in 2012

Country	Domestic Credit from Financial Institutions to GDP (%)	Stock Market Capitalization to GDP (%)	Stock Market Turnover Ratio (%)	Number of Listed Firms per Million in Population	Private Bond Market Capitalization to GDP (%)	Public Bond Market Capitalization to GDP (%)
Argentina	13.96	9.77	4.76	2.42	1.97	10.36
Brazil	56.04	49.62	69.29	1.86	21.68	39.81
Chile	79.94	107.60	18.60	13.26	14.76	18.81
China	121.49	46.29	188.21	1.74	23.08	22.44
Colombia	42.01	59.85	13.29	1.68	0.57	22.87
Czech Republic	.	17.75	38.01	1.42	12.81	25.44
Egypt	30.37	20.63	33.53	2.79	.	.
Hungary	.	13.54	83.86	5.21	5.92	43.61
India	47.15	54.22	56.26	4.11	4.89	29.64
Indonesia	28.25	46.09	37.21	1.81	1.41	10.79
Israel	92.54	59.68	58.14	74.17	.	.
Jordan	69.71	94.25	13.86	39.96	.	.
South Korea	98.43	89.22	195.14	35.99	59.25	44.81
Malaysia	106.40	137.21	32.00	32.60	58.09	54.02
Mexico	24.03	35.29	25.95	1.11	15.68	22.12
Morocco	68.72	60.57	9.78	2.32	.	.
Nigeria	22.91	16.10	9.21	1.20	.	.
Pakistan	18.05	15.55	28.59	3.60	.	30.70
Peru	24.16	44.84	5.49	6.87	3.32	11.33
Philippines	29.79	73.58	20.36	2.64	0.96	29.07
Poland	.	26.81	58.39	19.80	2.07	37.18
Russia	41.66	41.93	127.32	2.30	.	4.27
Saudi Arabia	52.44	58.75	84.65	5.34	.	.
Slovakia	48.24	4.93	6.06	14.88	4.96	29.25
Slovenia	91.46	12.58	6.50	32.16	7.35	10.51
South Africa	141.41	130.16	64.26	7.01	18.77	31.42
Sri Lanka	26.71	32.84	25.11	12.12	.	.
Taiwan	.	136.81	136.33	605.94	15.15	33.07
Thailand	130.87	77.67	85.11	7.83	12.73	49.78
Turkey	43.17	26.05	162.72	4.92	0.56	25.54
UAE	60.78	19.80	21.32	13.18	.	.
Venezuela	17.22	1.63	0.86	1.23	.	.
Vietnam	107.68	14.81	29.55	3.42	.	.
Emerging Median	*48.2*	*46.1*	*33.5*	*4.92*	*7.3*	*29.1*
Developed Median	*167.10*	*58.2*	*87.1*	*31.05*	*37.8*	*45.4*

Note: Appendix A details all data sources for the market capacity indicators. Some indicators are constructed from component data available as of the end of 2011.

48.2% for the median emerging market, less than one-third of that among developed markets. South Africa, Thailand, and China stand tall among emerging markets at 141%, 130%, and 121%, respectively. Each of those three would fit comfortably in the distribution among developed countries though their figures place them below the median. The market capitalization to GDP ratios among emerging markets (median of 46.1%) is closer to that for developed markets (median of 58.2%). The noteworthy right-tail outliers among the emerging markets are Malaysia (137%), Taiwan (136%), and South Africa (130%). But the story here is just as much about the developed market set, which features seven countries with equity market capitalization ratios below the median for emerging markets, including Austria, Belgium, Germany, Greece, Italy, Norway, and Portugal. Hong Kong, by contrast, is off the charts as a right tail with a ratio of 357% in 2012.

There are few eye-catching figures among the bond market capitalization ratios for emerging markets. The median size of the bond markets among developed countries far exceeds that in emerging markets (37% to 7% for private bonds, 45% to 29% for public bonds). What may be most noteworthy is the absence of data for many of the markets (actually 10 of the 37 countries listed). In fact, only the Brazilian, Malaysian, and South Korean bond markets would be comparable to the equivalent figures among the developed set. It is the underdeveloped private bond markets that bind more stringently. Turnover ratios in emerging equity markets are, on average, much lower than those for developed markets (33% versus 87% for developed markets). South Korea, China, Turkey, and Taiwan bring up the average with turnover ratios well above 100%. The number of listed companies per capita (in millions) has a lower median among emerging markets (4.92) compared to developed markets (31.05), but the cross-country dispersion among emerging markets is remarkable. In fact, Taiwan (605 firms per million) and even Israel (at 74 firms per million) both have counts that well exceed that for the typical developed market.

Distilling a Market Capacity Indicator with
Principal Component Analysis

Table 4.2 provides the summary statistics on the results of the PCA analysis for the market capacity indicator. There are two panels and this is will be the standard for presentation in the next several chapters. The first panel at the top lists the eigenvalues associated with the principal components chosen, the eigenvectors (or loadings, listed under coefficient heading) for each of the components, and a variety of statistics about their precision. The second panel gives some overall diagnostics about the reliability of the estimation.

You can see that only two components were selected for the market capacity indicator, because only two were needed to meet the arbitrary threshold

TABLE 4.2 Principal Component Analysis for Market Capacity Constraints

Eigenvalues	Coefficient	Std. Err.	z-statistic	p-value	(5%,	95%)
First Component	2.48964	0.46635	5.34	0.00	1.57560	3.40367
Second Component	1.32448	0.24810	5.34	0.00	0.83821	1.81074
First Component						
Domestic Credit	0.55575	0.05224	10.64	0.00	0.45337	0.65814
Stock Market Cap	0.40520	0.11458	3.54	0.00	0.18063	0.62977
Stock Market Turnover	0.42711	0.08634	4.95	0.00	0.25790	0.59633
Number of Listed Firms	0.32352	0.13360	2.42	0.02	0.06166	0.58538
Private Bond Market Cap	0.34824	0.12520	2.78	0.01	0.10286	0.59362
Public Bond Market Cap	0.34436	0.11807	2.92	0.00	0.11295	0.57578
Second Component						
Domestic Credit	−0.09045	0.14899	−0.61	0.54	−0.38247	0.20157
Stock Market Cap	0.48459	0.13112	3.70	0.00	0.22760	0.74158
Stock Market Turnover	−0.05435	0.20367	−0.27	0.79	−0.45353	0.34484
Number of Listed Firms	0.58647	0.12107	4.84	0.00	0.34916	0.82377
Private Bond Market Cap	−0.49016	0.18527	−2.65	0.01	−0.85328	−0.12705
Public Bond Market Cap	−0.41211	0.19516	−2.11	0.04	−0.79462	−0.02960

Diagnostics	
Number of observations	57
Number of components	2
Trace	6
Rho	0.6357
Std. Err. (Rho)	0.0396
Likelihood Ratio test for dependence: χ^2 (15)	84.69 p-value 0.00
Likelihood Ratio test for sphericity: χ^2 (20)	85.65 p-value 0.00

Note: For columns listed under the headings of 5% and 95%, the values of the coefficient at the 5% and 95% limits of the 90% confidence range are reported, respectively.

rule of at least 50% of the overall variability I discussed in Chapter 3. The first eigenvalue has a coefficient of 2.48, which represents 41.4% of the variation. It is precisely estimated, given its z-statistic of 5.34 and a 90% confidence range of 1.57 to 3.40. The second component is needed to get us over the 50% mark. The cumulative proportion—captured by the *Rho* statistic in the second panel—is 63.57%. I should mention that this particular indicator converged after two iterations with the EM algorithm, which suggests that the unbalanced nature of the sample across countries was not severe enough to impede the PCA approach.

There is interesting variation in the coefficients in the first principal component. Three of the coefficients are distinctly larger than the other three. The largest coefficient is for domestic credit as a fraction of GDP (0.55, associated z-statistic of 10.64). This domestic credit variable receives the heaviest weighting in my scheme. This gives nice support for the original Goldsmith and subsequent King and Levine studies that suggest the important position of the banking sector for development.[29] The two main stock market variables—market capitalization and turnover—receive the next-highest scores (0.41 and 0.43, respectively). Both are estimated with reasonable precision. The number of listed firms and the two variables on bond market capitalization have the lowest set of coefficients. It is interesting to contrast these eigenvector elements with those of the second principal component. The coefficients for domestic credit and turnover virtually disappear, and for those of the number of listed firms, the private bond capitalization increases to pick up the slack. In both components, stock market capitalization has an important place.

I caution, as in Chapter 3, that PCA constrains that the sum of the squared loadings add up to one, so you cannot interpret these as weights per se. The negative signs add to the confusion given the standardization. I will multiply these weights by the standardized values of the component variables to generate the index scores for the two components. I will also average the scores by country across the two components in a weighted-average fashion in which I assign greater weight to the first principal component by the relative fraction of the explained variation it contributes (41.49% of the total 53.57% explained by both, for a weight of 65.3%) and the same for the second component (34.7% weight).

Before I turn to the final market capacity risk indicator scores, note that I can easily reject the null hypothesis that both components are independent and, somewhat disappointingly, that the variables are normally distributed. It is not a surprise and reminds us it is fine to focus on the coefficients, but to be cautious about relying too much on the standard errors and inference tests.

Ranking Emerging Markets by Market Capacity Constraints in 2012

Figure 4.1 exhibits a full ranking of the 33 emerging markets by the principal component scores for the market capacity variables. The bar graph looks very much like the one I showcased in Chapter 1 for the overall risk indicators, but this one is built just from the subset of variables I feature here. I remind readers again that the PCA procedure delivers a unitless scale with its own range of possible values, so I normalize the scale for each variable by subtracting its mean and dividing by its standard deviation across all 57 countries. The resulting scale ranges with values on the standard normal range of –2.5 to +2.5, with an average around zero. Positive values indicate greater market capacity (fewer market capacity constraints) and negative values indicate lesser market capacity (more constraints). The ranks and the magnitudes of the differences in the scores, though unitless, will be meaningful.

Among emerging markets, there is substantial variation in the risk indicator scores in 2012. The highest positive value is for Taiwan (3.045, which is well into

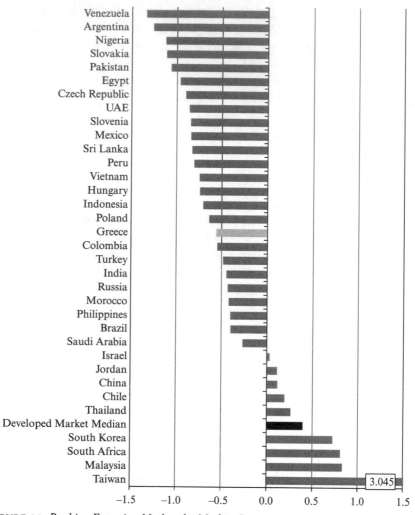

FIGURE 4.1 *Ranking Emerging Markets by Market Capacity Constraints in 2012.*

Note: The risk indicators are each computed on a standardized basis using a standard normal scale for the continuous index values. Negative (positive) values imply worse (better) scores, reflecting greater (lesser) risk. All scores are measured using data up to 2012.

the right tail) and the largest negative score is for Venezuela (–1.34). Though I suppress the scores for the developed markets from the graph, I do furnish the median for that set, which is a positive value of 0.395. That it is positive is not surprising, nor is it so that four of the emerging market countries have scores above that median, including South Korea (0.72), South Africa (0.81), and Malaysia (0.83). Their positions can be traced back to the component values of the domestic credit, stock market capitalization, and turnover variables for those countries, for which they ranked well. It is not uniformly so, but the implied weighting scheme from PCA is suggestive of the outcomes shown.

Taiwan is an illustrative case study of the role that the EM algorithm plays in my procedure. The EM algorithm deals with the problem of missing values in unbalanced samples, and I noted in Table 4.1 that Taiwan had no data for domestic credit. The World Bank's Database on Financial Development and Structure does not cover Taiwan, as it is not a World Bank member. The large loading or coefficient for domestic credit in the first principal component in Table 4.2 should adversely impact Taiwan's score. But the forecasted value from the EM algorithm delivers a value of 172.9%, a dramatic right-tail outlier among all emerging markets. This forecast arises from Taiwan's relative position among all markets with the other five variables for which viable data exist for Taiwan. A little due diligence suggests this forecast is not too far off base. According to end of 2012 statistics from the Central Bank of the Republic of China (Taiwan), total loans amounted to NT$22,604 billion or $745 billion at the prevailing exchange rate.[30] Relative to Taiwan's GDP of $464 billion (see Table 2.4), the implied ratio of domestic-credit-to-GDP is 160.8%, a difference of less than 10% not too far below that obtained from the EM algorithm.

The chapter led off with an intriguing case study about Greece's Folli Follie and the local capital constraints it faced before welcoming a PIPE investment by China's Fosun International. I plot Greece in Figure 4.1 in the relative ranking with its own negative score of –0.55, which hovers around the emerging market median and well below China's score (0.11). So which market is more of an emerging one: China or Greece? I take this as another telling sign about the importance of relying less on traditional classifications by commercial index vendors and of redirecting more attention to the relevant attributes of an emerging market—in this case, the market's capacity constraints on business and economic growth—to guide prospective investors or corporate entrants.

Assessing the Stability of Market Capacity Constraints over Time

In Chapter 1, I cautioned readers about the fact that some of the risk indicators I would build are more amenable to variation over time than others. You will see in upcoming chapters many variables that comprise the risk indicators are based on data from research studies that are not freshly updated each year. The market capacity constraints indicator in this chapter is one of the exceptions. These data come from public sources at the World Bank that are regularly updated. Truthfully, many of the components of this risk indicator—such as private credit, market capitalization, or turnover—move rather slowly over time. But they do move.

To gauge just how stable the relative rankings of the emerging markets are by market capacity constraints, I collected the relevant variables for each year between 2000 and 2012 and, for 2001 and 2006, I re-estimated the principal components and standardized and scaled the respective country scores. The scores are standardized to retain the same range, so one cannot decipher any trend by design. However, it is possible to compare the relative rankings of key countries by their scores to judge how their relative positions change. Figure 4.2 presents the rankings for the four countries of the BRIC (e.g., Brazil, Russia, India, and China) for the years 2001 (top bar, in each set of three), 2006 (middle bar), and 2012 (lowest bar).

These four countries are not the most interesting ones, as judged by the shifting ranks on market capacity constraints; I simply chose them because of their large profile before investors. India has traditionally had a poor score ranging around –0.5, and it has not changed very much over the decade. Brazil's range of scores over the decade has also been rather steady. The country that has made the greatest strides in relative terms of market capacity constraints is Russia. Its score was among the worst in 2001 (–1.24), and its relative position improved to become comparable to those of India and Brazil by 2012. China's relative position has shifted from a median position among emerging markets as of 2001 (–0.42) to one well above the median (0.11) in 2012.

Thinking about developments in Russia and China helps us to understand what is reflected back to us in the market capacity risk indicators. Russia's

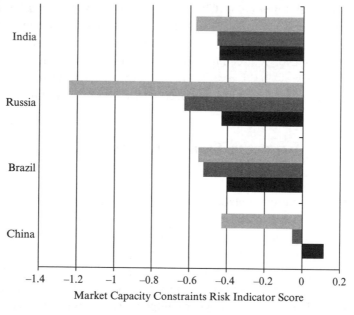

Market Capacity Constraints Risk Indicator Score

■ 2001 ■ 2006 ■ 2012

FIGURE 4.2 *Comparing the Rankings of the BRIC Countries by Market Capacity Constraints in 2001, 2006, and 2012.*

Note: The risk indicators are each computed on a standardized basis using a standard normal scale for the continuous index values. Negative (positive) values imply worse (better) scores, reflecting greater (lesser) risk. All scores are measured using data up to 2012.

domestic credit ratio has tripled in the decade from 13.71% to 41.66%, a rate of growth well above the pace of most emerging markets. The development of the MICEX (Moscow Interbank Currency Exchange) and RTS (Russian Trading System) stock exchanges has greatly promoted equity market capitalization (from 24.8% to 41.9% of GDP) and turnover rates (from 39.8% to 127.3%) in Russia. China has also seen improvements in domestic credit, equity market capitalization and turnover, but its greatest market capacity expansion arose in private bond capitalization (from 7.6% in 2001 to 23.1%) and public bond capitalization ratios (from 9.3% to 22.4%).

Figure 4.3 offers up another perspective across the broader cross-section of markets featured. There are two scatterplots of rankings by market capacity constraint: 2006 versus 2012 scores (top graph) and 2001 versus 2012 scores (bottom graph). The scores for all 57 countries—both developed and emerging markets—are plotted with a fixed range (for convenience, −2.0 to +2.0) and with a 45° line to help anchor them. For consistency, I place the 2012 scores along the x-axis and the earlier scores on the y-axis. If there was perfect agreement (or stability over time) in the relative rankings across the two periods compared, all of the country markers would lie along the 45° line. They clearly do not.

The fact that there are relatively more markers in the top-right and bottom-left quadrants of the plots suggests that there is some degree of stability. But many of the markers lie in a cloud around the line. If markers lie above the 45° line, those are countries that have seen erosion in their market capacity over time; if they lie below the line, those countries (like the BRICs in Figure 4.2) have experienced an expansion of market capacity over time. I place labels beside outliers visible by eye. I discussed the case study of Russia earlier; it is a notable outlier in the cloud in the bottom graph comparing 2001 and 2012, but it is not so for the top graph comparing 2006 and 2012. There has been relatively little change since 2006, and it is confirmed in Figure 4.2. Colombia appears as an outlier in both figures illustrating one of the greatest positive changes in market capacity scores with both reference points in time (2001 and 2006). The Philippines has also improved its score since 2006. The emerging market countries that have seen deterioration in market capacity over this decade include Pakistan, Egypt, South Africa, and Argentina. It is interesting that several key developed markets have taken a step backward since 2001 (the Netherlands, Japan) and 2006 (Denmark).

Is a Deep and Vibrant Capital Market Enough?

Probably not! The next five chapters will build on this opening measure of market capacity constraints. Investors and corporations, in sizing up an emerging market from the outside, not only care about whether the market is big enough but also about how operationally efficient it is, how accessible it is for foreign

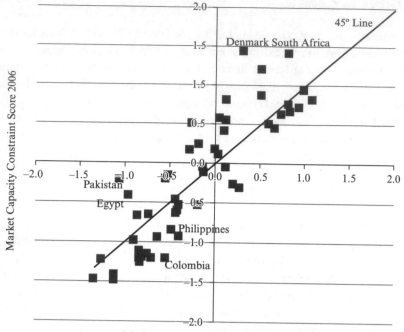

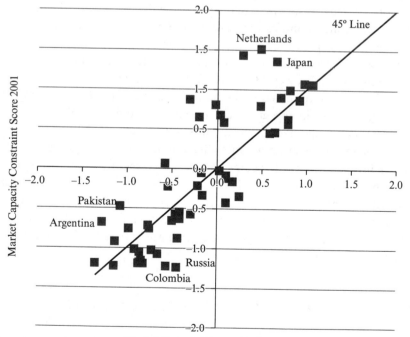

FIGURE 4.3 *Scatterplots Comparing the Rankings by Market Capacity Constraints in 2001,*
2006, and 2012.

Note: The scatterplots are for the scores of 2012 on the x-axis and corresponding scores for 2006 (2001) in the top
(bottom) graph y-axis. Perfect agreement on the scores across years would line up along the 45° line. Hong Kong and
Taiwan lie outside the range of the figures chosen.

interests, how poor the corporate transparency practices and disclosure rules are, the legal protections for stakeholders in dispute resolution, and political instability as a whole. It is also not unreasonable to think that market capacity constraints may, in fact, be a function of these other five risk factors, individually or in combination. After all, poor governance practices or tougher foreign investor restrictions may be a critical reason that an emerging market sees such limited participation, depth, and activity. This is a good start, but I need to move forward.

{ 5 }

Operational Inefficiencies

Operationally efficient markets are those in which transactions are executed at minimal costs. For any investor, this is a first-order concern. If the costs are prohibitive, domestic and foreign investors will be deterred from participating, the markets will be shallower and less vibrant, and capital formation will be adversely impacted as a result. Growth in an emerging market with severe operational inefficiencies may be stunted, even if the capacity of the market appears to be sufficiently large (see Chapter 4).

This chapter focuses on a wide range of potential operational inefficiencies in these markets. Some are more obvious than others. In my process toward constructing an operational inefficiency risk indicator, readers will see that some of the less obvious attributes of transacting in these markets do come to the fore. As in earlier chapters, I am unapologetic about the disproportionate emphasis I will place on cost inefficiencies in transacting by portfolio investors in emerging markets. Direct investments by corporations will undoubtedly be affected by these same concerns of portfolio investors. To be clear, by "operational" I do not mean challenges of doing business in emerging markets related to, for example, legal rights of borrowers and lenders, the existence of a private credit bureau, the prevalence of shareholder lawsuits, contract enforcement mechanisms, regulatory burdens, and the rule of law and control of corruption. I will follow up with these broader concerns in later chapters. Here, I really focus on what I like to call the "plumbing" in securities markets.

Operational Inefficiencies and Market Microstructure

Defining and measuring what constitute transaction costs is difficult.[1] The challenge of doing so has been a major focus of the subfield of market microstructure in finance for the past 30 years. Its theoretical foundation as a field is a good place to get a start. My Cornell colleague Maureen O'Hara, in her seminal book *Market Microstructure Theory*, defines market microstructure as "the study of the process and outcomes of exchanging assets under a specific set of rules. While much of economics abstracts from the mechanics of trading, microstructure theory focuses on how specific trading mechanisms affect the price formation process."[2] The market microstructure working group at the National Bureau of Economic Research devotes itself to "theoretical, empirical, and experimental research on the economics of securities markets, including the role of information in the price discovery process, the definition, measurement, control, and determinants of liquidity and transaction costs, and their implications for the efficiency, welfare, and regulation of alternative trading mechanisms and market structure."[3]

The breadth of these definitions or mission statements illustrates that the focus should not just be on transaction costs per se—like order processing costs for investors, or inventory holding costs for market-making dealers—but also on market structure and design, on price formation as well as on information and disclosure. Prices of assets are formed in different ways, by auction type methods or by negotiation, and these differences can drive transaction costs. The transparency of market information and how it impacts the behavior of market participants matters. There is also an important relationship between price determination and trading rules. How do different market designs give rise to different dimensions of trading costs? Is one design overall more operationally efficient than another?

With these guidelines in mind, I will include in my risk indicator explicit costs of trading, as well as implicit ones related to information and disclosure and rules of trading. Explicit costs are directly calculable, and include commissions paid to brokers, fees paid to exchanges, and taxes (like transactions taxes and value-added taxes on brokerage fees). Implicit costs are more difficult to pin down, and reflect any salient market features that prevent traders from executing their trades at the prices they want when they want to do so. I include in this category bid-ask spreads, market impact costs, various proxy variables for market illiquidity, and even the existence of restrictions on certain kinds of trades (such as short sales).

Transactions in equity markets are not only costly, but also risky. I define transaction risks as a failure to consummate a trade because the buyer could not arrange financing or because the seller failed to deliver. They arise in the process of clearing and settlement, where clearing refers to the processing of payment instructions and settlement refers to the actual discharge of the obligations of the buyer/seller through the transfer of funds and stocks. Transactions risks can inhibit the operational efficiency of emerging markets in particular, because the rules and conventions of clearance and settlement are so varied.[4] Unfortunately, there is still a relative dearth of academic research on these latter aspects of equity markets around the world.[5] I will construct components for my indicator of operational inefficiency that reflect important attributes of the clearance and settlement

systems in emerging markets, including settlement cycles, settlement methods, delivery-versus-payment procedures, and risk management practices for
central securities depositaries.

The Risk Indicator Scores for Operational Inefficiencies

I will change the lineup in this chapter. Instead of describing each of the component variables that constitute this risk indicator and how I estimate the
scores using principal components analysis (PCA), I will instead start with the
scores that result. Afterward, I will show you how I got there. A few interesting
surprises arise.

Figure 5.1 presents the principal component scores across the 33 emerging
and 24 developed markets for 2012. I chose to display all 57 markets for this
indicator to illustrate the intersecting ranges for the two groups of countries.
There is a nice range of outcomes, just as within the market capacity indicators
in Chapter 4. The scores for the emerging markets are skewed toward negative
values, scores which reflect greater operational inefficiencies.

According to the PCA scores there are well-separated clusters across the
various countries, which suggest that some emerging markets are more operationally efficient than a significant number of developed markets. The highest
value among emerging markets is for South Korea (0.81), followed closely by
those for Slovenia (0.75), Hungary (0.61), and Mexico (0.43). Several of these
names were not featured so prominently earlier in Chapter 4. All four of these
emerging markets lie below the developed market median, but not by much.
See how close to a third of the developed market scores lie below them, including Greece (–0.67) and even Singapore (–0.11). (More discussion on these will
come when I break the scores down.) There is a steady decline into the negative
range among scores for Brazil, China, Taiwan, and the Philippines. There is a
distinct break between the Philippines (–0.28) and Slovakia (–0.49). The scores
decline steadily again until that for Chile (–1.01), after which another discon-
tinuity arises to Jordan (–1.16). A final jump occurs following Russia (–1.35)
to the final cluster of countries at the bottom of the scale, which includes the
UAE, Egypt, Venezuela, and Nigeria. Perhaps these countries' appearing in
this range is not surprising at all.

How different are these rankings and scores on operational inefficiency from
those for the market capacity risk indicator? Quite a bit, it turns out. While
there is a tendency for the same countries with larger market capacity indicators to have better scores on operational efficiency, the correlation is only
0.33, which is far below a perfectly correlated value of +1.0. I compare the
risk indicators in Figure 5.2, which is a scatterplot with the scores for the market capacity risk indicator along the x-axis plotted against the country's score
for operational inefficiency on the y-axis. It is a diffuse cloud of points, which

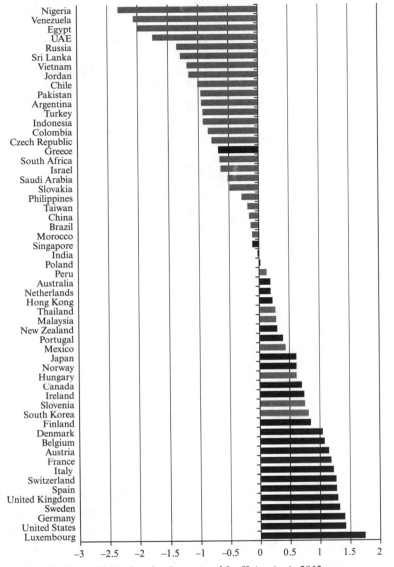

FIGURE 5.1 *Ranking All Markets by Operational Inefficiencies in 2012.*

Note: The operational inefficiencies risk indicator scores are computed on a standardized basis using a standard normal scale for the continuous index values. Negative (positive) values imply worse (better) scores, reflecting greater (lesser) risk. All scores are measured using data up to 2012.

means that the correlation itself (displayed by the slope of the line that runs through the cloud) is actually quite imprecisely estimated.

A helpful way to navigate around the scatterplot is to divide it into the four quadrants. If you want to look for the emerging markets that affirm the positive correlation between the two scores, you need to search in the top-right and bottom-left quadrants. South Korea has a solid positive score of 0.72 on

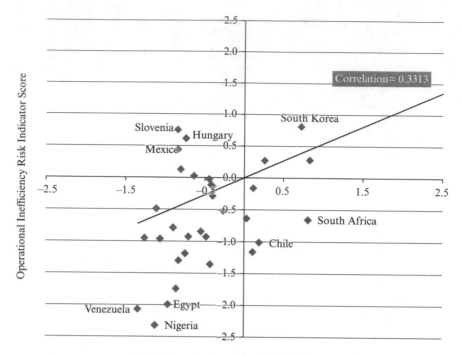

FIGURE 5.2 *Comparing Risk Indicators Scores on Operational Inefficiencies and Market Capacity in 2012.*

Note: The operational inefficiencies and market capacity risk indicator scores are both computed on a standardized basis using a standard normal scale for the continuous index values. The correlation between the two sets of scores is 0.3313, which represents the slope of the line exhibited through the scatterplot of scores for the two risk indicators. Taiwan's marker is not exhibited in the plot due to its very high market capacity score.

market capacity, and it is actually exceeded by its operational efficiency score of 0.81. By the same token, Nigeria, Venezuela, and Egypt can be seen in the bottom-left quadrant, indicating they have bottom-ranking scores for both indicators. In fact, they all three lie well below the line running through the scatterplot, which means that their negative scores on operational inefficiency are even worse than their relative scores on market capacity constraints. Take Venezuela, for example. Its market capacity constraints score of −1.34 (in Chapter 4) is even lower at −2.06 on operational inefficiency. This is why I mentioned earlier the lack of a surprise here.

The most interesting observations are those in the opposite quadrants. They weaken the positive correlation and have contrasting implications from their operational efficiency and market capacity scores. Countries in the bottom-right quadrant, such as South Africa and Chile, are countries that featured positive scores for market capacity but have weak, negative scores on operational efficiency. This arises in large part due to poor scores on proxy measures for the underlying liquidity of the shares traded on their major exchanges.

Conversely, in the top-left quadrant, take note of three emerging markets that improve their overall lot before investors by scoring positively on operational efficiency despite negative market capacity scores. The three markets, Slovenia, Hungary, and Mexico, were each mentioned above. These countries, you will come to learn, perform well on operational efficiency because of reasonable measures on commissions, fees, liquidity, and market impact costs, but also on market rules and the integrity of their clearance and settlement systems.

Let's turn the attention now to the components of the operational efficiency scores and the PCA estimation that delivers these scores.

Capturing *Explicit* Transaction Costs

Explicit transaction costs include commissions paid to brokers, fees paid to exchanges, and some taxes (like transaction taxes or value-added taxes on transactions costs). I obtain these data with permission from Elkins/McSherry LLC, a wholly owned subsidiary of State Street Corporation.[6] Their Global Trading Cost Analysis report contains information on the market impact costs, commissions, and other transaction-based fees for portfolios of over $7 trillion of principal for 1,500 pension funds, investment managers, banks, and 2,000 worldwide brokers from 208 exchanges in 42 markets. I obtained a summary statement provided to clients for peer-comparison benchmark purposes on a country-by-country basis from 1996 through the second quarter of 2011, the last snapshot of which is used in the computations for 2012.[7]

The brokerage commissions, transfer/other fees, and market impact costs are all measured as a percentage of the value of a transaction. No distinction is made for buyer- versus seller-initiated transactions in most cases, and the statistics are averaged when both are provided. Market impact costs are computed on a daily basis with every trade by every institution they track time-stamped to the closest second. The data is used to calculate the average prices and the volume-weighted average prices (VWAPs). VWAP is often used as a trading benchmark for institutional investors to ensure that a trader executing an order does so at a price that is in line with volume on the market over a particular time horizon (usually within that day).

Many research studies have successfully used the Elkins-McSherry proportional cost estimates to evaluate the profitability of trading strategies on a historical, back-testing basis. Consider, for example, my own study with Louis Gagnon in the *Journal of Financial Economics*.[8] My experiment measures the profitability of arbitrage trading strategies involving ordinary shares of stock from 35 different countries and their secondarily cross-listed pairs of stock trading on major US stock exchanges as American depositary receipts (ADRs). Over a more than a decade, from 1993 through 2004, we measure the price and return differentials of pairs of the identical stock from synchronous quotes in the two competing markets in which they trade on a currency-adjusted basis. The deviations from price parity average a modest 4.9 basis points (0.049%), but we show that they can be volatile and reach large extremes, even after accounting for the costs of executing the trades using the country-level aggregate costs of the Elkins-McSherry data. These cost estimates definitely take a big bite out of the profits of the arbitrage trading strategy.[9]

The trading cost estimates from the Elkins-McSherry data are computed in basis points, or in other words as a percentage of the value of the transaction. The overall median estimates for all emerging and developed markets are as expected, with the brokerage commissions are more than double the size in emerging markets (19.93 basis points) compared to developed ones (9.50 basis points). The transfer and other fees are more than ten times larger in the typical emerging market (1.95 basis points versus 0.16 basis points). Note how much smaller in absolute terms these fees are, however, relative to the commissions charged. The market impact costs computed relative to VWAP are closer in magnitude (6.91 basis points in emerging markets versus 5.89 basis points in developed).

It is worth lowering the microscope on what turned out to be the exceptional countries identified in Figure 5.2. Recall how Mexico scored well on operational efficiency relative to its emerging market peers. The brokerage commissions are very close to the emerging market median estimate (17.95 basis points), but the transfer fees are dramatically lower as are the market impact costs (only 1.99 basis points, even lower than the developed market median). By contrast, Chile, a country which had scored well on market capacity indicators, does not do so well on operational efficiency; indeed, at least part of the reason could be the relatively high brokerage commissions faced by investors there (over 20 basis points) and the higher market impact costs (around 10 basis points). The cost estimates for Venezuela are also higher than the typical emerging market.

Of course, the operational inefficiency scores cannot—and should not—line up perfectly with the Elkins-McSherry data, because it is after all only one set of components that enter into it. I will show you that they get a sizable weighting in the PCA scheme, but not as high as some of the other measures I will use.

Market Liquidity: Proxy Measures Judged in
the Eyes of the Beholder

If operationally efficient markets are those in which transactions are executed at minimal costs, then liquidity is an integral component of those costs. Unlike fees, it cannot be embodied in a single number for every transactional situation. In general, "Liquidity is the ability to trade large size quickly, at low cost when you want to trade," states Larry Harris, in Chapter 19 of his treatise *Trading and Exchanges.*[10] Harris adds that given its importance, one might expect that the term is well defined and universally understood; yet he asserts that there is confusion about the various dimensions of liquidity, whether about large size, trading quickly, or what low cost is. Market makers provide liquidity by taking the opposite side of a transaction, and, in exchange for this service, they extract a price concession in that they can buy at a lower bid price or sell at a higher ask price. The bid-ask spread is a transaction cost and is higher for less liquid securities. But, as Harris notes, there are other dimensions of liquidity, such as the market's *depth* (the quantity of the security available for purchase or sale at or near the current market price), its *breadth* (reflecting the number of participants available with which to transact), its *immediacy* (how quickly trades of a given size can be executed at a given cost), and its *resiliency* (how quickly prices revert to former levels after a change in response to large order flow imbalances).[11]

Liquidity proxy measures, in their estimation and use, are varied. Simple ones to choose (that are also more widely available in a cross-country study) would be trading volume, trading frequency (or the number of trades per specified time interval), the bid-ask spread, or quote size (the quantity of securities tradable at the bid and offer prices close to the market price). Trading volume is simple and available (see Chapters 2 and 4 of this book). Greater volume could imply higher liquidity. But volume is also correlated with price volatility, which can be a force that impedes liquidity. All in all I have several liquidity measures, each representing an important facet of liquidity, but each is imperfect, so I will consider a number of proxies in my analysis.

I use an annualized measure of daily turnover as the first proxy. The intuition, of course, is that higher turnover stocks are easier to liquidate, as more shares change hands every day. It comes from a study by Karolyi, Lee, and van Dijk in which daily (fractional) turnover of a representative stock (not that of the market as a whole, as in Chapter 4) is computed for a large cross-section of individual stocks from 40 countries around the world over the period from 1988 through 2009.[12] Half the countries represented are in my emerging market set. Daily turnover is the number of shares traded on a day as a fraction of the shares outstanding.

I also use two relatively more sophisticated liquidity proxies. My second measure is from Amihud, who introduces a measure of the price-impact of a trade defined as the absolute value of stock returns scaled by dollar volume.[13] It draws as its inspiration Pete Kyle's so-called "lambda," or the elasticity of the price change for a trade of a given magnitude.[14] The higher the ratio of absolute returns to dollar volume, the larger is the price impact of a trade of a given magnitude and the greater is the illiquidity of the market for that stock. While it is a unitless measure, being an elasticity coefficient, it still has some interpretability. It is more reliably comparable across countries, as it is a measure scaled by security price and dollar volume. I use the time-series average of daily estimates of the Amihud proxy from Karolyi, Lee, and van Dijk for the representative stock in each of the 40 countries the study covers.[15]

The third proxy is based on the work of Lesmond, Ogden, and Trczinka, who devise a count-based measure from daily securities returns in which one computes as a percentage of the number of available trading days over a month or quarter those that are zero, what they call the "zero-returns percentage."[16] The idea is that illiquidity inhibits investors with information from trading on it, so more zero returns will be observed because no new information, on average, has been incorporated into the price. Higher illiquidity is associated with proportionally more zero returns.

For the zero-returns proxy, I use the statistics in Table 1 from Lee for which the median zero-return proportions are measured on a monthly basis across 24,978 firms in 48 countries (28 emerging) during 1988 to 2004. His statistic is the median proportion across the firms in a given country averaged across the sample months available for that country.[17] He demonstrates that a series of liquidity risk measures built from this zero-return-proportions proxy, as components of the liquidity-adjusted capital asset pricing model (LCAPM) of Acharya and Pedersen, can reliably explain the cross-section of average returns across stocks in emerging markets.[18] From Table 2 in Fong, Holden, and Trczinka, I also use a new proxy with the acronym FHT (initials of the authors' names), which simplifies the existing zero-returns-proportion measure of LOT and which these authors show does well as a proxy for intraday effective spreads from Thomson Reuters Tick History global data.[19] The simplification rescales the zero-returns proportion to account for higher volatility of a representative stock; higher volatility implies that the transaction cost bounds and spreads must be larger in order to achieve the same proportions of zero returns as an equivalent lower-volatility stock.

Table 5.1 shows how these two proxies based on zero-returns proportions are typically higher for most emerging markets than for developed markets, but not always. The Lee measure actually averages 23.68% for the typical emerging market and 25.91% for the typical developed market.[20] As Lee himself points out, this inversion has to do with how deep the markets are in terms of the number of stocks covered. More stocks, including less liquid ones, make the cut in the developed markets. Colombia, Indonesia, Morocco, the Philippines, South Africa, and Sri Lanka are the six countries that have the highest zero-returns proportions for the median stocks in their respective samples.

Fong, Holden, and Trzcinka's streamlined versions of the zero-returns proportions are presented in the second column of the first panel. The scaling is different from that for Lee, but here emerging markets have higher estimates than developed. Among those emerging markets that have high FHT estimates are Indonesia, the Philippines, South Africa (as above), and Brazil.

The advantage of the Karolyi, Lee, and van Dijk measures—shown in the next two columns of the first panel of Table 5.1—is that they offer the most

TABLE 5.1 Measures of Operational Inefficiencies in 2012

Country	Zero-Return Proportions (Lee, 2011)[1]	Zero Returns Proportions (Fong et al., 2011)[2]	Karolyi, Lee, & van Dijk (2012)[3]		Cumming, Johan, & Li (2011)[4]	
			Annual Liquidity	Annual Turnover	Market Manipulation Index	Insider Trading Index
Argentina	24.08	0.023	1.4314	7.35%	3	3
Brazil	28.96	0.033	0.2863	73.50%	1	1
Chile	31.59	0.016	0.0009	17.43%	0	0
China	4.96	0.003	0.0022	438.48%	5	2
Colombia	38.08				2	0
Czech Republic	24.71					
Egypt	9.86				2	0
Hungary	20.86					
India	16.94	0.022	0.1138	28.35%	6	3
Indonesia	39.55	0.062	0.0013	48.09%	3	2
Israel	19.10	0.025	0.0865	47.88%	3	1
Jordan					2	5
South Korea	11.65	0.007	0.0003	194.04%	9	3
Malaysia	23.89	0.020	1.3729	30.24%	2	7
Mexico	15.58	0.019	0.0234	38.85%	6	2
Morocco	36.76					
Nigeria						
Pakistan	23.48		0.3481	84.63%		
Peru	18.64				0	0
Philippines	42.40	0.053	0.1334	22.89%	0	0
Poland	18.74	0.019	1.5340	58.38%		
Russia	20.22					
Saudi Arabia						
Slovakia						
Slovenia					13	3
South Africa	35.64	0.033	0.2447	77.49%		
Sri Lanka	38.58				4	4
Taiwan	10.32	0.007	0.0054	153.72%	2	0
Thailand	26.72	0.028	0.3610	80.85%	8	1
Turkey	18.95	0.010	0.1648	168.84%	0	0
UAE						
Venezuela	31.01					
Vietnam						
Emerging	23.69	0.021	0.1333	58.38%	2.5	1.5
Developed	25.91	0.013	0.5378	86.31%	12.0	3.0

(continued)

TABLE 5.1 Continued

| Country | Jain, Jain, McInish, & McKenzie (2013)[5] | | World Bank World Payments Survey[6] | | | | |
	Median Short-Borrowing Ratio	Short Sales Legal?	T+3 Cycle or Better?	CSD Integrated with RTGS?	Model 1+ Delivery Vs. Payment?	CSD Participants (3 points)	Risk Management (7 points)
Argentina	0	Legal					
Brazil	0	Legal	Yes	Yes	Yes	3	7
Chile	0	Legal	Yes	No	No	3	7
China	0.29	Illegal	Yes	Yes	Yes	3	7
Colombia	0	Illegal	No	Yes	Yes	3	7
Czech Republic	0.14	Legal	No	No	No	3	7
Egypt	0	Illegal	Yes	No	No	2	6
Hungary	2.58	Legal	Yes	Yes	Yes	3	7
India	0	Legal	Yes	Yes	No	3	7
Indonesia	0.02	Legal	No	Yes	Yes	2	5
Israel	0.16	Legal	No	Yes	Yes	0	0
Jordan	0	Illegal	Yes	Yes	No	2	7
South Korea	0	Legal	Yes	Yes	Yes	3	7
Malaysia	0	Legal	Yes	Yes	Yes	2	7
Mexico	0.28	Legal	Yes	Yes	Yes	3	6
Morocco	0.05	Legal	Yes	Yes	Yes	2	7
Nigeria	0	Illegal	Yes	No	No	1	0
Pakistan	0	Legal	Yes	No	No	3	7
Peru	0	Legal	Yes	Yes	Yes	3	6
Philippines	0.01	Legal	Yes	Ycs	Yes	3	7
Poland	0.01	Legal	No	Yes	Yes	2	6
Russia	0	Illegal	Yes	No	No	3	3
Saudi Arabia			Yes	Yes	No	3	7
Slovakia	0	Illegal	No	Yes	Yes	3	7
Slovenia	0	Legal	No	Yes	Yes	3	7
South Africa	0.32	Legal	No	Yes	No	1	7
Sri Lanka	0	Legal	Yes	No	No	1	7
Taiwan	0	Legal	Yes	Yes	No	3	7
Thailand	0.25	Legal	Yes	Yes	Yes	3	6
Turkey	0.25	Legal	Yes	No	No	3	7
UAE	0	Illegal	Yes	Yes	No	1	7
Venezuela	0	Legal					
Vietnam		Illegal					
Emerging Median	0.00		Yes	Yes	Yes	3	7
Developed Median	2.27		Yes	Yes	Yes	3	7

Note: Appendix B details all data sources for the operational inefficiency indicators.

[1] See Table 1 of Lee, "The World Price of Liquidity Risk." Zero-returns proportions are the fraction of trading days within a month with zero returns for the typical stock available 1988–2007; higher proportions denote greater illiquidity.

[2] See Table 2 in Fong, Holden, and Trczinka, "What Are the Best Proxies for Global Liquidity Research?" It gives a proxy for illiquidity scaling the zero-returns proportion measure by individual security price volatility.

recent estimates (through 2009) among the studies available. The two columns also juxtapose the Amihud illiquidity proxy with the annual turnover measure for the typical stock in a country, which are not negatively correlated as one might expect. China, South Korea, and Taiwan do have higher median turn-over rates and lower Amihud illiquidity ratios. Argentina stands out with a high Amihud ratio and low median-stock turnover (only 7.35%). Indonesia has a low Amihud illiquidity ratio, like the zero-returns proportions estimators from Fong et al. and Lee, yet it has only average turnover.

To my reading of this raw data, it seems that each of these important proxy measures for illiquidity in emerging markets—simple to complex, as they are—brings something to the table and is a welcome addition for the PCA analysis to follow.

The Stringency of Trading Rules and Market Integrity

Stock exchanges around the world invest considerable resources to curb market manipulation and to promote operational efficiency of their markets. Better rules and practices on trading are associated with greater integrity in the func-tioning of the markets. Greater integrity should, in turn, be associated with higher market liquidity. For this purpose, I will first examine sets of rules related to trading manipulation, which aim to curb unfair or malicious practices in the markets, and then restrictions related to short-selling, which can potentially hinder lawful attempts to correct market mispricing.

In a recent study, Cumming, Johan, and Li create a series of indices for trading rules that pertain to market manipulation and insider trading for 42 exchanges in both developed and emerging markets. Market manipulation rules refer to

---

[3] See data appendix of Karolyi, van Dijk, and Lee, "Understanding Commonality in Liquidity around the World." Illiquidity is computed as the average daily returns volatility per dollar value of trading for the typical stock over 1995–2009. Turnover is the ratio of the dollar value of trading relative to the market capitalization for the typical stock.

[4] From Table 2 of Cumming, Douglas, Johan, and Li, "Exchange Trading Rules and Stock Market Liquidity," who count up to five market manipulation rules for brokers on trade-through, improper execution, and fair dealing with customers, and up to seven exchange rules on insider trading.

[5] From Table 1 of Jain, Jain, McInish, and McKenzie, "Worldwide Reach of Short-Selling Regulations," the median of the aggregate dollar amount of short-selling-related borrowing of all stocks from each country and whether short-selling is illegal or not.

[6] World Bank's *Global Payments Survey 2010* asks whether the settlement cycle is three days or shorter for securities trading, whether the Central Securities Depository (CSD) is integrated with the country's real-time gross settlement (RTGS) system, whether a securities delivery system occurs simultaneously when fund payments are transferred or on a net basis (Model 1, 2, or 3 delivery versus payment model); whether CSD participants include commercial banks (1 point, if yes), broker-dealers (1 point), or other financial institutions (1 point); and whether up to seven different resilience and business continuity provisions are taken by the CSD.

"trading practices that distort prices and enable market manipulators to profit at the expense of other market participants."[21] Brokers, for example, could take actions while acting as the agent of a client that benefits the broker or some other affiliated party at the expense of a client, or the market more generally. Insider trading rules refer to "acting on material non-public information."[22] Some exchanges furnish detailed provisions that explicitly prohibit manipulative practices and curb insider trading; others are less precise. Detailed rules about prohibited conduct could give investors greater confidence and could help to improve trading activity, reduce uncertainty, and decrease operational inefficiencies. Of course, detailed regulations can just as easily create greater inefficiencies if market participants seek to exploit loopholes in the morass of the details. Cumming et al. devise a series of indices by scouring the trading handbooks of the individual stock exchanges (from the 2006 to 2008 period) to capture the stringency of rules and they show rules are reliably positively associated with improved trading activity.

I adopt two of the indices from Cumming et al.'s study: the market manipulation index and the insider trading index, which their paper lays out in detail. The market manipulation index has 14 elements that essentially are a tally of answers to yes/no questions. There are questions about *price manipulation*, such as ramping or gouging, in which a series of trades over a short time period generate unusual price movement given the security's history; *volume manipulation*, such as the explicit prohibition on wash sales (same client referenced on both sides of a trade); what they call *spoofing*, such as rules preventing brokers from staggering orders from the same client at different price and volume levels to give a false appearance of market activity; and *false disclosure*, such as rules prohibiting the hiding of the true ownership of securities with fictitious trades. The insider trading rules index tallies up a series of answers to 10 yes/no questions that relate to rules that preclude front-running (in which brokers buy or sell ahead of a client), trading ahead of research reports, and that impose a separation of trading and research, restrictions on affiliations between exchange members, and member companies.

The first panel of Table 5.1 (in Columns 5 and 6) shows that the median developed market scores 12 out of 14 on the market manipulation index and 3 out of 10 on the insider trading index. The respective scores for the median emerging market are 2.5 and 1.5. Higher scores on these indices imply more stringent trading rules. Slovenia scores well on the market manipulation index (13 points), and it is followed distantly by South Korea (9) and Thailand (8). Malaysia scores highest on the insider trading index, with 7 out of 10 points.

In addition to market malfunctions caused by insider trading, short sales restrictions and constraints can affect the operational efficiency of markets. Bris, Goetzmann, and Zhu survey the history of short-selling in 46 equity markets around the world (including legal restrictions as well as the practice over 1990–2001) to test this hypothesis.[23] They show that the easing of restrictions allows for improved price discovery across most countries, though also with a greater risk of skewed returns (or large negative price declines). However, despite the academic evidence that short-selling *in general* promotes well-functioning markets, it is a controversial trading strategy. Regulators around the world have at times reacted to periods of market turmoil (like during the 2008 global financial crisis) by banning short-selling, arguing that the practice exacerbates market volatility and, worse, destabilizes markets. The issue is complicated further by the fact that despite the clear motivations for short-selling bans, how effective the bans are in achieving the goal of market stability is unclear.

A recent study by Jain, Jain, McInish, and McKenzie provides useful evidence on the effectiveness of short-selling restrictions.[24] They characterize the legality and incidence of short-selling across a large cross-section of countries, and show how these restrictions do curtail the activity and even reduce short-selling of the country's securities that are secondarily trading in competing markets outside the country of domicile. I obtain two sets of data from their study. The first is an index that indicates whether, as of 2010 (the ending year of their sample), short-selling activity is legal or illegal. I ignore that there may have been some restrictions in one form or another at a particular time and focus on the existence of a straight-up ban or not. I also take the median daily average short-borrowing ratio, which (during 2006 to 2010, their period of analysis) is the daily average outstanding dollar value of shares borrowed summed across all stocks from that country divided by the country's total stock market capitalization. The higher is the short borrowing ratio, the more intense the activity.

Table 5.1, in the second panel (in Columns 1 and 2), presents their findings across the 33 emerging markets in the analysis. The median short-borrowing ratio across developed markets is 2.27%, well above the median ratio of 0% among emerging markets. None of the developed markets in the sample render the activity illegal as of 2010, but it is still so for over half of the emerging markets. Many emerging markets report 0% short-borrowing ratios for the median stock. One country, Hungary, stands out with a ratio that exceeds the median among developed markets. Other countries with more than negligible short-borrowing ratios are China, Mexico, South Africa, Thailand, and Turkey.

It is somewhat strange that short-selling is illegal in China as of 2010, according to Jain et al.'s index, yet its short-borrowing ratio is 0.29%. It turns out that this activity arose because China lifted its restrictions for 11 brokerage firms in 2008, when 19 countries imposed temporary restrictions on the activity during the global financial crisis.[25]

The Plumbing of Securities Markets: Scoring Clearance and Settlement Systems

Transactions in equity markets are not only costly, but also risky. Transaction risks represent a failure to consummate a trade because the buyer could not arrange financing, or because the seller failed to deliver the security after cash settlement. They arise in the process of clearing and settlement, where clearing refers to the processing of payment instructions and settlement refers to the actual discharge of the obligations of the buyer/seller through the transfer of funds and stocks. The fact that securities clearing and settlement systems typically handle large values creates the possibility that a failure in such systems could cause broader financial instability. Market liquidity is critically dependent on the confidence of investors in the safety and reliability of its clearing and settlement arrangements.

I construct components for my risk indicator of operational efficiency that reflect important attributes of the clearance and settlement systems in emerging markets, including settlement cycles, settlement methods, delivery-versus-payment procedures, and same-day turnaround trade capacity. I obtain these data from original sources, including Deutsche Bank's Trust and Securities Services Group, Citigroup's Payment Systems Group, a bienniel survey titled "The World's Clearing Houses" by FOW (a division of Metal Bulletin, PLC), but most prominently the World Bank's Global Payments Systems Survey in 2010.

The World Bank Group has been a leader in financial infrastructure development in emerging markets, including payment systems and remittances, credit reporting, and secured lending. Its Bank Payment Systems Development Group prepared the first report in 2008, titled *Payment Systems Worldwide: A Snapshot—Outcomes of the Global Payment Systems Survey 2008*, and this survey of over 132 central banks representing 139 countries worldwide participated in the 2010 iteration. The questionnaire included questions about the legal and regulatory framework, large-value funds transfer systems, retail payment systems, foreign exchange settlement systems, cross-border payments and international remittances, securities settlement systems, payment system oversight, and planned ongoing reforms to the national payments systems. My attention homed in on the questions about the securities settlement systems. Indeed, considerable attention in the 2010 report and its recommendations was devoted to this category in the aftermath of the global financial crisis.

The five components I build from the World Bank Payments survey are presented in Table 5.1 (second panel, last five columns).

Central securities depositories (CSD) are regularly used to transfer ownership following a transaction in the markets. Otherwise, ownership changes occur in a separate registry. All of the countries in the sample have a CSD in place. One of the main risk management features related to settlement of transactions was the rolling settlement cycle. ISSA, the International Securities Services Association, a global asset servicing association, recommends a rolling settlement cycle of "T+3" (trade date plus three days) or shorter, which means that the funds are transferred within three business days after the trade is executed. The World Bank reports that T+3 or shorter applies in 98 out of the 149 CSDs (66%) surveyed. In my sample of emerging markets, all but 11 markets, or 63% of the total, do so (Argentina, Vietnam, and Venezuela do not participate in the survey).

One way to mitigate trade risk is to integrate the CSD with the real-time gross settlement (RTGS) system. RTGS systems are funds-transfer systems where transfers of money or securities take place from one bank to another on a real-time basis (i.e., no waiting period) and as a gross settlement, or one transaction at a time, without bunching or netting with other transactions. The World Bank survey indicates that 90 out of 179 CSDs have a real-time interface with the RTGS system. The median emerging market is also so integrated, but there are interesting exceptions, like Chile, the Czech Republic, Russia, and Turkey. I will discuss shortly how I encoded this feature and other such features shortly in my risk indicators.

Simultaneous delivery-versus-payment (DvP) models are typically used as the method of settling all securities transactions in developed markets. A DvP mechanism minimizes transaction risk by ensuring that the final transfer of one asset (say, a security) occurs in real time if and only if the final transfer of another asset (say, funds) occurs simultaneously. Central banks call a simultaneous or near-simultaneous DvP a fully integrated securities-transfer and funds-transfer system to satisfy payment obligations. Only 8% of CSDs do *not* use a DvP model at all. However, more sophisticated models allow for simultaneous settlement (DvP Model 1), on a net basis (DvP Model 2), or at the end of the processing cycle (DvP Model 3).[26] These higher grades require more sophisticated optimization algorithms. I identify those that have at least one form of upgrade (denoted "Model 1+") on the basic DvP model. The World Bank points out that at least 35% of their survey respondents do not have one of these upgraded forms. In my sample, 14 of the 30 reporting emerging markets do not.

CSDs and securities settlement systems, in general, also attempt to control the risks in their systems by defining access criteria for participants. According to the World Bank survey, 86% of CSDs indicated that commercial banks are direct participants, whereas corresponding figures for broker-dealers and other financial institutions (like central banks, stock exchanges, and treasury departments) is only 66%. Direct participation by nonbanks is higher in more developed countries. I arbitrarily compile a score out of 3 points to the yes/no questions as to whether these three groups participate directly (commercial banks, broker-dealers, other financial institutions). The logic is simple: the greater is the level of participation, the more robust is the CSD and securities settlement system. In 11 of the 30 reporting emerging markets, full points are awarded. One surprising exception is

Israel (0 points), and other less surprising ones are Nigeria, South Africa, Sri Lanka, and the UAE (1 point each).

The investment in risk management systems in CSDs and securities settlement systems are more likely to assure the integrity of the process. The World Bank survey captures a number of assessments of the resilience and business continuity features of CSDs. They ask seven questions about whether they have routine procedures in place for periodic data backups, whether tapes are kept in sites other than the main processing site, whether backup servers are deployed, and even whether business continuity arrangements include procedures for crisis management and information dissemination. Not all countries respond to these questions, but among those that do, 71% to 82% answer affirmatively. In Table 5.1, I report that the median emerging market does score a full 7 points, but there are always noteworthy exceptions. Israel and Nigeria score low (0 points), as do Russia (3 points) and Indonesia (5 points).

Estimating the Operational Inefficiency Scores with PCA

I face an additional challenge with the prospect of reducing the cross-country variation across 16 different variables into a single index. The goal is honorable in seeking out a measure that encapsulates so many of the important aspects of doing business in emerging markets as investors. The challenge for the PCA procedure comes in two forms. So many of the variables chosen as components have observations only for a subset of the markets I survey. I am, in effect, putting a lot of pressure on the Expectations Maximization (EM) algorithm, discussed in Chapter 3, to deal with the unbalanced nature of this sample.

The second big challenge arises from the fact that there are 16 different variables. In order to get over the magic threshold of 50% cumulative proportion of the variation, I actually need to extract four principal components. The diagnostics in the final panel of Table 5.2 shows that even with four components I only hit the mark at 56.55% (see the *Rho* coefficient). A third challenge that is acute here—though it has nothing to do with the mechanics of PCA itself—comes from the fact that many of the variables rely on computations by different author teams from different sample periods. It should give my readers appropriate pause on the interpretations.

The first principal component is strongly dominant with its eigenvalue of 4.31 (and a 90% confidence range between 2.73 and 5.90). It picks up 26.9% of the variation. The next three components each contribute an additional 8.7% to 11.3% at best. I use them all. The coefficients are displayed in the next four parts of the table with their respective standard

TABLE 5.2 Principal Component Analysis for Operational Inefficiencies

Eigenvalues	Coefficient	Std. Err.	z-statistic	p-value	(5%	95%)
First Component	4.31657	0.80857	5.34	0.00	2.73181	5.90133
Second Component	1.82407	0.34168	5.34	0.00	1.15439	2.49376
Third Component	1.50231	0.28141	5.34	0.00	0.95076	2.05387
Fourth Component	1.40581	0.26333	5.34	0.00	0.88969	1.92193
First Component						
Brokerage Commissions	−0.38024	0.04685	−8.12	0.00	−0.47206	−0.28843
Transfer & Other Fees	−0.09138	0.08369	−1.09	0.28	−0.25541	0.07265
Market Impact Costs	−0.24858	0.06811	−3.65	0.00	−0.38208	−0.11509
Zero-Returns (Lee, 2010)	−0.18499	0.09043	−2.05	0.04	−0.36222	−0.00776
Zero-Returns (Fong et al., 2011)	−0.37647	0.05722	−6.58	0.00	−0.48861	−0.26433
Annual Liquidity	−0.00609	0.09105	−0.07	0.95	−0.18455	0.17237
Annual Turnover	0.21917	0.08046	2.72	0.01	0.06148	0.37687
Market Manipulation	0.39264	0.04770	8.23	0.00	0.29916	0.48613
Insider Trading	0.26465	0.06962	3.80	0.00	0.12820	0.40111
Short-Borrowing Ratio	0.35599	0.05496	6.48	0.00	0.24827	0.46371
Short Sales Legal	0.20516	0.07797	2.63	0.01	0.05234	0.35798
WB T+3 Cycle or Better	−0.00158	0.08892	−0.02	0.99	−0.17586	0.17270
WB CSD/RTGS Integrated	0.18497	0.08554	2.16	0.03	0.01731	0.35262
WB Model DvP	0.26720	0.07644	3.50	0.00	0.11739	0.41701
WB CSD Participants	0.19195	0.08264	2.32	0.02	0.02998	0.35393
WB Risk Management	0.16051	0.08398	1.91	0.06	−0.00408	0.32510
Second Component						
Brokerage Commissions	0.05943	0.14652	0.41	0.69	−0.22774	0.34660
Transfer & Other Fees	0.05068	0.27227	0.19	0.85	−0.48297	0.58433
Market Impact Costs	0.00540	0.17275	0.03	0.98	−0.33319	0.34398
Zero-Returns (Lee, 2010)	0.51169	0.14946	3.42	0.00	0.21876	0.80462
Zero-Returns (Fong et al., 2011)	0.31895	0.08389	3.80	0.00	0.15452	0.48337
Annual Liquidity	0.21806	0.37579	0.58	0.56	−0.51847	0.95460
Annual Turnover	−0.27517	0.26964	−1.02	0.31	−0.80366	0.25332
Market Manipulation	0.06902	0.19976	0.35	0.73	−0.32250	0.46055
Insider Trading	0.10451	0.24761	0.42	0.67	−0.38080	0.58982
Short-Borrowing Ratio	0.13715	0.17680	0.78	0.44	−0.20938	0.48367
Short Sales Legal	0.24629	0.22547	1.09	0.28	−0.19563	0.68820
WB T+3 Cycle or Better	−0.32340	0.22958	−1.41	0.16	−0.77338	0.12658
WB CSD/RTGS Integrated	0.38028	0.24424	1.56	0.12	−0.09842	0.85898
WB Model DvP	0.38394	0.16148	2.38	0.02	0.06746	0.70043
WB CSD Participants	−0.12345	0.38485	−0.32	0.75	−0.87775	0.63085
WB Risk Management	0.00677	0.37204	0.02	0.99	−0.72242	0.73595
Third Component						
Brokerage Commissions	0.14717	0.17038	0.86	0.39	−0.18678	0.48111
Transfer & Other Fees	0.18668	0.59032	0.32	0.75	−0.97032	1.34368
Market Impact Costs	−0.06943	0.26113	−0.27	0.79	−0.58122	0.44237

(*continued*)

TABLE 5.2 Continued

Eigenvalues	Coefficient	Std. Err.	z-statistic	p-value	(5%	95%)
Zero-Returns (Lee, 2010)	−0.04607	0.56979	−0.08	0.94	−1.16285	1.07071
Zero-Returns (Fong et al., 2011)	−0.00364	0.23931	−0.02	0.99	−0.47267	0.46539
Annual Liquidity	0.39212	0.97265	0.40	0.69	−1.51423	2.29848
Annual Turnover	0.19807	0.83009	0.24	0.81	−1.42889	1.82502
Market Manipulation	−0.24626	0.26165	−0.94	0.35	−0.75909	0.26656
Insider Trading	−0.29873	0.21183	−1.41	0.16	−0.71391	0.11645
Short-Borrowing Ratio	−0.20155	0.17247	−1.17	0.24	−0.53959	0.13649
Short Sales Legal	−0.01506	0.78565	−0.02	0.99	−1.55491	1.52479
WB T+3 Cycle or Better	0.14072	0.59248	0.24	0.81	−1.02052	1.30196
WB CSD/RTGS Integrated	0.27433	0.49919	0.55	0.58	−0.70407	1.25273
WB Model DvP	0.14896	0.41934	0.36	0.72	−0.67292	0.97085
WB CSD Participants	0.51320	0.49828	1.03	0.30	−0.46342	1.48981
WB Risk Management	0.41496	0.83482	0.50	0.62	−1.22126	2.05118
Fourth Component						
Brokerage Commissions	0.05509	0.32635	0.17	0.87	−0.58455	0.69473
Transfer & Other Fees	0.24668	0.55143	0.45	0.66	−0.83411	1.32747
Market Impact Costs	−0.06736	0.29460	−0.23	0.82	−0.64476	0.51004
Zero-Returns (Lee, 2010)	0.21588	0.31698	0.68	0.50	−0.40540	0.83715
Zero-Returns (Fong et al., 2011)	0.02008	0.19047	0.11	0.92	−0.35324	0.39340
Annual Liquidity	−0.47561	0.81144	−0.59	0.56	−2.06601	1.11478
Annual Turnover	−0.39607	0.46838	−0.85	0.40	−1.31409	0.52194
Market Manipulation	0.11797	0.50614	0.23	0.82	−0.87404	1.10999
Insider Trading	−0.02171	0.64070	−0.03	0.97	−1.27746	1.23404
Short-Borrowing Ratio	0.01937	0.43808	0.04	0.97	−0.83925	0.87799
Short Sales Legal	0.37722	0.21243	1.78	0.08	−0.03914	0.79358
WB T+3 Cycle or Better	0.24771	0.43348	0.57	0.57	−0.60189	1.09732
WB CSD/RTGS Integrated	−0.19515	0.61687	−0.32	0.75	−1.40420	1.01389
WB Model DvP	−0.15246	0.38046	−0.40	0.69	−0.89814	0.59323
WB CSD Participants	0.23406	1.04155	0.22	0.82	−1.80735	2.27547
WB Risk Management	0.40860	0.85548	0.48	0.63	−1.26811	2.08531

Diagnostics	
Number of observations	57
Number of components	4
Trace	16
Rho	0.5655
Std. Err. (Rho)	0.0301
Likelihood Ratio test for dependence: χ^2 (120)	296.31 p-value 0.00
Likelihood Ratio test for sphericity: χ^2 (135)	300.07 p-value 0.00

Note: For columns listed under the headings of 5% and 95%, the values of the coefficient at the 5% and 95% limits of the 90% confidence range are reported, respectively.

errors, z-statistics, p-values, and confidence ranges. The z-statistics show how much more statistically precise inferences can be with the coefficients in the first component. In fact, very few are reliably different from zero in the other four principal components. Seeing how this played out, I seriously considered using only the first principal component for this index. It turns out that the unconditional rank correlations between the one I use and this shortcut alternative is a very high 0.94. They are almost indistinguishably different, because the first principal component really delivers the biggest punch.

Among the coefficients in the first component, the largest weights (in the eigenvector) arise for the brokerage commissions from the Elkins-McSherry database (–0.38), the market manipulation index of Cumming et al. (0.39), the short-borrowing ratio of Jain et al. (0.35), and the zero-returns proportion measure of illiquidity of Fong et al. (–0.37).[27] The higher illiquidity or transaction cost variables gain the negative sign implying worse scores, all else being equal, and those revealing more stringent market trading rules and more active short-selling activity have positive signs implying better scores. I take reassurance that the World Bank Payments Survey constructs fare reasonably well, especially the item related to the DvP models (coefficient of 0.26). The most disappointing outcomes—at least from a personal standpoint—arise from the fact that the Amihud-based proxies that I build with my coauthors in the Karolyi et al. study receives negligibly small coefficients in the eigenvector. Better luck next time, I guess.[28]

Next Steps?

Having a deep capital market in order to realize the long-run growth potential of an emerging economy is job number one. Chapter 4 hopefully made this clear. What this chapter has uncovered is that not all emerging markets with sufficient capacity function well. At least, they do not from the perspective of portfolio investors who are likely to care how much the value of their (or their clients') capital might be eroded by operational inefficiencies. How large the commissions brokers charge are, how well the trades are executed in terms of their market impact costs, and how vague and how few are the rules governing trading processes, including clearance and settlement systems, all matter.

In the next chapter, I add another layer of concern for the foreign portfolio investor, in particular. Even if there is sufficient market capacity to attract interest and even if the markets function sufficiently well on an operational basis not to deter them, there is still the issue of accessibility. Investors from outside the country of domicile need to be able to get in the door. In the remaining three chapters after that, I broaden the perspective beyond just the concerns of portfolio investors to that of corporations sizing up these emerging markets for business. The focus shifts to corporate transparency and disclosure, legal protections, and political stability.

{ 6 }

Foreign Accessibility Restrictions

The most recent wave of financial globalization began in a serious way in the mid-1980s with the rise of cross-border financial flows between countries, and especially between developed and emerging economies. The process was spurred by the liberalization of capital controls in many of these countries that made it possible for better access to capital among corporations seeking funding and for a better sharing of risks among global investors wanting to deploy their savings. The traditional view among economists—and at its core my own view pushed throughout this book—is that the benefits of financial globalization were positive and substantial, especially for emerging economies in which the many growth opportunities were otherwise underfunded due to binding capital constraints. The flow of foreign capital relaxed these constraints imposed by all-too-shallow pools of local capital.

Of course, the story of financial globalization is not so simple.[1] A large number of currency, banking, and financial crises have dotted the global capital markets landscape since the 1980s, which has challenged the validity of the traditional view. A perception among leading economists such as Dani Rodrik, Jagdish Bhagwati, and Joseph Stiglitz, was that opening up many developing countries to capital flows has increased their vulnerability to these crises.[2] Increased capital account liberalization, they argue, allows capital to enter for investment, but also to swiftly exit during periods of domestic or foreign turmoil, giving rise to local and even global financial market instability. This opposing view holds that the instability has impeded the level of growth and increased its volatility. That is, a net negative, *not* positive, arises from greater financial globalization. The strongest opponents have argued for the reintroduction of capital controls, like a so-called Tobin's tax on international movement of capital.[3]

I will not arbitrate the debate for or against financial globalization in this chapter. I have already revealed my bias as a proponent. But out of the heat emanating from this debate comes some useful light about the manner in which the growth effects of access to more foreign capital really arise. I will focus my discussion around what Kose, Prasad, Rogoff, and Wei refer to as the "potential *collateral* benefits" of financial globalization that arise from a variety of *indirect* channels, as opposed to the *direct* channels, that drive the process.[4] Direct channels come from neoclassical models of macroeconomics: financial flows from abroad complement limited domestic savings in capital-poor countries to deepen the local capital pool, help reduce the cost of capital, and thus stimulate increased investment and overall growth. The indirect channels also come from greater foreign participation, but stem from externalities, like greater competition from more foreign entrants in financial services or from their demanding better corporate governance and transparency practices to justify their participation. In other words, financial globalization, my focus in this chapter, is a mechanism that exerts influence through other indicators already featured in Chapter 4 (market capacity constraints), Chapter 5 (operational inefficiencies), or in Chapter 7 (corporate opacity) to come.

This framing of the discussion is particularly helpful to me, as it helps organize thinking about how to measure financial openness in emerging markets. It turns out that there are many potential measures about the accessibility of markets for foreign investors that are based on the rules and legal restrictions that guide their flow. This inspires another bit of jargon often used in the financial globalization literature: de jure measures of capital account openness. De jure means rules "on paper." Consider in this category the existence of foreign investor registration requirements, foreign currency convertibility restrictions, or withholding taxes on dividends and interest income from foreign investments. These rules on paper are important to identify and measure. These are traditionally linked to the *direct* channels through which financial globalization plays a role in economic growth.

But even where de jure limitations on foreign access are not binding, the research evidence seems to point toward so-called de facto measures of openness as also having "bite in practice." De facto measures of foreign access are those that are not ordained by law, but which are complications faced by foreign investors, acting as inhibitors to doing business in a hassle-free manner. Some de facto measures evaluate the differences in prices of what would otherwise be identical securities except for the fact that they are exposed to different ownership restrictions, tax exposures, and position limits for foreign and domestic investors. Though it is hardly an exclusive connection, it turns out that many *indirect* channels through which financial globalization affects growth are linked to de facto measures of openness. These measures look at the quantity of the globalization activity, such as computing the external assets and liabilities relative to the GDP of a country. I harvest what I think are the best from the extensive work on this question—including a healthy mix of de jure and de facto measures—from the fields of development economics and international finance into building my risk indicator for foreign accessibility restrictions.

Spreadtrum Communications Sinks into
Muddy Waters in 2011

"We believe this organization is trying to target China companies with questionable accounting practices," stated Shannon Gao, chief financial officer at Nasdaq-listed Spreadtrum Communications (TICKER: SPRD), in response to a negative report issued by Muddy Waters LLC, a research firm specializing in uncovering investment value from identifying potential accounting or business fraud.[5] Gao added: "In this case, they picked the wrong company. We do not fit their profile." The reply from the executive at the Chinese-based semiconductor firm came on the heels of an open letter written by Muddy Waters' Carson Block to Spreadtrum chairman Leo Li. The letter points out "a high risk of material misstatement" in the reported financials of SPRD since the time of Dr. Ping Wu's February 2009 resignation as chief financial officer and founder of the company.[6] The letter contained nine specific questions expressing "grave" concerns about the 2010 and 2011 financial accounting statements for Spreadtrum.[7]

Spreadtrum was not the only Chinese company having to defend its financial statements during the summer of 2011. Sino-Forest had denied overstating its assets after a Muddy Waters report said city records did not match the amount of land the Hong Kong-based timber company said it owned in China's Yunnan province.[8] China Yurun Food Group's stock had fallen 20% on the Hong Kong Stock Exchange as of June 27, 2011, on speculation that Muddy Waters would issue a negative report on the pork producer.[9] Orient Paper, another US-listed Chinese company, had been the focus of another fraud allegation by Muddy Waters in 2010.[10]

But what caught many off guard in this case was that Spreadtrum's share price had jumped $2.76 to reach $24.38, or a 13% jump, on the news of its strong fourth-quarter earnings spike as recently as March 4, 2011.[11] The company said that it had earned $30 million, or 56 cents per share, compared to only $1.4 million, or 3 cents per share, in the fourth quarter of 2009.[12] Further, Spreadtrum's American depositary shares (ADRs)—the form in which SPRD and many other foreign-listed firms trade on US exchanges—had already appreciated 215% since January 2010 when it was trading at $6.76, its strongest performance run since its initial public offering on Nasdaq in July 2007.

Headquartered in Shanghai, Spreadtrum Communications was a "fabless" semiconductor company—in that it outsources the fabrication process—designing radio processing chips and chips capable of transmitting and receiving wireless signals, and developing turn-key solutions for the evolving standards in the wireless communications market in China (including GSM, GPRS, and TDSCDMA).[13] The firm was founded in 2001 by Drs. Ping Wu, Datong Chen, and Renyong Fan, and though most of its subsidiary operations were totally

in China, the holding company was incorporated in the Cayman Islands. The
two US-based subsidiaries—SPRD LLC, a Delaware limited liability company,
and Spreadtrum USA—were acquired in 2007 and 2008, respectively. In the
firm's 2009 annual report, Spreadtrum's holding company owned Spreadtrum
Shanghai, through which products reached their customers, and Spreadtrum
Shanghai owned 38% of Spreadtrum Beijing, a wholly domestic company
focused on research and development.[14] Each of three Chinese national nomi-
nee shareholders, family members of the cofounders, owned a direct 21% stake
in Spreadtrum Beijing.[15] The major individual shareholders in Spreadtrum
Communications, the holding company, included 4.6% by the cofounders and
another 34% by venture capital firms, such as New Enterprise Associates and
Silver Lake Partners.

Spreadtrum does not own or operate any fabrication, assembly, or testing
facilities. Instead it designs chips and outsources processing to foundries for
manufacturing. By outsourcing this expertise rather than developing it internally, Spreadtrum was able to wedge a position in the market before other
competitors and achieve stellar growth. The company's revenues increased
from $12.9 million in 2004 to over $105 million in 2009, a sixfold increase.
Its first-mover advantage and government support in the Chinese mobile
telecommunications market via tax exemptions, favorable lending terms, and
research grants comprised the basis of a rapid growth story. The company
targeted GSM/GPRS mobile handset baseband starting in 2004 and has
since invested heavily, ahead of its competitors, in developing products for
TD-SCDMA, China's homegrown 3G mobile telecommunications standard.
And with China being the largest mobile subscriber market in the world, with
over 795 million users in 2010 and over $84 billion in estimated revenues, the
pressure was always on to continue to invest and acquire additional market
share.[16]

Spreadtrum had some strong industry catalysts extending its stellar growth.
Surging TD-SCDMA handset sales and its increasing market share (especially
relative to key competitors MediaTek, MStar Semiconductor, and Infineon)
within this growing Chinese market were two main factors leading sell-side analysts to predict strong earnings in the next several years. Among the seven analysts following the stock in March 2011, five recommended buy or overweight
with price targets cushioned well above the prevailing $21.76 at the time.[17]
A surprisingly conflicted signal came from the uptick in the short-interest ratio
to 2% of outstanding shares, only a few weeks before the release of the open
letter from Muddy Waters.[18]

Following the intense exchange between Spreadtrum Management and
Muddy Waters,[19] SPRD's stock price had fallen over 30% from March to
under $13 by the end of June. The firm booked earnings declines in the second
quarter (as of June 30, net income fell to $21 million, or 41 cents per share),
and some analysts downgraded the stock to underperform.[20] Additional news

articles popped up about the recent accounting blowups facing US-listed Chinese firms registered in offshore tax havens, like the British Virgin Islands and the Cayman Islands, which in turn caught the eyes of key market regulators in the United States.[21] The pressures did not abate through to December 2013, at which point Spreadtrum Communications agreed to be acquired for $1.78 billion by and to be consolidated as a wholly owned subsidiary of Tsinghua Holdings, a Chinese state-owned corporation affiliated with Tsinghua University.[22]

The Two Sides of Financial Globalization

The complex story of Spreadtrum reveals some intriguing elements of the two views of financial globalization that I described at the start of the chapter. The traditional view describes the *direct* channels through which globalization can mobilize capital flows to stimulate economic growth. Spreadtrum's management team believed, like many, that there were inadequate funding opportunities for their business model in a blossoming Chinese telecommunications marketplace. A better opportunity was to take the fabless business model and the Chinese growth pitch directly to global investors and by means of a listing of the shares for trading, not on the Shanghai or Shenzhen stock exchanges, but as ADRs on the Nasdaq stock exchange in the United States. The transaction was inarguably a successful one from its IPO in 2007 through to the summer of 2011.

The second view of globalization is also revealed starkly for Spreadtrum in terms of *indirect* channels or its "potential collateral benefits," so coined by Kose et al.[23] In their case, however, the potential collateral benefits turned out to be effectively *net negative* as of 2011. Unanticipated, intense scrutiny by some capital market participants based in the United States challenged Spreadtrum—as well as that of a number of other Chinese firms that listed shares there—and its corporate governance and disclosure practices. In not making the mark on these standards, the firm's ability to secure long-term investor interest was likely hampered.

How this case study fits into the globalization paradigm is useful toward bringing out the challenges of measuring the extent of globalization. But before discussing the measures, I need to add some more color on the prevailing theoretical models about how financial globalization should affect growth.

As mentioned above, the traditional neoclassical framework in macroeconomics implies that financial globalization should lead to flows of capital from economics with fewer capital-market constraints to those with more constraints. The flows can basically supplement the limited domestic savings, thereby deepening the pool of capital for those (firms, governments) that need to draw from it, and along the way lowering the cost of capital to stimu-late more investment activity.[24] Globalization and the rise in capital flows can help promote industrial specialization by allowing some risk-sharing among global investors, which can lead to increased productivity and growth.[25] But greater specialization from globalization could just as easily hurt capital-constrained economies by exposing them to global industry-specific shocks.[26]

Theory does predict that globalization helps consumers who are risk averse to exploit global financial markets in order to insure themselves against local, home-country income risks. Income growth may be volatile, but consumption growth should be less so, as a result. Consumption patterns across countries should also become more correlated with globalization. But if investors do not exploit global markets to diversify their risks—an empirical reality that researchers term the "home-bias puzzle"—then all bets are off on these gains to consumption.

Why global investors choose not to take full advantage of the benefits of global risk-sharing to smooth their consumption is still an ongoing mystery.[27] Of course, I am confident that at least some of the home-bias mystery in emerg-ing markets can be solved with my risk indicators.

Distinguishing de Jure Versus de Facto Measures of Financial Openness

The de jure approach to measuring foreign accessibility restrictions is to focus on the legal blocks on cross-border capital flows. They come in all shapes. There are controls on outflows as well as on inflows, controls on prices as well as on quantities, and even limits on level of foreign ownership in differ-ent securities. There are two influential studies of de jure measures, and both use the International Monetary Fund (IMF)'s *Annual Report on Exchange Arrangements and Exchange Restrictions* (AREAER). The AREAER, since 1950, reports on restrictions in effect under Article XIV, Section 2, of the IMF's Articles of Agreement in accordance with Section 3 of Article XIV, which mandates annual reports on such restrictions. The AREAER includes over 60 different types of controls governing exchange and trade systems that come in the form of a yes/no question. Quinn was one of the first to use a quantitative approach, indexing countries by adding up yes/no values on select questions, and Chinn and Ito upgraded Quinn's approach using a principal components analysis, similar in spirit to what I do in this book.[28]

As Kose et al. point out, there are a number of shortcomings that arise from de jure measures.[29] For one, they do not reflect the degree of open-ness of the capital account as a whole, because by the nature of the data source from the IMF, the questions are disproportionately focused on foreign exchange restrictions. For another, one never really gets a good sense of the extent to which these rules and restrictions are enforced. Finally, they do not capture how much the restrictions actually have "bite" on actions and behaviors.

Financial economists have developed measures of capital account restrictions that focus on more than just foreign exchange restrictions. For example, Bekaert and Harvey and Henry compile dates from the AREAER and other sources of official equity market liberalization dates for developing economies. Bekaert and Harvey analyze changes in the dividend yield after liberalizations and report that the cost of capital declines by 5 to 75 basis points.[30] A lower cost of capital should be associated with a higher rate of investment activity, all else being equal. Indeed, Henry finds that in almost every emerging market country in his sample growth rates of private investment are larger in the first year after an equity-market liberalization event.[31] Bekaert, Harvey, and Lundblad uncover a positive 1% per year effect on real per capita growth using a broad sample of 95 countries over the period from 1980 to 1997.[32] These findings suggest that these signpost events—coarsely defined as they may be—are associated with important economic changes.

De facto measures of financial globalization skip over the letter of the law and focus on the actual changes in relevant economic measures, like the prices of securities subject to foreign accessibility restrictions or the quantities of capital flows or foreign portfolio holdings. Price-based measures are a natural choice, especially among the corps of asset-pricing specialists in financial economics. After all, in a perfect world without transaction costs, taxes, information, and agency (corporate governance-related) problems, an asset has the same price regardless of where it is traded and no finance is local.[33] Markets in which identical assets have the same price regardless of where they are traded are said to be *integrated*, while markets where the price of an asset depends on where it is traded are said to be *segmented*.

Though they have great intuitive appeal, price-based measures face a practical problem. Identical assets must be equivalently risky, so these measures must rely on a model of market equilibrium to define what risks may be priced and how so. Typically, academic studies assume a model of market equilibrium, such as the capital asset pricing model (CAPM), and estimate it to measure the average return for a unit of covariance with the rest of the market or with other state variables. If this premium is common across markets, they arguably are integrated. However, so far the empirical evidence on international asset pricing—particularly that of the last decade—has suggested that the workhorse CAPM or even the arbitrage pricing theory (APT) falls short when it comes to describing the actual prices and returns in global stock markets. Additionally, documented premiums to size, book-to-market values, price momentum, trading volume, or liquidity clearly complicate interpretations, as they may be evidence of additional risk factors I have to compare across countries or of deviations from fair pricing of risk.[34] As a result, some scholars have sought to deflect this problem by building price-based or return-based measures of integration that are "model-free."[35]

De facto quantity-based measures provide another set of useful measures of a country's integration with international financial markets that I will use. As Kose et al. articulate, there are distinct advantages to studying actual gross capital flows as a ratio of national GDP because they are relatively less volatile than net flows (defined as portfolio or direct capital inflows less outflows).[36] Others prefer to focus on the sum of gross stocks of foreign assets and liabilities as a ratio of GDP to dance around some of the measurement errors in the gross flow data. The stock measure is essentially a cumulated version of the periodic flows.

I, like many researchers before me, benefit here from the seminal work of Trinity College Dublin's Philip Lane and his IMF collaborator, Gian Milesi-Ferretti, on the External Wealth of Nations project.[37] They have carefully constructed an extensive dataset of stocks of gross liabilities and assets for 145 countries covering the period 1970 to now 2011. It contains information about the composition of international financial positions, including foreign direct investment, portfolio equity investment, external debt, and official reserves.

De Jure Openness Measures for the Foreign Accessibility Restrictions Indicator

I use a variety of de jure and de facto openness measures to construct my risk indicator for foreign accessibility restrictions. Some of these measures are commercial indices available from Standard & Poor's Emerging Market Database (EMDB), the foundations of which I described in Chapter 2; the Milken Institute, the World Bank Financial Development and Structure database, and the External Wealth of Nations database of Lane and Milesi-Ferretti.[38] A second set on the de jure taxes, regulations, and ownership restrictions faced by foreign investors I construct from a variety of original and web-based open sources, including Deloitte International Tax Services, World Bank Reports on Investing Across Borders, and the United Nations International Trade Center's Market Analysis Services. I build this new database to circumvent some of the concerns about the IMF's AREAER database and its overemphasis on foreign exchange markets. As elsewhere in this book, I face the ongoing challenge of mixing data sources with different horizons for the data-compression exercise that follows with principal component analysis (PCA). I start with the de jure measures.

Table 6.1 exhibits the de jure variables I use. The first eight are qualitative variables that I build from the web-based sources I listed above. One particularly useful source for me is the Deloitte International Tax Source (DITS), which is an online database featuring tax rates and information for 65 jurisdictions worldwide.[39] DITS includes current rates for corporate income tax, domestic withholding tax, withholding tax on dividends, interest and royalties under tax treaties, value-added taxes, goods and services taxes, sales taxes, and a five-year table of statutory corporate income tax rates. These taxes and tax rates are among the most common that arise in connection with international transactions. I supplement these data with other sources mentioned earlier.

The first component evaluates foreign investor registration requirements. A useful starting point for my research here is a series of Euromoney Institutional Investor books on World Equity Markets published in the early 2000s and late 1990s.[40] By country, information was supplied on taxation and regulations affecting foreign investors as well as listing and reporting requirements. For more recent years, I supplement these data with those from Bloomberg, a number of Form 20-F filings by foreign company registrants of the US Securities and Exchange Commission. I build an indicator variable, for which I assign one point, if any restrictions on foreign equity ownership exists across any sector; a second point if annual reviews of performance are needed for continued registration; and a third point if compliance requirements are mandated for clients or custodians toward registration. Many countries require foreign institutional investors to obtain licensing and certification. China, for example, mandates a Securities Investment License for foreign investors to be qualified, followed by a Foreign Exchange Registration Certificate, both requiring annual review by the China Securities and Regulatory Commission and the State Administration for Foreign Exchange. There are compliance requirements for custodians and clients independent of registration requirements in some countries. China scores two points. In India, monthly transaction reports must be filed to the Reserve Bank of India and the Securities and Exchange Board of India. India scores three points. The median developed market actually scores two points relative to the median emerging market, which scores only one, implying by this measure at least emerging markets are less restrictive.

The second component assesses foreign ownership restrictions. I rely extensively on data from the World Bank Group initiative Investing Across Borders, which compares regulations of foreign direct investment around the world. It presents quantitative indicators on economies' laws, regulations, and practices affecting how foreign companies invest across sectors, start green-field businesses, access industrial land, and even arbitrate commercial disputes.[41] I supplement this data with those from a 2013 report from the World Bank's Financial and Private Sector Development group on Converting and Transferring Currency (CTC), which complements the IMF's AREAER focusing on de jure measures of currency convertibility, but those more relevant for capital flows and FDI.[42] Ownership restrictions

TABLE 6.1 De jure Measures of Foreign Accessibility Restrictions in 2012

Country	Registration Requirements[1]	World Bank Ownership Restrictions[2]	World Bank Repatriation Cap Limits?[3]	IMF AREAER Currency Convertibility[4]	Deloitte DITC Withholding Taxes[5]	Double Taxation[6]	Foreign Capital Gains Tax[7]	Other Securities Taxes[8]	Capital Access Index[9]
Argentina	0	1	1	0	1	2	0	1	3.84
Brazil	2	1	0	0	0	2	0	1	5.14
Chile	1	2	1	1	1	2	0	2	6.36
China	2	2	1	2	0	3	0	1	6.00
Colombia	2	2	1	1	1	2	0	2	4.97
Czech Republic	0	1	0	0	2	0	1	0	5.72
Egypt	0	1	0	1	1	1	0	0	5.08
Hungary	0	1	0	0	2	0	0	0	5.82
India	3	3	1	1	1	0	1	1	5.51
Indonesia	0	1	1	0	1	0	1	2	4.60
Israel	0	0	0	1	1	1	0	1	6.66
Jordan	.	.	.	1	.	.	.	1	5.47
South Korea	2	1	0	0	2	0	1	1	7.39
Malaysia	0	3	0	0	2	0	0	1	7.06
Mexico	2	1	0	0	0	2	0	1	5.50
Morocco	.	.	.	1	.	.	.	.	4.74
Nigeria	1	.	.	2	1	.	0	.	3.73
Pakistan	0	1	1	1	2	0	1	1	3.93
Peru	1	1	0	1	1	2	0	1	4.86
Philippines	1	1	1	1	2	0	1	2	4.62
Poland	0	1	0	0	2	0	0	0	6.86
Russia	0	2	1	1	2	0	1	2	5.03

	[1]	[2]	[3]	[4]	[5]	[6]	[7]	[8]	[9]
Saudi Arabia	.	.	.	0	.	.	0	.	4.96
Slovakia	0	0	0	0	1	0	0	1	5.90
Slovenia	2	1	.	1	1	2	.	0	5.59
South Africa	.	.	0	.	.	.	0	.	5.53
Sri Lanka	1	0	0	1	0	1	0	1	6.15
Taiwan	2	0	1	1	1	1	1	0	3.96
Thailand	2	1	1	2	2	1	0	1	6.54
Turkey	2	1	0	2	1	0	1	2	6.51
UAE	1	1	0	1	.	0	0	1	4.27
Venezuela	0	1	0	0	0	0	0	1	5.02
Vietnam	2	1	1	2	1	1	2	0	3.36
Emerging Median	*1*	*0*	*0*	*1*	*1*	*0*	*0*	*1*	*5.47*
Developed Median	*2*	*1*	*0*	*0*	*1*	*0*	*0*	*0*	*7.23*

Notes: Appendix C details all data sources for the foreign accessibility restrictions indicators. The main sources include World Bank reports on *Investing Across Borders* (2010), *Converting and Transferring Currency Benchmarking Foreign Exchange Restrictions Transferring Foreign Direct Investment* (2013, CTC), the IMF's *Annual Report on Exchange Arrangements and Exchange Restrictions* (annual, AREAER), and Deloitte's online resource, Deloitte International Tax Service (DITS).

[1] Four-point scale: if any registration is required; if annual performance review mandated; and if compliance required for client/custodian.
[2] Four-point scale: if only some sectors are restricted for foreign investors; if broad-based restrictions exist with cap limits; and if other ownership restrictions exist.
[3] An indicator variable equals to one if any type of restriction on repatriation of investment profits exists.
[4] Three-point scale: if currency only partially or nonconvertible; and if not freely floating.
[5] Three-point scale: if withholding on dividend or interest income; and if no exemptions for tax-treaty country residents.
[6] Four-point scale: if no tax treaty exists; if tax treaties exist with fewer than 20 countries; and if tax treaties exist with fewer than 50 countries.
[7] Equals one if there exists a foreign capital gains tax and zero, otherwise.
[8] Three-point scale: if stamp duty exists; and if additional value-added tax on securities/broking service fees.
[9] *Capital Access Index 2009: Best Markets for Business Access to Capital,* James R. Barth, Tong Li, Wenling Lu, and Glenn Yago, eds. (Milken Institute, April 2010, www.milkeninstitute.org).

can be broad-based cap limits on the fraction of shares foreign investors can cumulatively hold (in which case I assign two points) and can reside in only some sectors (one point assigned). For example, Indonesia has had stringent foreign ownership ceilings on firms in the telecommunications, media, and broadcasting industries in 2012, whereas in Malaysia foreign ownership limits are capped across most of the marketplace, except in light manufacturing and transportation. India scores a full three points, while Russia, Chile, China, and Colombia get two.

I construct a third component that evaluates potential restrictions on the repatriation of investment profits. Some countries, like Russia, impose some restrictions on repatriation of funds from ordinary securities accounts denominated in local currency (roubles) whereas others, like Argentina, place absolute local-currency caps on profits that can be adjusted with regulatory approval. I assign one point for countries with any kind of restriction, and zero points for others. The median score among my set of emerging markets is zero. As you would expect, countries like the United Kingdom and the United States impose no foreign loan interest or capital gains outflow or dividend-payment restrictions

Finally, I create a variable that assesses the degree of currency convertibility in a country. The World Bank Group's CTC report is particularly helpful in compiling this information. I assign one point for countries with partially or nonconvertible currencies (as designated by the UN International Trade Center's Market Analysis Services) and another point if the currency is not freely floating. China scores two points, as does Nigeria. Many developed countries have no restrictions on domestic or even offshore foreign exchange bank accounts.

Tax exposures on foreign investors are not necessarily distinct from those of domestic investors, but they may affect the extent to which foreign investors are more welcome in some countries than others. Deloitte's DITS data comes in handy for these classifications. Withholding taxes (held at source) can be prohibitively high in some countries, such as Taiwan at 20% or Hungary at 25%, unless there are double taxation avoidance agreements (tax treaties) with the home countries of the foreign investors. Some countries are active in developing international tax treaties with other countries (Hungary, 50 countries); others not so much (Mexico, 3 countries). I create an index that assigns a point if the country applies any withholding tax on dividend income and a second point if no exemptions are applied for tax-treaty-country residents. Most countries do so with exemptions (the median score is one point). I create a second component that applies 3 points for countries with no declared tax treaty, two points for those with fewer than 20 signatories, 1 point for those with fewer than 50 signatories, and zero points otherwise. Mexico scores two points by this rule, and it is not alone despite the fact that the median emerging country scores one. Note that China alone scores three points on this dimension.

I also create a component from DITS in the form of a dummy variable for those countries that apply a capital gains tax to foreign investors (one point assigned) and those that exempt foreign investors (zero points). Only a few countries in my set record a point here. Finally, a component judges whether a country applies a stamp duty on securities transactions (one point assigned) with a second point for any kind of value-added-tax (VAT) applied on securities/brokering service fees. I call this index "other securities taxes." Eight emerging markets impose additional duties on securities/brokering service fees, though most simply apply a stamp duty.

Though they retain good logic and are constructed parsimoniously, there are many arbitrary choices I make in the construction of these indices. I counterbalance my choices with another variable built by an outside agency. Specifically, I obtain the Capital Access International (CAI) index of the Milken Institute. The index of 121 countries worldwide looks at seven key components that can make it easier or more difficult for entrepreneurs to access capital. Those components are the macroeconomic environment, economic institutions, financial and banking institutions, equity market, bond market, alternative capital, and, most interesting to us, international access. I specifically use the 2009 index from the Milken Institute report by James R. Barth, Tong Li, Wenling Lu, and Glenn Yago from their April 2010 report, the latest one available in the public domain.[43] Higher scores in this case indicate greater ease of access to capital. The median developed country score is 7.23 and that of an emerging market is only 5.47, which is not a wide range. Not surprisingly, the emerging markets with the highest scores are Israel, South Korea, Malaysia, Thailand, and Turkey. Vietnam, Argentina, and Nigeria fare poorly in their rankings. The CAI index is, as expected, negatively correlated with each of my constructed indices, except that associated with registration requirements.

De Facto Openness Measures for the Foreign Accessibility Restrictions Indicator

Table 6.2 presents six different variables based on the de facto measures of foreign accessibility restrictions. These will be a variety of measures that quantify the potential investable share of security markets and the degree to which these capital flows currently take place. The first measure is the fraction of the market capitalization of a country that is investable from the ratio of market capitalization of Standard and Poor's IFC Global to that of its Investable Indices. The S&P/IFC Global indices include securities without accounting for the stock's availability to overseas investors; coverage exceeds 75% of total market capitalization, drawing on stocks in order of their liquidity. The S&P/IFC Investable indices further screen stocks for foreign ownership restrictions factoring in minimum market capitalization and liquidity considerations. Stocks are assigned weights according to the amount foreign investors may buy, because of foreign investment restrictions at the national level or by the individual company's corporate statute. I follow Geert Bekaert and Hali Edison and Frank Warnock, who originally devised this simple measure of market openness.[44] My score is based on the market capitalization data from 2009, the last year for which this data exists. The median emerging market scores only 39%, despite countries like Hungary, South Korea, South Africa, and Taiwan, which all score above 60%.

My second measure of market openness is based on the US market presence of emerging market firms in terms of international cross-listings via ADR programs. Indeed, much research has shown that the pursuit of overseas listings and capital-raising opportunities by means of a firm's secondary stock market listing on a major market like the United States often signifies the earliest signpost of capital-market liberalization of a country, one that can even predate official government liberalization actions.[45] I define presence in terms of the market capitalization of all firms with US listings relative to the market capitalization of the home market and in terms of the count of the number of firms with US listings relative to the total number of home market listings. I originally proposed this alternative measure for this study of equity market development based on investability according to the number of domestically listed companies that had initiated US-traded ADR programs, both as a fraction of that of all domestic companies.[46] This is arguably a narrower (US cross-listings only) and more conservative (only cross-listings) measure of investability, but it is quite possibly more objective than the somewhat vague criteria outlined by the advisory panels of commercial index providers. I update these data for 2012 on the fraction of the count of firms with US ADR programs following the guidelines for what counts as such from Doidge, Karolyi, and Stulz.[47]

Many of my measures of financial openness until now rely on data from the capital markets. There has also been a rapid increase in international banking and financial flows over the past several decades. According to statistics from the Bank for International Settlements (BIS), international banks' foreign claims increased from $1.12 trillion in 1987 to just over $31 trillion as of September 2013, suggesting that the international banking system is as important a conduit for the transfer of capital across countries as debt and equity capital markets.[48] To gauge the breadth of this activity, I obtain two series from the World Bank's Financial Development and Structure database on the consolidated claims of foreign banks (at least, those that are BIS-reporting) and the loans from nonresident foreign banks. Banks' financial claims are extended to residents of a host country either cross-border or domestically via a local affiliate. The claims consist of financial assets such as loans, debt securities, properties, and equities, including equity participations in subsidiaries. I deflate this quantity as of the end of 2012 by the host country's GDP. A second measure is the international loans from nonresident banks, which is equal to the loans of BIS-reporting banks to a host country, again divided by the country's GDP.[49]

Table 6.2 shows that the typical developed market has much larger foreign bank claim and lending activity: the median fraction of GDP is 58% and 38%, whereas the respective numbers among my set of emerging markets

TABLE 6.2 De facto Measures of Foreign Accessibility Restrictions in 2012

Country	S&P/EMDB Investability Ratio[1]	Size of the ADR Market (Doidge et al., 2009)[2]	World Bank FD&S Database[3]		Lane & Milesi-Ferretti (2007)[4]	
			Consolidated Claims of Foreign Banks to GDP	Loans from Nonresident Foreign Banks to GDP	Total External Assets & Liabilities to GDP	Total External Portfolio & Direct Equity to GDP
Argentina	0.394	27.03	10.85	2.96	1.02	0.30
Brazil	0.495	20.82	21.77	7.43	0.89	0.50
Chile	0.392	5.34	52.09	18.91	2.11	1.31
China	0.147	9.90	8.92	5.08	1.10	0.39
Colombia	.	9.55	12.80	4.61	0.89	0.45
Czech Republic	0.327	19.05	86.85	13.46	1.64	0.74
Egypt	0.394	2.10	16.70	4.58	0.69	0.34
Hungary	0.644	12.00	77.32	31.28	4.62	3.04
India	0.298	0.35	16.75	9.31	0.73	0.36
Indonesia	0.368	7.18	13.55	6.67	0.80	0.39
Israel	0.569	3.47	8.69	6.96	1.99	0.96
Jordan	.	0.81	13.40	16.05	2.26	0.93
South Korea	0.624	0.73	29.68	12.54	1.41	0.58
Malaysia	0.397	0.95	53.07	12.66	2.38	1.13
Mexico	0.491	34.34	30.54	7.33	0.98	0.49
Morocco	0.342	0.00	29.31	9.18	1.11	0.54
Nigeria	.	0.00	3.94	3.12	0.88	0.41
Pakistan	.	0.28	6.70	2.36	0.53	0.13
Peru	0.303	2.90	26.59	11.68	1.17	0.56
Philippines	0.297	5.61	16.13	9.14	1.15	0.34
Poland	0.412	15.99	148.75	199.42	16.43	6.01
Russia	0.388	2.47	54.19	14.56	1.30	0.55
Saudi Arabia	0.000	13.99	11.08	6.94	1.36	0.65
Slovakia	.	0.00	12.57	13.88	2.33	0.79
Slovenia	.	0.00	72.68	12.60	1.67	0.65
South Africa	0.606	0.00	72.25	40.08	2.10	0.54
Sri Lanka	.	21.74	28.95	6.13	1.56	1.11
Taiwan	0.668	0.00	11.48	5.43	0.75	0.16
Thailand	0.316	0.08	.	.	3.60	1.38
Turkey	0.309	6.01	25.04	8.91	1.69	0.73
UAE	.	0.00	20.85	12.22	1.19	0.58
Venezuela	.	7.39	26.79	16.90	0.86	0.26
Vietnam	.	30.51	9.55	3.50	1.23	0.21
Emerging Median	*0.39*	*3.47*	*21.31*	*9.16*	*1.23*	*0.55*
Developed Median	*1.00*	*14.38*	*58.20*	*37.99*	*4.43*	*1.39*

Note: Appendix C details all data sources for the foreign accessibility restrictions indicator.

[1] *Source:* S&P Emerging Market Database, computed as fraction of market capitalization as at calendar year end designated as investable using S&P IFC Investable index inclusion criteria.

is only 21% and 9%. In terms of consolidated claims, the Czech Republic (87%) and Poland (148%) both stand out from the emerging markets pack. Slovakia and Slovenia also attract the attention of the foreign banking community. Poland is also in the right tail as a beneficiary of lending by foreign banks at a remarkable 199% of GDP. South Africa follows distantly at 40% and Hungary at 31%. The Czech Republic is now close to the median emerging market, interestingly. Of course, what this data does not detail is the country of origin for the BIS-reporting banks that target opportunities in Poland, Hungary, and the Czech Republic, which is definitely worthy of more study.[50]

As a final set of de facto measures, I obtain two series from Lane and Milesi-Ferretti's External Wealth of Nations database, which I described earlier in the chapter. One series is the total stock of external assets and liabilities relative to a host country's GDP. This measure is similar in spirit to the measures in the preceding paragraph, except here I focus on the total stock of capital flows, instead of only those of bank activities. One measure is not a complete subset of the other, of course. But this one allows us to capture multiple dimensions of cross-border capital sharing. The other focuses on just equity assets and liabilities, both in portfolio and direct foreign form. As of the end of 2011, the median ratio of the total external position to GDP across developed markets is 4.43, compared to only 1.23 for the median across the 33 emerging markets. The ratio for developed markets has increased dramatically from around 0.29 back in 1970. There are some noteworthy outliers among the developed markets that pull the median ratio up, including Luxembourg (231.4), Ireland (32.3), Hong Kong (22.1), Singapore (15.4), and the United Kingdom (14.0). Among the emerging markets, it is reassuring to see that Poland stands out again (like it did with the consolidated banking sector statistics), with a total external position of 16.4 times its GDP. Hungary and Thailand also score well. The same countries rank well on the external equity assets and liabilities ratio.

---

[2] Number of domestic listed firms with a US listing as an American depositary receipt (ADR) program on a major exchange, over-the-counter or SEC Rule 144a form as fraction of total count of all domestic listed companies (Doidge, Karolyi, and Stulz, "Has New York Become Less Competitive than London in Global Markets?"

[3] *Source:* World Bank's Financial Development and Structure Database obtain data from the Bank for International Settlement on foreign claims held by banks from OECD countries in the rest of the world. These claims represent banks' financial claims extended to residents of a host country either cross-border or domestically via a local affiliate. The claims consist of financial assets such as loans, debt securities, properties, and equities, including equity participations in subsidiaries.

[4] *Source:* Philip Lane and Gian Milesi-Ferretti, (www.philiplane.org/EWN.html). One measure computes all external assets and liabilities relative to GDP including foreign direct investment, portfolio equity investment, external debt, and official reserves; the second includes only foreign direct and portfolio equity investments, both assets and liabilities.

Using Principal Component Analysis for the
Foreign Accessibility Risk Indicator

Like with the operational inefficiency risk indicator in Chapter 5, I face the challenge of distilling down as many as 15 different variables into a single risk indicator for foreign accessibility risk. The good news is the data is readily available in this category, so the unbalanced nature of the sample across countries does not come into play as much as with earlier risk indicators. Table 6.3 presents the main findings. One helpful result right out of the gate is the dominance of the first principal component with its eigenvalue of 5.16, implying about 34.4% of the overall variation is captured by it alone. To get over the magic threshold of 50% that I set, only one additional component is needed. And it delivers, though just barely. The *Rho* coefficient that captures the cumulative explanatory power of the first two principal components is 50.34%.

The second panel of results shows the coefficients of the first and second principal components with their respective inferences. The largest coefficients for the first component clearly arise for the one de jure measure on capital access (CAI) from the Milken institute (0.373) and the five de facto measures from the World Bank's Financial Development and Structure database on banking, the two from Lane and Milesi-Ferretti (2007) on external balance, and the S&P/IFC openness ratio. Each of the coefficients exceeds 0.30 with z-statistics that imply they are reliably different from zero. Not far behind these are several de jure measures on repatriation limits, on currency convertibility restrictions, and on other securities taxes, like the VAT surcharge on brokering service fees. Of course, these scores are higher for countries that are more restrictive for foreign access, so negative coefficients naturally arise. It is comforting to see that a healthy mix of both de facto and de jure measures gets some weight in the first component.

Several of the de facto variables receive some weight with statistically significant coefficients in the second principal component. The one de jure measure on currency convertibility restrictions has one of the single largest coefficients (in absolute terms). This is important because the overall risk indicator balances the respective scores for each country across the two principal components weighted by their relative contribution to overall combined explanatory power.

The Foreign Accessibility Restrictions Indicator for 2012

Figure 6.1 displays the principal component scores across the 33 emerging markets for 2012. A couple of data points jump off the page. First, Poland's score (0.55) exceeds that of the median developed market (0.37), and no other

TABLE 6.3 Principal Component Analysis for Foreign Accessibility Restrictions

Eigenvalues	Coefficient	Std. Err.	z-statistic	p-value	(5%,	95%)
First Component	5.16479	0.96745	5.34	0.00	3.26862	7.06097
Second Component	2.38599	0.44694	5.34	0.00	1.51001	3.26197
First Component						
Milken Institute Capital Access Index	0.37300	0.03538	10.54	0.00	0.30367	0.44233
S&P/IFC Openness	0.32159	0.06119	5.26	0.00	0.20166	0.44153
Size of the ADR Market	0.19658	0.06347	3.10	0.00	0.07217	0.32098
Registration Requirements	0.17798	0.06736	2.64	0.01	0.04597	0.31000
Ownership Restrictions	-0.17983	0.06588	-2.73	0.01	-0.30895	-0.05071
Repatriation Cap Limits	-0.21658	0.07140	-3.03	0.00	-0.35651	-0.07664
Currency Convertibility Restrictions	-0.25178	0.07316	-3.44	0.00	-0.39516	-0.10840
Withholding Taxes	-0.08481	0.07649	-1.11	0.27	-0.23473	0.06510
Double Taxation Treaties	-0.12802	0.08576	-1.49	0.14	-0.29611	0.04007
Foreign Capital Gains Tax	-0.10194	0.07934	-1.28	0.20	-0.25745	0.05358
Other Securities Taxes	-0.25004	0.06484	-3.86	0.00	-0.37712	-0.12296
WB Consolidated Claims of Foreign Banks	0.34348	0.04174	8.23	0.00	0.26168	0.42528
WB Loans from Foreign Banks	0.35145	0.06227	5.64	0.00	0.22940	0.47349
Lane/Milesi-Ferretti Total External Balance	0.32708	0.06964	4.70	0.00	0.19059	0.46356
Lane/Milesi-Ferretti Equity External Balance	0.31548	0.07187	4.39	0.00	0.17462	0.45633
Second Component						
Milken Institute Capital Access Index	-0.05129	0.08737	-0.59	0.56	-0.22253	0.11994
S&P/IFC Openness	-0.31413	0.08044	-3.91	0.00	-0.47179	-0.15648
Size of the ADR Market	-0.05987	0.12939	-0.46	0.64	-0.31348	0.19374
Registration Requirements	-0.02567	0.15632	-0.16	0.87	-0.33205	0.28072
Ownership Restrictions	0.08530	0.13496	0.63	0.53	-0.17923	0.34982

					5%	95%
Repatriation Cap Limits	0.29814	0.10719	2.78	0.01	0.08804	0.50823
Currency Convertibility Restrictions	0.37224	0.08442	4.41	0.00	0.20678	0.53769
Withholding Taxes	0.03109	0.22152	0.14	0.89	-0.40307	0.46526
Double Taxation Treaties	0.34654	0.19729	1.76	0.08	-0.04015	0.73322
Foreign Capital Gains Tax	-0.15735	0.22645	-0.69	0.49	-0.60119	0.28648
Other Securities Taxes	0.24818	0.11125	2.23	0.03	0.03013	0.46623
WB Consolidated Claims of Foreign Banks	0.05973	0.09241	0.65	0.52	-0.12138	0.24084
WB Loans from Foreign Banks	0.35244	0.08415	4.19	0.00	0.18750	0.51737
Lane/Milesi-Ferretti Total External Balance	0.39773	0.08096	4.91	0.00	0.23905	0.55642
Lane/Milesi-Ferretti Equity External Balance	0.40785	0.08179	4.99	0.00	0.24755	0.56816

Diagnostics

Number of observations	57		
Number of components	2		
Trace	15		
Rho	0.5034		
Std. Err. (Rho)	0.0326		
Likelihood Ratio test for dependence: χ^2 (106)	790.95	p-value 0.00	
Likelihood Ratio test for sphericity: χ^2 (119)	800.05	p-value 0.00	

Note: For columns listed under the headings of 5% and 95%, the values of the coefficient at the 5% and 95% limits of the 90% confidence range are reported, respectively.

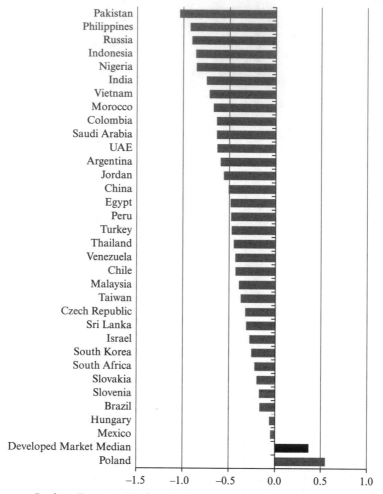

FIGURE 6.1 *Ranking Emerging Markets by Foreign Accessibility Restrictions in 2012.*

Note: The foreign accessibility restrictions risk indicator scores are computed on a standardized basis using a standard normal scale for the continuous index values. Negative (positive) values imply worse (better) scores, reflecting greater (lesser) risk. All scores are measured using data up to 2012.

emerging market scores close to either of them. Poland's outlier scores on the consolidated banking statistics and the Lane and Milesi-Ferretti data with the sizable coefficients from the PCA seem to carry the day. A second feature of the cross-country distribution is that there are no distinct tiers in the scores. Mexico and Hungary have small negative scores (–0.05 and –0.06 respectively), which are a good distance higher than that for Brazil (–0.17), which is ranked next. A third attribute of the distribution is how compressed it is relative to what was seen for the market capacity constraints indicator (Chapter 4) and the operational inefficiency indicator (Chapter 5). See how the lowest negative value reaches only –1.04 for Pakistan, which is not that far from the median emerging market score around –0.50.

To push this point about the compressed distribution one step further, consider Figure 6.2. I gathered scores from the two indicators from the previous two chapters for select countries. The countries were chosen as those that had the largest absolute difference in the standardized scores for the foreign accessibility restrictions relative to the average of the other two. In other words, I am looking to those countries for which the newest foreign accessibility scores would really shift priors. Four countries go in a positive direction and four others in a negative direction. Among the latter set, you see that China has a distinctly lower score for foreign accessibility restrictions (–0.49) than for its market capacity constraints or its operational inefficiencies (together averaging around 0.25). South Korea, Malaysia, and Taiwan also impose tougher restrictions on foreign access than their market capacity and operational efficiency would have led you to believe. By contrast, Egypt, Nigeria, Poland, and Venezuela offer greater openness by the rules in place and by the de facto actions of foreign market participants than their limited capacity and inefficiency of trading, clearance, and settlement systems would imply.

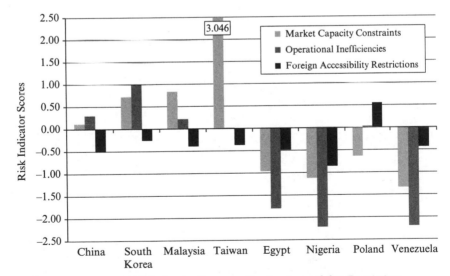

FIGURE 6.2 *Comparing Risk Indicators Scores on Foreign Accessibility Restrictions, Operational Inefficiencies, and Market Capacity in 2012 for Selected Markets.*

Note: The market capacity constraint, operational inefficiency, and foreign accessibility restrictions risk indicator scores are computed on a standardized basis using a standard normal scale for the continuous index values. Negative (positive) values imply worse (better) scores, reflecting greater (lesser) risk. All scores are computed using data up to 2012.

The Collateral Benefits (and Costs) of Financial
Globalization: Redux

The next step in our journey is to broaden the concept of financial globalization into the ancillary benefits (and costs) that might arise from greater participation of global investors. Remember that this is the central thesis of the book in defining emerging markets: countries with significant growth opportunities underfunded because of severe local market capacity constraints, and because of many problems that impede access of foreign capital. I have taken on the biggest constraint that binds in this chapter, which comprises the rules and restrictions that keep foreign investors out. I addressed operational inefficiencies in Chapter 4, a key deterrent for *any* market participant, but especially foreign investors who are likely to be unused to such inefficiencies. I now turn to other deterrence forces—what Kose et al. call "potential collateral benefits or costs"—that reveal just how fragile emerging markets can be.[51] These are corporate governance problems (Chapter 7), limits on legal protections for investors and corporations alike (Chapter 8), and political instability revolving around the role of the state in the markets (Chapter 9).

Corporate Opacity

Corporate governance deals with the mechanisms that ensure investors in corporations get a return on their investments.[1] Corporate governance practices vary widely across countries and across firms within any one country. Better governance enables firms to access capital markets on better terms, which is valuable for those intending to raise funds. Firms with valuable growth opportunities that cannot be financed internally have greater incentives to adopt mechanisms that commit them to better governance.[2]

What are credible ways in which firms can commit to better governance? There are many. But at the core of them all is the pursuit of greater transparency—or less corporate opacity—in the rights and protections afforded to outside, minority investors in the firm relative to others. After all, it is the outside, minority investors who need to be convinced to fund the growth opportunities in the first place. The more rights minority investors have and the more clearly those rights are communicated, the more easily their trust will be secured for the long haul. Firms can improve investor rights by increasing their disclosures of financial and even nonfinancial information to the marketplace, by selecting well-functioning and independent boards, by imposing disciplinary mechanisms to prevent management and large, controlling blockholders from investing in projects related to their private interests at the expense of minority shareholders. I will feature elements of each of these governance mechanisms in the corporate opacity risk indicator I build.

There are, of course, country-level reporting standards on financials and mandated disclosures about board structure, director compensation, and the extent of block ownership. But firms often have the flexibility in their corporate charters and bylaws to either choose to opt out and decline specific provisions, or adopt perhaps additional provisions not mandated in their country's legal code. The choices firms make depend on the benefits and costs, both direct and indirect. And firms, especially those domiciled in emerging markets with weak laws to protect minority investors or with poor economic and financial development, can face up to significant costs to improve their corporate transparency. For example, a firm in an emerging market might be unable to commit to external verification of its financial statement information via its auditors, if the necessary infrastructure for such verification is not available because regulatory authorities do not conduct regular audit inspections. Also, firms in countries with low financial and economic development will find it optimal to invest less in providing detailed and timely disclosures if the terms and minimal governance standards under which the capital would be raised are so poor. That is also why widening financial globalization could matter for governance choices of emerging-market firms, as they are presented with new *external* opportunities for raising capital.

Corporate transparency and disclosure choices are complex. The lines that might separate corporate opacity from capital market development, functional efficiency of the markets, financial openness, or the political and legal environment of business are blurred. My modest goal in this chapter is to *describe* differences in governance systems across countries, especially in emerging markets. Stated differently, my foremost goal is not to *explain* why those differences arise, though for completeness, later in the chapter, I will offer up a primer on various competing theories that have been put forward for why governance systems do differ across countries. I hope it helps not only to rationalize the choices I make for the variables that will comprise the corporate opacity risk indicator, but also to help delineate the broad distinctions I make with the other risk indicators I build in the book.

As the next case study demonstrates, international differences in corporate governance and the general quality of governance standards can give rise to complications with protracted, ongoing uncertainty for businesses and their investors.

Grupo Modelo: Trouble Brewing in the Global Beer Industry?

On June 20, 2008, Carlos Fernandez, chairman and CEO of Mexican brewer Grupo Modelo, unexpectedly announced his resignation from Anheuser-Busch's board of directors.[3] Anheuser-Busch (A-B), the US brewer best known for Budweiser, had received an uninvited offer at $65 per share for all outstanding shares from rival InBev, the Belgian-Brazilian conglomerate and the world's second-largest brewer of, among other brands, Stella Artois and Beck's. The mega-deal would have exceeded $52 billion in total value. Rumors were rampant that A-B would resist what it perceived to be a weak offer and that InBev, in turn, was maneuvering to bypass A-B's board by filing a case in a Delaware court to remove the current directors.[4] Some analysts were surprised by Fernandez's decision to resign, as they believed Fernandez was in favor of InBev acquiring A-B. This was the widely drawn conclusion, because Fernandez opted to not have A-B buy out the remaining 49.8% of Grupo Modelo's shares that they did not already own.[5] Buying out the remaining shares of Modelo, the analysts figured, would convert the Mexican brewer into a wholly owned subsidiary and thus might have made A-B too large for InBev to pursue.[6]

Cerveceria Modelo S.A. de C.V. was founded in 1925 in Mexico by a group of Spanish immigrants. By 1936, one of the founding members, Pablo Diez Fernandez, had bought out the other founders and was the majority shareholder until his death in 1972. During his lifetime Modelo acquired a number of competing breweries and invested in modernizing its plants, achieving leadership in the Mexican beer market by the 1950s. The elder Fernandez, Carlos' grandfather, allowed senior managers to become shareholders, resulting in the company being controlled by six families. These families had the first right of refusal for any significant management decisions through a voting trust. The breweries and distribution network were organized as Grupo Modelo S.A. in 1991, which subsequently listed on the Mexican stock exchange, the Bolsa Valores, in 1994.[7]

By 2008, Modelo led the Mexican beer market with a 57% market share of the domestic and export market, with revenues over $7 billion (as of 2007 year-end).[8] The firm had an installed production capacity of 60 million hectoliters and produced 12 brands, including Corona Extra, the best-selling Mexican beer globally. Modelo's global reach extended to more than 150 countries. FEMSA was Modelo's main domestic competitor with a 42% market share through its own leading brands, Dos Equis and Tecate. To broaden Modelo's distribution network in the United States, it created a joint venture with Constellation Brands, called Crown Imports LLC, with a renewable 10-year contract. If A-B were to buy Modelo, Constellation Brands would expect A-B to renew the contract or pay fair market value for its half of the venture.[9]

The relationship with A-B was forged on March 22, 1993, in the aftermath of the enactment of the North American Free Trade Agreement. A-B acquired a 17.7% interest in Grupo Modelo for $207 million, and a joint venture allowed A-B to buy additional shares in it and its operating subsidiary, Diblo. By 1998 A-B had secured its 50.2% ownership position in Modelo but only a 43.9% voting share, allowing the six families to retain their controlling position.[10] Carlos Fernandez took over as CEO in 1997 at age 31, though his uncle, Antonio, the immediately preceding CEO, remained heavily involved. At age 90, he continued to control the Modelo family voting trust.[11]

Anheuser-Busch, of course, had its own family legacy to deal with. A-B was now the world's third-largest brewer by volume, with $17 billion in annual sales. August Busch IV had only been CEO of A-B for 18 months when InBev made its takeover offer in June 2008. He was the fifth family member to run the business. And August Busch III, his father and former CEO, had declared himself openly opposed to the InBev deal.[12] Interestingly, while Carlos Fernandez held one seat on the A-B board, both Busches III and IV held two of the nonvoting seats on the Modelo board.[13]

The push for ever greater consolidation in the global beer industry weighed on the A-B-Inbev deal. Estimated to top $401 billion in sales worldwide, with most of it in the developed markets of North America and Europe, industry experts described the developed-world beer market as mature, growing at a modest 1.5% to 2% for the next several years.[14] On July 12, InBev raised its offer for A-B from $65 to $70 per share and it began syndicating a $45 billion loan that it would need to finance the deal.[15] The deal closed on November 18, 2008.[16]

During the acquisition process, Modelo's stock price had drifted downward from just under MXP (Mexican pesos) 55 (or $5.06, at 10.87 MXP per US dollar) on June 20 to under MXP 40 by November 18. On the announcement day, Grupo Modelo filed an arbitration notice against A-B, arguing that InBev's $52 billion takeover of A-B, which owned half of Grupo Modelo, violated the original 1993 investment agreement.[17] While the arbitration panel deliberated on the notice, market rumors swirled about the de facto new entity, A-B InBev, and the possibility that it would move to buy out the remaining half of Modelo shares it did not own for $10.8 billion.[18] Part of the motivation for this action was likely Heineken's simultaneous $7.7 billion deal to buy the beer operations of FEMSA, Modelo's main competitor at home.[19] Though the arbitration panel finally did rule in A-B InBev's favor to affirm the creation of the new company, and though it created a smoother path for it to pursue the controlling stake in Modelo, no offer was made until June 2012.[20] The $9.15 per share offer to be paid in cash represented a 30% premium to Modelo's closing price the day before making it a $20.1 billion deal. Carlos Fernandez welcomed the deal, saying: "We have worked together with AB InBev in a productive decades-long partnership and it is time to cement our relationship through this merger."[21]

Analysts rumored that in order to preempt antitrust issues, Modelo might have to sell its 50% stake in the Crown Imports joint venture with Constellation Brands.[22] And indeed the Department of Justice of the United States filed an antitrust lawsuit, challenging that the deal would "substantially lessen competition in the market for beer in the United States as a whole and in 26 metropolitan areas . . . resulting in consumers paying more for beer and having fewer new products from which to choose."[23] The deal closed once the suit was settled April 19, 2013, requiring A-B InBev to divest Modelo's entire US business, including its interest in Crown Imports, and other assets.[24]

International Corporate Governance Systems: A Bit of Theory

There are many aspects of the A-B InBev acquisition of Grupo Modelo that reveal the innate challenges of corporate governance in emerging markets. One aspect is about the complex ownership structure of Modelo. Family-centered, controlling blockholders are a common occurrence in many emerging market firms. Their presence creates an element of opacity about the firm's goals, and, specifically, the extent to which the controlling shareholders may pursue their private interests at the expense of other minority shareholders. That the family with the large voting trust also handled the responsibilities of management from one generation to the next is not unusual.

Multiple classes of shares of stock with differential voting and cash-flow ownership rights often arise in emerging market firms. Scholars refer to the wedge between the fraction of voting rights and that of the cash-flow rights as red flags for governance problems. Proportionally higher voting rights relative to cash-flow rights allow for one more degree of freedom for those with controlling interests to pursue corporate objectives that are not in the best interest of minority shareholders. Of course they really only come to the foreground around important transactions, like the A-B InBev acquisition, that could perturb those stakes. The relatively low fraction of shares listed and trading in the public markets (Modelo's Series C shares) implies a smaller float, so common in many emerging markets, that alerts investors to potentially unusual patterns in the returns and trading volume, on average, around key news events like acquisitions or earnings announcements, and especially during periods of market stress.

What I most value in the Modelo case is how a cross-border transaction organically brings out the stark differences in corporate governance and transparency systems across countries. But what is the best way to measure these differences? Is it important to understand how these differences in governance standards arise? Maybe theory can help.

A study by La Porta, Lopez-de-Silanes, and Shleifer in 1999 was one of the first to show that most firms outside the United States are controlled by large shareholders who may have the incentives to extract private benefits from the corporations they control.[25] Their finding laid the groundwork for a host of well-cited theoretical models of corporate governance by Johnson, Boone, Breach, and Friedman; La Porta, Lopez-de-Silanes, Shleifer, and Vishny; Shleifer and Wolfenzon; Doidge, Karolyi, and Stulz; Durnev and Kim; and Stulz.[26]

These models start with an assumption that there is a cost of extracting private benefits. Further, the controlling shareholders consume fewer private benefits in countries where the costs of extracting them are higher. The costs associated with the extraction of private benefits are what these theorists call "deadweight," and are lost to all or are wasted. They are assumed to increase the costs of raising outside funds for the controlling shareholder who bears them. So no one gains, and only the controlling shareholders lose. Controlling shareholders of firms with growth opportunities that cannot be financed internally have the greatest incentives to find ways to commit to lower extraction of private benefits. There are many ways they can commit to do so, but the most credible is by increasing the costs of doing so. In other words, they communicate to outsiders the penalty they themselves would suffer if they breached the trust of outside investors.

One way to increase the cost of extracting private benefits is by increasing their ownership of cash-flow rights relative to their voting rights, or by reducing or eliminating the wedge I mentioned earlier. Another way is to improve the firm's governance processes, which can be done several ways. Increasing a firm's disclosures beyond the minimum level mandated by law or convention, for example, makes it easier for outsiders to monitor the consumption of private benefits and to take actions to limit it.[27] As much as it is about the quality or number of the disclosures, another part of the credibility may come from the timeliness of their releases and the form in which it takes place. Other out-of-pocket costs to display self-discipline before outsider investors include the hiring of a higher-quality external auditor. After all, it will take more time for management to hire one, the auditor will charge higher fees than a lower-quality one, and a good one will make more demands on management's time. Finally, retaining more reputable, independent directors on a board will require appropriate compensation and will make more demands on management's time and limit their discretion in corporate policy choices.

Reality cannot be as simple as these models make it sound, of course. The measures that firms choose to take will also be a function of their country's institutional framework. Two firms that are otherwise identical (in terms of growth opportunities, say) except that they are domiciled in different countries may face very different costs of extracting private benefits, which will in turn impact their incentives to improve governance. There is an important literature that has focused on the level of economic and financial development as a determinant of the institutions that comprise the financial system. Franklin Allen and Douglas Gale specifically emphasize the importance of different governance systems across countries in their 2000 book *Comparing Financial Systems*, to help understand the functional efficiency of a financial system in an economy.[28] They argue how good quality market institutions impact the capital allocation mechanism, and how institutions are impacted by vibrancy capital allocation activities, in turn. And that complex cycle is what is crucial toward overcoming market imperfections or what I referred to earlier as deadweight costs.[29] If this is correct, there is some natural interdependence between separate measures of market capacity constraints (Chapter 4) and operational inefficiencies in a market (Chapter 5), and what I try to measure in this chapter.

A quality legal system may also be a critical ingredient for better governance standards. Making promises to investors that are *enforceable* in court is one way a firm can commit itself *credibly* to better behavior. But mechanisms to do so could be unavailable or prohibitively expensive in countries with poor legal protections for minority investors. Consider a firm that might be unable to commit to credible external verification of its financial statement disclosures if the necessary infrastructure for such verification is not available. Ray Ball, a thought leader on corporate disclosure choices, articulates what he thinks are the "infrastructure requirements" needed for an economically efficient system of public financial reporting and disclosure; Bernie Black, a legal scholar, delineates what he calls the "legal and institutional preconditions" for strong securities markets.[30] Some of the infrastructure or preconditions need to come from the state. In fact, in a model by Bergman and Nicolaievsky, firms gain more from investing in better governance-related monitoring (hiring good auditors, underwriters, and lawyers) in countries with better state-provided investor protection. For them, state-level investor protection and firm-level governance are complements.[31] This logic makes just a little harder the effort to define a difference between corporate governance measures in this chapter from limits to legal protections for minority investors in the next (Chapter 8).

Financial globalization—the limits of which were the focus in Chapter 6—throws another wrench into the exercise. Institution-based theories posit that differences in a country' laws, governance, disclosure, and enforcement standards can explain differences in financial and economic activity. Better institutions stimulate greater investment and greater economic output. But with financial globalization, these very same theories predict that differences in these standards should erode and make them less important determinants of economic output. Some scholars call this "functional convergence" in legal, disclosure, and governance institutions.

An archetypal model by Andrei Shleifer and Daniel Wolfenzon models how a country's governance standards affect the benefits and costs of raising outside capital for the owners of a firm (think of them as the controlling stakeholders).[32] The worry for the outside investors, as usual in such a model, is that the controlling shareholder can extract private benefits at their expense. So they coinvest only if they can buy in at a fair value, perhaps a discount relative to what they would otherwise be willing to pay. The stronger the governance system in the country in which the firm is domiciled means that the private benefits are likely lower, and so is the discount. The global free flow of capital allows firms to raise funds outside their country of domicile. They may choose to list their shares on a major stock exchange overseas that has much more stringent rules on disclosures. With this possibility of borrowing the tougher standards for governance outside, the importance of home country institutions wanes.[33]

Theory tells us that measuring the quality of corporate governance standards of a country with confidence is a chore. With all the warnings and cautions laid out before us, I now push forward to describe the specific governance metrics I use across the 57 countries in my analysis.

General, All-Purpose Governance Rankings

The surge of interest in the topic of corporate governance among investment banks, ratings agencies, and asset management firms made it viable for a number of private firms to start collecting firm-level data on differences in corporate governance scores across firms in different countries. The two I use are from Credit Lyonnais Securities Asia (CLSA) and Standard and Poor's (S&P's).[34] The CLSA survey was conducted over a six-week period ending in March 2001, and it rates the corporate governance practices of 495 firms from 25 countries. This survey has been used in a number of recent papers.[35] The main criteria for including firms in the CLSA survey are firm size and investor interest. The CLSA corporate governance rating is based on a questionnaire given to financial analysts who responded with "Yes" or "No' answers to 57 questions related to seven categories: management discipline, financial transparency, independence, accountability, responsibility, fairness, and social responsibility. A composite governance rating is computed by giving an equal weight of 15% to the first six categories and a weight of 10% to social responsibility. Percentage scores on the composite governance ratings range from 13.9 to 93.5. I obtain the median scores across the firms for a given country.[36]

Table 7.1 shows that the median CLSA score in emerging markets is 53.67, which is lower than that for the two developed markets in their sample (Hong Kong and Singapore, median 64.57). The scores cluster for the most part around the median, but outliers with low scores include China (46.22), South Korea (43.65), Poland (36.20), Turkey (43.67), and especially Russia (15.40). Peru (75.50) scores well above Hong Kong and Singapore.

Another set of governance ratings, Standard & Poor's Transparency and Disclosure ratings, constructed for a study by S&P launched in 2001, has also been used in recent research.[37] The sample provided by Standard & Poor's in April 2003 covers 901 firms from 40 countries. S&P compiles the ratings by examining firms' annual reports and standard regulatory filings for disclosure of 98 items, divided into three sections: financial transparency and information disclosure (35 items), board and management structure and process (35 items), and ownership structure and investor relations (28 items). S&P uses a binary scoring system in which one point is awarded if a particular item is disclosed or if the firm exhibits a particular positive feature with respect to its structure or management. The scores are added and converted to a percentage score, with a range from 15.22 to 88.78; the medians across firms in a given country are presented.

The coverage across countries in the emerging markets is spotty in Table 7.1 compared to CLSA. But there are many developed markets in this sample, so the comparison of the low emerging market median (34.33) compared to the high developed market median (58.71) is more meaningful. In this sample Colombia (19.15), Taiwan (21.63), and Mexico (24.77) score poorly and none of the emerging markets scores exceed the developed market median.

TABLE 7.1 Measures of Corporate Opacity in 2012

Country	CLSA[1]	S&P[2]	Bushman, Piotroski, and Smith (2004)[3]				CKP[4] Analyst Coverage	DKLMS[5] Blockholder Control	LLS[6] Top 3 Owners	WS[7] Closely Held	CIFAR[8] Accounting Standards	Karolyi, et al. (2012)[9]		IFRS Adoption?
			Timeliness	Measure	Govern	Disclose						R^2 Liquidity	R^2 Returns	
Argentina	66.70	28.63	91.30	100.00	68.12	70.65	12.73	0.6167	0.53	69.057	45	0.2616	0.2633	1
Brazil	61.91	32.75	86.96	100.00	65.94	57.25	16.10	0.4500	0.57	63.099	54	0.2207	0.2680	1
Chile	62.12	34.33	94.20	100.00	76.45	92.75	5.35	0.3929	0.45	66.458	52	0.2172	0.2600	1
China	46.22	48.58					5.36			48.164		0.4963	0.3877	0
Colombia	57.90	19.15	62.32	22.83	65.58	14.49	3.31		0.63	63.349	50			0
Czech Republic	51.40						8.33	0.2800		63.581	24			1
Egypt									0.62					0
Hungary	52.85						5.11			67.215				1
India	54.74	38.75	45.65	54.35	76.45	79.35	11.90		0.40	52.170	57	0.2443	0.2442	0
Indonesia	37.03	36.47					5.96	0.3642	0.58	68.575	65	0.2274	0.2888	0
Israel							3.19	0.3140	0.51	55.023	64	0.2410	0.2646	1
Jordan									0.52					1
South Korea	43.65	46.65	65.22	100.00	96.74	100.00	19.90	0.3254	0.54	45.019	76	0.2227	0.1940	1
Malaysia	55.25	45.44	84.78	100.00	65.58	68.12	18.53		0.64	50.799	60	0.2252	0.2408	1
Mexico	68.20	24.77								61.636		0.2398	0.3134	1
Morocco							3.40		0.40		59			0.5
Nigeria			51.45	46.74	92.75	68.48			0.37		61			1
Pakistan	34.69	39.76	71.74	54.35	65.58	53.99	8.10	0.3500	0.56	61.841	38	0.2232	0.3633	1
Peru	75.50	23.26	75.36	23.91	65.58	80.07	10.90	0.6281	0.57	75.764	65			1
Philippines	48.30	27.21					8.00			68.540		0.2366	0.2905	1
Poland	36.20						1.50			55.650		0.2086	0.1976	1
Russia	15.40									73.304				1
Saudi Arabia														0.5

(continued)

TABLE 7.1 Continued

Country	CLSA[1]	S&P[2]	Bushman, Piotroski, and Smith (2004)[3]				CKP[4] Analyst Coverage	DKLMS[5] Blockholder Control	LLS[6] Top 3 Owners	WS[7] Closely Held	CIFAR[8] Accounting Standards	Karolyi, et al. (2012)[9]		IFRS Adoption?
			Timeliness	Measure	Govern	Disclose						R² Liquidity	R² Returns	
Slovakia	.	.	.	.	.	.	.	.	.	.	.	.	.	1
Slovenia	.	.	86.96	100.00	94.20	88.41	7.40	0.5278	0.52	.	70	.	.	1
South Africa	68.45	.	17.39	39.13	77.90	65.22	9.90	0.2220	0.23	44.594	62	0.2132	0.2751	1
Sri Lanka	.	.	.	.	.	.	2.40	0.1800	0.60	.	65	.	.	1
Taiwan	55.97	21.63	17.39	46.74	69.93	59.78	6.80	0.2524	0.18	26.650	65	0.2295	0.2258	1
Thailand	54.49	51.63	89.13	23.91	68.12	51.07	9.77	0.2476	0.47	52.212	64	0.2282	0.2828	0
Turkey	43.67	.	17.39	68.48	67.03	59.06	7.97	0.2000	0.59	66.502	51	0.2345	0.2574	1
UAE	.	.	.	.	.	.	.	.	.	.	.	.	.	1
Venezuela	.	30.65	17.39	100.00	69.57	36.23	1.67	.	0.51	76.140	40	.	.	1
Vietnam	.	.	.	.	.	.	.	.	.	.	.	.	.	1
Emerging Median	53.67	34.33	65.22	54.35	69.57	65.22	7.40	0.32	0.52	63.097	60.50	0.23	0.27	1.00
Developed Median	64.57	58.71	76.09	69.57	84.24	100.00	16.90	0.38	0.41	47.979	69.00	0.22	0.27	1.00

Note: Appendix D details all data sources for the foreign accessibility restrictions indicators.

[1] Credit Lyonnais Securities Asia Governance Score is on a standardized scale of 0 (bad) to 100 (good) and is based on a survey of 57 questions on management discipline, accountability, fairness, and social responsibility.

[2] Standard & Poor's Transparency score is on a scale of 0 (bad) to 100 (good) and includes data from corporate filings on 98 items related to disclosure, board, and ownership structure.

[3] Bushman, Piotroski, and Smith, in "What Determines Corporate Transparency?," create scale from 0 (bad) to 100 (good) on timeliness of disclosures, on consolidated reporting, on disclosures of management, officers, and directors, and on nonmandated disclosures.

[4] Number of analysts following the largest 30 companies in each country in 1996, from Chang, Khanna, and Palepu, "Analyst Activity Around the World," and using data from Bailey, Karolyi, and Salva, "The Economic Consequences of Increased Disclosure."

[5] Fraction of shares outstanding controlled by the largest blockholder for the largest firms. Doidge, Karolyi, Lins, Miller, and Stulz, "Private Benefits of Control, Ownership and the Cross-Listing Decision."

[6] Percentage of shares owned by three largest blockholders among the largest 30 firms in each country. La Porta, Lopez-de-Silanes, and Shleifer, "Corporate Ownership around the World."

[7] Thomson Reuter's Worldscope computes shares held by officers, directors, and other beneficial owners, as a percentage of all shares outstanding.

[8] Center for International Financial Analysis and Research (CIFAR) index runs from 0 (bad) to 90 (good) of 1995 annual reports for inclusion or omission of financial statement items.

[9] Karolyi, Lee, and Van Dijk, "Understanding Commonality in Liquidity around the World." Across the listed stocks in a given market with daily returns and trading volume, monthly averages of the firm-level R² of returns (Amihud illiquidity) on value-weighted market returns (Amihud illiquidity).

Corporate Reporting Practices Around the World

Corporate reporting practices vary widely across countries. Researchers construct different metrics of corporate transparency in terms of the collection, production, gathering, validation, and dissemination of information to market participants. They also track unusual practices, such as earnings management, which some associate with incentives of dominant controlling shareholders or other corporate insiders to conceal their private benefits of control from outsiders. I collect and use four different sets of measures.

My first two measures relate to practices of disclosure and accounting. First, Bushman, Piotroski, and Smith analyze an extensive range of measures of corporate reporting practices, including (1) disclosure intensity, which relate to reporting of segment information, R&D, capital expenditures, subsidiaries and overall accounting policy ("Disclose" heading in Table 7.1); (2) governance disclosures on major shareholders, management information, names of board members, remuneration of directors/officers ("Govern"); (3) timeliness of disclosures, including frequency of reporting, consolidation of interim reports, and the number of disclosed items ("Timeliness"); and (4) reporting of consolidation and discretionary reserves ("Measure").[38] These measures are standardized, scale-free factors (ranging from zero to 100, where 100 indicates high transparency) extracted from a principal components analysis procedure across 203 firms in 46 countries.

The median scores among emerging market firms in each of the four categories are distinctly lower than for those of developed markets. The sparseness of the coverage across my 33 countries is a cause for some concern. But the dispersion is quite dramatic. Venezuela scores low on the timeliness score, but so does Turkey, South Africa, and Taiwan (all four average around 17). A number of the countries tracked do report consolidated statements for the "Measure" category, but not Colombia, Peru, and Thailand, each of which scores well on timeliness. There is a strong clustering of scores among emerging markets around their median (69.7), but South Korea, Nigeria, and Slovenia stand out. This one of the four measures is correlated most weakly (–0.02) with the CLSA Governance score among the countries both have in common. Colombia (14.49) and Venezuela (36.23) score particularly poorly on the disclosure intensity measure.

Second, the Center for International Financial Analysis and Research (CIFAR) constructs an index based on an average number of 90 accounting and nonaccounting items disclosed by a sample of large companies in their annual reports. It draws from their 1995 International Accounting and Auditing Trends Report and has been used in many academic research studies.[39] It is a broad set of disclosures, including general information, items from the income statement, balance sheet and funds flow statement, accounting standards, stock data, governance data, and special items. The index, presented under the column heading "CIFAR Accounting Standards" in Table 7.1, runs from a low value of 40 (Venezuela) to a high value of 76 (South Korea). Egypt and Pakistan are big outliers (24 and 38, respectively). One caution, of course, is that the data presented characterize accounting standards across countries, when the new millennium was marked by coordinated adoption of new standards. I address this concern shortly, but I still believe the variation across countries provides a meaningful contrast.

Disclosure of information in a transparent manner, with well-defined accounting standards, of course, plays a large part in corporate governance. But, as in the United States, investors often partly delegate interpretation of that information gathering to analysts. Financial analysts specialize in processing and interpreting financial information reported by firms and in collecting additional information through discussion with firms' managers, suppliers, and customers. I use a measure of the amount of private information acquired by financial analysts with the average number of analysts following the largest firms in a country as reported by Chang, Khanna, and Palepu and Bailey, Karolyi, and Salva.[40] Both studies obtain these data based on stocks available in the International File of the Institutional Brokers' Estimate System (I/B/E/S) database.

The column in Table 7.1 with the heading "CKP Analyst Coverage" summarizes this data. The median emerging market country firm has a following of 7.40 analysts, less than half that of the typical developed market firm (16.9 analysts). Venezuela (1.67) and Sri Lanka (2.40) score low on analyst following, especially compared to South Korea (19.90) and Malaysia (18.53), which are comparable with most developed market firms.

The introduction of international financial reporting standards (IFRS) for listed companies in many countries around the world was one of the most significant regulatory changes in accounting history. Over 100 countries have moved to IFRS reporting, or have decided to require the use of these standards in the near future. Even the US Securities and Exchange Commission (SEC) has been considering allowing US firms to use IRFS reporting standards. The argument for harmonization of standards is to make easier comparisons across countries, to improve transparency, and to increase the quality of reporting. Daske, Hail, Leuz, and Verdi examine the effects on market liquidity, cost of capital, and Tobin's q, a valuation metric, for a large sample of firms that were mandated to adopt IFRS. They found positive consequences, but only for those firms that voluntarily switched to IFRS before it became mandatory.[41]

I collect information as of the end of 2012 from PriceWaterhouseCoopers report *IFRS Adoption by Country*, which provides a narrative for each country on the extent of their IFRS practices.[42] I score a variable as "1" if full adoption has occurred with few exceptions, and "0.5" if there are many exceptions, if IFRS is encouraged, or if plans for IFRS adoption are underway. The last column of Table 7.1 shows that the median emerging market as well as the median developed market country is a full IFRS adopter. But some countries, like Morocco and Saudi Arabia, are partly there, and six others are not there at all (China, Colombia, Egypt, India, Indonesia, and Thailand). Interestingly, the IFRS indicator variable

I build has a positive but modest correlation with the CIFAR accounting standards (0.034), but it is more reliably positively correlated with several of the Bushman, Piotroski, and Smith reporting standards scores, all of which predate IFRS.[43]

Where Are the Large, Controlling Blockholders?

If corporate transparency reflects the extent to which firms' reported economic performance is altered by insiders to either mislead stakeholders or to influence contractual outcomes, the incentives to do so likely increase when there is a large controlling stake by a corporate insider, who with a large stake can more easily extract private benefits. Many of the theories on international corporate governance have the existence of a controlling stakeholder as a starting point. A corporate insider can be a large blockholder of shares, such as a founder or family of a founder, government, management, officers, or directors. Unfortunately, there exists no uniform data on large blockholders that cover my country set. As a result, I draw data from several different studies, each of which spans different countries and years, and apply different definitions.

One of the first studies to attempt measuring large blockholder interests is La Porta, Lopez-de-Silanes, Shleifer, and Vishny, which identified the top three blockholders and their stakes (percentage of shares held) in 1995.[44] They consider the 10 largest firms in a country with at least $500 million in market capitalization, and a sample of 540 firms in 27 countries. In the column in Table 7.1 under the heading "LLS Top 3 Owners," the average percentage of shares held exceeds 52%. The countries for which the firms bring up this average are Colombia (63%), Egypt (62%), Sri Lanka (60%), and Turkey (59%). It is surprising that there is so little dispersion in these levels among the countries in their sample. Taiwan (18%) and South Africa (23%) score low on top-three blockholder presence.

Second, I use data from the studies by Faccio and Lang for mostly European firms on the largest controlling blockholder (minimum 10% stake) and the fraction of shares outstanding that they control.[45] Claessens, Djankov, and Lang perform the same computation for Asian firms.[46] Together, these data are collected around 1996 and in pooled form comprise 4,280 companies from 22 countries. Lins focuses on emerging market companies, but defines controlling shareholders in terms of the family/management group and their stake.[47] He evaluates for what fraction of the firms in the sample the family/management group is the largest blockholder in the firm. These data are collected around 1997, and in pooled form comprise 4,516 companies from 31 countries. I use the country-level summary statistics from my study with Doidge, Lins, Miller, and Stulz, in which we build a composite database for our analysis of international cross-listings activity.[48] I only use the blockholder rights series from that study.

The countries that stand out in terms of blockholder presence (column heading "DKLMS Blockholder Control") are Argentina (61.7%) and Peru (62.8%)

on the high end, with Sri Lanka (18%) and Turkey (20%) on the low end. It is quite possible that Turkey and Sri Lanka would score high on the top-three ownership stake from La Porta et al., but low on the fraction of control rights held by the largest blockholder.[49] The two series are capturing related, but different elements of the controlling blockholder's stake. It turns out these two series are strongly positively correlated in any case (0.49).

I also obtain data from Thomson Financial's Worldscope database on what they call "closely held shares."[50] Worldscope defines corporate insiders as officers, directors, and immediate families; the company (except held by banks and custodians in a fiduciary capacity); pension/benefit plans; and individuals with over 5% stakes. These data are collected for a large cross-section of publicly listed firms from around the world on an annual basis from 1990 through 2010.[51] The median emerging market firm has 63% of its shares in closely held form by one of the insider or outside blockholders. Venezuela has a relatively high fraction (76%), as do Russia (73%) and Peru (75%). As with the DKLMS Blockholder Control series and the LLS top-three ownership stake, Taiwan scores low (26%).

Commonality in Returns and Liquidity

Another way to gauge the transparency of the information environment in a country is not by studying *quantity*-based measures, like the number of corporate insiders, analysts, or outside directors on a firm's board, but by *price*-based measures. An influential study by Morck, Yeung, and Yu gives us an opening to consider some. In their study, they argued that information acquisition by market participants is an endogenous choice. Specifically, they offered that there are fewer incentives to collect firm-specific information (on the firm's management, operations, marketing, or financial policy choices) in countries with weaker disclosure rules and poorer legal standards. What protections are in place for minority investors to give them the confidence to gather information and to then capitalize on what they think is an arbitrage opportunity? Morck et al. construct a measure of the extent to which the high-frequency returns across the breadth of stocks in a given market comove together, on average. They call this measure *synchronicity*, or a commonality in returns. The higher is the level of synchronicity in returns across stocks in a market, the less transparent the information environment and the fewer protections are in place for minority investors.[52]

In my own study with Kuan-Hui Lee and Mathijs van Dijk, we hypothesize that investor protection and transparency also affect the commonality in liquidity (the same concepts outlined in Chapter 5) through the very same influence on the incentives to trade individual stocks.[53] If firm-specific information acquisition is impeded by low transparency or by uncertainty about whether investors can actually reap the benefits of firm-specific arbitrage, investors are more likely to engage in market-wide basket trading. Countries with greater synchronicity in returns or higher commonality in liquidity (our author team's preferred term) are associated with weaker investor protections and lower transparency. Needless to say, these synchronicity measures are not without their critics.[54]

I add two variables from the Karolyi et al. study: one measures the commonality in liquidity and the other commonality in returns, just like Morck et al., but for an updated sample period. For each of almost 27,447 publicly traded stocks across 40 countries from 1995 through 2009, we compute daily returns and daily changes in liquidity using the Amihud proxy for illiquidity (a reasonable choice, based on arguments in Chapter 5).[55] Each month, we estimate a simple univariate regression model of the individual stocks returns or innovations in liquidity on the market-wide equivalent; the coefficient of determination, or R^2, measures this common comovement. We average across the R^2 of the individual stocks in a market and average these across the months of a given year. A lower score means that the market as a whole is more transparent, since individual stocks are being traded and there is less market-wide trading.

The numbers by country for the last year in the Karolyi et al. study are presented in Table 7.1 under the headings "R^2 Liquidity" and "R^2 Returns." There is not a lot of dispersion in these measures across emerging markets, and it is not clear that in this year (2009) the differences for the typical emerging and developed market exist. Rest assured that Figure 2 and Table 2 of the Karolyi et al. study do show the cross-country relationships are statistically significant across all years in the sample period.[56] The higher are the disclosure standards and investor protections in a country, the lower the average R^2. What you can see from the data is that China stands on the right tail with estimates of 49% and 38% for liquidity and returns, well above the cluster of the other emerging markets. Pakistan and Mexico also exhibit high R^2 in returns.

While I have high hopes for this measure as one of its proponents as an author, its limited cross-country variation will probably adversely impact its candidacy for much weight in the principal component analysis for the corporate opacity risk indicator. This analysis comes next.

The Principal Component Analysis Delivers the Corporate Opacity Scores

I face the challenge of reducing 14 different variables into a single indicator for corporate opacity. Like in previous chapters, the sample across countries is unbalanced, so I lean heavily on the EM algorithm.

Table 7.2 presents the PCA results. Two principal components are enough to get us over the threshold of 50% of the unconditional variation across all 14 variables. Together they deliver 52.87% of the variation (see *Rho* in the bottom panel). The eigenvalue for the first component (5.57) is almost three times

TABLE 7.2 Principal Component Analysis for Corporate Opacity

Eigenvalues	Coefficient	Std. Err.	z-statistic	p-value	(5%,	95%)
First Component	5.57551	1.04439	5.34	0.00	3.52854	7.62247
Second Component	1.82677	0.34218	5.34	0.00	1.15610	2.49744
First Component						
Credit Lyonnais Securities Asia (CLSA)	0.31252	0.04327	7.22	0.00	0.22771	0.39733
S&P Transparency & Disclosure	0.32771	0.04154	7.89	0.00	0.24629	0.40913
Bushman, et al. (2004) Timeliness	0.24823	0.05587	4.44	0.00	0.13873	0.35772
Bushman, et al. (2004) Measurement	0.07848	0.07085	1.11	0.27	-0.06038	0.21734
Bushman, et al. (2004) Governance	0.31835	0.04227	7.53	0.00	0.23549	0.40120
Bushman, et al. (2004) Disclosure	0.38110	0.02769	13.76	0.00	0.32682	0.43538
Chang, et al. (2000) Analyst Coverage	0.30248	0.04727	6.40	0.00	0.20984	0.39513
DKLMS Blockholder Control Rights	-0.08267	0.07510	-1.10	0.27	-0.22986	0.06452
La Porta et al. (1999) Top 3 Blockholders	-0.29077	0.05224	-5.57	0.00	-0.39316	-0.18837
Worldscope (WS) Closely Held Shares	-0.34142	0.04213	-8.10	0.00	-0.42400	-0.25884
CIFAR Accounting Standards	0.35990	0.03208	11.22	0.00	0.29703	0.42277
Karolyi et al. (2012) R^2 Liquidity	-0.15092	0.06799	-2.22	0.03	-0.28417	-0.01766
Karolyi et al. (2012) R^2 Returns	-0.16785	0.06530	-2.57	0.01	-0.29583	-0.03986
IFRS Adoption by 2012	0.02574	0.07373	0.35	0.73	-0.11876	0.17025
Second Component						
Credit Lyonnais Asia (CLSA) Governance	0.03087	0.14166	0.22	0.83	-0.24677	0.30851
S&P Transparency & Disclosure	-0.08298	0.12789	-0.65	0.52	-0.33365	0.16768
Bushman, et al. (2004) Timeliness	0.20277	0.21832	0.93	0.35	-0.22514	0.63068
Bushman, et al. (2004) Measurement	0.34152	0.20461	1.67	0.10	-0.05951	0.74256
Bushman, et al. (2004) Governance	-0.01331	0.13364	-0.10	0.92	-0.27525	0.24862
Bushman, et al. (2004) Disclosure	0.12638	0.06931	1.82	0.07	-0.00947	0.26223

Chang, et al. (2000) Analyst Coverage	0.11247	0.19840	0.57	0.57	-0.27639	0.50133
DKLMS Blockholder Control Rights	0.49237	0.25549	1.93	0.05	-0.00838	0.99311
La Porta et al. (1999) Top 3 Blockholders	0.33785	0.11937	2.83	0.01	0.10389	0.57181
Worldscope (WS) Closely Held Shares	0.28921	0.07133	4.05	0.00	0.14941	0.42901
CIFAR Accounting Standards	-0.02843	0.08745	-0.33	0.75	-0.19982	0.14296
Karolyi et al. (2012) R^2 Liquidity	-0.35103	0.24493	-1.43	0.15	-0.83109	0.12902
Karolyi et al. (2012) R^2 Returns	-0.28008	0.21494	-1.30	0.19	-0.70136	0.14120
IFRS Adoption by 2012	0.40364	0.26757	1.51	0.13	-0.12079	0.92807

Diagnostics

Number of observations	57
Number of components	2
Trace	14
Rho	0.5287
Std. Err. (Rho)	0.0405
Likelihood Ratio test for dependence: $\chi^2(91)$	408.96 p-value 0.00
Likelihood Ratio test for sphericity: $\chi^2(104)$	414.06 p-value 0.00

Note: For columns listed under the headings of 5% and 95%, the values of the coefficient at the 5% and 95% limits of the 90% confidence range are reported, respectively.

as large as that for the second (1.83), so it is natural to focus attention on the first one.

Looking down the column of coefficients in the first principal component, you see that the largest (and most precise, as judged by the p-values on the respective z-statistics) arise for the disclosure index for Bushman et al., the CIFAR Accounting Standards, the S&P Transparency and Disclosure scores, and the series for closely held shares from Worldscope.[57] Each of these loadings in the eigenvector for the first component exceeds 0.30 with p-values below 1%. The signs revealed (notwithstanding the warnings about PCA, from Chapter 3) seem to make sense. Higher scores on the index if I used these loadings as weights would arise from higher accounting and disclosure standards, better transparency scores, and less closely held shares. The loadings for two of the Bushman et al. indicators on disclosure and transparency fare well, as does the CLSA governance score. Disappointingly, the IFRS Adoption indicator fails to deliver any punch, perhaps because of the way this variable was coded. The Chang et al. variable on analyst coverage gets sizable positive weight, and the La Porta et al. top-three blockholder does as well, on a negative basis.[58] The Worldscope closely held shares variable also gets a large negative and precise coefficient. The Karolyi et al. R^2 measures are statistically significant with a fair confidence level, but their weights are distinctly smaller.[59]

Among the coefficients in the second principal component, only the Doidge, Karolyi, Lins, Miller, and Stulz blockholder control rights variable; the La Porta et al. top-three blockholder and Worldscope closely held shares series are precise.[60] One can essentially chalk this second component up as the blockholder component, while the first component retains more balanced weightings across the kinds of variables represented.

Figure 7.1 ranks the resulting principal component scores for corporate opacity. As in Chapter 5, I furnish the scores across all emerging and developed markets in the sample, so readers can see their intersection across the two groups. Four countries have standardized scores in the positive range: South Korea (1.05), Slovenia (0.73), Chile (0.21), and Malaysia (0.20). Only South Korea gets a score that is higher than the developed market median, but see how well over half of the developed market countries fall below that median score of 0.97. Indeed, Greece scores poorly deep in the negative range, and comfortably among the emerging markets. Argentina and Brazil rank relatively well with the next grouping (scores around –0.15). This is not surprising, based on how they showed on the rankings for the Bushman et al. scores as well as on analyst coverage, controlling ownership blocks, and R^2 measures. There is a noteworthy plateau among all countries around a score of –0.5. It drops away when one reaches Indonesia (–1.04). The countries in the next cluster are all ones that I referenced above when discussing individual variables, so there are no real surprises here.

If there is one thing that catches my eye, it is that China ranks lowest on corporate transparency with a low score of (–1.98). I brought this up in earlier

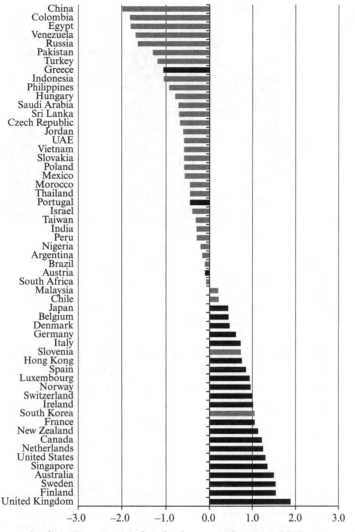

FIGURE 7.1 *Ranking Emerging Markets by Corporate Opacity in 2012.*

Note: The foreign accessibility restrictions risk indicator scores are computed on a standardized basis using a standard normal scale for the continuous index values. Negative (positive) values imply worse (better) scores, reflecting greater (lesser) risk. All scores are measured using data up to 2012.

chapters. Now, you can see that some more caution is in order because of the sparseness of the data for some of these worst performing countries on corporate opacity. Indeed, what likely drives China's score into the left tail are its poor outcomes on the CLSA and S&P governance scores, the weak numbers on analyst coverage, and the very high scores on R^2 in returns and liquidity. Some of these metrics reflect institutional features likely present still today, but some are likely to change in the future, such as analyst coverage and large blockholder stakes.

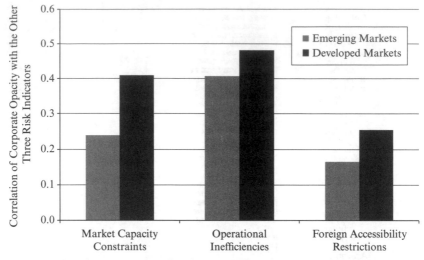

FIGURE 7.2 *Correlations among Risk Indicators Scores on Corporate Opacity, Foreign Accessibility Restrictions, Operational Inefficiency, and Market Capacity in 2012.*

Note: The market capacity constraints, operational inefficiency, and foreign accessibility restrictions risk indicator scores are computed on a standardized basis using a standard normal scale for the continuous index values. Negative (positive) values imply worse (better) scores, reflecting greater (lesser) risk. All scores are computed using data up to 2012.

As a final thought before I move us to the next risk indicator on limits to legal protections, I want to point out the bigger argument to which I am building. These four risk indicator scores from this and preceding chapters on corporate opacity, foreign accessibility restrictions, operational inefficiencies, and market capacity are empirically distinctive. I mention this point because so much of the theory of international corporate governance points to the fact that the standards adopted have a fundamental related to the level of economic and financial development, and the extent to which the countries are open to foreign investment. In other words, they are naturally interrelated conceptually. Figure 7.2 shows the actual cross-country correlations separately across emerging and developed market countries for the corporate opacity indicator and the preceding three. They are all positive, which makes sense. But the correlations are below 0.50; that between corporate opacity and foreign accessibility restrictions is below 0.30, in fact. Another encouraging sign for their distinctiveness is that among emerging markets, the correlations tend to be lower than among the more developed countries.

This matters because my goal in Part III of the book will be to cross-validate these risk indicators with actual data on foreign holdings by investors around the world. Some of these indicators will perform better in explaining those holding biases across countries, but what you will see is that each of them brings important *incremental* explanatory power to the table. Before I get to Part III, however, I still need to build two more indicators for legal protections and political instability, which come next.

{ 8 }

Limits on Legal Protections

Legal protections for public investors and corporations vary widely across countries. Some of these differences stem from different legal systems that are in place around the world, others from the quality of enforcement of the laws on the books. Some countries have better protections of creditor rights, while others enforce more stringently the protections of public shareholders. Some systems seek to protect public shareholders primarily from corporate insiders and the risk of their expropriating resources from the firms they control, while others limit shareholders and their abilities to pursue actions with burdensome numbers of procedures, delays, and prohibitive costs.

In this chapter, I construct a market indicator of the legal protections for public investors that comprehensively incorporates all of these different attributes of legal systems, laws, and their enforcement. I am influenced by the research of the collaborative team of Simeon Djankov, Rafael La Porta, Florencio Lopez-de-Silanes, Andrei Shleifer, and Robert Vishny, which has investigated whether and how securities laws matter for the performance of capital markets, typically in a cross-country setting. They examine attributes of the legal systems around the world (English common law versus French civil law, for example), and they construct indices based on the efficiency of the judiciary, tradition of law and order, minority shareholder rights relative to corporate directors and officers, creditor rights, legal procedures imposed on litigants and courts for dispute resolution, public and private enforcement mechanisms, and even characteristics of the supervisory powers, such as securities regulatory commissions. The team identifies empirically the potential consequences of these attributes of the legal system for corporate ownership, valuations, corporate financial policies (capital structure choice, dividend payout), and the overall economic and financial development of capital markets. A second key data source I use is the World Bank Doing Business Indicators. These have been compiled by the Private Sector Group of the World Bank headed for many years by Simeon Djankov, an important member of the collaborative team above.[1]

The metrics from these sources capture features of legal institutions in each country that mitigate risks in doing cross-border deals. As the next case study suggests, the absence of these protections can create major headaches.

Pulkovo Airport's Expansion Project in 2010

On April 15, 2010, the board of directors of the International Finance Corporation, a member of the World Bank Group, was to vote to approve €70 million in debt financing for a €1.2 billion expansion project for the Pulkovo Airport outside St. Petersburg, Russia.[2] As Pulkovo had already reached capacity years before, IFC's financing would help to not only stimulate development in the local St. Petersburg economy, but also to facilitate the city's goal of becoming a major transport hub. On a wider scale, Pulkovo would be one of the first public-private partnership (PPP) deals in Russia, and if successful, the IFC believed it could serve as a model for other infrastructure projects through the country.[3] This was important given Russia's need to upgrade infrastructure to help diversify its commodity-dependent economy. Some analysts, however, expressed doubts about the adequacy of Russia's legal framework for dispute resolution given the large scale of the investments, the number of parties involved in the deal, and the overall complexity of its financing structure.[4]

Pulkovo Airport began operations as Shosseynaya Airport back in 1932, with its first passenger flight to Moscow.[5] The airport ceased operations due to its proximity to the front lines during World War II, but resumed flights to over 30 destinations within the Soviet Union once war damages were repaired. The new terminal—Pulkovo I, the domestic passenger terminal—was constructed in 1973 in the Soviet modernist style referred to endearingly by locals as the "steamship," for its tubular roof. By 2009 the terminal was annually serving 6.7 million passengers for a city with a population of roughly 6 million, and it was the fourth busiest Russian airport behind Moscow's three main airports. With the Russian and local economy growing rapidly, Pulkovo Airport was unable to meet demand during peak times due to insufficient terminal capacity.[6]

Traffic was split evenly between international and domestic destinations and attracted 42 international airlines, 29 Russian carriers, and served 130 regular destinations. Over 43% of the airport's traffic was accounted for by state-owned Rossiya Airlines passenger traffic.[7] Before the financial crisis affected Russia, the Russian air transport sector was one of the fastest growing in the world. Between 1999 and 2008, passenger traffic grew by 130% to 45.1 million. While traffic declined sharply the following year, certain factors boded well for continued growth such as a relatively low number of international routes (which current market liberalization measures intended to change), and Russia's huge landmass, making air travel economical. There were also heavy market access restrictions and regulations on international routes, complicating market entry for potential new entrants.[8]

Russia's Minister of Economic Development and Trade, German Gref, stated that the country's infrastructure spending would need to exceed $1 trillion to keep pace with demand and the country's rapid growth path.[9] City and airport authorities chose a public-private partnership (PPP) structure to mobilize financing for Pulkovo's expansion. PPP deals allow private investors and operators to provide financing and services for a public sector authority, and are often used to fund infrastructure projects. The model presents an attractive alternative to local governments willing to cede some or total control over public assets to attract financing, which in turn can help alleviate public financing deficits and allow gains in private sector efficiencies. As with many project finance PPP deals, the government does not typically provide any investment guarantee to outsider investors; they are to be repaid solely by generated cash flows.[10] Investors have no recourse to the project sponsor's nonproject-related cash flows or assets.

A competitive bidding process was conducted to screen potential private partners in April 2008. The winner of the tender would modernize the existing infrastructure, revamping the interior of Pulkovo I, and extend it with a new 100,000 square meter terminal expansion with 20 gates, a hotel, business center, and parking facilities to be built by 2013.[11] Pulkovo's capacity was expected to expand to 22 million passengers per year and the winner would operate the airport, including both aviation and nonaviation activities, for a 30-year period.[12] Nine parties bid—most of them consortia composed of investors, like banks and investment funds, and airport operators as partners. Macquarie Renaissance, Germany's Hochtief, and the pension fund of Russia's own national champion energy company, Gazprom, were among the bidders.[13] In July 2009, the governor of St. Petersburg signed a memorandum of understanding awarding the contract to the Northern Capital Gateway (NCG) consortium before dignitaries like German Chancellor Angela Merkel and Russian President Dmitri Medvedev.[14] The main stakeholders in NCG were VTB Capital (50% ownership), the strategic business arm of Russia's state-owned investment bank VTB Group; Fraport AG (35.5%), a German airport operating company with 11 management contracts globally; and two other lesser known investors, Koltseva Holdings (7.5%) of Cyprus and Horizon Air Investments (7%) of Greece's Copelouzos Group.[15]

The financing was complex. Of the roughly €1.2 billion being invested in the project, NCG would contribute initial equity capital amounting to €440 million. The IFC, together with European Bank for Reconstruction and Development (EBRD), had initially expressed interest in lending to the project in August 2008 during the tender process.[16] The IFC often partnered with EBRD, a major regional international financial institution with a similar organizational mission and capital base of €20 billion, on various financing projects in Eastern Europe. Also expressing interest in providing debt financing was the Russian state-owned bank Vneshekonombank (VEB). The proposed deal eventually presented to IFC's board called for IFC, EBRD, three smaller international financial institutions, and VEB to arrange €750 million in long-term debt financing. IFC and EBRD were also arranging a joint syndication of international commercial banks to provide €200 million of the total in the form of a "B loan" with a 12-year maturity. IFC would lend €70 million from its own account as an "A loan" carrying a 15-year maturity; the EBRD would directly lend €100 million of the total.[17]

Some investors had expressed concern about Russia's statutory framework for PPPs. Russia established its PPP framework in 2005 with passage of the Federal Law on Concession Agreements (FCLA) setting forth guidelines for granting concessions in PPP deals. Following passage of the FCLA, experts noted several inadequacies compared to other countries' legislation in areas such as securing assets, step-in rights, and dispute resolution.[18] To assuage these concerns, several regional bodies in Russia have promulgated more investor-friendly legislation to supplement the national framework. In 2006, St. Petersburg passed a law permitting concessionaires to transfer ownership of assets and grant security over ownership.

An important additional consideration for IFC was the environmental and social consequences of its investment projects. While the project feasibility study did not reveal any environmental risks atypical for an airport expansion project, it did indicate a greater likelihood for increased noise and air pollution and for local opposition because of the expected doubling of airport traffic.[19] This was a particularly acute concern given IFC's nearing decision to fund another major project: the Moscow–to–St. Petersburg Motorway, which was to be constructed through the Khimki Forest, a natural, protected area northwest of Moscow. Upon discovering the motorway plans in 2007, local residents and environmentalists organized an opposition movement that attracted international support. Local protests were regularly broken up by police, and three journalists covering the protests had recently been badly beaten.[20] The IFC had been in talks to finance the motorway, but eventually decided against participating.[21]

On April 28, 2010, the IFC Board voted to support the Pulkovo PPP deal and announced that the B loan commercial syndicate had been completed.[22] "This was the first Russian public-private partnership transaction financed by commercial lenders, and the fact that this benchmark transaction for a landmark Russian infrastructure project was heavily oversubscribed sends a positive signal about the market's potential appetite for such deals," said Lorenz Jorgensen, EBRD Director of Syndications.[23] The commercial banks participating in the €200 million loan included UniCredit, Standard Bank, Espirito Santo Investments, and Nordea Bank, as mandated lead arrangers.[24]

Law and Finance

What the Pulkovo Airport expansion case brings to the forefront is the importance of a strong, reliable legal system to support outside funding for major infrastructure investment projects so critical for emerging market growth. Project finance deals like Pulkovo are really nothing more than a "contractual bundle," Harvard's Ben Esty states in his book *Modern Project Finance*.[25] Some reliable dispute resolution mechanism is needed because the raising of funds occurs on a limited- or nonrecourse basis in which the providers of the funds look to the cash flow of the project to support their decision. Inter-creditor agreements need the court's backbone, shareholder agreements must bind, and supplier and purchase contracts must be protected to ensure the reliability of cash flows. Many emerging markets, like Russia, may not have the legal system in place that allays concerns for all contracting parties, which is why organizations like the IFC and EBRD step in to fill the gap.

How can I measure the quality of the legal environment for creditors, investors, and corporations? For the past 20 years, academic research on corporate governance has focused on the problem of investor expropriation, sometimes known as "self-dealing" or "tunneling." That is, those who control a corporation, as managers or controlling shareholders, can use their power to divert corporate assets to themselves rather than sharing it with the other stakeholders. These expropriations can also include excessive executive perquisites or compensation, transfers of corporate opportunities, financial transactions such as directed equity issuance or personal loans to insiders, and outright theft.[26] Economists have followed legal scholars in emphasizing the crucial role played by the law in the control of expropriations of this kind. The early research argued theoretically and showed empirically that differences in legal protections across countries shape the ability of corporate insiders to expropriate outsiders and thus determine investor confidence in markets, and, as a result, market development.

The seminal work came in two studies in late 1990s by the team of Rafael La Porta, Florencio Lopez-de-Silanes, Andrei Shleifer, and Robert Vishny (the so-called LLSV team). Their body of work has inspired many of us who work in the field of international corporate finance, and it lays the groundwork for the discipline referred to as law and finance. The first study by LLSV argued that a country's legal origin, which could be English common law, French civil law, German civil law, or Scandinavian law, is an important determinant of the country's strategy for protecting investors.[27] The authors find systematic differences among legal origins in the protection of both minority shareholders and creditors through corporate and bankruptcy laws. Common law countries, they showed, were associated with larger market capitalizations, more dispersed ownership structures, higher valuations, and especially lower market declines during periods of financial distress, like the Asian financial crisis of 1997. In this work, they also built somewhat ad hoc indices to capture the intensity of shareholder protections by creating a list of laws pertaining to antidirector rights, creditor rights, and efficiency of the judiciary, and counting the number of these attributes a country's legal system has. However, their ambitious attempt was met with heavy criticism for the ad hoc nature of the indices, for mistakes in its coding, and for conceptual ambiguity in the definitions of some of its components.[28]

Revisions and extensions to focus more directly on formalism in the court system as well as on anti self-dealing by corporate insiders followed in later work, but this newer work began with a deeper base. The authors, together with Simeon Djankov at the World Bank, contracted with *Lex Mundi*, an association of international law firms with members in 108 countries, to execute a survey of legal procedures. They would present the law firms with stylized transactions between two companies, many detailed facts, and an obvious conflict of interest. To a series of questions about minimum legal requirements in force in such a case, the lawyers based their answers on all binding (not voluntary guidelines) laws applicable and were asked to substantiate their answers with references to relevant legal provisions. These results were featured in three well-cited studies by Djankov, La Porta, Lopez-de-Silanes, and Shleifer (hereafter, DLLS).[29]

The third stage of development in the field of law and finance took a practical turn in the development of the Doing Business Indicators by the Private Sector Group of the World Bank, headed at the time by Simeon Djankov.[30] These indices on protecting investors, getting credit, enforcing contracts, and a host of other attributes of business transacting were built into a readily accessible database based on research of laws and regulations, with input and verification from more than 3,000 local government officials, lawyers, business consultants, and other professionals who routinely administer or advise on legal and regulatory requirements. These data have been collected each year since 2004.

I will harvest data from each of these three stages of development of the law and finance literature for my own risk indicator for limits on legal protections. Details follow.

Antidirector and Creditor Rights

From the original LLSV study, I use four indices of antidirector, credit rights, and of the efficiency of the judiciary.[31] The antidirector rights index runs on a scale from 0 to 5 points, with high scores for good protection. It is formed by adding one point when the country allows shareholders to mail their proxy vote, one if shareholders are not required to deposit their shares prior to a general meeting, one if cumulative voting or proportional representation for minorities on the board of directors is allowed, one if oppressed minorities have mechanisms in place, one if the minimum percentage of share capital needed for a shareholder to call for an extraordinary meeting exceeds 10%, and one when shareholders have preemptive rights that can only be waived by a shareholders' meeting. The later study by Djankov, La Porta, Lopez-de-Silanes, and Shleifer updates the original antidirector rights index based on feedback and criticism from legal scholars and others.[32] I use this updated index for the whole sample.

The creditor rights index (0 to 4 points, with high scores for good protection) determines whether there are no automatic stays on assets, whether secured creditors get paid first, whether there are restrictions for going into reorganization, and whether or not management stays in reorganization. This measure is naturally related to creditor protection and has been shown to shape foreign bank lending, the terms and conditions of loans, and the enforcement of rental contracts in the rental housing market. Of particular note, given the case study analysis of Pulkovo Airport, Subramanian and Tung find that stronger creditor rights significantly mitigate the effect of managerial self-dealing in project finance deals.[33]

I also use two indices on the efficiency of the judiciary (EJ) and a tradition of law and order (RL, for rule of law), both of which are drawn from the International Country Risk (ICR) Guide by La Porta, Lopez-de-Silanes, Shleifer, and Vishny.[34] The EJ index (0 to 10 points, with low scores representing lower efficiency) measures the efficiency and integrity of the legal environment as it affects business, particularly foreign firms, and the RL index (0 to 6 points, with low scores for less tradition for law and order) assesses the law and order tradition.

Table 8.1 presents these four indices for my emerging market country set in the first three columns and the second-to-last column. The EJ index does have a much higher median score among developed markets (10.00) than emerging markets (6.50), as expected, but there is also considerable cross-country variation among emerging market countries. Indonesia scores low (2.50), as does Thailand (3.25), but it reaches a high with Israel (10.00). The RL index is similar, but the low scores obtain for Sri Lanka (1.90), Peru (2.50), the Philippines, and Nigeria (both 2.73). Uncovering that for both the creditor rights and antidirector rights indices, the median scores among emerging markets are in fact higher than among developed markets is surprising. It implies that the efficiency of the judicial system and the rule of law are more robust in emerging than developed countries. The LLSV and DLLS studies do show reliably positive correlations with GDP per capita, as well as other measures of financial development. On creditor rights Peru and the Philippines again score poorly, but in this category Mexico and Colombia join them (all four have scores of 0 points on the 4-point scale). With the revised antidirector rights index in Djankov, La Porta, Lopez-de-Silanes, and Shleifer, the low scores arise for Jordan and Venezuela (both with only 1 point out of a potential 5 points).[35]

TABLE 8.1 Measures of Limits on Legal Protections in 2012

Country	LLSV (1998)[1]			DLLS (2003)[2]		DLLS (2008)[3]		LLS (2006)[4]
	Judicial Efficiency Index	Rule of Law	Creditor Rights	Formalism Index	AntiSelf-Dealing Index	Public Enforcement	Antidirector Rights Index	Supervisory Powers
Argentina	6.00	5.35	1.00	5.40	0.44	0.00	3.0	0.67
Brazil	5.75	6.32	1.00	4.57	0.29	0.50	5.0	0.33
Chile	7.25	7.02	2.00	4.57	0.63	1.00	4.0	0.33
China	.	5.83	.	3.41	0.78	0.00	.	.
Colombia	7.25	2.08	0.00	4.11	0.58	0.00	3.0	0.33
Czech Republic	.	8.30	3.00	4.06	0.34	1.00	.	.
Egypt	6.50	4.17	4.00	.	.	.	3.0	.
Hungary	.	8.70	3.75	3.42	0.21	0.00	.	.
India	8.00	4.17	4.00	3.34	0.55	0.50	5.0	0.33
Indonesia	2.50	3.98	4.00	3.90	0.68	0.00	4.0	0.33
Israel	10.00	4.82	4.00	.	.	.	4.0	.
Jordan	8.66	4.35	.	.	.	.	1.0	.
South Korea	6.00	5.35	3.00	3.37	0.46	0.50	.	0.33
Malaysia	9.00	6.78	4.00	2.34	0.95	1.00	5.0	0.33
Mexico	6.00	5.35	0.00	4.71	0.18	0.50	3.0	0.00
Morocco	.	.	.	.	.	.	.	.
Nigeria	7.25	2.73	4.00	.	0.41	.	4.0	.
Pakistan	5.00	3.03	4.00	3.76	0.41	0.75	4.0	0.67
Peru	6.75	2.50	0.00	5.60	0.41	0.25	4.5	0.67
Philippines	4.75	2.73	0.00	5.00	0.24	0.00	4.0	0.67
Poland	.	8.70	2.25	4.15	0.30	1.00	.	.
Russia	.	3.70	2.50	3.39	0.48	1.00	.	.
Saudi Arabia	.	.	.	.	.	.	.	.

Slovakia	.	.	.	.	.	.	.	.
Slovenia	.	.	.	.	.	.	.	.
South Africa	6.00	4.42	3.00	1.68	0.81	0.00	5.0	0.33
Sri Lanka	7.00	1.90	3.00	.	.	.	4.0	.
Taiwan	6.75	8.52	2.00	2.37	0.56	0.00	3.0	0.33
Thailand	3.25	6.25	3.00	3.14	0.93	0.00	4.0	0.67
Turkey	4.00	5.18	2.00	2.53	0.43	0.00	3.0	0.67
UAE	.	.	.	.	.	.	.	.
Venezuela	6.50	6.37	.	6.01	0.09	0.00	1.0	0.33
Vietnam	.	.	.	.	.	.	.	.
Emerging Median	6.50	5.18	3.00	3.83	0.45	0.13	4.00	0.33
Developed Median	10.00	10.00	2.00	3.02	0.46	0.50	3.50	0.33

Note: Appendix E details all data sources for the limits to legal protections indicator.

[1] In La Porta, Lopez-de-Silanes, Shleifer, and Vishny, "Law and Finance," judicial efficiency (10 point scale, bad to good) measures integrity of the legal environment, rule of law (6 point scale, bad to good) assesses law and order tradition, and creditor rights (4 point scale, bad to good) includes no automatic stays on assets, and secured creditors getting priority.

[2] In Djankov, La Porta, Lopez-de-Silanes, and Shleifer, "Courts," procedural formalism (7 point scale, good to bad) measures the expected duration of proceedings due to more corruption, less consistency, less honesty, and less fairness in decisions.

[3] In Djankov, La Porta, Lopez-de-Silanes, and Shleifer, "The Law and Economics of Self-Dealing," anti self-dealing (0 to 1 scale, bad to good) measures the extent of private enforcement mechanisms such as disclosure, approval, and litigation on dealings by insiders; enforcement (0 to 1 scale, good to bad) indicates more stringent fines, prison terms for self-dealing transactions, and antidirector rights; (0 to 5 scale, bad to good) measures whether shareholders can mail proxy votes, whether shareholders must deposit shares prior to vote, if cumulative voting is the rule, and if shareholders have preemptive rights that can only be waived in general meetings.

[4] In La Porta, Lopez-De-Silanes, and Shleifer, "What Works In Securities Laws?," supervisory powers (0 to 1 scale, good to bad) averages across one point if majority of members of supervisory are appointed by the executive branch, another if members cannot be dismissed at the will of the appointing authority, and a third if separate government agencies are in charge of supervising banks and stock exchanges.

Courts and Formalism

The sources of data on legal rules and institutions vary across studies. Some rules, like those above, come from national laws. They are the "laws on the books," as La Porta, Lopez-de-Silanes, and Shleifer put it.[36] Other indicators are mixtures of national laws and actual experiences, and tend to combine substantive and procedural rules. It is this latter construction through collaborative efforts with the *Lex Mundi* network of international law firms that led Djankov, La Porta, Lopez-de-Silanes, and Shleifer to build their index of "formalism."[37] They define formalism as the burden of procedures needed for dispute resolution.

Using data on exact procedures used by litigants and courts to evict a tenant for nonpayment of rent and to collect a bounced check, the authors construct an index (0 to 7 points, 7 is associated with higher procedural formalism) to capture higher expected duration of judicial proceedings, more corruption, less consistency, less honesty, less fairness in decisions, and inferior access to justice. The measure is about the efficiency of contract enforcement by courts. DLLS demonstrates that this element of formalism (with respect to the time to collect on a bounced check) is reliably negatively related to the market capitalization-to-GDP ratio and positively related to the level of ownership concentration among the largest firms in a country.

Table 8.1 provides DLLS's index for my 33 emerging markets. It is higher for the median emerging market (3.83) than for that of the developed markets (3.02), but not by much. Venezuela (6.01 out of a possible 7) scores high on formalism, while countries like Malaysia (2.34) and South Africa (1.68) would score more favorably than most of the developed markets in the analysis.

Anti Self-Dealing and Public Enforcement

Djankov et al. present a new measure of legal protection of minority shareholders against expropriation, or "self-dealing," by corporate insiders, which they call their "anti self-dealing" index.[38] Self-dealing represents actions by managers or controlling shareholders to divert corporate wealth to their own pockets without sharing it with other investors. The Djankov et al. index is compiled using surveys distributed to lawyers of *Lex Mundi* law firms, and focuses on private enforcement mechanisms. These mechanisms include disclosure, approval, and litigation governing a specific self-dealing transaction. The specific deal involves an asset sale in which the buyer and seller have a common large block shareholder, who serves as the director of one (buyer) and who benefits financially if the buyer overpays for the assets of the seller. The case has a business purpose, but involves an obvious conflict of interest.

The authors use the first principal component from these elements to build the index and standardize it to lie in a range from 0 to 1. A higher score indicates better control of self-dealing.

DLLS also construct their own public enforcement index using these data.[39] Public enforcement deals with the criminal sanctions when a self-dealing transaction is in violation of the law. A higher score (on a scale of 0 to 1) indicates more stringent fines and prison terms for self-dealing transactions. The authors argue that the anti self-dealing index is better grounded in legal theory, and they show that it predicts a variety of stock market outcomes well—generally better than the antidirector rights index presented above.

I use both the anti self-dealing and public enforcement indices, and show them in Table 8.1. Emerging markets with good scores on anti self-dealing include Malaysia (0.95), South Africa (0.81), and Thailand (0.93), all three of which happen to be common law regimes. Interestingly, South Africa and Thailand both score a zero on the public enforcement index, though the median across all emerging markets is 0.13. Brazil, Hungary, Mexico, and especially Venezuela score poorly on anti self-dealing (respectively, 0.29, 0.21, 0.18, and 0.09). For contrast, readers might find it interesting to know that countries like the United Kingdom or Hong Kong score well on anti self-dealing (0.93 and 0.96, respectively) and that countries like Sweden or Singapore do so as well on public enforcement (both a full one point).

As a complement to the measure on public enforcement for dispute resolution in general, I also draw another on supervisory powers for the markets, in particular involving the securities regulatory commission or equivalent body in a country. Mandating disclosure and facilitating private enforcement rules through central agencies may benefit stock market development and economic growth. In yet another contribution by La Porta, Lopez-de-Silanes, and Shleifer, the authors focus efforts on the characteristics of the supervisory power, like the securities regulatory commission, and build an index of their powers.[40] The index of the characteristics of the supervisor of financial markets equals the mean of three components: (1) appointment, (2) tenure, and (3) focus. Higher scores indicate weaker powers. Appointment equals one if a majority of the members of the supervisory agency are unilaterally appointed by the executive branch of government, and equals zero otherwise. Tenure equals one if members of the supervisory agency cannot be dismissed at the will of the appointing authority, and equals zero otherwise. Focus equals one if separate government agencies or official authorities are in charge of supervising commercial banks and stock exchanges, and equals zero otherwise.

In Table 8.1, the supervisory powers index is spotty in coverage across my emerging markets sample. The country with the lowest score among those is Mexico (0.0). It clearly stands out among the pack of emerging markets, which averages around 0.33, and which is very similar to that for developed markets.

The World Bank's Doing Business Indicators

The World Bank's Doing Business indicators are designed to measure government regulations and their effect on businesses, especially on small- and medium-size domestic firms. The Doing Business data is based on research of laws and regulations, with input and verification from more than 3,000 local government officials, lawyers, business consultants, and other professionals who routinely administer or advise on legal and regulatory requirements. Standard templates and questionnaires have been developed for all topics and were applied over the years from 2003 to 2013. I collect data on three components of the ten that focus on getting credit, protecting investors, and enforcing contracts, as these are most directly related to my interest on limits to legal protections.[41]

The getting credit indicator is composed of a legal rights index (LR) and a credit information (CI) index. Together, they capture the legal rights of borrowers and lenders with respect to secured transactions through one set of indicators and the sharing of credit information through another. The LR index (0 to 10, high scores with better laws designed to expand access to credit) reflects the legal rights of borrowers and lenders and measures the degree to which collateral and bankruptcy laws facilitate lending.[42] The CI index (0 to 6, higher values indicate more credit information) focuses on information available on the credit-worthiness of borrowers from a public registry or private bureaus to facilitate lending decisions. Public registry coverage measures the percent of adult population covered by a registry managed by the central bank or a superintendent of banks collecting information on the creditworthiness of borrowers that is made available to financial institutions. Private bureau coverage captures the fraction of the adult population in a database managed by private firms or nonprofit organizations collecting information on the creditworthiness of borrowers that is made available to financial institutions.

Table 8.2 shows that the typical (median) emerging market furnishes weaker legal rights than the typical developed country and that the depth of credit information via private credit bureaus is starkly lower, but that related to public credit registries is not so. On legal rights (LR), the median score for an emerging market is 5 out of 10 points and there is large cross-country dispersion. Jordan and Venezuela score as low as a 2 and Malaysia gets full points (10). There is by contrast very little dispersion in the credit information index (CI). Jordan receives the median score on public credit registry coverage at a meager 2% of the adult population. Many of the emerging markets, therefore, have 0% coverage. Malaysia scores well on this dimension (53%), but South Korea remarkably records 100% of the adult population on this dimension. A recent study by Han, Lee, and Park analyzes the link between public credit registries and credit bureaus in Asia and uncover a significant *negative* relationship with the development of financial markets: the lower the income level, the heavier is the

TABLE 8.2 Selected World Bank Measures of Limits on Legal Protections in 2012

Country	World Bank Getting Credit[1]					World Bank Protecting Investors[2]				World Bank Enforcing Contracts[3]		
	Legal Rights	Credit Info	Credit Registry	Private Bureau	Disclosure Index	Director Liability	Shareholder Lawsuits	Protection Index	Number of Procedures	Time to Resolution	Cost (as % of Debt)
Argentina	4	6	41.9	100.0	7	2	6	5.0	36	590	20.5
Brazil	3	5	50.4	63.4	5	8	3	5.3	44	731	16.5
Chile	6	5	40.5	5.9	8	6	5	6.3	36	480	28.6
China	5	5	30.2	0.0	10	1	4	5.0	37	406	11.1
Colombia	5	5	0.0	83.8	9	8	8	8.3	34	1,288	47.9
Czech Republic	6	5	6.4	76.0	2	5	8	5.0	27	611	33.0
Egypt	3	6	5.3	19.6	5	3	3	3.7	42	1,010	26.2
Hungary	7	4	0.0	73.2	2	4	7	4.3	35	395	15.0
India	8	5	0.0	19.8	7	4	8	6.3	46	1,420	39.6
Indonesia	5	4	41.2	0.0	10	5	3	6.0	40	498	139.4
Israel	9	5	0.0	100.0	7	9	9	8.3	35	890	25.3
Jordan	2	2	2.0	0.0	4	4	1	3.0	38	689	31.2
South Korea	8	6	100.0	100.0	7	4	7	6.0	33	230	10.3
Malaysia	10	6	52.9	77.2	10	9	7	8.7	29	425	27.5
Mexico	6	6	0.0	100.0	8	5	4	5.7	38	400	31.0
Morocco	3	5	0.0	19.6	6	2	6	4.7	40	510	25.2
Nigeria	9	5	0.1	4.9	5	7	5	5.7	40	447	92.0
Pakistan	6	4	8.0	2.1	6	6	7	6.3	46	976	23.8
Peru	7	6	31.7	41.5	9	6	6	7.0	41	426	35.7
Philippines	4	5	0.0	9.3	2	3	8	4.3	37	842	26.0
Poland	9	6	0.0	82.8	7	2	9	6.0	33	685	19.0
Russia	3	5	0.0	59.2	6	2	6	4.7	36	270	13.4

(continued)

TABLE 8.2 Continued

Country	World Bank Getting Credit[1]					World Bank Protecting Investors[2]			World Bank Enforcing Contracts[3]		
	Legal Rights	Credit Info	Credit Registry	Private Bureau	Disclosure Index	Director Liability	Shareholder Lawsuits	Protection Index	Number of Procedures	Time to Resolution	Cost (as % of Debt)
Saudi Arabia	5	6	0.0	44.3	8	8	4	6.7	40	635	27.5
Slovakia	8	4	2.7	61.6	3	4	7	4.7	32	545	30.0
Slovenia	4	4	3.3	100.0	5	9	8	7.3	32	1,270	12.7
South Africa	7	6	0.0	55.6	8	8	8	8.0	29	600	33.2
Sri Lanka	5	5	0.0	39.0	6	5	7	6.0	40	1,318	22.8
Taiwan	5	5	0.0	94.1	9	5	5	6.3	45	510	17.7
Thailand	5	5	0.0	49.2	10	7	6	7.7	36	440	15.0
Turkey	4	5	27.0	71.7	9	5	5	6.3	36	420	24.9
UAE	4	5	5.8	27.0	6	7	2	5.0	49	524	19.5
Venezuela	2	5	0.0	16.7	3	2	2	2.3	30	610	43.7
Vietnam	8	4	39.1	0.0	7	1	2	3.3	36	400	29.0
Emerging Median	*5.00*	*5.00*	*2.00*	*49.20*	*7.00*	*5.00*	*6.00*	*6.00*	*36.00*	*545.00*	*26.00*
Developed Median	*7.00*	*5.00*	*0.00*	*89.00*	*7.00*	*5.00*	*7.00*	*6.15*	*30.00*	*395.00*	*21.50*

Note: Appendix E details all data sources for the limits to legal protections indicator.

[1] World Bank Getting Credit Indicators (www.worldbank.org) measure the strength of credit reporting systems and the effectiveness of collateral and bankruptcy laws in facilitating lending including legal rights (10 point scale, bad to good) on rights of borrowers and lenders; credit information (6 point scale, bad to good) on information available from public registry or private bureaus to facilitate lending; public registry (% of adults) measures adult population for which superintendent of banks or central bank collects info on creditworthiness; private bureau (% of adults) on databases managed by private or nonprofit firms collecting info on creditworthiness. It is based on the work of Djankov, McLiesh, and Shleifer, "Private Credit in 129 Countries."

[2] World Bank Protecting Investors measure protections for minority investors against directors misuse of assets at their expense, including disclosure (0 to 10 points, bad to good) on disclosure required about potential transactions by managers or directors; director liability (0 to 10 points, bad to good) of plaintiffs' abilities to hold a director liable for damages to a company if he influenced a deal or was negligent; shareholder lawsuits (0 to 10 points, bad to good) on ease of shareholder suits on documents available to plaintiff from defendant or witnesses in trial; investor protection (0 to 10 points, bad to good) on extent of disclosure requirements, director liability, and shareholder suits.

[3] World Bank Enforcing Contracts measure assesses the efficiency of the judicial system by following the evolution of a commercial sale dispute over the quality of goods and tracking the time (in days), cost (attorney fees, administrative costs as % of debt value), and number of procedures involved from the moment the plaintiff files the lawsuit until payment is received.

government's hand in financial markets, and the greater is the need for public registries.[43] The presence of private bureaus is positively correlated with the public registries, but the level of coverage among adults across all emerging markets is much higher at 49%. Argentina, Israel, South Korea, Mexico, Slovenia, and Taiwan have well over 90% of the adult population covered.

The protecting investors indicator measures the strength of minority shareholder protections against directors' misuse of corporate assets for personal gain.[44] It comprises a disclosure index (DI) about reporting transactions by directors and officers, an index of director liability (DL) if damages are claimed, an index of the ease of shareholder lawsuits (SS), and a composite index (PI). The DI index (0 to 10, with higher values indicating greater disclosure) measures the extent of disclosure about potential transactions by managers or directors that misuse corporate assets for personal gain. The DL index (0 to 10, with higher values indicating greater liability of directors) captures plaintiffs' abilities to hold a director liable for damages to the company if he or she influenced approval of a transaction or was negligent. The SS index (0 to 10, with higher values indicating greater powers of shareholders to challenge a transaction) assesses the ease of shareholder suits in terms of range of documents available to plaintiffs from defendants and witnesses during trial, the ability to engage in direct examination during trial, and other related measures. The PI index is a composite index (0 to 10, with higher values indicating better investor protection) of DI, DL, and SS.

The middle four columns of Table 8.2 provide data for 2012. China, with its score of 10 points on disclosure (DI), is stringent on the approval process and on disclosure requirements for related-party transactions. So are Indonesia, Malaysia, and Thailand. The scores are comparable on this dimension for emerging and developed markets. Interesting standouts with weak related-party disclosure rules are the Czech Republic, Hungary, and the Philippines (all with scores of 2 out of 10). The cross-country differences in director liabilities relative to minority shareholders (DL) are also wide. It is relatively more feasible for minority investors to file a direct or derivative lawsuit to hold interested parties accountable in Israel, Malaysia, and Slovenia (9 points out of 10), but relatively less so in China and Vietnam (each with 1 point only). Access to internal corporate documents that might ease shareholder suits against corporate insiders is made more difficult in Jordan, Venezuela, Vietnam, and the UAE (two points or less on this 10-point scale for shareholder suits, SS).

The overall investor protection index published with the Doing Business Indicators is a simple average of the three components, as I mentioned above. But an inadvertent consequence of averaging is that the dispersion across countries gets suppressed along the way. The lowest scores do still accrue to Venezuela, Vietnam, and Egypt, but their scores on this 10-point scale are not very different from the top scorers in Colombia, Israel, Malaysia, and Slovenia. I debated whether or not to include the averaged PI index in the principal component analysis (PCA) to follow and decided to keep it in the mix, as opposed to disaggregating the component indices. As a matter of principle, I want to let the data-driven distilling exercise take its full course. If some of these indices furnished less cross-country dispersion, they would appropriately gain less weight (smaller coefficients in absolute values) in the PCA estimation and thus in the resulting risk indicator scores.

The enforcing contracts indicator includes three components including a count of the mandatory procedures needed for legal action, the time needed for dispute resolution, and an estimate of the cost of legal action.[45] The last three columns of Table 8.2 showcase these data for 2012. The count comprises the number of procedures mandated by law that demand interaction between parties and a judge or court officer. The median emerging market requires just as many steps to file and serve a case or take it to trial and judgment as that of developed markets (36 procedures to 30, on average). Some countries require as many as 45 procedures, including India, Pakistan, and Taiwan.

The time variable estimates the time required for dispute resolution in calendar days from moment of a plaintiff filing of lawsuit in court to settlement or payment. Five countries report over 1,000 days duration, though the median country reports 545 days (versus only 395 days in developed countries). The long-duration outliers are Colombia, Egypt, India, Slovenia, and Sri Lanka. Recall how well Slovenia scored on the getting credit indicators. To my reading, these business indicators are picking up different economic forces around the legal system. A cost indicator computes the cost of going through court procedures, attorney fees, and administrative debt recovery procedures, as a percentage of the debt value. The median fraction of debt for cost is 26% among emerging markets, but, as is the case so often, the outliers catch one's eye. On this variable, Indonesia reports costs of 139%. I should add that Indonesia is not the only country that reports costs that exceed debt value in 2012 (others include Cambodia, the Democratic Republic of the Congo, Mozambique, Papua New Guinea, Sierra Leone, Timor-Leste, and Zimbabwe), but it is the only such country that comprises the 33 emerging markets in this book. To give readers some perspective, note that the United States requires only 32 procedures averaging about 300 days, and the cost of these proceedings represent as low as 14.4% (all as of 2012).

Building the Risk Indicator for Limits to Legal Protections

The magnitude of the challenge of data compression with PCA for 19 different variables is one that I have not yet faced in the previous four chapters. It is true that many of these variables are closely related, so the challenge may not be as daunting as at first blush. After all, many of the World Bank's Doing Business Indicators in Table 8.2 are constructed using the very same methodology for the indices underlying the studies that built up the law and finance literature in the first place (in Table 8.1). The only difference is that they are regularly updated. What I do find more reassuring about the limits to legal protection indicator compared to earlier ones is that the missing values are relatively fewer, so I am leaning less heavily on the filling-in by the EM algorithm I discussed in Chapter 3.

At the top of Table 8.3, I report the eigenvalues for the first three components. Recall my implicit rule that I need sufficient numbers of components to achieve a cumulative overall explanatory power over 50%. This number gets us to 52.87% (see *Rho* in the last panel). Not surprisingly, the largest eigenvalue of the first component (5.92) is much larger than the other two and it delivers 31.12% of the overall punch.

The coefficients for the first component are the most interesting to study. A good number of the 19 variables report statistically significant and large coefficients (at least, in absolute value). I would judge that more of the statistical energy comes from the World Bank indicators than those of the original studies from which they are built, which is somewhat reassuring. The timeliness of these scores seems to matter. Of the original indices the DLLS 2003 formalism index of the procedural rules has an estimated coefficient over 0.30, as does DLLS's 2008 anti self-dealing index. The formalism index coefficient gets a negative coefficient, which is the appropriate sign given the overall risk indicator score's purpose (greater limits to legal protections, lower scores on the standardized scale). The revised version of LLSV's 1998 antidirector rights index that was rebuilt in the 2008 DLLS study also gets a statistically reliable positive coefficient, though not as large in size.

Among the World Bank indicators, the legal rights index among the getting credit variables has a reliably estimated and large positive coefficient, perhaps also that for the private bureau coverage variable, but the other two in that category definitely do not. Each of the four variables from the protecting investors group has reliable positive coefficients, including the overall averaged PI index, about which I was worried earlier for its potential redundancy. My own prior would have been that the enforcing contracts variables would receive reliable weight, but this does not happen. The only variable that has a statistically significant and appropriately negative coefficient is that for the number of procedures.

Among the coefficients that make up the second and third components, there are relatively few and it is hard to detect some kind of pattern among those that show up as statistically significant. If anything, the World Bank enforcing contracts variables get more weight in this second component, possibly also those for protecting investors. But the most interesting loadings arise for the original LLSV study on judicial efficiency and rule of law, for which both coefficients are significantly negative.[46] The only two coefficients that are significant for the third principal component are the World Bank's getting credit variable for the

TABLE 8.3 Principal Component Analysis for Limits on Legal Protections

Eigenvalues	Coefficient	Std. Err.	z-statistic	p-value	(5%,	95%)
First Component	5.92527	1.10991	5.34	0.00	3.74990	8.10065
Second Component	2.60836	0.48859	5.34	0.00	1.65074	3.56598
Third Component	1.64463	0.30807	5.34	0.00	1.04083	2.24844
First Component						
LLSV 1998 Judicial Efficiency	0.24701	0.06626	3.73	0.00	0.11714	0.37689
LLSV 1998 Rule of Law	0.18803	0.07688	2.45	0.01	0.03735	0.33870
LLSV 1998 Creditor Rights	0.12798	0.06719	1.90	0.06	-0.00371	0.25968
DLLS 2003 Formalism Index	-0.33774	0.03540	-9.54	0.00	-0.40713	-0.26836
DLLS 2008 Anti Self-Dealing Index	0.31533	0.05069	6.22	0.00	0.21597	0.41469
DLLS 2008 Enforcement Measures	0.03830	0.07050	0.54	0.59	-0.09988	0.17649
DLLS 2008 Antidirector Rights	0.25355	0.05798	4.37	0.00	0.13992	0.36718
LLS 2006 Supervisory Powers	-0.19541	0.05896	-3.31	0.00	-0.31098	-0.07985
WB Getting Credit Legal Rights Index	0.32405	0.03933	8.24	0.00	0.24696	0.40114
WB Getting Credit Information	0.11879	0.06599	1.80	0.07	-0.01055	0.24814
WB Getting Credit Registry	-0.06011	0.06872	-0.87	0.38	-0.19479	0.07458
WB Getting Credit Private Bureau	0.23017	0.05831	3.95	0.00	0.11589	0.34445
WB Protecting Investors Disclosure Index	0.21642	0.06439	3.36	0.00	0.09021	0.34263
WB Protecting Director Liability	0.25321	0.05512	4.59	0.00	0.14517	0.36125
WB Protecting Shareholder Lawsuits	0.30706	0.04339	7.08	0.00	0.22201	0.39210
WB Protecting Protection Index	0.35468	0.04232	8.38	0.00	0.27173	0.43763
WB Enforcing Contracts Procedures	-0.21802	0.06495	-3.36	0.00	-0.34533	-0.09072
WB Enforcing Contracts Time to Resolution	-0.12192	0.07100	-1.72	0.09	-0.26108	0.01723
WB Enforcing Contracts Cost % of Debt	-0.02573	0.07617	-0.34	0.74	-0.17502	0.12355

Second Component

LLSV 1998 Judicial Efficiency	-0.36590	0.07558	-4.84	0.00	-0.51403	-0.21778
LLSV 1998 Rule of Law	-0.44816	0.06515	-6.88	0.00	-0.57585	-0.32048
LLSV 1998 Creditor Rights	0.17776	0.14541	1.22	0.22	-0.10725	0.46276
DLLS 2003 Formalism Index	0.04018	0.08571	0.47	0.64	-0.12781	0.20816
DLLS 2008 Anti self-Dealing Index	0.24836	0.08939	2.78	0.01	0.07316	0.42356
DLLS 2008 Enforcement Measures	-0.20206	0.13843	-1.46	0.14	-0.47338	0.06926
DLLS 2008 Antidirector Rights	0.25261	0.09420	2.68	0.01	0.06798	0.43724
LLS 2006 Supervisory Powers	0.11743	0.12252	0.96	0.34	-0.12270	0.35757
WB Getting Credit Legal Rights Index	-0.05473	0.09499	-0.58	0.56	-0.24092	0.13145
WB Getting Credit Information	0.11189	0.15110	0.74	0.46	-0.18426	0.40805
WB Getting Credit Registry	0.06692	0.16695	0.40	0.69	-0.26030	0.39414
WB Getting Credit Private Bureau	-0.10472	0.15014	-0.70	0.49	-0.39899	0.18956
WB Protecting Investors Disclosure Index	0.26876	0.11671	2.30	0.02	0.04001	0.49752
WB Protecting Director Liability	0.19780	0.09981	1.98	0.05	0.00217	0.39343
WB Protecting Shareholder Lawsuits	0.01314	0.11106	0.12	0.91	-0.20454	0.23081
WB Protecting Protection Index	0.22484	0.07809	2.88	0.00	0.07179	0.37789
WB Enforcing Contracts Procedures	0.31367	0.09088	3.45	0.00	0.13555	0.49179
WB Enforcing Contracts Time to Resolution	0.23770	0.15631	1.52	0.13	-0.06867	0.54407
WB Enforcing Contracts Cost % of Debt	0.32249	0.13158	2.45	0.01	0.06459	0.58039

Third Component

LLSV 1998 Judicial Efficiency	0.03735	0.25277	0.15	0.88	-0.45807	0.53277
LLSV 1998 Rule of Law	-0.07450	0.19973	-0.37	0.71	-0.46596	0.31695
LLSV 1998 Creditor Rights	-0.24833	0.52713	-0.47	0.64	-1.28148	0.78483
DLLS 2003 Formalism Index	0.07629	0.13620	0.56	0.58	-0.19064	0.34323
DLLS 2008 Anti self-Dealing Index	-0.17363	0.20039	-0.87	0.39	-0.56640	0.21913
DLLS 2008 Enforcement Measures	-0.09252	0.35437	-0.26	0.79	-0.78707	0.60204

(continued)

TABLE 8.3 Continued

Eigenvalues	Coefficient	Std. Err.	z-statistic	p-value	(5%,	95%)
DLLS 2008 Antidirector Rights	-0.13580	0.17654	-0.77	0.44	-0.48181	0.21020
LLS 2006 Supervisory Powers	0.03520	0.41081	0.09	0.93	-0.76996	0.84037
WB Getting Credit Legal Rights Index	-0.16164	0.16974	-0.95	0.34	-0.49432	0.17104
WB Getting Credit Information	0.34826	0.31424	1.11	0.27	-0.26764	0.96415
WB Getting Credit Registry	-0.27468	0.66707	-0.41	0.68	-1.58212	1.03276
WB Getting Credit Private Bureau	0.46413	0.13993	3.32	0.00	0.18987	0.73839
WB Protecting Investors Disclosure Index	-0.13849	0.44948	-0.31	0.76	-1.01947	0.74248
WB Protecting Director Liability	0.13678	0.19570	0.70	0.49	-0.24679	0.52034
WB Protecting Shareholder Lawsuits	0.27630	0.11228	2.46	0.01	0.05625	0.49636
WB Protecting Protection Index	0.11736	0.18385	0.64	0.52	-0.24298	0.47769
WB Enforcing Contracts Procedures	0.14175	0.17234	0.82	0.41	-0.19602	0.47953
WB Enforcing Contracts Time to Resolution	0.46767	0.25334	1.85	0.07	-0.02886	0.96421
WB Enforcing Contracts Cost % of Debt	-0.24916	0.42071	-0.59	0.55	-1.07374	0.57541

Diagnostics

Number of observations	57
Number of components	3
Trace	19
Rho	0.5357
Std. Err. (Rho)	0.0338
Likelihood Ratio test for dependence: χ^2 (171)	882.10 p-value 0.00
Likelihood Ratio test for sphericity: χ^2 (189)	893.59 p-value 0.00

Note: For columns listed under the headings of 5% and 95%, the values of the coefficient at the 5% and 95% limits of the 90% confidence range are reported, respectively.

coverage by private bureaus and that from the protecting investors category on shareholder suits.

Figure 8.1 displays the rankings of the countries by the resulting scores on limits to legal protections in 2012. The range of scores is as wide as ever to now among any of the five risk indicators I have built. I see about half of the 33 countries with positive scores, many of which well exceed that for the median developed country (0.11). Three countries stand out in the positive range: Malaysia (1.64), South Africa (1.37), and Israel (1.36). Consider the number of times I mentioned these countries in discussing the outliers among the component scores, and there should be no surprise here. Other countries with good scores that compete well with developed markets are Slovenia, India, Thailand, and Colombia.

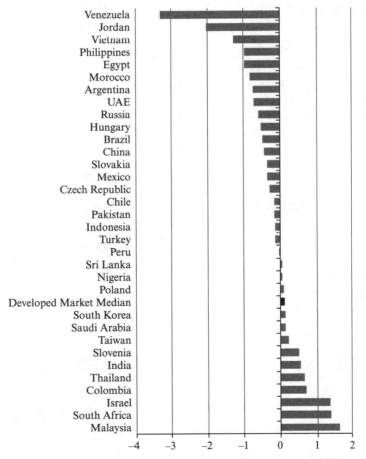

FIGURE 8.1 *Ranking Emerging Markets by Limits on Legal Protections in 2012.*

Note: The limits on legal protections risk indicator scores are computed on a standardized basis using a standard normal scale for the continuous index values. Negative (positive) values imply worse (better) scores, reflecting greater (lesser) risk. All scores are measured using data up to 2012.

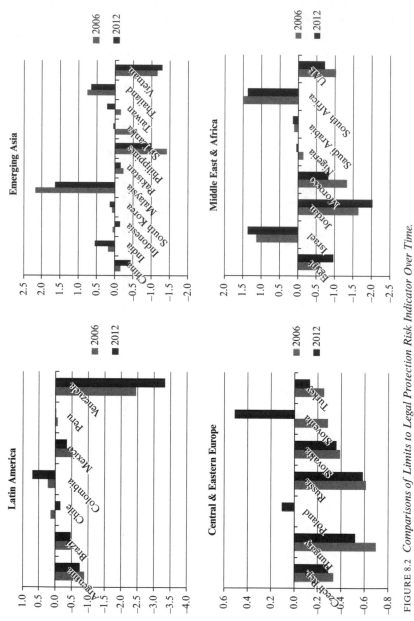

FIGURE 8.2 *Comparisons of Limits to Legal Protection Risk Indicator Over Time.*

Note: The limits on legal protections risk indicator scores are computed on a standardized basis using a standard normal scale for the continuous index values.
Negative (positive) values imply worse (better) scores, reflecting greater (lesser) risk. All scores are measured using data in 2006 and in 2012.

The figure shows a steady decline in the scores until one gets to the bottom tail, which features Vietnam (–1.28), Jordan (–2.02), and Venezuela (–3.32). Consider again how many times they were mentioned in my discussion above. It is intriguing to see how three of the BRIC countries (China, Brazil, and Russia) are so closely clustered around –0.50. The dispersion of these scores on legal protections across countries gives me hope of their potential for Part III of the book in terms of the explanatory power of the risk indicators for foreign investors' cross-country holdings in 2012 and 2013. Consider how compact the scores were around the median for the foreign investability restrictions indicator, by contrast. It turns out the correlation between the legal protection and investability restrictions indicator for 2012 is low (0.10).

Stability of Legal Protections over Time

I mentioned in Chapter 1 that the data underlying some of my risk indicators are more naturally accommodating for analysis of how these scores might fluctuate over time. I would offer that the legal protection index is definitely one of those, thanks to the efforts made at the World Bank's Private Sector Group to keep the Doing Business Indicators fresh and relevant. This gives us an opportunity to study how things might be changing over time.

Figure 8.2 showcases how stable the index scores are for my countries by contrasting them for two years 2012 and 2006. I will save you the details of how the principal component weights may have changed with the 2006 scores and any discussion of the component variables and data. There are some interesting shifts and in both directions across this six-year span. I cluster the countries in my emerging market set for the first time by geographic region: Latin America (top left), Asia (top right), Eastern Europe (bottom left), and the Middle East and Africa (bottom right). For each country, the left bar is for 2012 and the right is for 2006. Among Latin America, the limits to legal protections for Colombia have eased and those for Venezuela have worsened. The scores for the China and Malaysia (already a positive score that is off the charts for emerging markets) have taken a turn for the worse in Asia, but India and especially the Philippines have seen an improvement. In Eastern Europe, I can see improvements in all seven countries, but especially in Slovenia. Among the Middle East and Africa countries in my sample, many saw improvements in these scores, but not Jordan or Egypt, for which the scores went in the wrong direction in 2012.

The next step in the journey is to build my last major risk indicator—and it is indeed an important one—in political instability.

Political Instability

Global investors increasingly view political stability as the most critical aspect of the investment climate. Politicians can and do change laws that affect investors, including foreign investors, which can inhibit long-term investment plans. It is critical to understand the behavior of voters and politicians and how they maximize their economic interests to understand when and why they decide to change those laws, and how policy changes occur within the bounds of existing laws.

In this chapter, I build my risk indicator of political instability that draws on the burst of academic research on political economy from the last decade. Political economy models have been useful in understanding the design and execution of fiscal and monetary policy, but they are now helpful in studying investor-protection laws and overall economic and stock market development.[1] The basic idea is that countries with constraints on policy change (through veto powers in executive, lower, or upper legislative chambers) adopt policies with more credible commitments to the returns to private property and enterprise. It is in this way the political environment can maximally facilitate growth. Out of this academic output has arisen a number of intriguing databases of democracy versus autocracy, such as the Polity IV Democracy index developed by of the Political Instability Task Force at the Center for Global Policy.[2] Another database in wide use by scholars is the Database of Political Institutions from the World Bank's Development Research Group.[3] It focuses on the concentration and fractionalization of legislatures around the world. These authors and their respective think tanks and organizations thankfully update their data on a regular basis and share it with scholars.

I also use various measures of political stability, civil unrest and violence, government effectiveness, and corruption control. Some of these measures are commercially available indices, such as those of Transparency International, the Heritage Foundation, and the International Country Risk Guide (ICRG) of the PRS Group. ICRG's political risk index measures the rule of law, likelihood of government expropriation, likelihood of government contract repudiation, and the extent of government corruption and bureaucratic competence (they also build economic and financial risk indices). Critics argue against the construction of the indices (due to their subjective weightings), their lack of focus on political systems they purport to measure, and their poor performance in being able to predict currency crises, banking crises, and expropriation events, for which they are purportedly designed. Throughout this book my inclination has been to give these data a chance, and it is no different in this chapter. I also collect data on indices that have been constructed in response to these criticisms, such as the World Bank Governance Indicators developed primarily by the current and former members of the World Bank team of Daniel Kaufmann, Aart Kraay, Massimo Mastruzzi, and Pablo Zoido-Lobatón.[4]

Most times it is hard to perceive how political instability can impact an investment decision. Fortunately, there are other times, like in the case study that follows, when it seems quite clear.

Trouble Off the Vietnamese Coast in 2011

On September 15, 2011, the Chinese government issued diplomatic protests directed toward India over the continued exploration by the state-controlled Oil and Natural Gas Company (ONGC) of India in Blocks 127 and 128 off the Vietnamese coast in the South China Sea.[5] Many years of conflict between China, Vietnam, and other Southeast Asian countries over territorial rights in the waters of the South China Sea had escalated with a high potential for the conflict to boil over in regional and even global instability. One week earlier, the government of India had filed a prospectus for a secondary issue of 5% of its stake in ONGC to raise US$ 2.5 billion to help fill dwindling government coffers.[6] While the Indian government was dealing with a rising fiscal deficit and inflationary fears, its long-term interests were to manage energy security to fuel its rapidly growing economy. Chinese protests could threaten the security of ONGC's assets and create doubts in their investors' minds. Given that previous equity issues of energy companies in India were highly oversubscribed, the government had to decide whether or not to go ahead with the secondary offering.[7]

ONGC was founded in 1956 by the government of India under the provisions of a legislative act to develop, produce, and sell petroleum products within India.[8] Starting with a few oil fields in Digboi in northeast India, ONGC transformed India's upstream sector by developing onshore fields in the western state of Gujarat and the Assam-Arakan Basin in northeastern India. In 1974 ONGC discovered a giant oil field 75 kilometers (kms) long and 25 kms wide off the coast of Bombay, which subsequently helped catapult the company into major offshore energy development. As part of an economic liberalization program initiated in the 1990s, the Indian government launched an initial public offering (IPO) of ONGC on the Bombay Stock Exchange (BSE) in 1994, offloading a 20% stake in the company and making ONGC then the second-largest Indian company by market capitalization at $47 billion (behind Reliance Industries).

ONGC was at the time ranked second worldwide among global exploration and production (E&P) companies, behind the China National Offshore Oil Corporation (CNOOC) in terms of total assets. It was the largest public-sector company in India, with net income of US$4.3 billion on revenues of US$22.6 billion in 2010. The company has over 32,000 employees distributed across operations in 15 countries outside India. It specialized in exploration of new oil fields, or "upstream activities," in the petrochemical chain and does not directly engage in the retail sale of petroleum products. It primarily served domestic demand in India, where downstream production was handled by other state-owned companies including Indian Oil, Bharat Petroleum, and Hindustan Petroleum. To date, India had been a net importer of oil and it supported consumption of 2.9 million barrels per day against production of only 878,000 barrels per day. In addition, the government controlled production and pricing through the so-called administered pricing mechanism (APM).[9] Through the APM, ONGC conceded via subsidies over 30% of its revenues to downstream operations, thus reducing its overall profitability. Investors have historically complained about these subsidies and have expressed concern that with an ever increasingly lower ownership stake, the government may not be able to pressure ONGC as easily through the APM program.[10]

As of July 2011, the Indian government owned 74.14% of ONCG shares, with state-owned oil and financial institutions maintaining an additional 7.37% stake in the company. Foreign institutional investors and the Indian public made up the balance of the holdings.

ONGC's first overseas venture dated back to a highly successful 1988 production-sharing contract in offshore Block 6.1 in Vietnam, producing over 50% of Vietnam's natural gas requirements.[11] The following year, ONGC established ONGC Videsh (OVL), a 100% subsidiary to control overseas assets.[12] Since then, OVL had regularly won exploration and drilling rights, both individually and as part of a consortium. Over the preceding 23 years, OVL expanded operations globally to over 33 projects in Vietnam, Russia, Sudan, Syria, and Venezuela. However, many of OVL's exploratory fields were located in politically sensitive zones such as Libya, Iraq, Egypt, and Myanmar. The recent deterioration of the political situation in Libya, Egypt, and Iraq forced OVL to relinquish fields in those countries, making existing exploratory rights in Russia, Venezuela, Brazil, and Vietnam even more critical to OVL's operations.

The South China Sea is a body of water in the southwestern Pacific Ocean stretching from the Straits of Melaka near Singapore to the Straits of Taiwan. It encompasses over 1.4 million square miles of open water and sees more than one-third of the world's seaborne shipping traffic annually. The South China Sea lies at a strategic crossroads with conflicting claims of ownership between nearly all of its bordering nations, including China, Taiwan, Malaysia, Brunei, Indonesia, Singapore, Vietnam, and the Philippines. Historically, the economic importance of the South China Sea has been the abundant biodiversity because of its position at the confluence of the Indian and Pacific Oceans, which resulted in an abundance of vital fisheries stocks. However, when large reserves of fossil fuels were discovered under the seas in the 1990s, it prompted many countries to reassess their territorial claims. Vying nations quickly developed small, uninhabited, and loosely claimed islands overnight, turning them from refueling and supply depots for fishing fleets into armed military outposts.

Part of Vietnam's growth in the late 1990s could be linked to its export of oil and gas resources. British Petroleum (BP) was a key partner during the initial set-up stages of PetroVietnam in providing technology and governance.[13] PetroVietnam had granted exploration rights to BP for the Phu Kanh Basin, approximately 140 miles from Vietnam's coast at water depths of 50 to 2,500 meters. In 2006, as the basin was previously unexplored and no wells had been drilled, PetroVietnam chose a bidding route to sell rights for nine blocks at an average area of 7,000 square kms per block. The reserves in the basin were estimated at 2.5 billion barrels of oil and 18 trillion cubic feet of gas. Out of the nine bids presented, ONGC's proposal was accepted. OVL signed a production-sharing contract with Vietnam to obtain seven years of exploration and 30 years of production rights. The rights include an option for Petro Vietnam to take up to 20% participating interest in operations if oil was discovered in the blocks.

China's Nine-Dotted Line Policy is a highly contested territorial claim by the government of the People's Republic of China on a large U-shaped section of the South China Sea.[14] The claim is based on historical access and control over key island groups that the line encompasses—including the Spratly Islands, the Paracel Islands, and Scarborough Reef. The Chinese government based the boundary line for this claim on a historical map entered into the Chinese government archives in the 1940s, and recently presented it to the United Nations in 2009 in a move to make the territorial claim official.[15] The most heated of these territorial claims to date had been between China and Vietnam. The majority of the clashes between the governments have been centered on the Spratly Islands, due to the largely unexplored deposits of oil and natural gas that are reported to exist beneath the surrounding waters.

In late May 2011, tensions escalated when three Chinese state-operated ocean marine surveillance vessels encountered a survey vessel owned by the oil company PetroVietnam, cutting a towed survey cable that had been mapping oil deposits in the development blocks leased by ONGC.[16] Vietnam claimed that a Chinese fishing vessel intentionally rammed into the exploration cables of a vessel chartered by PetroVietnam and engaged in seismic surveys inside Vietnamese waters.[17] Two Chinese fisheries enforcement vessels were reportedly in the area and aided the vessel. In July 2011, upon the announcement that

ONGC had signed a long-term cooperative agreement with PetroVietnam to continue offshore oil and gas exploration, Chinese Foreign Ministry spokesperson Jiang Yu stated: "China enjoys indisputable sovereignty over the South China Sea. China's stand is based on historical facts and international law. . . . As for oil and gas exploration activities, our consistent position is that we are opposed to any country engaging in oil and gas exploration and development activities in waters under China's jurisdiction. We hope the foreign countries do not get involved in the South China Sea dispute."[18]

On September 16, 2011, the ONGC share sale that was expected to raise $2.5 billion for government coffers was suspended due to "poor market conditions."[19] Despite the fact that the delay would slow the broader federal government plan to raise about $9 billion from share sales in the fiscal year to help plug India's fiscal gap, investors cheered the delay, pushing ONGC shares up 8% on the day.[20] Five months later, the Indian government approved a second attempt at the 5% equity sale, offering the shares at a premium this time, and ONGC shares rose 3.5% to its highest price in nine months to 293 rupees per share.[21] The auction was not heavily subscribed, and the exercise was marred by glitches raising questions about the future of stake sales.[22]

The stock reached a near peak of 330 rupees per share up to June 28, when CNOOC, China's state-owned oil company, issued its own tender to invite foreign companies to jointly develop blocks in the western part of the South China Sea.[23] Vietnam declared the move illegal because the blocks tendered encroached on what it claimed were its own territorial waters; "the area that the China National Offshore Oil Corporation announced to open for international bidding lies entirely within Vietnam's 200 nautical mile exclusive economic zone and continental shelf in accordance with the 1982 United Nations Convention on the Law of the Sea," declared Vietnamese Foreign Ministry spokesperson Luong Thanh Nghi.[24] Street protests in Hanoi ensued. CNOOC reported that South China block tenders were progressing well through 2013, while ONGC's stock sagged to as low as 249 rupees through November of that year.[25] South China Sea tensions continue.[26]

Measuring Political Risk

The ONGC case study brings to the fore the issue of business and security risks associated with operating in emerging markets. Whether it was a first- or second-order driver of the valuation of ONGC stock during the $2.5 billion secondary offering is worthy of debate and further discussion. But the intensity of the geopolitical backdrop undoubtedly weighed on the minds of current and prospective investors for that issue. What I want to measure is the risk that an investment's return for portfolio investors—say, in ONGC stock or for a corporation like ONGC investing its resources in the South China Sea off the coast of Vietnam—could suffer as a result of political changes or instability in a country or region. The instability could stem from a change in government, legislative bodies, other foreign policymakers, or even a military conflict.

Political risks are notoriously hard to quantify, because the incidents that define them are idiosyncratic and necessarily constitute limited sample sizes or case studies, like that of ONGC. You know it when you see it through an action taken, but it is challenging to decipher such risks before the fact. In their book's chapter on political risk, Geert Bekaert and Robert Hodrick outline several factors that constitute political risk: expropriation or nationalization of assets of a firm without compensation, contract repudiation, changes in taxes, restrictions, and regulations governing foreign firms and investors, exchange controls, corruption and legal inefficiencies, ethnic violence and terrorism, and home-country restrictions.[27] I have addressed legal inefficiencies in Chapter 8, and exchange controls with home-country restrictions in Chapter 6. What about the other elements?

When corporations and investors undertake international investments, a project's feasibility is judged by the future cash flows it generates and how those cash flows may be discounted by an appropriate risk-adjusted discount rate. Many researchers propose that a country's political risk should be incorporated using a discount-rate adjustment reflecting a systematic risk exposure to a country's sovereign bond's yield spread.[28] Of course, as Bekaert and Hodrick rightly point out, if the risk of loss from political risk is not linked to international, systematic risks, the firm or investor faces (such as the world market return in a global version of the Capital Asset Pricing Model) no adjustment to the discount rate.[29] Instead, the project's cash flows should be adjusted to cover all contingencies directly or by political risk insurance premiums that cover such unforeseen contingencies.

There are many potential sources of data on political risk insurance, including international organizations designed to promote foreign direct investing like the World Bank's Multilateral, Investment Guarantee Agency (MIGA), the Inter-American Development Bank, and the Asian Development Bank. National agencies include the Overseas Private Investment Corporation (OPIC) in the United States, Lloyd's of London, Sovereign Risk Insurance Limited, or Zurich Emerging Market Solutions.[30] Insurance programs are typically available for currency inconvertibility, expropriation, and war and political violence, but it is not possible to insure all expected cash flow losses. Each of these public and private organizations invests considerable in-house resources for research on identifying and measuring how political actors or conditions can affect a firm's goals. They empirically link measurable attributes to future political risk events.

What measurable attributes matter? Consider the example of the Political Risk Services Group (PRS Group), a New York–based firm, which produces a monthly report, *International Country Risk Guide* (ICRG), along with an annual yearbook, with periodic country fact sheets, datasets, and alerts.[31] ICRG ratings are split up into economic, financial, and political risk components; they have been available since 1980, and are developed from 22 different underlying variables. The political risk measure has 12 subcomponents; government stability, socioeconomic conditions, investment profile (risk of expropriation or contract violation), and internal and external conflicts are the most heavily weighted ones. Though their focus is on how equity market liberalizations are associated with boosts in real GDP per capita growth, Bekaert, Harvey, and Lundblad build their own categories from these subcomponents to study how correlated they are across countries and over time. They show that the growth response to a liberalization event is considerably greater in those countries with higher-quality institutions, as measured by the extent of political risk using ICRG ratings.[32]

It is common in the international finance literature to use a country's sovereign bond yield spread—that is, the country's bond yield relative to that of, say, the equivalent maturity US Treasury note or bond—as a market-based, observable, and forward-looking assessment of a country's overall political risk.[33] Adjustments can be made to the spread to account for accessibility to the market in question, the importance of the market for the investor or corporation, and for the susceptibility of the investment to political risk. Bekaert, Harvey, Lundblad, and Siegel argue that sovereign spreads are impacted by many factors beyond political risk, and estimate that they lead to discount rates being overstated by 2% to 5% potentially leading to substantial misallocations of capital.[34] They devise a statistical procedure to extract a component of the sovereign yield spread that is linked to political risk—their so-called political risk spread is about one-third of the total spread—and uncover that a 1% increase in this spread is associated with a 10% drop in net foreign direct investment flows.

What is the takeaway? For one thing, mine can only be a partial summary of this broad literature that spans the fields of economics, finance, international business, strategy, and political science. For another, my choice set of variables that is to follow has to be seen as an arbitrary subset of what is possible. It is not an optimal set by any stretch, but once distilled into the political instability risk indicator, it may work reasonably well when it comes to explaining how investors allocate their investments across emerging markets.

Political Constraints

Political constraints indices incorporate information on the number of independent branches of government with veto power and the distribution of preferences across and within those branches. I use four different indices of those constraints.

Henisz builds a political constraint index (Polcon) by assigning those countries without effective veto points with the lowest score.[35] He relies on what he calls a spatial model of political interaction to derive the extent to which any one political actor (e.g., the executive branch or a chamber of the legislature) is constrained in his or her choice of future policies. The first step is to identify the number of independent branches of government, their preferences, and status quo policies. The second step is to account for alignments across branches using data on party composition of executive and legislative branches. The index ranges from 0 to 1 where 1 equals countries with most constraints via veto powers in executive, lower, or upper legislative chambers over policy change. I specifically use Henisz's 2012 version of the data (PolconV).[36]

He argues in his article that indices that measure the rule of law and the likelihood of government expropriation or contract repudiation (like, for example, the PRS Group's ICRG) may very well be influenced by private sector perceptions of such economic outcomes, but it "does not, by itself, establish the inferred link between investment and political institutions." He calls his structural model of political interaction a new measure of credible commitment by political actors and a "robust determinant of cross-national variation in economic growth."[37] Indeed, his panel regression analysis of 157 countries over the period from 1960 to 1994 empirically shows a reliable positive relationship to his Polcon index even after controlling for a whole host of other factors. The more tightly the political constraints in a country bind, the greater the presence of checks and balances on political actors, and the higher its real per capita GDP growth.

Table 9.1 shows a large cross-country variation in the Polcon scores. The median across developed markets is only modestly higher than for that of emerging markets (0.765 versus 0.681). Egypt scores a zero as of 2012, though it has always had a low score through most of the 2000s (an average of 0.189). China and Saudi Arabia have both consistently scored zero. Other countries with low levels of constraints include Argentina (0.167), Peru (0.167), and Pakistan (0.209). On the other end of the scale, there are only a few countries that score better than the median developed market, such as Malaysia (0.837), but many that hover in that range. The United States scores one on this metric. Next, I obtain the Polity IV Democracy index, which was originally developed by Ted Robert Gurr with the Inter-University Consortium for Political and Social Research at the University of Colorado and the Center for International Development and Conflict Management at the University of Maryland. Since 1998, the dataset has been maintained and updated (now to 2010) by the Center for Global Policy.[38] His team codes annual information on regime and authority characteristics for all independent states that exist and have existed in the world from 1800 to 2011. The index ranges from –10 to 10: –10 represents high autocracy, and 10 high democracy. To score a perfect –10, citizens' participation is sharply restricted or suppressed; chief executives are selected according to

TABLE 9.1 Measures of Political Instability in 2012

	Henisz[1] Political Constraints	Polity IV Democracy Index[2]	Database of Political Institutions[3] Herfindahl	Database of Political Institutions[3] Fractionalize	Pagano-Volpin[4] Proportionality Index	World Bank's World Governance Indicators[5] Voice & Account	World Bank's World Governance Indicators[5] Political Instability	World Bank's World Governance Indicators[5] Government Effectiveness	World Bank's World Governance Indicators[5] Regulatory Burden	World Bank's World Governance Indicators[5] Rule of Law	World Bank's World Governance Indicators[5] Control of Corruption	Transparency International Corruption[6]	Heritage Freedom Index[7]
Argentina	0.166	8	1.000	0.899	3	0.353	0.198	-0.159	-0.736	-0.560	-0.394	3.0	48.0
Brazil	0.681	8	0.312	0.633	2	0.501	-0.036	-0.009	0.166	0.013	0.173	3.8	57.9
Chile	0.725	10	1.000	0.097	0	1.058	0.558	1.173	1.538	1.371	1.571	7.2	78.3
China	0.000	-7	1.000	.	.	-1.644	-0.698	0.119	-0.203	-0.428	-0.620	3.6	51.2
Colombia	0.394	7	0.383	0.540	3	-0.148	-1.254	0.244	0.353	-0.264	-0.289	3.4	68.0
Czech Republic	0.762	8	0.364	0.438	2	0.984	1.118	1.018	1.252	1.013	0.316	4.4	69.9
Egypt	0.000	-2	1.000	0.680	0	-1.127	-1.286	-0.602	-0.333	-0.419	-0.676	2.9	57.9
Hungary	0.733	10	1.000	0.605	2	0.849	0.749	0.705	1.046	0.774	0.342	4.6	67.1
India	0.702	9	1.000	0.543	1	0.405	-1.201	-0.029	-0.340	-0.081	-0.562	3.1	54.6
Indonesia	0.560	8	0.229	0.490	3	-0.082	-0.820	-0.241	-0.325	-0.662	-0.656	3.0	56.4
Israel	0.781	10	0.227	0.612	3	0.652	-1.297	1.203	1.348	0.981	0.678	5.8	67.8
Jordan	0.700	-3	1.000	0.000	.	-0.879	-0.418	0.049	0.250	0.238	0.041	4.5	69.9
South Korea	0.755	8	1.000	0.518	1	0.708	0.233	1.232	0.953	1.010	0.452	5.4	69.9
Malaysia	0.837	6	1.000	0.670	0	-0.444	0.156	0.999	0.658	0.518	0.003	4.3	66.4
Mexico	0.711	8	1.000	0.520	1	0.090	-0.696	0.324	0.348	-0.489	-0.363	3.0	65.3
Morocco	0.780	-4	0.348	0.797	2	-0.712	-0.467	-0.219	-0.094	-0.209	-0.260	3.4	60.2
Nigeria	0.433	4	1.000	0.738	0	-0.757	-1.940	-1.124	-0.685	-1.248	-1.137	2.4	56.3
Pakistan	0.209	6	1.000	0.707	0	-0.830	-2.697	-0.817	-0.610	-0.899	-1.003	2.5	54.7
Peru	0.167	9	1.000	0.713	3	0.050	-0.689	-0.151	0.501	-0.605	-0.204	3.4	68.7
Philippines	0.361	8	0.583	0.958	1	-0.015	-1.386	-0.003	-0.265	-0.512	-0.784	2.8	57.1
Poland	0.744	10	0.790	0.469	2	1.036	1.090	0.676	0.961	0.733	0.514	5.5	64.2
Russia	0.752	4	1.000	0.654	3	-0.942	-0.875	-0.404	-0.354	-0.780	-1.092	2.4	50.5

Saudi Arabia	0.000	-10	1.000	.	.	-1.843	-0.300	-0.431	0.005	0.068	-0.291	4.4	62.5
Slovakia	0.768	10	0.271	0.225	3	0.950	0.965	0.856	1.032	0.646	0.293	4.0	67.0
Slovenia	0.693	10	0.433	0.564	3	1.028	0.845	0.985	0.633	1.072	0.930	5.9	62.9
South Africa	0.412	9	0.971	0.675	3	0.569	0.021	0.369	0.436	0.100	0.034	4.1	62.7
Sri Lanka	0.347	4	1.000	0.419	3	-0.535	-0.542	-0.084	-0.094	-0.075	-0.423	3.3	58.3
Taiwan	0.724	10	0.909	0.000	1	0.875	0.893	1.168	1.167	1.041	0.904	6.1	71.9
Thailand	0.407	7	0.869	0.428	0	-0.448	-1.020	0.103	0.237	-0.241	-0.367	3.4	64.9
Turkey	0.373	9	1.000	0.407	3	-0.168	-0.927	0.409	0.422	0.077	0.100	4.2	62.5
UAE	0.667	-8	0.500	.	.	-0.977	0.957	0.952	0.400	0.464	1.085	6.8	69.3
Venezuela	0.327	-3	1.000	0.059	2	-0.924	-1.301	-1.103	-1.492	-1.630	-1.215	2.0	38.1
Vietnam	0.688	-7	1.000	.	0	-1.483	0.169	-0.279	-0.612	-0.465	-0.593	2.9	51.3
Emerging median	*0.681*	*8*	*1.000*	*0.543*	*2*	*-0.082*	*-0.467*	*0.103*	*0.250*	*-0.075*	*-0.260*	*3.6*	*62.7*
Developed median	*0.765*	*10*	*0.675*	*0.505*	*2*	*1.362*	*0.985*	*1.684*	*1.629*	*1.725*	*1.762*	*8.2*	*72.8*

Note: Appendix F details all data sources for the political instability indicator.

[1] Range of 0 to 1, where 1 has more constraints via veto power in executive/legislature on policy change. Henisz, "The Institutional Environment for Economic Growth."

[2] Range of −10 (high autocracy) to +10 (high democracy). See Marshall and Cole, *Global Stability Report*.

[3] Herfindahl annually measures the concentration of seats held by governing party; fractionalization, the likelihood that two random draws from opposition parties in legislature are from different parties. See Beck, Clarke, Groff, Keefer, and Walsh, "New Tools in Comparative Political Economy."

[4] Equals 3 if 100% of seats are assigned via a proportional rule, 2 if the majority are assigned by this rule, 1 if minority assigned proportionally, 0 if no seats assigned this way. Pagano and Volpin, "Political Economy of Corporate Governance."

[5] All scores on a scale of −2.5 to +2.5 from weak to strong on voice and accountability on civil liberties in political process, political instability on likelihood of violent threats like terrorism, government effectiveness on quality of bureaucracy, regulatory burden on incidence of market-unfriendly policies, rule of law on confidence in rules of society, control of corruption on exercise of public power for private gain.

[6] Scale 0 to 100, 100 is low perceived corruption. *Corruption Perception Index 2011*. Source: www.transparency.org.

[7] Score of 100 (more conducive to economic freedom) to 0 (less conducive) using 10 factors from four categories of rule of law, limited government, regulatory efficiency, and open markets, www.heritage.org/index/about.

clearly defined rules of success from within the political elite; and, once in office, they exercise power with no meaningful checks from legislative, judicial, or civil society institutions. By contrast, a perfect +10 is a country with institutionalized procedures for open, competitive political participation; chief executives are chosen and replaced openly; competitive elections are held; and substantial checks and balances are imposed on their discretionary powers. Examples of these countries include the United States and the United Kingdom.

The Polity dataset has been and continues to be commonly used in time-series analyses of political behavior. Most often, Polity indices are used to provide such analyses with a measure of regime democracy and/or autocracy. I use the 2012 version of the data (Polity IV).[39] The second column in Table 9.1 presents the scores. The median among developed markets is a 10, the highest score possible on the Polity IV scale. Seven of the emerging markets in my sample gain that same top score (Chile, Hungary, Israel, Poland, Slovakia, Slovenia, and Taiwan), which helps to raise the emerging market median to an 8 out of 10. Only Saudi Arabia scores a perfect –10. There are some fascinating, conflicting signals when comparing Polity IV to Henisz's Polcon scores. Relatively high Polcon scores arose for countries that scored poorly on the Polity IV scores, such as UAE (–8 on Polity IV), Vietnam (–7), Morocco (–4), and Jordan (–3).

There are several other takes on ways to benchmark political systems. In two influential studies, Marco Pagano and Paolo Volpin argue that political outcomes are a function of the electoral system itself, and, specifically, whether it is proportional (where winning a majority of the votes is crucial) or majoritarian (where winning a majority of districts ensures victory).[40] Proportional representation systems lead to more common and more uncertain policy change and thus weaker investor protections, they argue. Such systems push political parties to cater more to the preferences of social groups with homogeneous preferences (like entrepreneur associations or worker unions), unlike majoritarian systems in which keen competition is for the votes of a pivotal district, which often coincides with a heterogeneous residual group.

They develop a proportionality index, which they build from variables in the World Bank's Database on Political Institutions (DPI). (I will describe DPI in more detail below.) The index equals 3 points if 100% of seats are assigned via proportional rule, 2 points if the majority of seats are so assigned, 1 point if only a minority of seats is so assigned, and no points if no seats are. I reconstruct and update their index using the World Bank's DPI database, which I obtain with permission.[41]

The fifth column in Table 9.1 reveals a nice range of scores among the emerging market countries despite the narrow scale of 3 points. Eleven countries score high on the proportionality index, including Argentina, Indonesia, Israel, Russia, Slovakia, Slovenia, and Turkey (all with 3 points). Malaysia gets zero points, but yet scores well on Polcon and the Polity IV. Across all 57 countries in my sample using the latest scores available, the correlation between the proportionality index and the other two are negative (–0.34 and –0.20, respectively).

I also use two variables from the World Bank's Database of Political Institutions, the source for Pagano and Volpin's proportionality index. DPI was compiled in the late 1990s by a team of researchers in the Development Research Group of the World Bank, led by Thorsten Beck, George Clarke, Alberto Groff, Philip Keefer, and Patrick Walsh.[42] The original mandate of the project was to answer two fundamental questions: which political institutions are most conducive to development and reform, and, under what conditions do such institutions emerge? DPI originally contained 113 variables for 177 countries over the years 1975 to 1995, and it has been regularly updated since (to 2012).[43] The researchers describe their variables as "nearly all objective and their construction is entirely transparent," and it allows researchers to use "precise and concrete institutional features of countries . . . to combine them in ways appropriate to theories they are examining."[44] So I accept their invitation to choose with discretion.

One variable I choose from DPI is a Herfindahl index of the concentration of seats held by the governing and opposition parties in the legislature: a highly concentrated (i.e., single party) legislature equals one, whereas a less-concentrated legislature is closer to zero. I focus my choice here on the governing party, and DPI uses the code name HERFGOV. The second is the fractionalization of the legislature. Fractionalization measures annually the likelihood that two random draws from the legislature are from different parties. I choose to focus on the degree of fractionalization of the opposition parties, using the code OPPFRAC. Greater fractionalization and less concentration are likely to be associated with more political constraints, all else being equal. This follows the intuition borne from Henisz's research.

These two series are presented in two columns on the left side of Table 9.1. Several important facts jump out. There are a number of countries that have very high levels of concentration in the governing party (100%) and no fractionalization among the opposition parties (missing data); these include China, Saudi Arabia, and Vietnam. The UAE split the governing party at 50%, but still has no opposition from which to compute the fractionalization. A second salient fact from these data is that many emerging market countries have 100% Herfindahl scores for the governing party. This is not surprising, and implies that few allow for governing coalitions. Those that score low on government party's Herfindahl are themselves notable (Indonesia, Israel, and Slovakia). The median fractionalization among emerging markets is 0.543, not too much higher than for developed countries (0.505), but several countries have low rates, including Jordan and Taiwan (both zero), Venezuela (0.059), and Chile (0.097).

World Governance Indicators

In the 1990s, the Macroeconomics and Growth Team of the Development Research group of the World Bank launched a series of studies by their team members Daniel Kauffman, Aart Kraay, Pablo Zoido-Lobaton, and Massimo Mastruzzi to try to understand the causes and consequences of good governance for development.[45] The indicators are based on 352 different underlying variables measuring perceptions of a wide range of governance issues drawn from 31 separate data sources constructed by 30 different organizations worldwide. Some of these organizations include the PRS Group's International Country Risk Guide and *The Economist*'s Economic Intelligence Unit's data, two of which I have discussed earlier. Each measure is constructed on a scale of –2.5 to 2.5 with a standard deviation of 1.0 using standard unobserved components models. I use each of these six measures and describe them as in Kaufman, Kraay, and Mastruzzi.[46] Their scores for 2012 are all presented on the left side of Table 9.1.

Voice and accountability measures various aspects of the political process, civil liberties, and political rights in year 2000. This variable measures the extent to which citizens of a country are able to participate in the selection of governments. Also included in this category are three indicators measuring the independence of the media. The median score for the emerging markets is low (–0.082) relative to that for developed markets (1.362). The lowest scores—not surprisingly, given the other data analyzed above—arise for China (–1.64), Saudi Arabia (–1.84), and Vietnam (–1.48). Political instability measures the likelihood of violent threats to or changes in government, including terrorism. The range between emerging and developed market median scores for this index is also large. The negative median score for the emerging markets (–0.467) is influenced by a large negative score for Pakistan (–2.697). Pakistan has scored among the lowest in this set of countries for most of the 2000s, but its own score has declined over this period. Very few of the 33 emerging markets score as well as the median score for the developed markets (with the UAE Slovakia, and Poland as exceptions).

Government effectiveness measures the quality of public service provision, the quality of the bureaucracy, the competence of civil servants, the independence of the civil service from political pressures, and the credibility of the government's commitment to policies. The main focus of this index is on the inputs required for the government to be able to implement good policies and deliver public goods. Several emerging markets score well on government effectiveness, including Chile (1.173), Israel (1.203), South Korea (1.232), and Taiwan (1.168). A related measure is regulatory burden, which measures the incidence of market-unfriendly policies. It captures perceptions of the ability of the government to formulate and implement sound policies and regulations that permit and promote private sector development. The same countries that score high on government effectiveness do so also on regulatory burden. In fact, in 2012, the correlation among these two sets of scores is 0.95. It will be interesting to see how well the principal component analysis (PCA) will be able to separate out the distinctive elements of these two measures.

Rule of law measures the extent to which agents have confidence in and abide by the rules of society. At face value, I worry about the extent to which this measure may be too closely related to my risk indicator for the limits to legal protections. But this variable focuses on perceptions of the population at large (not the perceptions on case law of the legal teams of the *Lex Mundi* project) about the incidence of both violent and nonviolent crime, the effectiveness and predictability of the judiciary, and the enforceability of contracts. On this variable Nigeria scores relatively poorly (–1.248), and not one other of the 32 emerging markets come close (the second worst, Russia, scores –0.780).

Finally, the corruption index measures "the exercise of public power for private gain."[47] It measures aspects ranging from the frequency of additional payments to get things done to the effects of corruption on the business environment. The perceptions that matter are the extent to which public power is exercised for private gain, including both petty and grand forms of corruption, and the "capture" of the state by elites and private interests. According to the World Bank, the countries with the worst control of corruption are Venezuela (–1.215), Saudi Arabia (–1.092), and Nigeria (–1.137). Only Chile scores within striking distance of the median score among developed markets (1.762).

Corruption

The last index in the World Bank's World Governance Indicators emphasizes a dimension of political instability that has received considerable attention among scholars. Empirical studies have shown how corruption is associated with higher borrowing costs, lower stock valuations, and worse corporate governance.[48] Ciocchini, Durbin, and Ng decompose a country's sovereign yield spreads into that related to corruption after controlling for default rates from credit ratings, GDP growth, and external debt burdens.[49] They estimate that a one-unit decrease in the level of corruption can be linked with a 20% lower yield spread.[50] Charles Lee and David Ng use firm-level data from 43 countries to show how firms in more corrupt countries trade at significantly lower market multiples after controlling for other factors.[51] This relatively large body of research compels me to add more emphasis to it in building my risk indicator of political instability.

Transparency International conducts an annual survey (since 1995) of more than 150 countries by their perceived levels of corruption, as determined by expert assessments and opinion surveys. Sixteen surveys and expert assessments are used and at least 3 are required for a country to be included in the index. The corruption perception index score relates to perceptions of the degree of corruption as seen by business people and country analysts, and ranges between

10 (highly clean) and 0 (highly corrupt). I obtain the 2011 scores from *Corruption Perception Index 2011*, which is available from the organization's website.[52]

The second-last-column of Table 9.1 presents the scores. The median score among emerging markets is much lower than that for developed markets (3.6 versus 8.2). Not one of the emerging markets scores at the level of the median of developed markets, though Chile (7.2) comes closest of the pack. The countries with the lowest scores include Russia (2.4), Nigeria (2.4), and Pakistan (2.5). The correlation with the World Bank's variable on the Control of Corruption is 0.98, which is very high.

Economic Freedom

The Heritage Foundation has constructed since 1995 an Index of Economic Freedom.[53] Economic freedom is defined as the absence of government coercion or constraint on the production, distribution, or consumption of goods and services beyond the extent necessary for citizens to protect and maintain liberty itself. They build indices of ten factors: trade policy, fiscal burden of government, government intervention in the economy, monetary policy, capital flows and foreign investment, banking and finance, wages and prices, property rights, regulation, and informal market activity. All 10 factors are equally important to the level of economic freedom in any country, and are weighted equally. Each factor is graded according to a scale that runs from 1 to 100, where a score of 100 signifies an economic environment or set of policies that are most conducive to economic freedom. I obtain the overall scores for 2012.

The last column of Table 9.1 exhibits the scores for my 33 emerging market countries. There is limited dispersion across the markets and a range that runs from a low of 39.1 for Venezuela to a high of 78.3 for Chile. As an all-encompassing index, there is a risk that it does not fit well into this risk indicator for political instability. However, its correlations with the World Bank World Governance Indicators are positive, and reliably so; the correlation with the voice and accountability index is 0.58, and that with the regulatory burden index is 0.89.

Together, we have worked long and hard to identify a set of variables that capture this amorphous concept called political instability. I now turn my attention to estimation with the data-reduction exercise using principal component analysis (PCA) to build the political instability risk indicator.

Principal Component Analysis of the Political Instability Indicator

Table 9.2 presents the estimation for the first principal component of the 13 variables that go into this indicator. It turns out that one component is enough; the eigenvalue of that component (7.97) implies that it singly delivers 61% of

TABLE 9.2 Principal Component Analysis for Political Instability in 2012

Eigenvalues	Coefficient	Std. Err.	z-statistic	p-value	(5%,	95%)
First Component	7.97265	1.49341	5.34	0.00	5.04561	10.89968
First Component						
Henisz Political Constraints Index	0.26183	0.03413	7.67	0.00	0.19493	0.32873
Polity IV Democracy Index	0.20922	0.04376	4.78	0.00	0.12345	0.29499
DPI Herfindahl Index	-0.15002	0.05137	-2.92	0.00	-0.25070	-0.04934
DPI Fractionalization Index	-0.06759	0.05515	-1.23	0.22	-0.17568	0.04051
Pagano-Volpin Proportionality Index	0.06016	0.05698	1.06	0.29	-0.05152	0.17185
WB Voice & Accountability	0.30979	0.02620	11.82	0.00	0.25843	0.36114
WB Political Instability	0.30461	0.02537	12.01	0.00	0.25489	0.35434
WB Government Effectiveness	0.34457	0.01141	30.19	0.00	0.32220	0.36694
WB Regulatory Burden	0.34194	0.01298	26.35	0.00	0.31651	0.36737
WB Rule of Law	0.34468	0.01158	29.76	0.00	0.32197	0.36738
WB Control of Corruption	0.34059	0.01410	24.15	0.00	0.31295	0.36824
Transparency International Corruption Index	0.33063	0.01862	17-.76	0.00	0.29414	0.36712
Heritage Economic Freedom Index	0.29740	0.02856	10.41	0.00	0.24143	0.35337

Diagnostics

Number of observations	57
Number of components	1
Trace	13
Rho	0.6133
Std. Err. (Rho)	0.0489
Likelihood Ratio test for dependence: χ^2 (78)	1101.08 p-value 0.00
Likelihood Ratio test for sphericity: χ^2 (90)	1114.69 p-value 0.00

Note: For columns listed under the headings of 5% and 95%, the values of the coefficient at the 5% and 95% limits of the 90% confidence range are reported, respectively.

the explanatory power of the variation across all the variables. The confidence interval implies that it is likely to be quite high, even if the point estimate does not seem quite right. The coefficients in the eigenvector reveal a striking pattern. The coefficients for each of the six World Bank's World Governance Indicators are reliably positive and precisely estimated. The same can be said for the Transparency International Corruption Index and the Heritage Foundation's Economic Freedom Index. These eight variables have coefficients around 0.30, and with very large z-statistics associated with them.

Perhaps just as interesting is the fact that among the other five variables, only the Henisz Polcon index receives a coefficient close in magnitude.[54] That for the Polity IV Democracy index is 0.21, and the three for the variables from the Database for Political Institutions (DPI) are much lower and not reliably estimated. I remind readers that these cannot be directly interpreted as weights in the usual sense, as they are forced to sum to one only in their squared form. However, it is sensible that the coefficients on the DPI variables are negative in value given that higher concentration and greater fractionalization should, in principle, be associated with greater—not less—political instability.

There is a large range of scores that obtain for the political instability indicator, shown in Figure 9.1. The median score for developed markets is shown at the bottom of the figure (a 0.95 value). Chile—so often among the variables on political constraints, democracy, corruption, and economic freedom—scored well, so it is not surprising that it tops out all emerging markets with a score of 0.70, just below that for the developed market median. Many of the countries with positive scores on the index were also mentioned frequently in my discussion of the variables above. Taiwan, the Czech Republic, Slovenia, Slovakia, Israel, Poland, South Korea, and Hungary stand tall among the next set. There is a drop to the UAE (−0.13), and yet another to Malaysia (−0.27) and Brazil (−0.41). The set of countries becomes a crowded pack around the emerging market median of −0.68.

The countries at the left tail of the distribution on the political instability scores will also not surprise readers, given the low ratings they received on the democracy, political constraints, and corruption variables. Venezuela scores lowest (−2.09), but it is joined closely by Pakistan (−1.79), Nigeria (−1.74), Egypt (−1.64), and China (−1.57). I remind readers that these scores have no unit measure per se, so they have no economic meaning by construction. I create a standard normal scale from the principal component scores, which means that the ordinal rankings are meaningful as are the resulting gaps between the scores.

One More Thing

I am almost ready to transition to the next part of the book, which seeks to understand whether and how these risk indicators work. How they work will

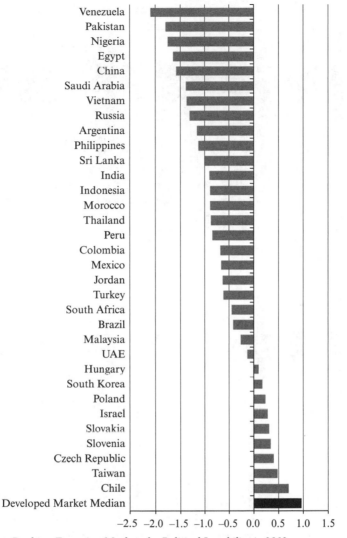

FIGURE 9.1 *Ranking Emerging Markets by Political Instability in 2012.*

Note: The political instability risk indicator scores are computed on a standardized basis using a standard normal scale for the continuous index values. Negative (positive) values imply worse (better) scores, reflecting greater (lesser) risk. All scores are measured using data up to 2012.

be judged by how well they explain how global investors actually behave. But before I close out the chapter on political instability, I want to reveal a couple of interesting facts about my newly constructed collection of six risk indicators.

The first fact is exhibited in Figure 9.2. What I have computed is the pairwise correlations between each of the six indicators, but separately for the 33 emerging markets and the 24 developed ones. The figure is a bit difficult to read for the individual data points, but I believe it is worth the effort. If you look at the top graph for the emerging markets, you can see that the vertical axis shows the

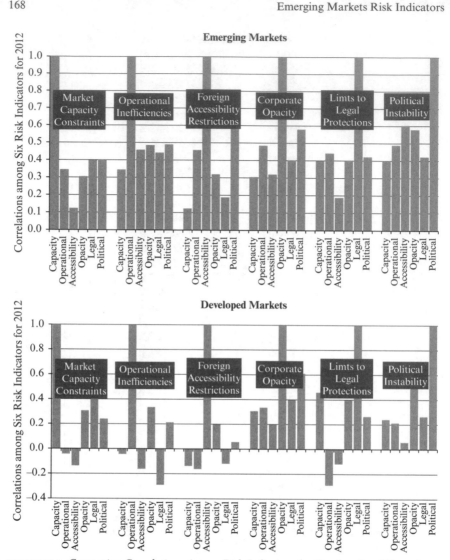

FIGURE 9.2 *Comparing Correlations Among Risk Indicators for Developed and Emerging Markets in 2012.*

Note: The six risk indicators are as reported in this chapter and the previous five chapters. Correlations range from a minimum of –1 to a maximum of +1. The correlation of one risk indicator with itself is indicated with a perfect positive correlation of +1. The statistics are reported separately for the 33 emerging countries and the 24 developed ones as outlined in Chapter 2.

correlations. Correlations can range by constructions from –1.0 to +1.0, but all of these are positive. There are six clusters of six correlations, and each cluster organized by one of the indicators in the box displayed.

The way to read this figure is as follows. In the first cluster for market capacity constraints, the correlation with market capacity constraints (denoted "Capacity" as a label along the x-axis) is +1.0. This is the correlation of the risk

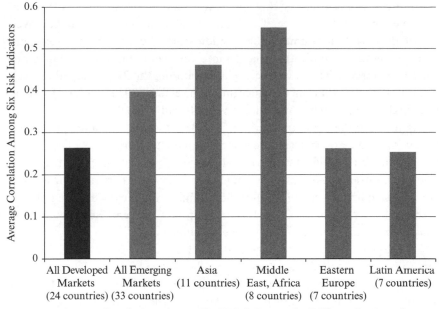

FIGURE 9.3 *Average Correlations Among Six Risk Indicators for Different Regions of Emerging Markets in 2012.*

Note: The six risk indicators are as reported in this chapter and the previous five chapters. Correlations range from a minimum of −1 to a maximum of +1. The correlation of one risk indicator with itself is indicated with a perfect positive correlation of +1. The statistics are reported separately for the 33 emerging countries, separately by geographic region within that group, and for the 24 developed ones as outlined in Chapter 2.

indicator with itself, so it has to be perfectly positively correlated. The correlation of market capacity constraints with operational inefficiencies (the second bar, "Operational") is 0.35. It is positive, but closer to zero than 1.0. You can see that most of the correlations among the risk indicators are positive, average around 0.40, and range between a low of 0.12 between market capacity and foreign accessibility ("Accessibility" for short) and a high of 0.60 between foreign accessibility restrictions and political instability ("Political"). Of course, you have to exclude the correlations of each of the risk indicators with themselves, which are +1.0 by construction and which are therefore not interesting to study. By contrast, study the bottom figure for developed markets. Readers beware: the range on the y-axis has been adjusted to account for the fact that there are negative correlations in this set. But overall, the correlations are lower, averaging around 0.25. The range is from a negative value of −0.25 between operational inefficiencies and legal protections and a high of +0.60 between corporate opacity (labeled "Opacity" on the x-axis) and political instability. Overall, the correlations among developed market risk indicator scores are lower than the same scores among emerging markets. What's the takeaway? Emerging market risk indicators have more in common with each other than those among developed markets.

Figure 9.3 shows further that this is not even across different regions of the emerging markets space. The figure exhibits a simple arithmetic average of the correlations among the six indicators (there are 30 different pairings among the six indicators that go into the averaging) for developed and emerging markets. The average correlation among the 24 developed markets is about 0.26 and that for the emerging markets is 0.39, an order of magnitude higher. This is what one can see visually in Figure 9.2.

As you read the figure to the right, it is clear that the commonality among the six risk indicator scores in the emerging markets is driven to a large extent by the Middle East's eight countries. The correlations average more than 0.55. The 11 countries in Asia also have higher than average common correlations among the indicator scores (around 0.46). It falls dramatically to the equivalent averages for Latin America and Eastern Europe (both with seven countries), which are correlations like those for the developed ones.

This degree of correlation may matter as I now proceed to take the indicators to actual data on foreign portfolio holdings. The higher is the correlation, the less may be the independent variation among the indicators that one can identify. It makes it more difficult to understand what factors really shape how investors think about these markets.

PART III

Validating the Risk Indicators

Do the Emerging Market Risk Indicators Work?

In Part II of the book, I built the emerging market indicators. Now what? The goal of this chapter is to assess the validity of the indicators. The real question is how best to take them for a test drive. I can take two possible routes: an easier one that is less likely to impress any reader and a harder one that potentially will. I am always inclined toward the latter. Therefore, I choose to try to explain what is known affectionately in the world of international finance as the "home-bias puzzle." That is: why do global investors choose disproportionately to invest in securities at home? It has a companion phenomenon called the "foreign bias," which relatedly asks why global investors disproportionately invest in securities that are familiar or proximate (literally and more broadly) to their country of domicile. These two phenomena have dogged researchers for decades. Wish me luck!

What exactly is the *puzzle* of the home and foreign biases? Since the waves of market liberalization events in the 1990s, many emerging markets have become increasingly open to foreign investors. Classic models of portfolio choice predict that under these circumstances, investors should ideally hold portfolios that are well-diversified internationally, so that risk is shared across countries efficiently and so that capital flows where it can be used most profitably. Yet there is much evidence that investors still hold portfolios that are overweighted in the country in which they are domiciled. This is the home bias. It is not just about holding much of one's wealth in his or her home country's securities, but also relative to what a rational, risk-averse, optimizing global investor should hold. Of course, the benchmark is the key. I will discuss this more below, but the relative market capitalization of the home market is a common benchmark choice. There is also evidence that investors systematically bias their foreign portfolio holdings away from some countries and toward other countries relative to their market capitalization weight in the world market portfolio based on geographic proximity, similarity of national language, and even similar colonial links. This is the foreign bias, and it is similarly benchmarked against the weight of the target country in the capitalization of the world market. I cite a number of studies on the foreign bias in the discussion below.

The challenge of explaining the home bias, and maybe the foreign bias, is a robust one. Do market capacity constraints, operational inefficiencies, foreign investability restrictions, corporate opacity, limits to legal protections, and political instability represent "hard" or "soft" constraints that bind foreign investors and that therefore challenge the basic assumptions underlying the classical models? Do they do so in a way that makes intuitive sense? That's my test. I evaluate the integrity of my six market indicators by assessing whether they have any explanatory power for the actual foreign portfolio holdings of global investors.

To this end, I conduct two simple experiments in this chapter. First, from annual surveys conducted jointly by the Board of Governors of the Federal Reserve System, the Federal Reserve Bank of New York, and the US Treasury Department since 1994, I collect data on aggregate portfolio holdings of foreign bonds and equities by US residents in 2012. These so-called Treasury International Capital (TIC) surveys are done at the individual security level through the largest US custodians, a relatively small group of institutions (about 220) that collectively report on the vast majority of total US financial holdings at home and abroad. The survey is conducted under the authority of the International Investment and Trade in Services Survey Act.

Using this data, I compute the percentage of total foreign equity holdings in each market relative to all foreign equity holdings in the survey and perform regression analysis on each of my indicators. I control for the percentage of total foreign equity market capitalization in each market (from Chapter 2) relative to the market capitalization of all markets, so that my scores for each indicator need to explain the bias or excess in the actual holdings of US investors. That is, if the weight of Russian long-term securities in actual US investor portfolios is 10% and the actual relative market capitalization of Russia in the world market portfolio as a benchmark is 7%, then US investor excess holdings of Russian securities are a positive 3%, or an overweighting of Russian securities.

Next I obtain a second dataset, because I want to make sure that the relevance of these risk indicators for emerging markets goes beyond just understanding how US investors allocate their investments. Specifically, I collect stock holdings data from the FactSet Ownership (formerly, Lionshares) database, which is a leading information source for global institutional ownership. Institutions, which are defined as professional money managers with discretionary control over assets like mutual funds, pension funds, bank trusts, and insurance companies, are frequently required to disclose publicly their holdings in many countries around the world. In the United States, FactSet secures data on institutional holdings from the mandatory quarterly 13F filings with the Securities and Exchange Commission (SEC), as well as by rolling up the holdings by individual mutual funds (N–30D filings with the SEC) managed by a particular fund management company. Outside the United States, FactSet collects holdings data from sources such as national regulatory agencies, stock exchange announcements, local and offshore mutual funds, mutual fund directories, and company proxies and annual reports. To the best of my knowledge, it is the most comprehensive source available outside the United States.

These FactSet Ownership data represent a nice complement to the TIC data from the United States, even though it is only for equities and not bond holdings and even though it is only for institutional holdings (not including retail) individual investors. The data run through 2012, with holdings data for over 5,000 different institutions in over 35,000 stocks worldwide representing a total market value of $19 trillion as of December 2012. I perform similar regression analysis with the risk indicators as explanatory variables for the foreign bias in emerging and developed markets computed with FactSet holdings data.

Before I describe the foreign holdings data I use and how well my risk indicators do, a brief review of the home-bias literature may be worthwhile. It helps to justify the experiments I run.

A Primer on the Home Bias

Domestic investors hold a disproportionate share of their portfolios in domestic assets. This observation was made for US investors at least as far back as Herbert Grubel in 1968 and by Haim Levy and Marshall Sarnat in 1970.[1] And though globalization of international portfolios has increased international investment activity dramatically in the almost 50 years since, the phenomenon persists.[2] No single explanation that scholars have put forward seems to resolve the puzzle completely. The competing explanations have addressed information problems, behavioral aspects of decision-making, corporate governance issues, and barriers to foreign investment. As Cooper, Sercu, and Vanpée argue, each explanation on its own falls short, suggesting that the home bias probably reflects "a combination of factors."[3] Maybe, just maybe, the *combination* of my risk indicators in this book can deliver the goods?

The departure points for most of this research are the elegant models of portfolio choice and asset pricing developed in the 1970s for a world without barriers for the free flow of capital. In my survey study with René Stulz, we refer to these as the "perfect models" of globally integrated markets in which "an asset has the same price regardless of where it is traded and in which no finance is local."[4] In a world of perfect financial markets globally, the key assumptions one makes about how goods prices in different currencies are related are those that have important implications for how individuals choose portfolios and how asset prices are determined. Investors want to smooth out their consumption spending in spite of bumpy and unexpected changes in their income flow, and it is the capital markets (global, if possible) that help them get there. If consumption and investment opportunity sets are the same for all investors across countries—a highly unrealistic assumption—it cannot matter where an investor is located. If consumption and investment opportunity sets do differ across countries and investors are not mobile, then an investor's expected lifetime depends on where he or she is located.

A kind of counterfactual experiment is what defined the early theoretical models of Bruno Solnik and Frederick Grauer, Robert Litzenberger, and Richard Stehle.[5] The studies were typically developed in the world of the single factor model, the capital asset pricing model (CAPM), and its global equivalent, the global CAPM. The implication of the model is that the rational, risk-averse mean-variance optimizing global investor would hold securities on a market-value-weighted basis. Shares of Brazilian equities held by global investors, for example, should be commensurate with the market capitalization of the Brazilian equity markets relative to that of the world. However, home bias exists; global investors severely underweight Brazil, so one must turn to these models and their underlying assumptions for guidance on why they must be wrong.

The first reason investors may hold portfolio allocations that differ from the world market portfolio defined by the global CAPM is that the returns they face differ by their location. Michael Adler and Bernard Dumas derived equilibrium portfolio holdings for investors facing shocks to their purchasing power due to real exchange rate risk.[6] In their world, an investor not only maximizes risk-adjusted returns across all investors, but also minimizes real exchange rate risk. Cooper and Kaplanis evaluate equity returns and portfolio holdings across a number of developed markets to ask whether currency risk can explain the home bias, and find that it cannot.[7] Currency risk seems to be too small to explain why mean-variance optimizing investors would choose not to diversify more.

Baxter and Jermann, Glassman and Riddick, and Jermann proposed that there may be other country-specific risks that are unrelated to real exchange rate fluctuations and that might yet influence portfolio choices and pricing.[8] They propose that nontradable goods like an investor's own human capital (local job market prospects, for example) may lie at the core of the problem in the perfect markets model. Maybe the country-specific risk is not a risk, but a benefit? After all, some domestically traded assets could provide the kind of diversification benefits of investing abroad without investors' having to go there? Coca-Cola, Walmart, and McDonald's have globally diversified operations as US listed and traded stocks. Errunza, Hogan, and Hung explore this kind of "home-made diversification" using optimally weighted portfolios of US traded securities—US multinational, foreign stocks listed secondarily on US stock exchanges, and country funds—that are likely to have foreign risk components.[9] Interestingly, they find that there are domestic portfolios that can mimic the risk profile of international portfolios, except for those in emerging markets.

Another issue is that information problems naturally arise between domestic and foreign investors: local investors may have a natural advantage that deters global investors from competing with them. This idea is very much in the spirit of the transparency and disclosure components of my corporate opacity risk indicator of Chapter 7. Gehrig showed how if domestic investors have more precise information about domestic equity markets compared to foreign investors, they will choose to weight their portfolios more heavily toward domestic equities—or, at least, foreign equities in which they have less of a disadvantage relative to locals.[10] Dahlquist, Pinkowitz, Stulz, and Williamson, and another study by Stulz, build on the information problem story by pointing out that in most countries, firms have controlling shareholders who do not trade their shares.[11] The impact of corporate opacity and limits to their legal protections as minority investors (Chapter 8) may not only rationalize why global investors cannot invest directly in local shares (due to absence of shares that float), but actually choose not to do so (for fear of expropriation by insiders).[12]

Additionally, even if information acquisition costs are not prohibitive, agency issues can give rise to home bias if monitoring is costly. Governance problems, as opposed to information problems, sit at the center of an analysis of institutional investor equity holdings around the world by Ferreira and Matos.[13] Theirs is one of the first to use the FactSet Lionshares Ownership data on institutional holdings that I will showcase below. The data runs from 2000 through 2005 for 5,337 different institutions in over 35,000 stocks worldwide representing about $18 trillion in investments. They find that institutional investors have a strong preference for holdings in large firms and firms with good governance. Foreign institutions significantly overweight holdings in firms that are secondarily cross-listed in the United States and that are members of a major global index, such as Morgan Stanley Capital International's all-capital world index, including all the features that lead to such associations.

A final, somewhat related but subtly different rationalization for the home- and foreign-bias puzzles is a behavioral one; namely, a lack of familiarity with foreign markets. Grinblatt and Keloharju have shown that in Finland, investors are more likely to trade stocks of firms that share the investor's same language and cultural background. For example, Finnish investors whose native language is Swedish are more likely to own stocks of companies listed on the Helsinki Stock Exchange that have annual reports in Swedish with Swedish-speaking CEOs than are investors whose native language is Finnish.[14] Chan, Covrig, and Ng study how mutual funds from 26 developed and emerging markets allocate their investments in 1999 and 2000 between domestic and foreign markets and show that familiarity factors like geographic distance, common language, common culture, and strong bilateral trade activity play a significant role.[15]

I have clearly only scratched the surface of a large body of research on the home-bias puzzle. All this primer can simply do is to establish that an analysis of foreign investor holdings is a reasonable setting in which to assess the usefulness of my emerging market risk indicators.

The First Test: Explaining US Foreign Investor Holdings in 2012

Table 10.1 displays the data on total foreign debt (both short-term and long-term) and equity holdings of US residents as of the end of 2012. I present a column for the total foreign holdings and separately another for just equity holdings along (all in US$ millions). Beside both columns, I report the fraction of the total that each country constitutes.

The first important fact to note is that US residents now hold $7.9 trillion of foreign securities. The equity holdings alone excluding the debt securities are $5.3 trillion, or comprise 67% of the total. These data include foreign securities from almost 215 countries outside the United States. The foreign holdings have doubled since the end of 2008 ($3.6 trillion), and almost quadrupled since 2001 ($2.01 trillion). Part of the story no doubt stems from fluctuations in the valuations over the decade, but a big part stems from US residents actively diversifying their financial wealth overseas. Second, at the bottom of the table I show that the US holdings of the 57 countries on which I focus my analysis add up to $6.5 trillion in 2012, representing 82% of all foreign holdings ($4.2 trillion of equities, or 80%).

From a quick glance, US residents clearly favor the developed markets in their mix of foreign holdings. The United Kingdom is of primary interest at $1 trillion (12.6%); Canada follows next ($800 billion, 10%); and the next cluster of countries includes Japan, France, Australia, Switzerland, and Germany (all around 5% of the total). Looking at the top of the table among the emerging markets, US residents favor Brazil ($216 billion, 2.7%) and South Korea ($174 billion, 2.2%). There is a drop-off to the next tier of active interest in Mexico, China, South Africa, and Taiwan.

Of course, this analysis fails to recognize the relative sizes of these bond and equity markets, which clearly matters. After all, the $2.4 trillion in total equity market capitalization of the United Kingdom represents 3.7% of the world equity market capitalization ($65.9 trillion) as of the end of 2011, and 4.8% of the world excluding the United States. So it is important to calibrate the raw allocation of US residents to the United Kingdom of 11.8% (see Table 10.1 for equity holdings only) against the 4.8% of the world equity market capitalization pie that is available to be had. I call the difference of 7% the *excess* foreign equity holdings of US residents in the United Kingdom. As I already mentioned above, these *excess* equity holdings will be the object of interest in my regression analysis to come.

TABLE 10.1 Total Foreign Debt and Equity Holdings of US Residents in 2012

Country	Total Debt & Equity Holdings (US$ millions)	% of Total	Equity Holdings Only (US$ millions)	% of Total
Argentina	7,110	0.09%	1,610	0.03%
Brazil	216,116	2.72%	150,015	2.82%
Chile	27,912	0.35%	14,049	0.26%
China	120,392	1.52%	119,360	2.25%
Colombia	19,996	0.25%	7,406	0.14%
Czech Rep.	4,420	0.06%	3,506	0.07%
Egypt	4,655	0.06%	3,283	0.06%
Hungary	13,082	0.16%	2,556	0.05%
India	78,847	0.99%	75,686	1.42%
Indonesia	44,991	0.57%	30,342	0.57%
Israel	56,544	0.71%	37,309	0.70%
Jordan	231	0.00%	142	0.00%
South Korea	174,689	2.20%	141,077	2.66%
Malaysia	42,418	0.53%	25,445	0.48%
Mexico	157,089	1.98%	76,835	1.45%
Morocco	1,012	0.01%	523	0.01%
Nigeria[2]	4,048	0.05%	1,781	0.03%
Pakistan	1,323	0.02%	1,027	0.02%
Peru	10,830	0.14%	3,418	0.06%
Philippines	22,417	0.28%	14,583	0.27%
Poland	33,664	0.42%	10,209	0.19%
Russia	66,532	0.84%	54,717	1.03%
Saudi Arabia[1]	15,451	0.19%	3,069	0.06%
Slovakia	651	0.01%	–	0.00%
Slovenia	1,360	0.02%	161	0.00%
South Africa	85,830	1.08%	71,286	1.34%
Sri Lanka	2,638	0.03%	557	0.01%
Taiwan	87,640	1.10%	87,433	1.65%
Thailand	36,731	0.46%	33,322	0.63%
Turkey	50,124	0.63%	30,788	0.58%
UAE[1]	.	.	.	.
Venezuela	13,607	0.17%	47	0.00%
Vietnam	1,804	0.02%	1,074	0.02%
Australia	351,065	4.42%	146,943	2.77%
Austria	14,408	0.18%	8,824	0.17%
Belgium	45,545	0.57%	38,755	0.73%
Canada	808,023	10.17%	375,567	7.07%
Denmark	49,270	0.62%	43,318	0.82%
Finland	26,578	0.33%	20,241	0.38%
France	374,753	4.72%	257,137	4.84%
Germany	329,575	4.15%	228,202	4.30%
Greece	4,629	0.06%	3,622	0.07%
Hong Kong	144,743	1.82%	139,420	2.62%

(continued)

TABLE 10.1 Continued

Country	Total Debt & Equity Holdings (US$ millions)	% of Total	Equity Holdings Only (US$ millions)	% of Total
Ireland	180,851	2.28%	133,928	2.52%
Italy	109,564	1.38%	54,066	1.02%
Japan	520,713	6.56%	427,249	8.04%
Luxembourg	100,431	1.26%	32,663	0.61%
Netherlands	286,055	3.60%	145,503	2.74%
New Zealand	17,967	0.23%	3,870	0.07%
Norway	73,282	0.92%	24,420	0.46%
Portugal	6,426	0.08%	4,528	0.09%
Singapore	72,896	0.92%	59,482	1.12%
Spain	98,894	1.25%	63,350	1.19%
Sweden	121,568	1.53%	66,354	1.25%
Switzerland	333,492	4.20%	322,226	6.07%
United Kingdom	1,001,456	12.61%	626,428	11.79%
Total (57 Countries)	6,476,338	81.55%	4,228,712	79.61%
World Total (215 Countries)	7,941,441		5,311,509	

Note: The data were obtained from US Treasury website at www.treas.gov/tic/. I have computed aggregate statistics from this database for this exercise.

[1] The UAE is included with Saudi Arabia and is reported as Middle East Oil Exporting Countries.
[2] Nigeria includes other African Oil Exporting Countries.

What do the actual excess foreign holdings of US residents look like? Figure 10.1 gives us a clear picture for the 33 emerging markets in this book. Many of the excess holdings are negative. In fact, there are only four markets that have positive excess holdings: Israel, South Korea, South Africa, and Taiwan. Several of these countries are not surprising choices, given that they had relatively high raw (not excess) foreign portfolio holdings among US residents. I did mention Brazil, China, and Mexico in the same breath as these others, however, and they are associated with negative excess holdings. China's excess holding of –12% is literally and figuratively off the charts. Brazil, India, and Russia are also significantly underweight relative to their equity market capitalizations: each of them faces negative excess holdings greater than –2%.

There is some irony in these findings. In spite of the great interest that the BRIC countries receive, US residents do not invest in them, at least in a way commensurate with their relative importance in global equity markets. It will be of great interest to see how large my prediction errors ultimately are from the regression analysis of my six risk indicators for these four countries, in particular.

Before I turn to the details of the regression analysis to follow, I do need to offer fair warning (and one that I mentioned earlier) that the benchmarking I do may not be completely right. My literature survey of the home- and foreign-bias phenomenon comments on the limitations of

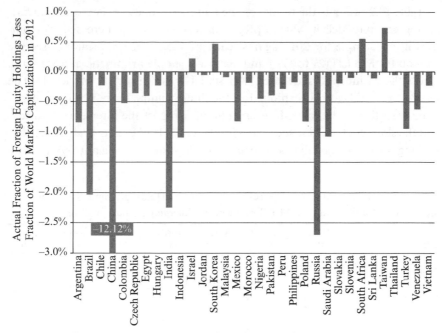

FIGURE 10.1 *Foreign Bias in Emerging Markets of US Residents in 2012 Using Treasury International Capital Data.*

Note: To compute the actual excess holdings, the fraction of total world equity market capitalization for 2011 for each market is subtracted from the fraction of total foreign holdings by US residents, which in turn is aggregated by country and computed as a fraction of the total.

relying on right-sizing these actual holdings against the fraction of the world equity market capitalization to get an over- or underweighting. Many of the shares of the stocks that comprise the respective markets are not free-floating, and therefore not readily available for US residents even if they were so inclined. My counterargument is that the float is a manifestation of more important fundamentals in those countries. In fact, it is quite possibly an important element of the corporate opacity risk indicator I built in Chapter 7. Some critics may argue that holdings should be defined by the real economy and not the equity markets for which the valuations fluctuate so dramatically. I could have recalibrated the actual holdings against the benchmark of the relative size of the country's GDP as a fraction of the world's GDP in 2012. But it is not clear to me that this fits with the mind-set of US or global investors as they size up a target investment market. I should also add that the relative size of the equity markets to the GDP of a country is an important ingredient in the building of my market capacity constraints risk indicator (Chapter 4). So odds are that I will pick this up in my regression analysis for perhaps mechanical reasons.

Table 10.2 presents the results of the regression analysis. These are univariate regression models in which I project the excess holdings across all 57 countries in my sample for 2012 against each of the six risk indicators—see the column for Models (2) to (7)—and against a simple arithmetic average score across the six indicators, denoted "All Six Risk Indicators" in Model (1). The relevant risk indicator is exhibited in the first column. There is a host of relevant statistics in the table. In each column, I report the intercept coefficient and the slope coefficient associated with the variable in each model. What I am looking for is whether the slope coefficient is positive or negative. A positive

TABLE 10.2 Regression Analysis of Excess Foreign Equity Holdings from US Treasury International Capital Database of US Residents in Emerging Markets in 2012

Variable	Model (1)	Model (2)	Model (3)	Model (4)	Model (5)	Model (6)	Model (7)
Intercept	−0.0033	−0.0034	−0.0034	−0.0035	−0.0032	−0.0034	−0.0034
	(−1.14)	(−1.13)	(−1.11)	(−1.13)	(−1.17)	(−1.12)	(−1.18)
All Six Risk Indicators	0.0124 (3.15)***						
Market Capacity Constraints		0.0068 (2.24)***					
Operational Inefficiencies			0.0036 (1.16)				
Foreign Investability Restrictions				0.0047 (1.53)			
Corporate Opacity					0.0109 (3.85)***		
Limits to Legal Protections						0.0057 (1.87)*	
Political Instability							0.0091 (3.15)***
Observations	56	56	56	56	56	56	56
F-statistic	9.9470	5.0170	1.3360	2.3427	14.8451	3.4973	9.9496
p-value	0.0026	0.0292	0.2528	0.1317	0.0003	0.0669	0.0026
Adj. R^2	0.1556	0.0850	0.0241	0.0416	0.2156	0.0608	0.1556

Note: The *excess* foreign equity holdings of the global institutional investors are obtained from raw data of the US Treasury International Capital database (in Table 10.1). I compute aggregate summary statistics. The excess holdings measure subtracts from the fraction of equity holdings invested in each country the relative market capitalization of that country in 2012. All 56 countries, excluding the United States, are included in the cross-country regressions. Standard errors and associated t-statistics (reported below the coefficients in parentheses) are heteroscedasticity consistent and robust. The F-statistic evaluates the joint significance of the explanatory variables with its associated p-value reported below it. R^2 is the adjusted coefficient of determination that accounts for the number of degrees of freedom.

coefficient implies that higher scores on the risk indicator of interest—fewer market capacity constraints, less corporate opacity, stronger limits to legal protections—are associated with greater positive (or less negative) excess foreign holdings. This is what I expect if the indicators are sensible and my intuition is right.

I am also interested in the statistical precision with which I can draw any of those inferences. Below each coefficient is a *t*-statistic (in parentheses) that evaluates how many standard errors from zero that coefficient is. In such tests I would be looking for *t*-statistics that are above +1.64 or below –1.64 to feel reasonably confident. Beside these statistics, I denote their reliability with a superscript "*" if they are reliable at the 90% confidence level, two "**" at the 95% level, and "***" at the 99% level. At the bottom of the table, I report the number of country observations in the regression, the *F*-statistic (and its associated *p*-value), which evaluates the statistical reliability of the regression model. The *p*-value represents the complement of the confidence with which a statistical statement is made: a value of 0.01 implies a confidence of 99% that the regression model is well specified. Lastly, the adjusted R^2 at the bottom captures the explanatory power of the model; it ranges in value from zero (no explanatory power) to one (perfect explanatory power). All else being equal, it would be desirable to have bigger *F*-statistics, lower *p*-values for those *F*-statistics, and larger adjusted R^2.

Model (1), which uses the average of all six indicators as the explanatory variable, sets the stage. It is in the first column of the table. The intercept coefficient is indistinguishable from zero at a value of –0.33% and a *t*-statistic of –1.14. However, the slope coefficient of 0.0124 is positive, as hoped for, and statistically significant at the 99% confidence level (*t*-statistic of 3.15, well above 1.64). The *F*-statistic is large and has a *p*-value below 1%, which means the model is acceptable. The adjusted R^2 is fair at 15.6% explanatory power. I would like it to be higher, but it is not an easy thing to pin down these excess holdings across 57 countries, as my literature review should have conveyed, much less with a single explanatory variable. I will show you where the problems lie in some residual diagnostics later on. How do I interpret the coefficient of 0.0124? Since the risk indicators are standardized to have a unit standard deviation, I can state that a one-unit increase in the average risk indicator—say, from a score for the Philippines to that of South Africa—is associated with a 1.24% higher positive excess holding or a 1.24% lower negative excess holding (depending on the starting point). For the Philippines, for example, which had a negative excess holding of –0.7% in Figure 10.1, an improvement in its overall risk indicator scores of this magnitude could have put it in positive excess holding territory.[16]

Looking across the table at the regression models for each indicator, the respective slope coefficients are always positive, but not always reliably so. Their statistical reliability is closely connected to the overall explanatory power in the adjusted R^2 values. For example, the slope coefficient for market capacity constraints in Model (2) is reliably estimated with a value of 0.0068, but the adjusted R^2 is half the size of that for Model (1). These market capacity constraints matter in explaining foreign equity holdings, but not as much as some of the other indicators. It turns out that for US residents, operational inefficiencies and foreign investability restrictions do not seem to matter at all for their country allocation decisions. The slope coefficients are indistinguishable from zero, and the R^2 values are quite low (under 5%). The limits to legal protections in Model (6) offer some use, but it is in Models (5) and (7) where really important benefits arise. The coefficients for the corporate opacity and political instability risk indicators are large, statistically reliable, and offer good explanatory power overall. A one-unit increase in the corporate opacity score—approximately from China (–1.98) to Hungary (–0.79)—is associated with a 1.09% increase in the excess holdings. Now, China has a huge underweight (–12.12%) with respect to US residents investing abroad, so investing in corporate governance reforms might not make but a small dent.

Before I move on, study the figure at the top of Figure 10.2. (Do not peek ahead at Panel B's figure just yet.) This is a graphical illustration of the explanatory power of the risk indicators. It is a scatterplot of the actual excess holdings for a given emerging market from one of the regression models against its predicted value obtained from the equation of the best-fitting line. In this particular example, I estimate a regression model including all six of the risk indicators individually in a multivariate model. An ideal situation of perfect explanatory power would be if the individual dots line up along a 45° line in the scatter, implying a 1-to-1 relationship. Just by looking at the figure, you can see that this does not happen. I actually allow the figure to display a line through the cloud of dots, and it is clear that this line is not a 45° line. The actual slope of the line is described in the box to the left; it is 0.9702, which is close to 1-to-1, though a little flatter. The R^2 in the box tells us that only 26.48% of the variation in the actual holdings is captured by this best-fitting line. Not bad, but it could be better.

For some of the scattered dots that are furthest away from the line—those that are most likely to be influencing the 73.52% (the complement of 26.48%) that cannot be explained—I indicate the country name. Russia plots below the line, as does India. They have negative excess holdings that are large in magnitude, but they are so large that my six risk indicators cannot meet this challenge well. The same goes for China, which has a huge underweight (–12.12%) that is not even displayed. Colombia, Pakistan, and Venezuela distantly plot above the line, which means that I would have predicted their negative excess holdings to be much more severe than they actually were. My risk indicators and the regression model would have predicted a positive excess holding for Chile, but US investors actually underweighted their Chilean holdings in 2012 by a sizable margin.

Panel A: Treasury International Capital Holdings Data

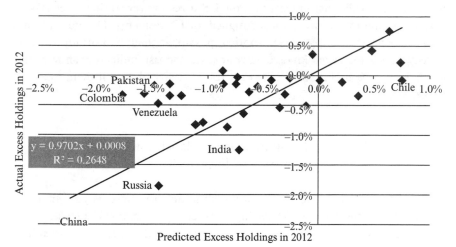

Predicted Excess Holdings in 2012

Panel B: Fact Set Institutional Holdings Data

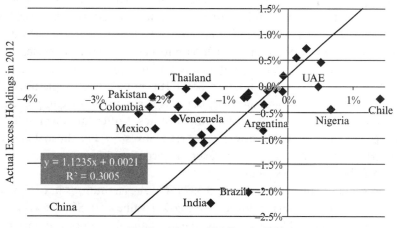

Predicted Excess Holdings in 2012

FIGURE 10.2 *Predicting Excess Foreign Holdings for Emerging Markets in 2012 Using Risk Indicators.*

Note: To compute the actual excess holdings, the fraction of total world equity market capitalization for 2011 for each market is subtracted from the fraction of total foreign holdings by US residents (Panel A) or institutional investors around the world (Panel B), which in turn is aggregated by country and computed as a fraction of the total. The predicted excess equity holdings are generated as fitted values from a multivariate regression model on all six risk indicators. The equation in the respective boxes in the figures shows that the slope coefficient is 0.9702 (1.1235), the intercept coefficient is 0.08% (0.21%), and the overall explanatory power of the risk indicators jointly (denoted by the coefficient of determination, or R^2) is 26.48% (30.05%).

For the most part, these are encouraging first signs of success.[17] The risk indicators are valid instruments for how US investors reveal their preferences. But my risk indicators are not just designed for US residents. The concepts and ideas are universally applicable. Another, possibly equally important question to ask then is for which kinds of investors do the risk indicators show themselves not to be useful at all. The next test is designed to roll them out on a bigger stage.

The Second Test: Explaining Global Institutional Investor Holdings in 2012

To get a truly global perspective on investing activities in emerging markets, I turn next to the FactSet Ownership (formerly Lionshares) database, which is a leading information source for global institutional ownership. Institutions are defined as professional money managers with discretionary control over assets such as mutual funds, pension funds, bank trusts, and insurance companies. As I mentioned earlier in the chapter, in the United States the FactSet/ Lionshares database for equities gathers mandatory quarterly filings with the Securities and Exchange Commission, and outside the United States it collects holdings data from sources such as national regulatory agencies, stock exchange announcements, local and offshore mutual funds, mutual fund directories, company proxies, and annual reports. It is not a complete picture of the global institutional investor universe, but it is easily the most comprehensive one available, especially outside the United States. I offer fair warning that it includes only institutional investors, so no retail investors, like those that would report through the custodians to Treasury International Capital in the United States, will be part of this picture.

I aggregate holdings from among 5,337 different institutions in over 35,000 individual stocks worldwide, for a total market value of US$ 23.6 trillion as of December 2012. Table 10.3 presents the total and foreign-only equity holdings of those global institutional investors by the target country in which they invest. At the very bottom of the table, the total assets across all 115 countries that report to FactSet is the figure I quote above. Note that the 58 countries that are *not* included in my set of 57 total $134 billion. This is not a trivial sum, but the 57 target countries in my sample represent 99.4% of the FactSet universe on a cap-weighted basis.

Looking up from the last row of the table, the reader's eye notes the large total holding for the United States at $18.2 trillion. This number includes all domestic and foreign equity holdings of these US institutions. Now look to the next column to the left. Of that total, more than $1.8 trillion of US investment assets are deployed into overseas markets. This figure compares favorably to the $4.2 trillion reported for all US investors going overseas in Table 10.1. In

TABLE 10.3 Total and Foreign Only Equity Holdings of Global Institutional Investors in Emerging Markets in 2012

Country	Foreign Holdings (US$ millions)	% of Total	Total Holdings (US$ millions)	% of Total
Argentina	8,623	0.14%	8,643	0.04%
Brazil	215,277	3.44%	216,912	0.92%
Chile	19,163	0.31%	19,165	0.08%
China	194,403	3.10%	194,542	0.83%
Colombia	11,434	0.18%	11,434	0.05%
Czech Republic	2,958	0.05%	3,077	0.01%
Egypt	1,854	0.03%	1,885	0.01%
Hungary	2,342	0.04%	2,358	0.01%
India	99,417	1.59%	139,806	0.59%
Indonesia	28,093	0.45%	28,093	0.12%
Israel	45,117	0.72%	45,238	0.19%
Jordan	76	0.00%	76	0.00%
South Korea	119,514	1.91%	119,930	0.51%
Malaysia	21,031	0.34%	22,005	0.09%
Mexico	88,612	1.41%	95,683	0.41%
Morocco	267	0.00%	267	0.00%
Nigeria	1,465	0.02%	1,465	0.01%
Pakistan	1,324	0.02%	1,349	0.01%
Peru	21,876	0.35%	21,876	0.09%
Philippines	12,234	0.20%	12,234	0.05%
Poland	8,884	0.14%	10,189	0.04%
Russia	64,014	1.02%	64,242	0.27%
Saudi Arabia	155	0.00%	404	0.00%
Slovakia	4	0.00%	4	0.00%
Slovenia	163	0.00%	163	0.00%
South Africa	64,813	1.03%	69,555	0.30%
Sri Lanka	391	0.01%	391	0.00%
Taiwan	90,892	1.45%	90,899	0.39%
Thailand	31,282	0.50%	31,326	0.13%
Turkey	23,757	0.38%	24,135	0.10%
UAE	509	0.01%	549	0.00%
Venezuela	2,202	0.04%	2,221	0.01%
Vietnam	2	0.00%	2	0.00%
Australia	102,580	1.64%	111,090	0.47%
Austria	8,809	0.14%	8,833	0.04%
Belgium	35,880	0.57%	38,479	0.16%
Canada	442,957	7.07%	912,970	3.87%
Denmark	43,548	0.70%	45,704	0.19%
Finland	21,806	0.35%	30,311	0.13%
France	229,203	3.66%	267,800	1.14%
Germany	210,979	3.37%	233,118	0.99%
Greece	4,599	0.07%	4,599	0.02%

(*continued*)

TABLE 10.3 Continued

Country	Foreign Holdings (US$ millions)	% of Total	Total Holdings (US$ millions)	% of Total
Hong Kong	143,205	2.29%	163,008	0.69%
Ireland	213,289	3.41%	213,764	0.91%
Italy	52,833	0.84%	54,851	0.23%
Japan	244,535	3.90%	251,900	1.07%
Luxembourg	27,389	0.44%	27,556	0.12%
Netherlands	250,640	4.00%	257,426	1.09%
New Zealand	2,242	0.04%	2,434	0.01%
Norway	21,226	0.34%	31,784	0.13%
Portugal	5,642	0.09%	5,652	0.02%
Singapore	51,528	0.82%	54,543	0.23%
Spain	54,466	0.87%	61,338	0.26%
Sweden	65,093	1.04%	144,675	0.61%
Switzerland	375,207	5.99%	385,644	1.64%
United Kingdom	527,304	8.42%	703,312	2.98%
United States	1,811,665	28.93%	18,192,549	77.16%
All Other Countries (58 countries)	133,943	2.14%	134,176	5.21%
World Total (All 115 countries)	6,262,714		23,577,629	

Source: FactSet Lionshares Database. See http://www.factset.com/websitefiles/PDFs/brochures/ownership.

other words, almost half of the overseas investing by US residents takes place through reporting of equity holdings of US institutions to FactSet. The foreign holdings of these institutions—$1.8 trillion out of $18.2 trillion, or 9.8%— reveals starkly the home bias in the United States. Almost 91% of the assets of these institutions are invested domestically, and the United States is far less than 91% of the world's investment opportunities. Looking up the two columns in this table one can see that many other countries also reveal a home bias, but it is not as dramatic as in the United States. Canada's institutions reporting to FactSet invest abroad $442 billion of their $912 billion in total assets, or almost 48%. To a large extent, this may reflect the reporting biases associated with FactSet's data collection outside the United States. Hopefully, it is not too severe, nor too skewed.

What I am most interested in is the allocation of foreign holdings by target country. These are the data in the first column and the associated fraction it constitutes. This is useful to me because it includes institutional investors distributed around the globe and the investment assets that they allocate beyond their own domicile. I have Japanese pension funds investing in the Czech Republic, South African bank trusts investing in Venezuela, and Canadian insurance companies investing in the United States. I want to know which markets are the strongest magnets for the foreign equity investor's dollar, euro, yuan, or rand regardless of where it comes from. The United States attracts almost 29% of the $6.3 trillion.

This is something I could not have known with the Treasury International Capital (TIC) data involving just US residents. The United Kingdom captures its own healthy 8.4% market share, Canada does well at 7%, Switzerland comes next at $400 billion (6%), and several other countries follow with around $200 billion (about 4%). Among the emerging markets at the top of the table, China draws the most interest at $194 billion (3.1%), followed by South Korea ($119 billion, 2%).

Following the protocol set in the earlier test from this chapter, I cannot just study the raw foreign allocations as a fraction of the total. Rather, I need to calibrate them against a benchmark, and the best candidate is the relative market capitalization of the target country of interest. This time, however, I must include the United States and its $14 trillion market capitalization contribution to the $66 trillion world market pie in 2012. Figure 10.3 reveals the foreign bias, or excess foreign portfolio holdings, among the 33 emerging markets in my analysis using the FactSet holdings data. China is still a large underweight at −8.01%, though it is much lower than among just US residents in the TIC data (−12.12%, as you will recall). This means that institutions outside the United States have a stronger preference (less of a negative preference, perhaps) for

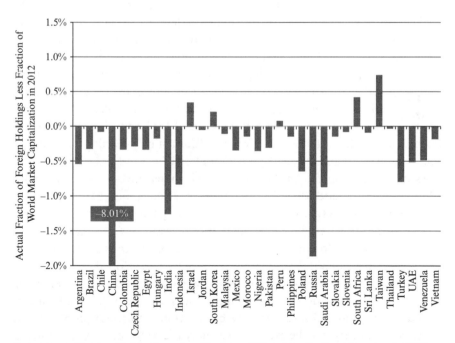

FIGURE 10.3 *Foreign Bias in Emerging Markets of Global Institutional Investors in 2012 Using FactSet Data.*

Note: To compute the actual excess holdings, the fraction of total world equity market capitalization for 2011 for each market is subtracted from the fraction of total foreign holdings by institutional investors around the world, which in turn is aggregated by country and computed as a fraction of the total.

investing in Chinese equities than those in the United States alone. Most of the emerging markets have a negative excess holding, as witnessed in Figure 10.1. Russia's negative excess holding is 1.9%. India, Indonesia, Saudi Arabia, and Turkey are underweighted by about 1%. Not surprisingly, the same four countries among global institutional investors show up with positive excess holdings: Israel, South Korea, South Africa, and Taiwan. Peru has a slight overweight in this figure compared to Figure 10.1.

In Table 10.4, I estimate the very same regression models as I did earlier for the TIC data in Table 10.2. The seven model specifications are the same, as are the reporting metrics and statistics on model inference. Panel A at the top shows that the risk indicators have greater reliability for explaining the excess foreign equity holdings of global institutional investors than for US investors alone. The coefficients for all six risk indicators are positively estimated and statistically significant by conventional criteria. The sizes of the slope coefficients are larger in magnitude, which means that the sensitivity of foreign excess holdings to a one-unit increase in any of the risk indicator scores is greater. Even those associated with operational inefficiencies and foreign investability restrictions are estimated with some precision, though they were not in Table 10.2. Each of the F-statistics is large enough to be able to say that the models are reasonable, and every one of the adjusted R^2s is higher than its counterpart in the earlier test.

If you turn back to Figure 10.2 from my earlier test, you can see the exact same kind of scatterplot of actual and predicted excess holdings for 2012. There is still a cloud of scattered dots around the line in the plot, so they do not line up one-to-one—frankly an unrealistic expectation. China is still a large underweight that even the best-fitting model cannot come close to explaining, and the Latin American outliers above the line—Colombia, Mexico, and Venezuela—are still out of range. But the slope of the best fitting line is 1.1235, which is steeper than that for the Treasury International Capital data experiment. And the overall adjusted R^2 is higher at 30.05%.

As interesting it is for us that global institutional investor foreign equity holdings are even better described by my six risk indicators than that for US residents, it is also useful to do a deeper dive among the global investors themselves. One question I ask is whether institutional investors from emerging markets are as sensitive to concerns about market capacity constraints, limits to legal protections, or political instability as those from developed markets. After all, emerging market institutional investors are well versed in these kinds of problems in their own domestic investing choices. On the other hand, emerging market institutional investors may be so attuned to those problems and constraints that they may be even more acutely averse to them in their foreign investment activities. To get at this question, I split the FactSet Ownership data on global institutional investors by domicile into two groups: those based in developed and emerging markets. I then study separately their foreign equity holdings, and specifically their foreign excess equity holdings.

TABLE 10.4 Regression Analysis of Excess Foreign Equity Holdings of Global Institutional Investors from FactSet Database in Emerging Markets in 2012

Panel A: All Institutional Investors

Variable	Model (1)	Model (2)	Model (3)	Model (4)	Model (5)	Model (6)	Model (7)
Intercept	-0.0004 (-0.15)	-0.0004 (-0.14)	-0.0004 (-0.14)	-0.0004 (-0.14)	-0.0004 (-0.15)	-0.0004 (-0.14)	-0.0004 (-0.15)
All Six Risk Indicators	0.0124 (3.72)***						
Market Capacity Constraints		0.0069 (2.65)***					
Operational Inefficiencies			0.0047 (1.73)*				
Foreign Investability Restrictions				0.0066 (2.49)***			
Corporate Opacity					0.0098 (4.01)***		
Limits to Legal Protections						0.0055 (2.04)***	
Political Instability							0.0081 (3.15)***
Observations	57	57	57	57	57	57	57
F-statistic	13.8580	7.0048	3.0016	6.2160	16.1018	4.1537	9.9096
p-value	0.0005	0.0106	0.0888	0.0157	0.0002	0.0464	0.0027
Adj. R²	0.2013	0.1130	0.0518	0.1015	0.2265	0.0702	0.1527

(continued)

TABLE 10.4 Continued

	Panel B: Emerging Market Institutional Investors Only						
Variable	Model (1)	Model (2)	Model (3)	Model (4)	Model (5)	Model (6)	Model (7)
Intercept	-0.0003 (-0.04)	-0.0003 (-0.04)	-0.0003 (-0.04)	-0.0003 (-0.04)	-0.0003 (-0.04)	-0.0003 (-0.04)	-0.0003 (-0.04)
All Six Risk Indicators	0.0131 (1.31)						
Market Capacity Constraints		0.0078 (1.04)					
Operational Inefficiencies			0.0069 (0.91)				
Foreign Investability Restrictions				0.0042 (0.55)			
Corporate Opacity					0.0102 (1.36)		
Limits to Legal Protections						0.0090 (1.21)	
Political Instability							0.0058 (0.77)
Observations	57	57	57	57	57	57	57
F-statistic	1.7055	1.0791	0.8291	0.3059	1.8461	1.4540	0.5882
p-value	0.1970	0.3035	0.3665	0.5825	0.1798	0.2330	0.4464
Adj. R²	0.0301	0.0192	0.0149	0.0055	0.0325	0.0258	0.0106

Note: The *excess* foreign equity holdings of the global institutional investors are obtained from the FactSet Lionshares database (in Table 10.2) and subtracts from the fraction of equity holdings invested in each country the relative market capitalization of that country in 2012. All 57 countries are included in the cross-country regressions. Institutional investors from 61 countries are included in Panel A; those domiciled in 30 emerging markets only are included in Panel B. The emerging market investors include 23 of the 33 in our sample, plus Bolivia, Cyprus, Estonia, Croatia, Lebanon, Latvia, and Romania. Standard errors and associated *t*-statistics (reported below the coefficients in parentheses) are heteroscedasticity consistent and robust. The *F*-statistic evaluates the joint significance of the explanatory variables with its associated *p*-value reported below it. R² is the adjusted coefficient of determination that accounts for the number of degrees of freedom.

Figure 10.4 juxtaposes those foreign biases on a country-by-country basis for emerging market investors (always the left bar for a given country) and for developed market investors (right bar). China is, as always, a huge underweight, but it is a higher one (–8.54%) among emerging market investors than developed ones (–8.01%). The most striking contrasts between the two arise for Brazil, for which emerging market institutional investors have a great appetite (+3.39% overweight) compared to developed investors (–0.33% underweight). A similar rank ordering arises for Chile, Hungary, Mexico, Poland, and Russia, each of which is overweighted among emerging investors and underweighted by developed market investors. Turkey is a less severe negative excess holding among emerging market investors. India is clearly a preferred target market for developed market institutional investors compared to emerging ones, for which there is a large negative excess holding of –2.4%. Indonesia, Israel, South Korea, South Africa, and Taiwan are like India. I must remind readers that the *absolute* magnitudes of the investment dollars flowing overseas from emerging market institutional investors are still rather small ($20.6 billion) compared to

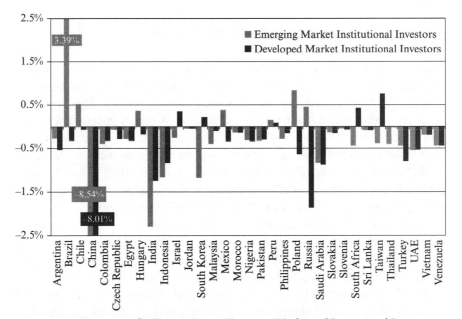

FIGURE 10.4 *Comparing the Foreign Bias in Emerging Markets of Institutional Investors Domiciled in Emerging versus Developed Market in 2012 Using FactSet Data.*

Note: To compute the actual excess holdings, the fraction of total world equity market capitalization for 2011 for each market is subtracted from the fraction of total foreign holdings by institutional investors around the world, which in turn is aggregated by country and computed as a fraction of the total. Institutional investors from 61 countries are divided into two groups; those domiciled only in developed markets and those domiciled in 30 emerging markets only. The emerging market investor set includes 23 of the 33 in our sample, plus Bolivia, Cyprus, Estonia, Croatia, Lebanon, Latvia, and Romania.

194

those of developed markets ($6.2 trillion). But remember it is about under-standing better the choices being made.

With these data in hand, I now turn attention back to Table 10.4 and the bottom panel devoted to a regression analysis of the foreign excess holdings for the emerging market institutional investors. I do not report it, but the overall variation in these excess holdings is much larger than for the whole sample, so I know I have a big challenge on my hands with these simple regression models and the six indicators. But the results for the six indicators are even more reveal-ing that I would have expected.

In not one of the seven models for emerging-market institutional investors do the slope coefficients (all positive in value) attain any statistical precision. The F-statistics are small and can easily lead us to reject that these models are reliable, and the adjusted R^2 point out the low explanatory power from the risk indicators. These findings clearly indicate that emerging market institutional investors are influenced less by the concerns about market capacity constraints, limits to legal protections, and foreign investability restrictions. I cannot report here what may explain how they over- and underweight the markets in which they do invest (or not), but it is not these risk indicators.

Some Validation for the Risk Indicators

These risk indicators have some useful explanatory power for the foreign port-folio holdings of investors in 2012. That is the good news. Their explanatory power is far from perfect. So there is some bad news as well. It is natural to wonder whether there are aspects of the building of the indicators that I might now have chosen differently with this validation experiment available in hind-sight. That is, after all, how science evolves: a never-ending feedback loop.

But instead of revising and rebuilding the risk indicators to reinforce the feedback loop, I turn to another experiment that unexpectedly arose for me during the writing of this book. It is what I refer to as the emerging mar-ket swoon of 2013. With the May 2013 announcement of the likely start to tapering of monthly asset purchase programs of the US Federal Reserve by Chairman Ben Bernanke, a large withdrawal of almost $73 billion in emerging market stocks and bonds took place, a significant market dislocation.[18] The capital flows receded with the increased uncertainty about those markets and the prospect of renewed higher investment yields in the United States and other developed markets. Why this is interesting as a kind of out-of-sample experi-ment is that some emerging markets were more severely impacted by Chairman Bernanke's announcement than others.

An interesting question, which I leave to the next chapter, is whether the differential intensity of the capital flow exit across emerging markets in 2013 is related to the risk indicators that I have built. The answer is a reassuring yes.

{ 11 }

Making Sense of the Emerging
Market Swoon of 2013

The year 2013 was a tough one for emerging markets. Of course, they are always supposed to be more volatile markets than what investors experience in developed markets, but that year was unusual. The Morgan Stanley Capital International (MSCI) all-capital World Index was up 22.9% in US dollar-denominated terms, while the MSCI Emerging Market index in US dollar-denominated returns was down 7.2%. These markets moved in distinctly different directions. The MSCI BRIC index, including Brazil, China, India, and Russia, was down –9.5% and Latin America was hit even harder at –20.4%. Most emerging market currencies tumbled relative to the US dollar, especially if they had the word "peso" in their currency names.[1] The Argentine peso depreciated almost 24%, the Indonesian rupiah 19%, and the South African rand 18%, followed closely by the Chilean, Colombian, and Philippine pesos.

What happened? According to the Bank for International Settlements, net bond and stock portfolio flows to emerging markets receded and withdrew over the course of the year by almost $29 billion, following almost three years of positive net inflows totaling almost $122 billion. More than $38 billion left emerging markets in June alone.[2] The pace of withdrawals has not eased well into 2014 (at least to the time of this writing), but portfolio flows are still negative.[3] What *specifically* happened in the spring of 2013? Officials of the Federal Reserve System first began to deliberate on the possibility of the US central bank tapering its securities purchase program, known to most as part of an unconventional policy practice called "quantitative easing." For several years post-crisis, the Fed had been regularly purchasing long-term securities at a rate of $85 billion per month to stimulate the economy. Many Fed watchers pointed to Chairman Ben Bernanke's testimony before Congress on May 22, 2013 as the catalyst point when he raised the possibility of a tapering, or an easing of the stimulus program, by the end of the year. Indeed, on December 18, the Federal Reserve Open Market Committee announced that it would begin to reduce its bond-buying program by $10 billion per month starting in January 2014, so the early hints turned out to be credible.[4]

The "taper talk" had a notable adverse impact on economic and financial conditions in emerging markets. The impact was sharp, and in the view of many commentators, surprisingly large.[5] Another intriguing aspect of the taper talk and its fallout in emerging markets was the uneven nature of it *across* different emerging markets. And the complaints from policymakers in emerging markets about the Fed's intentions were robust. Of note were the comments from—among others—China's deputy finance minister Zhu Guangyao, who stated: "We hope that the issuing country of the largest reserve currency in the world should be mindful of the spillover effect of its macroeconomic policies."[6] US government officials challenged these claims, arguing that the Fed's pro-growth policy was ultimately good for the global economy, including emerging markets.[7]

Nevertheless, the so-called taper tantrums continued.[8] Alexandre Tombini, governor of the central bank of Brazil, asserted that "a lack of a coordinated exit from exceptionally loose monetary policies was done at the expense of emerging markets," and Raghu Rajan, newly appointed governor of the Reserve Bank of India, argued that "international monetary cooperation has broken down" and that "industrial countries have to play a part in restoring that [cooperation], and they can't at this point wash their hands off and say, we'll do what we need to and you do the adjustment."[9] Some economic leaders, like Mexico's Finance Minister Luis Videgaray, recognized that some markets, like his with "stronger fundamentals," would likely fare better with the unwinding of the Treasury bond-buying program.[10] Indeed, scholars have written about the weak fundamentals underlying many of these markets, as well as the anemic pace of their capital market and economic reforms as the root causes of the problems.[11]

An Out-of-Sample Experiment?

These three features of the tapering events of 2013—the surprise, the scope of the fallout, and the reaction in its aftermath—make the year in emerging markets a useful out-of-sample experiment in which to assess the validity of my emerging market risk indicators. It is the goal of this chapter. I specifically ask whether these indicators can explain which of the emerging markets global investors exited in larger numbers in 2013. It is the parallel exercise to that in Chapter 10 in which I ask whether these indicators can explain into which emerging markets accumulated their investment flows to the stock of holdings they had as of 2012. Except this experiment predicts flows in the opposite direction.

Data on purchases and sales of foreign debt and equity securities by US residents between January and November 2013 are drawn from the US Treasury's

Treasury International Capital (TIC) database. I confirm that there is significant cross-country variation in the experiences among 26 of the 33 emerging markets in my sample (for which TIC has reliable data). And even though these risk indicators were built using data from 2012 without any look-ahead biases (honest!), they have reasonable explanatory power for the out-of-sample 2013 experiences.

There are of course many possible determinants of investor choices, including observable macroeconomic fundamentals like the budget deficits, public debt burdens, foreign exchange reserves, and GDP growth rates, none of which are featured among my set of indicators. So I could easily miss explaining most of the cross-country variation among emerging markets in their reactions to the taper. However, it is also possible that what matters more to investors were the dimensions of risk in the face of uncertainty, embedded in such measures as the relative size of the markets, the operational inefficiencies in their trading systems, the restrictiveness of access for foreign investors, the corporate governance problems, and limits to legal protections or political instability. I will show you that the last three indicators—what I have often called the *softer* constraints for global investors—are perhaps surprisingly more important than the first three.

I need to duly acknowledge that mine is not the first study of the 2013 experiment. There are at least two other studies that have gone before me, though my effort differs substantially in approach and scope from theirs. The first is by Robin Koepke of the Institute for International Finance.[12] The Koepke report presents evidence that the Fed's impact on portfolio inflows may be more complex than at first blush. Koekpe estimates an econometric model to quantify the impact of the shifts in market expectations about future monetary policy using federal funds futures contracts as a proxy for expectations. A one percentage point shift in expectations for the federal funds rate three years forward is associated with a $12 billion increase in fund outflows from emerging markets. The study also shows that the shift toward *tighter* monetary policy exerts a greater impact on EM portfolio *outflows* than an equivalent shift toward *easier* monetary policy for EM *inflows*. An asymmetric effect, Koepke calls it.

The second study is by Barry Eichengreen of Berkeley and Poonam Gupta of the World Bank. It was made publicly available on December 21, 2013.[13] Their objects of forecast were as much the depreciation in emerging market currencies as the stock index returns, and the changes in foreign currency reserves as the increases in sovereign bond yields and sovereign credit default swap spreads. Their study focuses on asset pricing and specifically does not examine fund flows into and out of emerging markets like the Koepke study above and my exercise below. The remarkable finding (their Tables 6, 7, and 8) is that the only reliable predictor in the changes in these price-based outcomes is the degree of openness of the capital markets. The more open is the emerging market (gross assets and liabilities as a fraction of GDP, per the data of Philip

Lane and Gian Milesi-Feretti featured in Chapter 6), the larger the depreciation of the emerging market currency. This means that many other important
measures—such as the institutional quality of the market, the intensity of its
capital controls, or the country's scores on the World Bank's World Governance
Indicators (featured in Chapter 9)—had no explanatory power whatsoever. The
country's external balance, its fiscal deficit position, and general public debt
burden were statistically insignificant in every one of their tests.

These two studies did not have my emerging market risk indicators at their
disposal. Based on the Eichengreen and Gupta findings, my priors were low
that these indicators would explain the flows in 2013.

Which Emerging Markets Did US Residents Exit in 2013?

My starting point is the data on net purchases by US residents of foreign debt
and equity during each month of 2013. The data come from the US Treasury's
Treasury International Capital (TIC) database. As of the writing of the book,
the data was available through November of 2013. I need to mention for completeness that TIC data is not available for eight of the emerging market countries in the sample of 33: Jordan, Saudi Arabia, Nigeria, the UAE Slovenia,
Slovakia, Sri Lanka, and Vietnam. However, I do have data on all of the developed countries in my sample, and I use them in the regression analysis that
follows.

Table 11.1 presents summary statistics on the data. For each country and
each month of 2013, I obtain net inflows from a country by subtracting the
gross purchases by foreigners from US residents from the gross sales by foreigners to US residents of *foreign* bond and stock securities. I cumulate across
those months and report it for the 25 countries available. A second column
does the same for only equity purchases and sales. Beside each column, I compute the fraction of the net inflows (or negative outflows) across the 25 countries of the total outstanding holdings by US residents as of the end of 2012.
These holdings data were featured in Table 10.1 in the previous chapter. The
question is whether US investors demobilized out of a country in a big way, as
judged relative to the position that they had accumulated to that point.

China experienced the largest cumulative net sales by US residents in 2013 at
$17.7 billion. This sell-down represented about 15% of their total 2012 end-of-
year holdings. The relative importance of the US investor in Chinese securities markets is debatable, of course, but based on this statistic, it may not be
surprising that Deputy Finance Minister Zhu Guangyao stepped up to express
his concerns in the G20 St. Petersburg Summit. It turns out that China did
not experience the largest withdrawal by US residents on a percentage basis.
Argentina, Pakistan, the Czech Republic, and especially Venezuela experienced
net outflows at least as great as 15% of outstanding holdings. The absolute

TABLE 11.1 Net Purchases of Foreign Debt and Equity Securities by US Residents in 2013

Country	Net Flows Foreign Debt & Equity January to November (US$ millions)	As a Percentage of 2012 Total Foreign Holdings[1]	Net Flows Foreign Equity Only January to November (US$ millions)	As a Percentage of 2012 Foreign Equity Holdings[2]
Argentina	−1,094	−15.39%	−924	−0.59%
Brazil	7,232	3.35%	4,904	13.43%
Chile	−2,467	−8.84%	735	2.86%
China	−17,675	−14.68%	−4,279	−36.85%
Colombia	922	4.61%	204	0.44%
Czech Republic	−661	−14.95%	−	−0.89%
Egypt	219	4.70%	8	−0.28%
Hungary	−304	−2.32%	−	−0.27%
India	6,403	8.12%	5,557	24.69%
Indonesia	818	1.82%	638	0.66%
Israel	−1,796	−3.18%	254	−2.27%
South Korea	−6,266	−3.59%	2,800	2.10%
Malaysia	1,691	3.99%	−70	−2.96%
Mexico	28,938	18.42%	123	−7.00%
Morocco	−	−7.61%	−	−0.09%
Pakistan	−235	−17.76%	−	−0.33%
Peru	2,127	19.64%	1,238	6.85%
Philippines	76	0.34%	623	2.16%
Poland	−2,515	−7.47%	369	1.12%
Russia	1,267	1.90%	−	−5.88%
South Africa	1,934	2.25%	687	−3.17%
Taiwan	−503	−0.57%	2,847	7.76%
Thailand	1,927	5.25%	1,186	3.54%
Turkey	−1,345	−2.68%	993	2.68%
Venezuela	3,823	−28.10%	−474	−2.76%

Note: Total Debt and Equity Holdings were obtained from US Treasury website (www.treas.gov/tic). These were presented in Table 10.1 in Chapter 10. From the original data, I construct aggregate summary statistics. I further compute the fraction of total positive and negative net flows across the 26 countries for the months from January to November 2013 for a given country and subtract its fraction of total foreign debt and equity holdings as of the end of 2012.

sizes of these outflows are smaller, ranging from $3.8 billion in Venezuela to $235 million in Pakistan.

Turning to the right side of the table, one's eye refocuses on China again for the equity-only outflows. China's equity withdrawal of $4.2 billion was easily the largest relative to the outstanding foreign equity holdings by US residents (−36% of their total holdings). None of those four other countries that experienced withdrawals were as large. On a percentage basis, equity outflows were largest for Mexico (−$70 million) and Russia (−$66 million).

Which countries were the winners? I do not show you the developed market net flows in the table, but it is clear that they were the big winners of US resident investor dollars with the emerging market fallout. Among the emerging

market set, however, the countries that *attracted* significant debt and equity
flows were Brazil ($7.2 billion, of which $4.9 billion were equity alone); India
($6.4 billion, of which $5.6 billion in equity); and Mexico, at a remarkable
$28.9 billion. Mexico's inflows are almost all in debt securities.

The Koepke study I cited above from the Institute of International Finance
emphasizes that the emerging market swoon of 2013 is more complex than
at first blush. Indeed, Figure 11.1 points us to this conclusion as well. For a
select set of interesting markets, I display the cumulative monthly net debt and
equity flows. The left-hand side scale changes for each country according to
how important they are for US investors overall, but it is the timing of the flows
that is instructive to study.

In Argentina, the net outflows began in February well before the early taper
talk began in May with Chairman Bernanke's testimony. In China, which had
the largest cumulative outflows, the positions began to shift in April, though
they clearly accelerated between June and August after the onset of the taper
talks. Undoubtedly, fears of slowing economic growth, rising property-sector
valuations, and the expansion of shadow-bank lending in China had been
weighing on global investors' minds beyond just the taper talk.[14] South Korea
looks like the case study I would expect based on the event of the taper talk
fallout. Its cumulative net flows were shifting between small positive and negative amounts in each month except June, in which the large $4.5 billion outflow
resulted. Mexico's flows were positive in each month of the year, but really
increased during the September to November period—well outside the immediate window of the concerns over the taper earlier in the year.

Do the Emerging Market Risk Indicators Explain the
Outflows in 2013?

Table 11.2 closes out the analysis in this chapter. The table reports univariate
regression tests of the six risk indicators as explanatory variables for the net
equity flows in 2013. The dependent variable is the normalized cumulative net
equity flows in 2013 by country as a fraction of total equity flows across the 48
countries. From this fraction, I subtract the fraction of total equity holdings
this country constitutes as a fraction of all $5.3 trillion in foreign equity hold-
ings by US residents in 2012. This latter adjustment captures whether the size of
the US investor exit was proportional or not to the relative importance of that
market in terms of its overall world market capitalization. Remember that eight
emerging markets drop out since the TIC data is unavailable, and the United
States is lost as a developed market as it is their investors on which I focus. The
table's format is exactly what I showed in the equivalent tests of Chapter 11. I
report the intercept coefficient, the slope coefficient for each of the six indicators, and the overall average indicator separately by model, and I offer a series

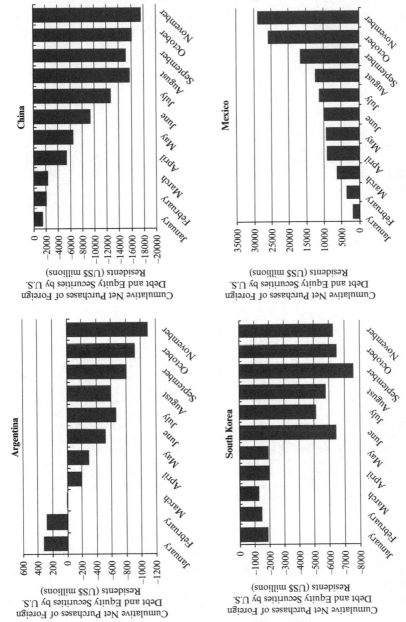

FIGURE 11.1 *Monthly Net Purchases of Foreign Debt and Equity Securities by US Residents in 2013. (Source: Treasury International Capital, www.treas.gov/tic.)*

Note: Total Debt and Equity Holdings were obtained from US Treasury website. I compute monthly the total net equity and debt flows from US residents to a country from January to November 2013. All data are obtained from US Treasury website (www.treas.gov/tic). From the original data, I construct aggregate summary statistics.

TABLE 11.2 Regression Analysis of Cumulative Net Equity Flows in 2013 of US Residents in Emerging Markets

Variable	Model (1)	Model (2)	Model (3)	Model (4)	Model (5)	Model (6)	Model (7)
Intercept	−0.2521 (−1.27)	−0.2190 (−1.05)	−0.2717 (−1.36)	−0.1972 (−0.92)	−0.2038 (−0.98)	−0.2259 (−1.22)	−0.2330 (−1.15)
All Six Risk Indicators	0.7715 (2.87)***						
Market Capacity Constraints		0.3135 (1.52)					
Operational Inefficiencies			0.5982 (2.73)***				
Foreign Investability Restrictions				0.0988 (0.49)			
Corporate Opacity					0.3472 (1.73)*		
Limits to Legal Protections						0.7225 (3.89)***	
Political Instability							0.4757 (2.34)***
Observations	48	48	48	48	48	48	48
F-statistic	8.2169	2.3019	7.4331	0.2371	2.9964	15.1131	5.4816
p-value	0.0062	0.1361	0.0090	0.6286	0.0902	0.0003	0.0236
Adj. R^2	0.1516	0.0477	0.1391	0.0051	0.0612	0.2473	0.1065

Note: The dependent variable in this regression is the total net equity flows from US residents to a country from January to November 2013 as a fraction of total equity holdings of US residents as of the end of 2012. All data are obtained from US Treasury website (www.treas.gov/tic). From the original data, I construct aggregate summary statistics. All emerging and developed countries (excluding the United States) for which the Treasury compiles holdings and flow data are included in the cross-country regressions. Jordan, Saudi Arabia, Nigeria, UAE Slovenia, Slovakia, Sri Lanka, and Vietnam are excluded. Standard errors and associated t-statistics (reported below the coefficients in parentheses) are heteroscedasticity consistent and robust. The F-statistic evaluates the joint significance of the explanatory variables with its associated p-value reported below it. R^2 is the adjusted coefficient of determination that accounts for the number of degrees of freedom.

of inference statistics like the coefficient t-statistics, the F-statistic for the overall reliability of the regression model, and the adjusted R^2 of the risk indicators overall explanatory power.

Model (1) confirms that the simple average of the six component risk indicators has reasonable explanatory power for the cumulative net equity flows. The intercept coefficient is insignificant (t-statistic of −1.27 is within the range of −1.64 to +1.64, or essentially zero), but that of the slope coefficient is 0.7715 with its t-statistic of 2.87. My interpretation of this coefficient is that a one-unit increase in the risk score—from, say, Greece at –0.51 to Germany at 0.52—is associated with a 0.56% increase in net inflows as a fraction of outstanding holdings.[15] The positive slope coefficient is of course further reinforced by higher net outflows for countries with relatively poorer risk scores, as I hypothesized. This average result is equivalent to the differences in the actual experiences of Russia, which saw a decline of 0.12% of its outstanding equity holdings in 2013, and Taiwan, which saw a 0.96% increase in the same. Russia and Taiwan, in fact, have about a one-unit difference in their overall risk indicator score.

I should point out that the F-statistic is large enough to be able to reject the hypothesis that the model is useless. The overall explanatory power is not high, however. The R^2 of 15.2% implies that about 85% of the cross-country variation in the net flow experience has nothing to do with my risk indicators. (Though I cannot compare my success rate with that of Eichengreen and Gupta, since they look at completely different metrics of the emerging market experience, I do have to concede that my overall explanatory power is a step down from theirs, which ranges from 26% to 32% for exchange rate depreciations and stock market returns.[16]) Maybe none of this low explanatory power is a surprise since my risk indicators only focus on the downside, not the potential upside that undoubtedly pervades the mind-set of global investors targeting these emerging markets.

Studying the different regression models for each of the six indicators shows us that they are not uniformly important in capturing how investors changed their positions in 2013. The slope coefficients are usually positive, which again is a good sign for the risk indicators, but they are larger and more precise for some risk indicators over others. Interestingly, by comparison with one of Eichengreen and Gupta's main conclusions, the size of the markets in my market capacity constraints factor does not matter. The slope coefficient is small—statistically insignificant—and the adjusted R^2 is only 5%. Recall how Eichengreen and Gupta found that the size of the markets was positively linked to the size of the market decline and currency depreciation. I venture a similar inference for Model (4) for my foreign investability risk indicator. How open the country is and how difficult it is for foreign investors to access those markets (currency convertibility restrictions, withholding taxes on capital gains and dividend income, ownership limits) does not matter for what happened in 2013.

The most dramatic positive findings uncovered are for operational inefficiencies in Model (2), limits to legal protections in Model (6), and political instability in Model (7). The slope coefficient for the corporate opacity measure in Model (5) is statistically significant at a low level of confidence and the explanatory power is low. For these other three indicators, the adjusted R^2 range from 11% for political instability to as high as 25% for legal protections. Consider the economic effects of the relationship: a one-unit increase in the limits to legal protections—from, say, Hungary to India—is associated with a

0.72% increase in net equity flows as a fraction of total holdings. In fact, the increase for India was as high as 7.3% compared to outflows of –0.12% for Hungary, so my measures would have severely understated the experiences of these two countries (though I would have forecast the right ranking).

These findings for operational inefficiencies, legal protections, and political instability are robust, and likely drive the explanatory power of the overall risk indicator.

Learning from the Taper Talk of 2013

Exploring the effects of the Fed's tapering talk in the summer of 2013 yields a few surprising conclusions. First, the experiences of emerging markets were very different across the set of countries. US resident outflows from some emerging markets were large and impactful, and those for others were neutral and benign. Second, the risk indicator measures can explain a healthy fraction of the reactions of US investors to the unexpected policy shift that took place in 2013. But, third, the risk indicators are not uniformly useful in explaining those reactions. What US investors appear to have prioritized in their cross-country reallocations were fundamentals that related to the operational inefficiencies of those markets, corporate opacity, the limits to legal protections, and political instability.

I offer it up as a quasi-out-of-sample experiment with lots of warnings. It is not pure, as there were undoubtedly lots of hints about the US Federal Reserve's impending reduction in its bond-buying program. Partial anticipation of the taper was undoubtedly possible, which means that much of the investor reactions would have preceded the window of analysis I employ for 2013. The findings also make me wonder about whether the decision-making of US investors is representative of what one saw among all global investors. It is clear from the TIC data from the US Treasury that US investors were not the leaders among those investors that really flocked to the exits in emerging markets. Others from around the world must have been part of the $71 billion exit that some analysts have reported for this period. Finally, I claim that mine is an out-of-sample forecast experiment—and this may be a bit too much to claim. The indicators were designed and built to work in previous years, and indeed none of the data used information from after 2012, but I may have been influenced by the events of the day in 2013 during the writing of this book that may have affected my choice of inputs into my risk indicators.

An out-of-sample forecast worth its weight would have to be for the experiences of 2014, 2015, and beyond, which will follow the completion of this book. If my analysis has a message, it would be to encourage my readers to pay close attention to the root causes of the anxieties of foreign investors in emerging markets, which are the fundamentals about market size and structure, the rules limiting foreign investor participation, and the legal, regulatory, and political environment. A corollary to that message is that simple labels such as "emerging" and "developed" really ought to be de-emphasized. While convenient, the differences among countries in terms of the actual risks they pose to investors are multifaceted and quite fluid. Think about which risk metrics to focus on when you size up these markets.

PART IV

The Emerging Markets Enigma Cracked?

{ 12 }

Final Remarks and a Few Cautions

Truthfully, I am not confident that this book has cracked the emerging markets enigma. But I believe I have met my commitment of delivering a rigorous, comprehensive, and practical framework with which to assess the risks associated with investing in emerging markets. That is what I promised in the first chapter. The rigor comes from the foundation of sound academic research by a large number of scholars of foreign direct and portfolio investment flows to and from emerging markets over the past two decades. My approach is comprehensive in that it incorporates an empirically coherent framework involving multiple dimensions of the potential risks that a prospective corporation or investor faces when walking into those markets. At its core, these risks reflect the uneven quality or fragility of the various institutions built to assure the integrity of the functioning of a country's capital markets. The practicality arises from the fact that I distill these various dimensions of risk into an internally consistent scoring system that ranks emerging markets by each dimension of risk, and overall across all dimensions. Throughout the book I have tried to bring this risk indicator framework to life, featuring recent case studies of corporations and investors that have done deals in the emerging markets.

The philosophical underpinning has also been consistent. What fundamentally characterizes countries as emerging markets are not the *realized* economic growth rates, but rather the even higher rates of *potential* economic growth that remain unrealized by underdeveloped capital markets that are needed to fuel them. Emerging markets are underfunded growth opportunities with problems. The problems arise from the fragility of the institutions that support the markets, I assert. The market's capacity may be inadequate relative to the overall economic needs. Binding capacity constraints locally necessitate the engagement of multinational corporations and foreign investors to help fund the shortfalls that impede growth at home. But the capital that might flow from these corporations and investors may in turn be stunted by operational inefficiencies, such as of the trading systems, the clearing and settlement facilities, and the high costs of transacting in that market. Foreign accessibility restrictions may impede the free flow of capital due to unusually tough owner-ship limits, burdensome withholding taxes, and extra securities taxes and fees for foreign participants. Poor governance and transparency rules, weak legal protections for dispute resolution, and overall political instability can also deter foreign corporations and investors. These are the six risk indicators that comprise my framework.

Empirically, I use a tried-and-tested methodology in principal component analysis (PCA) to build scaled, standardized indices from dozens of individual economic, political, or institutional indices and data. Why do I choose these component data to distill down using into each of the indicators? Existing academic research has shown reliably that they have consequences for actual outcomes, like valuations or investment choices, in emerging markets. A nice feature of PCA is that the statistical technique is built to assign weights to the component data. It defines an objective function to choose linear combinations of component scores to maximize the explanatory power of the data across variables and countries. In other words, I do not arbitrarily assign the weights based on my own subjective judgments, but rather let the data tell us what they are. Sure, I use some discretion in choosing which component variables enter the analysis, but apply little once they are selected.

How well do the risk indicators work? Not too badly, in fact. And I would add that some work distinctly better than others, which is another intriguing finding of the book. I take my risk indicators built from data up through 2012 to see how well they can actually explain how global investors have chosen to invest or not invest across the emerging markets. The main validation experi-ment applies them to the portfolio holdings of US investors as of the end of 2012 obtained from the Treasury International Capital (TIC) survey. It is a fairly accurate depiction of the $7.9 trillion in foreign portfolio holdings of US residents distributed across the world. I control for the relative market capi-talization of each market to assess the over- and underweighting by US resi-dents by target country. Using a completely different ownership database from FactSet on global institutional assets of over $19 trillion across 5,000 institu-tions in over 35,000 publicly traded equities worldwide, I conduct a second similar exercise.

The regression analysis in this validation exercise shows that my risk indica-tors fare reasonably well. They can explain up to as much as 25% of the cross-country variation in these holdings in both datasets. Further, the risk indicators for corporate opacity, for limits to legal protections, and for political instability really drive their success. Their explanatory power is much greater than the market capacity constraints or the foreign accessibility restrictions, which many market-watchers naturally focus on first when they think of emerging markets.

I conduct one more bonus experiment. The year 2013 was a turbulent one in emerging markets. The announcement by the US Federal Reserve in May that it would scale back or taper its quantitative easing program in 2014 appears to have inspired a large shift in portfolio flows into and out of emerging markets. What I showed is that global investors exited some emerging markets with much greater intensity than others, an unexpected phenomenon that allowed a quasi-out-of-sample experiment of my risk indicators. It turns out that they offered some useful predictive power for why investors chose to exit some countries, like Argentina, China, the Czech Republic, South Korea, Turkey, and Venezuela, and why they chose to double-down and invest more in other countries like Malaysia, Mexico, South Africa, and Thailand. Once again, my risk indicators on operational inefficiencies, corporate opacity, limits to legal protections, and political instability showed themselves to be the most successful.

A Few Cautions

I have scattered throughout this book my cautions and warnings about the potential weaknesses of the approach I take. I have already mentioned in this concluding chapter one of them. I have a discretionary role in deciding which component data are drawn from original sources or from existing academic research studies to enter the statistical analysis. I offer my arguments for those choices, but as reader you have the right to judge their integrity and validity. I have also disclosed the potential weakness of the PCA procedure that I use to reduce these various sources of data into a single index. I hide behind the cloak of objectivity in PCA and declare that I have no subjective role in determining the weights that these component data get in the indices that result. But it may be a bit of false objectivity. PCA defines a goal to maximize the variability of the component scores that may not be correct or even sensible. I give you my logic for preferring it: greater variability of the component scores will give my risk indicators a better chance to explain foreign portfolio holdings or flows to those countries. But greater variability could just as easily imply greater noise.

There are five additional warnings that need to be issued to be fair to you. The first one is about the passage of time. It is natural to wonder how these risk indicators change over time. What I have explained is that some of these indicators are more accommodating than others. Why is that? The answer stems from the fact that the input metrics that enter into the data reduction are regularly updated at their respective sources. Consider, for example, the World Bank's World Governance Indicators for the Political Instability indicator that are updated annually by the Macroeconomics and Growth teams in their Development Research Group. Some are updated only irregularly, such as the World Bank's Global Payment Systems survey. It is an understandable problem, but it leaves us all wanting more.

The real holdup on the timeliness of some of my scores is the data that I extract from published research papers. Some variables from published research papers do embed time series in their output variables of interest, such as my own with Kuan-Hui Lee and Mathijs van Dijk in our 2012 study on market liquidity and turnover. But with the passage of time, these results become naturally dated. Most of these studies are static in which their cross-country analysis takes place as a snapshot. One solution is to disregard this valuable research as being necessarily dated, but that seems to me to be the wrong answer. Truthfully I have no obvious solution to this problem, except to stand on the soapbox and call for more support for the kind of research these scholars lead. The cost of doing business for many of these researchers is so high that only the wealthiest schools and departments with large research budgets can afford to subscribe to the expensive databases that give us the answers those in industry crave. I plan to continuously update my risk indicator scores by taking into account the newest research on market capacity constraints, liquidity and trading, corporate governance, and legal protections, slow moving as it may be.

A second warning is also about timeliness. The best result I have ever suggested is an annual update of the risk indicator scores. This choice reflects a trade-off in which I judge that the annual frequency is the modal choice among all the data I harvest for the indicators. I am sure my colleagues in industry would very much like a higher-frequency alert when there is a major political or macroeconomic development, a substantial regulatory reform, or new legislation that affects foreign investor participation. There is nothing magical about the idea that these scores would be annually updated, which is understood to be the base frequency throughout the book.

Third, my set of 57 emerging and developed countries is an arbitrary choice. I worked hard in Chapter 2 to justify how I size up the emerging market landscape, but know that I excluded some markets that my readers would have liked to include. It is, of course, possible to include them. It is also possible that the validation experiment would deliver even stronger results than what I showed if I did. Data limitations on most of the variables in my six indicators governed my choices. I hope to do better in the future as I update these indicators. As a passing note, let me add that I was purposeful to include both emerging and developed countries, as there are strong common elements among many of the countries that outside agencies declare above or below the official line of economic and financial development. As a result, I would only ever seek to add new emerging market countries in the future and never to exclude the most developed countries from the analysis.

The book has been silent about the ever-evolving composition of the emerging markets, not only by asset classes (bank assets, debt, and equity securities), but also in the industrial composition of the firms that constitute the debt and equity markets. I discussed extensive research in the macroeconomics and international finance fields about how globalization has allowed for a potential shift toward industrial specialization that could be a healthy development, but also one that might expose countries to global shocks. It is a natural force of change, but one that has not factored in any way into how I built the emerging market risk indicators and validated them. I wonder—and worry about—how this changing industrial landscape across emerging market economies may affect how these indicators perform in the future.

Finally, I warn readers about shifting sands under our feet. I have worked hard to justify my six distinct risk indicators, though I fully acknowledge some common elements among subsets of them. Intellectually, there is nothing that separates them in any official way. Market capacity constraints that bind (Chapter 4's indicator) are quite likely to influence how market regulators might loosen up foreign investability restrictions (Chapter 6), for example. I could easily imagine in future iterations of my risk indicator framework that I reassign some variables in one indicator to those of another. What makes me more anxious—and, as a scholar, most excited—is the possibility that a whole new research paradigm arises in financial economics and development economics that justifies a new risk indicator altogether. Consider the possibility of having ignored a whole risk indicator dedicated to the study of the limits to legal protections in different emerging markets without the influence of the law and finance literature that spawned from the work of La Porta, Lopez-de-Silanes, Shleifer, and Vishny (featured in Chapter 8). I do not think I would need to scrap the framework I have built, but amend it to incorporate a new dimension, maybe one that subsumes an existing one.

The Future as Epilogue

I hope these risk indicators have some life beyond this book. I wish for my colleagues in industry—whether corporations doing business in emerging markets, those domiciled in emerging markets looking for opportunities outside, or investors deploying their assets there—to find some usefulness in rethinking their country allocation strategies. At least, I hope it stokes some discussion and debate about their choices. Market regulators and policymakers around the world may reject the simplicity of my approach and the answers I have given specifically about the markets for which they have oversight responsibility. I will enjoy meeting that challenge. And perhaps my colleagues in the academy will use these indicators as useful summary measures for their own research pursuits. If I am lucky, some may take me on and refine them further. Do not be surprised if I chip in on this initiative myself. I definitely expect to be updating them to keep the premise alive and to maintain their freshness for decision-makers.

Variable Definitions and Data Sources

Measures of Market Development and Market Capacity Constraints

Category	Variable	Definition and Source
Emerging Market Classification	Standard & Poor's/ International Finance Corporation	The Emerging Markets Database (EMBD) was launched by the International Finance Corporation (IFC) in 1981 to collect data on emerging markets for in-house use. Over time, outside demand from the financial and academic community for this data increased. In 1987, IFC began offering its indices and underlying data as a commercial product. Using a sample of stocks in each market, the various indices gave investors a transparent, standardized methodology for performance benchmarks across markets. EMDB was acquired by Standard & Poor's in January 2000. The S&P/IFCG Indices coverage of foreign equity markets exceeds 75% of total foreign market capitalization. The S&P/IFCI Indices screen stocks for foreign ownership restrictions, factoring in minimum market capitalization and liquidity parameters. Stocks are assigned weights representing the amount foreign institutional investors may buy because of foreign investment restrictions either at the national level or by the individual company's corporate statute. Frontier markets tend to be relatively small and illiquid by emerging market standards, and information is generally less available than in other markets. For these reasons, S&P calculates indices on a monthly basis, rather than a daily basis. Frontier markets are not currently included in the daily S&P/IFCG composite, although a monthly Frontier Composite Index is calculated. They are not considered investable under the S&P's definition, although they may be open to foreign portfolio investment. S&P currently covers 20 frontier markets. S&P strives for a methodology that is consistent and transparent. The *S&P Emerging Markets Index Methodology* is a continuously updated factsheet explaining in detail the methodology and selection criteria for the markets and stocks that make up the various S&P Emerging Market Indices. It also elaborates on the need for a standard measure of performance in emerging markets and describes the basic characteristics and weights of the indices. *Source:* http://us.spindices.com/indices/equity/sp-ifci-composite-price-index-in-us-dollar. More details are available in their publication *S&P Frontier Indices Methodology* (July 2013). I also recommend the table of Appendix A of a second publication, *S&P Global BMI, S&P/IFCI Indices Methodology* (July 2013).
	Economist Intelligence Unit	The Economist Intelligence Unit provides a constant flow of analysis, ratings and forecasts on more than 200 countries and eight key industries. The ratings span subjects such as risk, political climate, and credit. *Source:* http://country.eiu.com/AllCountries.aspx. This link provides a country list from which data on individual countries (where available) in my study can be found.
	Morgan Stanley Capital International	Morgan Stanley Capital International (MSCI) is one of the leading providers of investor support tools, including index construction and portfolio analytics. They provide a very comprehensive framework for country classification that emphasizes economic development, liquidity and size factors, and foreign accessibility criteria. See details in the June 2013 Global Market Accessibility Review, available at http://www.msci.com/resources/products/indexes/global_equity_indexes/gimi/stdindex/MSCI_Global_Market_Accessibility_Review_June2013.pdf.

FTSE International	See FTSE International's FTSE Frontier 50 Index Fact Sheet (December 31, 2013) and their FTSE Emerging Market Index (December 31, 2013) for a general discussion of their country classifications, their country breakdowns and some index characteristics. One notable feature is that FTSE International designates markets as "advanced emerging," distinct from "secondary emerging." Available: http://www.ftse.com/products/indices/frontier
JP Morgan	The JP Morgan GBI EM Broad is an all-encompassing index with all eligible countries included regardless of capital controls, taxes, or replicability issues that limit inclusion for the Narrow. Details are available in *JP Morgan Securities' Local Markets Guide: Emerging Markets Research* (9th edition, September 2013). Pages 38–42 detail the construction of the composite indices.
International Monetary Fund	The International Monetary Fund actually defines Emerging and Developing Countries as one classification in their World Economic Outlook (October 2013). See page 137 in the *Statistical Appendix of the IMF's World Economic Outlook: Transitions and Tensions* (October 2013). In the WEO statistical appendix, detailed discussion follows on the challenge of classifying countries that are not included in the analysis (such as the Democratic People's Republic of Korea, Cuba) because they are not IMF members or because of data limitations (Somalia). The WEO also emphasized how "country" and "economy" do not always refer to a territorial entity that is a state as understood by international law and practice (see footnote 4, page 137).
Economic Development	GDP is denominated in current US dollars at prevailing market exchange rates. It is denominated in dollars per person.
GDP Per Capita	Both population counts (for 2000) and GDP are obtained from the World Bank World Development Indicators.
Stock Market Development	Market capitalization to GDP is the value of listed shares divided by GDP. This is a unitless ratio. These data are from
Stock Market Capitalization-to-GDP Ratio	the World Federation of Exchanges and the World Bank World Development Indicators. I include data on the value of listed shares for all stock exchanges associated with a country including multiple exchanges (e.g., Shanghai and Shenzhen for China), alternative markets, and correspondent markets. Data for Taiwan comes from www.twse.com.tw/en/statistics/statistics.php?trm=07.
Listed Companies-to-Population Ratio	I count the number of domestically listed companies for all equity markets (WFE members, affiliates, and correspondents) designated for a given country in Table 1 and deflate the count by the population in tens of thousands. It is a unitless ratio. These data are from the World Federation of Exchanges and the World Bank World Development Indicators.
Financial Development	Domestic credit to the private sector refers to financial resources provided to the private sector, such as through
Domestic Credit from Financial Institutions-to-GDP	loans, purchases of nonequity securities, trade credit, and other accounts receivable, all of which establish a claim for repayment. In many countries, these claims include credit extended to public enterprises. I deflate this by the GDP of each country and it thus becomes a unitless ratio. The data come from the World Bank's World Development Indicators.

Category	Variable	Definition and Source
Bond Market Development	Private Bond Market Capitalization-to-GDP	Bond market capitalization is a measure of the depth of financial markets. Beck, Demirgüç-Kunt, and Levine describe the origination of the data in "A New Database on the Structure and Development of the Financial Sector." The same authors update their analysis in "Financial Institutions and Markets across Countries and Over Time," and a thorough benchmarking analysis is found in Čihák, Demirgüç-Kunt, Feyen, and Levine "Benchmarking Financial Systems around the World."
		The Financial Development and Structure database comes from the World Bank. This database was my starting point for many of the basic indicators of size, activity, and efficiency of financial intermediaries and markets. Beck, Demirgüç-Kunt, and Levine describe the sources and construction of and the intuition behind different indicators and present descriptive statistics. Private domestic debt securities issued by financial institutions and corporations as a share of GDP, calculated using a specific deflation method. Data for Taiwan comes from www.gretai.org.tw/storage/publish/others/2011_introduction_en.pdf.
	Public Bond Market Capitalization-to-GDP	See above. Public domestic debt securities issued by government as a share of GDP, calculated using a specific deflation method.
	Number of Bond Issuers	The total number of bond issuers represents the number of organizations that issued the fixed-income instruments listed on the exchange. These issuers are broken down into domestic private, public, and foreign entities. Domestic private bonds include corporate bonds, bonds issued by domestic banks, and financial institutions; domestic public bonds include government state-owned organizations bonds and bills, state-related institutions whose instruments are guaranteed by the state, and municipal bonds; foreign bonds listed on the exchange are issued by nonresident institutions such as foreign governments, banks, financial institutions, and supranational organizations (EIB, EBRD, World Bank). They also include Eurobonds (bonds issued under a law of a state different from the one of the issuer and placed in a foreign country inside the euro zone). An issuer may list bonds with different maturities, but the total number of issuers is unchanged.
Trading Activity	Stock Market Turnover Ratio	Turnover measures the value of total shares traded divided by market capitalization and is expressed as a percentage. These data are from the World Federation of Exchanges and the World Bank World Development Indicators.

{ APPENDIX B }

Measures of Operational Inefficiencies

Category	Variable	Definition and Source
Transaction Costs	Brokerage Commissions	Trading cost measures is a country-level measure of trading costs, expressed in raw form (e.g., 0.0110 is 110 basis points), which includes commissions, transfer and other related fees, and market impact costs in each home market, compiled by Elkins/McSherry LLC. The author is grateful to Dick McSherry for providing this data for 1997. I subsequently purchased access to this summary data through 2011. Now a wholly owned subsidiary of State Street Corporation, some database details are available at www.elkinsmcsherry.com/em/methodology.html. Some data is supplemented with *Salomon Smith Barney Guide to World Equity Markets*, Euromoney Books.
	Transfer/Other Fees	See above.
	Market Impact Costs	See above.
Liquidity Measures	Zero Return Proportions (Fong, Holden, and Trczinka, 2014)	Their proxy with the acronym FHT (from the authors' names) simplifies the existing zero-returns-proportion measure of LOT. These authors show it does well capturing intraday data on effective spreads from Thomson Reuters Tick History global data. The simplification rescales the zero-returns proportion to account for higher volatility of a representative stock; higher volatility implies the transaction cost bounds and spreads must be larger in order to achieve the same proportions of zero returns as an equivalent lower-volatility stock. See Table 2 in Fong, Holden, and Trczinka, "What Are the Best Proxies for Global Liquidity Research?" which gives a proxy for illiquidity. This measure is defined as scaling the zero-returns proportion measure by individual security price volatility.
	Zero Return Proportions (Lee, 2011)	Zero return proportions (in percent) represents the number of zero returns over one month scaled by the total number of available trading days averaged across all the months for which the stocks that comprise a country have available data. For each country, the median of the time-series averages of the measure is reported. Table 1 of Kuan-Hui Lee, "The World Price of Liquidity Risk." Zero-returns proportions are the fraction of trading days within a month with zero returns for the typical stock available 1988–2007; higher proportions of zero returns denote greater illiquidity.
	Annual Liquidity (Karolyi, Lee, and van Dijk, 2012)	Amihud, in "Illiquidity and Stock Return," introduces a measure of the price-impact of a trade defined as the absolute value of stock returns scaled by dollar volume. It draws as its inspiration Pete Kyle's so-called lambda, or the elasticity of the price change for a trade of a given size. A more liquid market has a lower price impact for a given trade size. I use the time-series average of daily estimates of the Amihud proxy from Karolyi et al. for a large panel of representative stocks in each of the 40 countries the study covers. See data appendix of Karolyi et al., "Understanding Commonality in Liquidity around the World." Illiquidity is computed as the average daily return volatility per dollar value of trading for the typical stock over 1995–2009.
	Annual Turnover (Karolyi, Lee, and van Dijk, 2012)	See above. Turnover is the ratio of the dollar value of trading relative to the market capitalization for the typical stock. I use an annualized measure of daily turnover as the first proxy. It comes from a study by Karolyi et al., "Understanding Commonality in Liquidity around the World," in which daily turnover rates of representatives stocks (not that of the market as a whole) are computed for a large cross-section of individual stocks from 40 countries around the world over the period from 1988 through 2009.

Short-Selling Restrictions	Median Short-Borrowing Ratio (Jain et al., 2013)	I take the median daily average short-borrowing ratio, which (during 2006 to 2010, their period of analysis) is the daily average outstanding dollar value of shares borrowed summed across all stocks from that country divided by the country's total stock market capitalization. A higher short borrowing ratio indicates more intense the short-selling activity. From Table 1 of Jain, Jain, McInish, and McKenzie, "The Worldwide Reach of Short Selling Regulations," the median of the aggregate dollar amount of short-selling-related borrowing of all stocks from each country and whether short-selling is illegal or not.
	Short Sales Legality (Jain et al., 2013)	An index that indicates whether, as of 2010 (the ending year of their sample), short-selling activity is legal or illegal. I ignore that there may have been some restrictions in one form or another at a particular time. I flag whether or not there existed a ban on short selling for a large fraction of the equity market. From Table 1 of Jain et al., "Worldwide Reach of Short-Selling Regulations," which lists the median of the aggregate dollar amount of short-selling-related borrowing of all stocks from each country and a description of short-sale legality and institutional details surrounding restrictions, if any.
Market Manipulation	Market Manipulation Index (Cumming, Johan, and Li, 2011)	Cumming, Johan, and Li, in "Exchange Trading Rules and Stock Market Liquidity," create a series of indices for trading rules that pertain to market manipulation and insider trading for 42 exchanges in both developed and emerging markets. Market manipulation rules refer to "trading practices that distort prices and enable market manipulators to profit at the expense of other market participants" (p. 652). Brokers, for example, could take actions while acting on behalf of a client that benefits the broker or some other affiliated party at the expense of a client or the market more generally. Insider trading rules refer to "acting on material nonpublic information" (also, p. 652). The market manipulation index is the tally of "yes" responses to 14 questions concerning the presence of price manipulation, such as ramping or gouging, in which a series of trades over a short time period generate unusual price movement given the security's history; volume manipulation, such as the explicit prohibition on wash sales (same client referenced on both sides of a trade); what they call "spoofing," such as rules preventing brokers from staggering orders from the same client at different price and volume levels to give a false appearance of market activity; and false disclosure, such as rules prohibiting the hiding of the true ownership of securities with fictitious trades. The insider trading rules index represents a tally of 10 yes/no questions that might preclude front-running (in which brokers buy or sell ahead of a client) and trading ahead of research reports, and that impose a separation of trading and research, restrictions on affiliations between exchange members, and member companies. From Table 2 of Cumming et al., "Exchange Trading Rules and Stock Market Liquidity," count up to five market manipulation rules for brokers on trade-through, improper execution, fair dealing with customers and up to seven exchange rules on insider trading.
	Insider Trading Index (Cumming et al., 2011)	See above. The insider trading rules index represents a series of 10 yes/no questions that might preclude front-running (in which brokers buy or sell ahead of a client) and trading ahead of research reports, and that impose a separation of trading and research, restrictions on affiliations between exchange members, and member companies. From Table 2 of Cumming et al., "Exchange Trading Rules and Stock Market Liquidity."

(continued)

Category	Variable	Definition and Source
Clearance & Settlement Procedures	Settlement Cycles: World Bank T+3 Cycle or Better	From the World Bank's Global Payments Survey 2010. A risk in settlement can be capital risk where only one side of a transaction settles, credit risk where a transaction has to be replaced due to default of one party or operational risk when it is not completed on the due date due to failure of one party to settle. Shorter settlement cycles can help minimize credit risk. ISSA recommends a rolling settlement cycle of T+3 (trade date plus three days) or shorter, which means that the funds are transferred within three business days after the trade is executed. One point is given if cycle exceeds T+3 days.
	Settlement Methods: World Bank CSD Integrated with RTGS	RTGS (real time gross settlement) systems are funds transfer systems where transfer of money or securities takes place from one bank to another on a real-time basis (no waiting period) and as a gross settlement, or one transaction at a time without bunching or netting with other transactions. The World Bank survey indicates that 90 out of 179 CSDs (Central Securities Depositories) have a real-time interface with the RTGS system. One point is given if a country has this interface.
	Delivery vs. Payment (DvP): World Bank Model 1 DvP	A risk in settlement can be capital risk where only one side of a transaction settles, credit risk where a transaction has to be replaced due to default of one party, or operational risk when it is not completed on the due date due to failure of one party to settle. A DVP mechanism in a settlement system minimizes credit risk by ensuring that the final transfer of one asset (security) occurs if and only if the final transfer of another asset (monetary, e.g., foreign exchange) occurs. Only 8% of CSDs do not use a DvP model at all. However, more sophisticated models allow for simultaneous settlement (DvP Model 1), on a net basis (DvP Model 2) or at the end of the processing cycle (DvP Model 3). One point is given for those countries that have at least one form of upgrade (denoted Model 1+) on the basic DvP model.
	Participation: World Bank CSD Participants	CSDs and securities settlement systems, in general, also attempt to control the risks in their systems by defining access criteria for participants. According to the World Bank survey, 86% of CSDs indicated that commercial banks are direct participants, whereas corresponding figures for broker-dealers and other financial institutions (like central banks, stock exchanges, treasury departments) is only 66%. Direct participation by nonbanks is higher in more developed countries, they find. I arbitrarily compile a score out of 3 points to the yes/no questions as to whether these three groups participate directly (commercial banks, broker-dealers, other financial institutions).
	Risk Management; World Bank Risk Management Systems	See above. An investment in risk management systems in CSDs and securities settlement systems is more likely to ensure the integrity of the process. The World Bank survey captures a number of assessments of the resilience and business continuity features of CSDs. They ask seven questions about whether they have routine procedures in place for periodic data backups, whether backup tapes are kept in sites other than the main processing site, whether backup servers are deployed, and even whether business continuity arrangements include procedures for crisis management and information dissemination. Up to seven points are possible, with one point for each positive answer.

Measures of Foreign Investability Restrictions

Category	Variables	Sources and Definitions
Capital Access	Milken Institute Capital Access International Index	The index of 121 countries worldwide (including 18 in Latin America) looks at seven key components that can make it easier or more difficult for entrepreneurs to access capital. Those components are macroeconomic environment, economic institutions, financial and banking institutions, equity market, bond market, alternative capital, and international access. See Barth, Li, Lu, and Yago, eds., *Capital Access Index 2009*.
	Investability Ratio (Standard & Poor's Emerging Market Database)	The measure of openness is equal to the fraction of the market capitalization of the market at the end of 2002 that is investable as dictated by the Standard and Poor's Emerging Markets Database (EMDB). My score is based on the market capitalization data from 2009, the last year for which this data exists. The Emerging Markets Database (EMBD) was launched by the International Finance Corporation (IFC) in 1981 to collect data on emerging markets for in-house use. Over time, outside demand from the financial and academic community for this data increased. In 1987, IFC began offering its Indices and underlying data as a commercial product. Using a sample of stocks in each market, the various Indices gave investors a transparent, standardized methodology for performance benchmarks across markets.
EMDB was acquired by Standard & Poor's in January 2000. The S&P/IFCG Indices coverage of foreign equity markets exceeds 75% of total foreign market capitalization. The S&P/IFCI Indices screen stocks for foreign ownership restrictions, factoring in minimum market capitalization and liquidity parameters. Stocks are assigned weights representing the amount foreign institutional investors may buy because of foreign investment restrictions either at the national level or by the individual company's corporate statute.
Size of the ADR Market	Count of US-listed ADRs as % of Total Count of All Domestic Firms	Number of domestic listed firms with a US listing as an American depositary receipt (ADR) program on a major exchange, over-the-counter or SEC Rule 144a form as fraction of total count of all domestic listed companies (Doidge, Karolyi, and Stulz, "Has New York Become Less Competitive than London in Global Markets?").
Foreign Banks	World Bank Financial Development & Structure: Consolidated Claims of Foreign Banks to GDP	The World Bank's Financial Development and Structure Database obtains data from the Bank for International Settlement on foreign claims held by banks from OECD countries in the rest of the world. These claims represent banks' financial claims extended to residents of a host country either cross-border or domestically via a local affiliate. The claims consist of financial assets such as loans, debt securities, properties, and equities, including equity participations in subsidiaries.
	World Bank Financial Development & Structure: Loans from Nonresident Foreign Banks to GDP	See above.

External Balance	
Lane & Milesi-Ferretti: Total External Assets & Liabilities to GDP	From a set of indicators created by Philip Lane and Gian Milesi-Ferretti, (www.philiplane.org/EWN.html). One measure computes all external assets and liabilities relative to GDP including foreign direct investment, portfolio equity investment, external debt, and official reserves.
Lane & Milesi-Ferretti: Total External Portfolio and Direct Equity Investment to GDP	See above. This variable considers only foreign direct and portfolio equity investments, on both the assets and liabilities side.
Regulations Affecting Foreign Investors	
Registration Requirements	From series of Euromoney Books published in early 2000s and late 1990s. For example, in 1999, *The Salomon Smith Barney Guide to World Equity Markets 1999*, was published by Euromoney Institutional Investor PLC and Salomon Smith Barney, edited by Jacqueline Grosch Lobo and Rob Irish (Euromoney Books, Nestor House, London). Earlier editions were published jointly with different firms, such as *The LGT Guide to World Equity Markets 1996* (Euromoney Books, Nestor House, London). For more recent years, I supplement these data with those from Bloomberg and a number of Form 20-F filings by foreign company registrants of the US Securities and Exchange Commission.
Ownership Restrictions	See the World Bank report at http://iab.worldbank.org/~/media/FPDKM/IAB/Documents/IAB-report.pdf, titled *Investing Across Borders 2010*. See Table 2.1 in particular, and the supplementary appendix on methodology, which outlines the survey approach by email, phone, or personal interviews and the team's composition, the survey instruments, and the survey respondents. Table 7.1 outlines each of the indicators and their type as to whether de jure or de facto. See also *Converting and Transferring Currency* (CTC, September 2013) by lead author John Anderson, of the Global Indicators and Analysis Department in Financial and Private Sector Development of the World Bank Group (http://iab.worldbank.org/~/media/FPDKM/IAB/Documents/FDI-Converting-and-Transferring-Currency.pdf). Four-point scale: if only some sectors are restricted for foreign investors; if broad-based restrictions exist with cap limits; and, if other ownership restrictions exist.
Repatriation Cap Limits	See above. Equals one if any limits on repatriation of profits.
Currency Convertibility Restrictions	See CTC report above. Three-point scale: if currency only partially or nonconvertible, and if not free-floating.

(continued)

Category	Variables	Sources and Definitions
Taxation Affecting Foreign Investors	Withholding Taxes (Equities)	See country reports and various available historical information sources from https://dits.deloitte.com/#TaxGuides. The Deloitte International Tax Source (DITS) site is updated regularly. My information was drawn as of January 2014. See also the United Nations International Trade Center's Market Analysis Services (http://www.intracen.org/itc/market-info-tools/tariff-data/). Three-point scale: if withholding on dividend or interest income, and if no exemptions for tax-treaty country residents.
	Double Tax Avoidance	See DITS above. Four-point scale: if no tax treaty exists, if tax treaties exist with fewer than 20 countries, and if tax treaties exist with fewer than 50 countries.
	Foreign Capital Gains Tax	See DITS above. Equals one if there exist any taxes on foreign capital gains.
	Other Securities Taxes	See DITS above. Three-point scale: 1, if stamp duty exists, and 2 if additional value-added tax on securities/broking service fees; zero, otherwise.

Measures of Corporate Opacity

Category	Variable	Source and Definition
Governance Rankings	Credit Lyonnais Securities Asia Governance Score	The CLSA corporate governance rating is based on a questionnaire given to financial analysts who responded with "Yes" or "No" answers to 57 questions related to seven categories: management discipline, transparency, independence, accountability, responsibility, fairness, and social responsibility. A composite governance rating is computed by giving an equal weight of 15% to the first six categories and a weight of 10% to social responsibility. *Source:* Doidge, Karolyi, and Stulz, "Why Do Countries Matter So Much for Corporate Governance?"
	Standard & Poor's Transparency & Disclosure Score	S&P compiles the ratings by examining firms' annual reports and standard regulatory filings for disclosure of 98 items, divided into three sections: financial transparency and information disclosure (35 items), board and management structure and process (35 items), and ownership structure and investor relations (28 items). S&P uses a binary scoring system in which one point is awarded if a particular item is disclosed. *Source:* Doidge, Karolyi, and Stulz, "Why Do Countries Matter So Much for Corporate Governance?"
Corporate Transparency	Timeliness Score	A scaled, standardized index from 0 to 100, where 100 represents high levels of transparency in terms of timely disclosures. Based on survey data average ranking of answers to questions on the likelihood of interim reporting items, including frequency, count of disclosed items, and consolidation of interim reports. *Source:* Bushman, Piotroski, and Smith, "What Determines Corporate Transparency?"
	Measurement Score	A scaled, standardized index from 0 to 100, where 100 represents high levels of transparency in terms of reporting consolidated disclosures. Survey data average ranking of answers to questions on consolidation and discretionary reserves. *Source:* Bushman, Piotroski, and Smith, "What Determines Corporate Transparency?"
	Governance Score	A scaled, standardized index from 0 to 100, where 100 represents high levels of transparency in terms of disclosures about management, officers, directors and large shareholders. Survey data ranking answers to questions on range of shareholdings, major shareholders, management information, list of board members, remuneration of directors and officers, and shares owned by directors and employees. *Source:* Bushman, Piotroski, and Smith, "What Determines Corporate Transparency?"
	Disclosure Score	A scaled, standardized index from 0 to 100, where 100 represents high levels of transparency in terms of nonmandated financial disclosures. Survey data ranking answer to questions on capital expenditures, R&D, subsidiaries, segment products, segment-geographic, and accounting policy. *Source:* Bushman, Piotroski, and Smith, "What Determines Corporate Transparency?"
Monitoring by Analysts	CKP Analyst Coverage	The number of analysts following the largest 30 companies in each country in 1996. *Source:* Number of analysts following the largest 30 companies in each country in 1996, from Chang, Khanna, and Palepu, "Analyst Activity Around the World," and using data from Bailey, Karolyi, and Salva, "The Economic Consequences of Increased Disclosure."

Monitoring by Large Blockholders	Blockholder Control Rights (Doidge, Karolyi, Lins, Miller, and Stulz, DKLMS, 2009)	The fraction of shares outstanding controlled by the largest blockholder for the largest firms from a given country. I obtain raw ownership and control data available for Western European firms from Faccio and Lang, "The Ultimate Ownership Of Western European Corporations"; for emerging market firms from Lins, "Equity Ownership and Firm Value in Emerging Markets"; and for East Asian firms from Claessens, Djankov, and Lang, "The Separation of Ownership and Control in East Asian Corporations." Ownership and control data for East Asian and emerging market firms are from the 1995 and 1996 period and those from Western Europe range from 1996 to 1999, with the majority of sample observations occurring in 1996. Claessens et al., Faccio and Lang, and Lins report ownership and control statistics that could proxy for a firm's internal corporate governance environment. For instance, they compute the percentage of total ultimate control rights held by the following types of blockholders: family/management, government, widely held corporations, widely held financials, and miscellaneous (which include ownership by trusts, cooperatives, foundations, employees, etc.). From these data it is possible to identify the largest blockholder of a firm's control rights. Faccio and Lang and Claessens et al. report the separation of ownership and control only for the largest blockholder of their sample firms (which may not be the family/management group), while Lins reports this measure for all holdings of the family/management group (which may not be the largest blockholder). See Doidge, Karolyi, Lins, Miller, and Stulz, "Private Benefits of Control, Ownership and the Cross-Listing Decision."
	LLS Top Three Blockholders Control Rights	Percentage of shares owned by three largest blockholders on average among the largest 30 firms in each country. *Source:* LaPorta, Lopez-de-Silanes, and Shleifer, "Corporate Ownership Around the World."
	WS Closely Held Shares (Worldscope)	This variable represents shares held by insiders as a percentage of all shares outstanding. It includes but is not restricted to shares held by officers, directors, and their immediate families; shares held in trust; shares of the company held by any other corporation (except those held in a fiduciary capacity by banks or custodians); shares held by pension/benefit plans; and shares held by individuals who hold more than 5% of outstanding shares. It excludes shares under option exercisable within 60 days, and preferred stock or debentures convertible into common shares. For Japanese companies it includes holdings of the ten largest shareholders. For companies with more than one class of common stock, closely held shares for each class are added together (Worldscope Annual Stock Data Item #05475). Worldscope data definition guide can be found here: http://extranet.datastream.com/Data/Worldscope/index.htm. Worldscope is a database currently owned by Thomson Reuters.
Accounting Standards	Center for International Financial Analysis and Research (CIFAR) Accounting Standards	Index (from 0 to 90, where 90 represents high standards) created by International Accounting and Auditing Trends, Center for International Financial Analysis and Research based on rating companies 1995 annual reports on their inclusion or omission of 90 items such as general information, income statements, balance sheets, fund flow statements, accounting standards, stock data, and special items. A minimum of three companies in each country were studied.

(continued)

Category	Variable	Source and Definition
	IFRS Adoption	I collect information as of 2013 from PriceWaterhouseCoopers report *IFRS Adoption by Country* (April 2013), which provides a narrative for each country on the extent of their IFRS practices. I score a variable as 1 if full adoption has occurred with few exceptions, and 0.5 if there are many exceptions, if IFRS is encouraged, or if plans for IFRS adoption are underway.
Commonality in Liquidity and Returns	R^2 in Liquidity (Karolyi et al., 2012)	From Karolyi, Lee, and van Dijk, "Understanding Commonality in Liquidity around the World." For each of almost 27,447 publicly traded stocks across 40 countries from 1995 through 2009, we compute daily returns and daily changes in liquidity using the Amihud ("Illiquidity and Stock Return") proxy for illiquidity (a reasonable choice, based on arguments in Chapter 5). Each month, we estimate a simple univariate regression model of the individual stocks returns or innovations in liquidity on the market-wide equivalent; the coefficient of determination, or R^2, measures this common comovement. We average across the R^2 of the individual stocks in a market and average these across the months of a given year. The R^2 is a statistic that ranges from zero (low level of commonality in liquidity or returns across stocks) to one (perfect synchronicity in liquidity or returns across stocks).
	R^2 in Returns (Karolyi et al., 2012)	See above. The dependent variable of my regression model is in this case returns instead of liquidity.

Measures of Limits to Legal Protections

Category	Variable	Definition and Source
Legal Protection of Minority Rights	Antidirector Rights Index (LLSV, La Porta, Lopez-de-Silanes, Shleifer, and Vishny 1998; DLLS, Djankov, La Porta, Lopez-de-Silanes, and Shleifer 2008)	The index (0 to 5) of antidirector rights is formed by adding one point when the country allows shareholders to mail their proxy vote, one if shareholders are not required to deposit their shares prior to a general meeting, one if cumulative voting or proportional representation for minorities on the board of directors is allowed, one if oppressed minorities have mechanisms in place, one if the minimum percentage of share capital needed for a shareholder to call for an extraordinary meeting exceeds 10%, and one when shareholders have preemptive rights that can only be waived by a shareholders' meeting. The original source is La Porta et al., "Law and Finance." I use the revised version in Djankov et al., "The Law and Economics of Self-Dealing."
	Judicial Efficiency Index (La Porta et al., 1998)	An index (0 to 10, with low scores representing lower efficiency) of the efficiency and integrity of the legal environment as it affects business particularly foreign firms produced by the country risk rating agency International Country Risk (ICR). *Source:* La Porta et al., "Law and Finance."
	Rule of Law (La Porta et al., 1998)	An index (0 to 6, with low scores for less tradition for law and order) assessing the law and order tradition in the country produced by the country risk rating agency International Country Risk (ICR). *Source:* La Porta et al., "Law and Finance."
	Creditor Rights (La Porta et al., 1998)	A creditor rights index (0 to 4, with high scores for good protection) considering whether there are no automatic stays on assets, secured creditors get paid first, there exist restrictions for going into reorganization, and management does not stay at the firm during reorganization. *Source:* La Porta et al., "Law and Finance."
	Formalism Index (Djankov et al., 2003)	Using data on exact procedures used by litigants and courts to evict a tenant for nonpayment of rent and to collect a bounced check, DLLS construct an index of procedural formalism of dispute resolution for each country. The data are combined into a unitless scale from 0 to 7, where higher procedural formalism is associated with higher expected duration of judicial proceedings, more corruption, less consistency, less honesty, less fairness in decisions, and inferior access to justice. *Source:* Djankov et al., "Courts."
	AntiSelf-Dealing Index (Djankov et al., 2008)	The index is computed for 72 countries based on legal rules prevailing in 2003 and focuses on private enforcement mechanisms such as disclosure, approval, and litigation governing a specific self-dealing transaction by corporate insiders. In Djankov et al., "The Law and Economics of Self-Dealing," anti self-dealing (0 to 1 scale, bad to good) measures extent of private enforcement mechanisms such as disclosure, approval and litigation on dealings by insiders.
	Public Enforcement Index (Djankov et al., 2008)	Public enforcement deals with the criminal sanctions when a self-dealing transaction (see above for definition) that has been approved is in violation of the law. In Djankov, La Porta, Lopez-de-Silanes, and Shleifer, "The Law and Economics of Self-Dealing," where enforcement (0 to 1 scale, good to bad) indicates more stringent fines, prison terms for self-dealing transactions.

Supervisory Powers (La Porta, Lopez-de-Silanes, and Shleifer, 2006)	The index of characteristics of the Supervisor of financial markets equals the arithmetic mean of (1) appointment, (2) tenure, and (3) focus. Higher scores indicate weaker powers. Appointment equals one if a majority of the members of the Supervisor are unilaterally appointed by the executive branch of government; it equals zero otherwise. Tenure equals one if members of the supervisor cannot be dismissed at the will of the appointing authority; it equals zero otherwise. Focus equals one if separate government agencies or official authorities are in charge of supervising commercial banks and stock exchanges; it equals zero otherwise. *Source:* La Porta, Lopez-De-Silanes, and Shleifer, "What Works in Securities Laws?"
World Bank Getting Credit Indicator — Legal Rights Index	An index (0 to 10, high scores with better bankruptcy laws to expand access to credit) reflects legal rights of borrowers and lenders, and measures the degree to which collateral and bankruptcy laws facilitate lending. Collateral and insolvency laws with support of a survey on secured transactions laws. *Source:* http://www.doingbusiness.org/methodology/getting-credit.
Credit Information Index	An index (0 to 6, higher values indicate more credit info) on information available from a public registry or private bureaus to facilitate lending decisions. *Source:* http://www.doingbusiness.org/methodology/getting-credit.
Public credit registry coverage (% adults)	A number as % of adult population of a registry managed by central bank or superintendent of banks collecting info on the creditworthiness of borrowers in the financial system made available to financial institutions. *Source:* http://www.doingbusiness.org/methodology/getting-credit.
Private bureau coverage (% adults)	A number as % of adult population of a database managed by a private firm or nonprofit organization collecting info on the creditworthiness of borrowers in the financial system made available to financial institutions. *Source:* World Bank Doing Business Indicators, http://www.doingbusiness.org/methodology/getting-credit.
World Bank Protecting Investors Indicator — Disclosure Index	An index (0 to 10, with higher values indicating greater disclosure) of extent of disclosure about potential transactions by managers or directors that misuse corporate assets for personal gain. *Source:* World Bank Doing Business Indicators, http://www.doingbusiness.org/methodology/protecting-investors.
Director Liability Index	An index (0 to 10, with higher values indicating greater liability of directors) of plaintiffs' abilities to hold a director liable for damages to the company if he influenced approval of a transaction or was negligent. *Source:* World Bank Doing Business Indicators, http://www.doingbusiness.org/methodology/protecting-investors.
Shareholder Suits Index	An index (0 to 10, with higher values indicating greater powers of shareholders to challenge a transaction) of ease of shareholder suits in terms of range of documents available to plaintiff from defendant and witnesses during trial, ability to engage in direct examination during trial and other related measures. *Source:* World Bank Doing Business Indicators, http://www.doingbusiness.org/methodology/protecting-investors.

(continued)

Category	Variable	Definition and Source
	Investor Protection Index	A composite index (0 to 10, with higher values indicating better investor protection) of the extent of disclosure requirements, the extent of director liability and the ease of shareholder suits. *Source:* World Bank Doing Business Indicators, http://www.doingbusiness.org/methodology/protecting-investors.
World Bank Enforcing Contracts Indicator	Procedures (number)	A count of the number of procedures mandated by law that demand interaction between parties and/or judge and/or court officer. *Source:* World Bank Doing Business Indicators, http://www.doingbusiness.org/data/exploretopics/enforcing-contracts.
	Time (days)	The time required (in days) for dispute resolution in calendar days from moment of plaintiff filing of lawsuit in court to settlement or payment. *Source:* World Bank Doing Business Indicators, http://www.doingbusiness.org/data/exploretopics/enforcing-contracts.
	Cost (% of debt)	A cost indicator of going through court procedures, attorney fees, administrative debt recovery procedures, as a percentage of the debt value. *Source:* World Bank Doing Business Indicators, http://www.doingbusiness.org/data/exploretopics/enforcing-contracts.

Measures of Political Instability

Category	Variable	Source and Definition
Political Constraints	Constraints Index (Henisz, 2000)	Range 0 to 1 (1 equals countries with more constraints via veto powers in executive, lower, or upper legislative chambers over policy change). *Source:* Henisz, "The Institutional Environment for Economic Growth." I specifically use Henisz's 2012 version of the data (PolconV). Links to download page can be found and data manuals: http://www-management.wharton.upenn.edu/henisz/. Direct download link: http://mgmt5.wharton.upenn.edu/henisz/POLCON/ContactInfo.html.
	Polity IV Democracy Index	Range = −10 to 10 (−10 = high autocracy; 10 = high democracy). The Polity dataset has been and continues to be commonly used in time-series analyses of political behavior; most often Polity indices are used to provide such analyses with a measure of regime democracy and/or autocracy. Researchers are reminded that Polity annual scores code the authority characteristics of the regime in place on December 31 of the coded year. See Marshall and Cole, *Global Stability Report*; the 2014 report can be found at: http://www.systemicpeace.org/vlibrary/GlobalReport2014.pdf. DEMOC (numeric) Range = 0–10 (0 = low; 10 = high), Democracy Score: general openness of political institutions. The 11-point democracy scale is constructed additively. The operational indicator is derived from coding of authority characteristics according to the following criteria: AUTOC (numeric) Range = 0–10 (0 = low; 10 = high) Autocracy score: general closeness of political institutions. The 11-point autocracy scale is constructed additively; POLITY (numeric). Combined polity score: computed by subtracting AUTOC from DEMOC; includes "standardized codes" (i.e., −66, −77, and −88) for special polity conditions. *Source:* http://www.systemicpeace.org/polity/polity4.htm. I use the 2011 version of the data (Polity IV), as available at the time of writing.
	Herfindahl Index Total of the Governing Party in the Legislature (Database of Political Institutions)	Measures annually the concentration of the seats held by the governing parties in the legislature. Highly concentrated (i.e., single party) legislature = 1, low concentrated legislature = 0. *Source:* Beck, Clarke, Groff, Keefer, and Walsh, "New Tools in Comparative Political Economy"; World Bank Economic Review. Direct download: http://econ.worldbank.org/WBSITE/EXTERNAL/EXTDEC/EXTRESEARCH/0,,contentMDK:2 0649465~pagePK:64214825~piPK:64214943~theSitePK:469382,00.html.
	Total Fractionalization of the Opposition Parties in Legislature (Database of Political Institutions)	Fractionalization measures annually the likelihood that two random draws from the opposition parties in the legislature are from different parties. *Source:* Beck, Clarke, Groff, Keefer, and Walsh, "New Tools in Comparative Political Economy"; World Bank Economic Review. Direct download: http://econ.worldbank.org/WBSITE/EXTERNAL/EXTDEC/EXTRESEARCH/0,,contentMDK:2 0649465~pagePK:64214825~piPK:64214943~theSitePK:469382,00.html.

Proportionality Index (Pagano & Volpin, 2005)	The Proportionality Index is computed from World Bank Database on Political Institutions (DPI) variables PR (Proportionality)—PLURALTY—HOUSESYS + 2, where plurality (1 if yes, 0 if no), proportional representation (1 if yes, 0 if no), and HOUSESYS if plurality and proportional Representation that governs the majority/all of the House seats (1 if plurality, 0 if proportional). *Source:* Pagano and Volpin, "Political Economy of Corporate Governance." Download: https://www.aeaweb.org/aer/data/sept05_data_pagano.zip.
Kauffmann-Kraay Governance Indicators	Kaufmann, Kraay, and Mastruzzi, "Governance Matters IV." The authors present the latest update of their aggregate governance indicators, together with new analysis of several issues related to the use of these measures. The governance indicators measure the following six dimensions of governance: (1) voice and accountability, (2) political instability and violence, (3) government effectiveness, (4) regulatory quality, (5) rule of law, and (6) control of corruption. They cover 209 countries and territories for 1996, 1998, 2000, 2002, and 2004. They are based on several hundred individual variables measuring perceptions of governance, drawn from 37 separate data sources constructed by 31 organizations. The authors present estimates of the six dimensions of governance for each period, as well as margins of error capturing the range of likely values for each country. The main studies are Kaufmann, Kraay, and Zoido-Lobaton, "Aggregating Governance Indicators"; Kaufmann, Kraay, and Zoido-Lobaton, "Governance Matters"; Kaufmann, Kraay, and Mastruzzi, "Governance Matters III"; and Kaufmann, Kraay, and Mastruzzi, "The Worldwide Governance Indicators." *Source:* http://info.worldbank.org/governance/wgi/index.aspx#home. Download: http://info.worldbank.org/governance/wgi/wgidataset.xlsx.
Voice & Accountability	Measures various aspects of the political process, civil liberties, and political rights in a given year. "This variable measures the extent to which citizens of a country are able to participate in the selection of governments. We also include in this category three indicators measuring the independence of the media." The indicators are based on 352 different underlying variables measuring perceptions of a wide range of governance issues drawn from 32 separate data sources constructed by 30 different organizations worldwide. Each measure is constructed on a scale of −2.5 to 2.5 with a standard deviation of 1.0 using standard unobserved components models. *Source:* http://info.worldbank.org/governance/wgi/index.aspx#home. Download: http://info.worldbank.org/governance/wgi/wgidataset.xlsx.
Political Instability	Measures the likelihood of violent threats to government including terrorism. The indicators are based on 352 different underlying variables measuring perceptions of a wide range of governance issues drawn from 32 separate data sources constructed by 30 different organizations worldwide. Each measure is constructed on a scale of −2.5 to 2.5, with a standard deviation of 1.0 using standard unobserved components models. *Source:* http://info.worldbank.org/governance/wgi/index.aspx#home. Download: http://info.worldbank.org/governance/wgi/wgidataset.xlsx.

(*continued*)

Category	Variable	Source and Definition
	Government Effectiveness	This variable measures the quality of public service provision, the quality of the bureaucracy, the competence of civil servants, the independence of the civil service from political pressures, and the credibility of the government's commitment to policies. The main focus of this index is on inputs required for the government to be able to produce and implement good policies and deliver public goods. This variable ranges from −2.5 to 2.5, where higher values equal higher government effectiveness. This variable is measured in 2000. *Source:* http://info.worldbank.org/governance/wgi/index.aspx#home. Download: http://info.worldbank.org/governance/wgi/wgidataset.xlsx.
	Regulatory Burden	Measures the incidence of market-unfriendly policies. The indicators are based on 352 different underlying variables measuring perceptions of a wide range of governance issues drawn from 32 separate data sources constructed by 30 different organizations worldwide. Each measure is constructed on a scale of −2.5 to 2.5, with a standard deviation of 1.0 using standard unobserved components models. *Source:* http://info.worldbank.org/governance/wgi/index.aspx#home. Download: http://info.worldbank.org/governance/wgi/wgidataset.xlsx.
	Rule of Law	Rule of law measures the extent to which agents have confidence in and abide by the rules of society in the year 2000. These include perceptions of the incidence of both violent and nonviolent crime, the effectiveness and predictability of the judiciary, and the enforceability of contracts. The indicators are based on 352 different underlying variables measuring perceptions of a wide range of governance issues drawn from 32 separate data sources constructed by 30 different organizations worldwide. Each measure is constructed on a scale of −2.5 to 2.5, with a standard deviation of 1.0 using standard unobserved components models. *Source:* http://info.worldbank.org/governance/wgi/index.aspx#home. Download: http://info.worldbank.org/governance/wgi/wgidataset.xlsx.
	Control of Corruption	The Corruption index measures the extent of exercise of public power for private gain in year 2000. It captures aspects ranging from the frequency of additional payments to get things done, to the effects of corruption on the business environment. The indicators are based on 352 different underlying variables measuring perceptions of a wide range of governance issues drawn from 32 separate data sources constructed by 30 different organizations worldwide. Each measure is constructed on a scale of −2.5 to 2.5, with a standard deviation of 1.0 using standard unobserved components models. *Source:* http://info.worldbank.org/governance/wgi/index.aspx#home. Download: http://info.worldbank.org/governance/wgi/wgidataset.xlsx.

| Corruption | Transparency International Corruption Index | Transparency International (www.transparency.org) conducts an annual survey (since 1995) of more than 150 countries by their perceived levels of corruption, as determined by expert assessments and opinion surveys. Sixteen surveys and expert assessments are used, and at least three are required for a country to be included in the index. The corruption perception index score relates to perceptions of the degree of corruption as seen by business people and country analysts and ranges between 0 (highly corrupt) and 10 (largely clean of corruption). I obtain the 2011 scores from *Corruption Perception Index 2011*, which are available from the organization's website. In particular the 2011 data is from the interactive data tool shown on: http://www.transparency.org/cpi2011. |
| | Heritage Foundation Index of Economic Freedom | The scale runs from 1 to 100: a score of 100 signifies an economic environment and set of policies that are most conducive to economic freedom, while a score of 0 signifies a set of policies that are least conducive to economic freedom. Since 1995, the Index of Economic Freedom has offered the international community an annual in-depth examination of the factors that contribute most directly to economic freedom and prosperity. Economic freedom is defined as the absence of government coercion or constraint on the production, distribution, or consumption of goods and services beyond the extent necessary for citizens to protect and maintain liberty. In other words, people are free to work, produce, consume, and invest in the ways they feel are most productive. Trade policy, fiscal burden of government, government intervention in the economy, monetary policy, capital flows and foreign investment, banking and finance, wages and prices, property rights, regulation, and informal market activity. All 10 factors are equal-weighted in the measure of economic freedom for a country. Each factor is graded according to a unique scale. Score of 0 (more conducive to economic freedom) to 100 (less conducive), using 10 factors from four categories of rule of law, limited government, regulatory efficiency, and open markets. Raw data downloads are available here, for most recent year: http://www.heritage.org/index/download. However, the following data tool can be used to extract all prior years for all countries in the dataset: http://www.heritage.org/index/explore?view=by-region-country-year. |

{ NOTES }

Chapter 1

1. "Bharti-Zain Deal to Add Punch to India Growth Story: India Inc.," *Economic Times of India*, March 31, 2010. See http://articles.economictimes.indiatimes.com/2010-03-31/news/28494886_1_india-growth-story-bharti-zain-deal-kuwait-s-zain-telecom. All of this discussion is based on the case study, titled "India Dials Africa: Bharti Airtel Acquires Zain's African Assets," coauthored with Saurabh Arora, Chiropriya Dasgupta, Anuj Jain and Glen Dowell. It is available upon request from the Emerging Market Institute at the Johnson Graduate School of Management at Cornell University.

2. Press release, "Bharti Set to Acquire Zain Africa BV," March 30, 2010 at http://www.airtel.in/about-bharti/media-centre/bharti-airtel-news/corporate/pg-bharti-set-to-acquire-zain-africa-bv.

3. See "Sunil Mittal Profile," at http://www.iloveindia.com/indian-heroes/sunil-mittal.html.

4. See "Bharti Minutes in Africa," www.Forbes.com, April 28, 2010. See http://www.forbes.com/2010/04/27/forbes-india-bharti-minutes-factory-goes-to-africa.html.

5. *Finance Asia Magazine*, "Asia's Best Managed Companies: Singapore and India," April 30, 2010. See http://www.financeasia.com/News/173383,asias-best-managed-companies-india-and-singapore.aspx.

6. "Zain poised to lead telecom emerging markets by 2011," www.ghanaweb.com Business News, November 18, 2008. See http://www.ghanaweb.com/GhanaHomePage/NewsArchive/artikel.php?ID=153246.

7. "S&P, Crisil place Bharti's Debt Programmes on 'Rating Watch'," February 20, 2010. See also *Economic Times of India,* May 11, 2010, "(This) reflects CRISIL's belief that Bharti Airtel's proposed acquisition of Zain Africa BV's business for an enterprise value of US$10.7 billion will be largely debt-funded; the acquisition can thereby adversely affect Bharti Airtel's gearing [debt-to-equity ratio] and debt protection indicators over the short term." See http://articles.economictimes.indiatimes.com/2010-02-20/news/27577612_1_risk-profile-crisil-standard-poor.

8. "Bharti Faces Hurdle in Bid for Zain's $10.7b Asset," NigeriaBusiness.com, February 10, 2010. See http://www.thenigeriabusiness.com/tnit114.html. See also "Congo Republic Says Zain-Bharti Deal Breaks Law," Reuters, April 12, 2010. See http://in.reuters.com/article/2010/04/12/telecom-bharti-congo-idUSLDE63B1SD20100412. In Bharti's press release (see footnote 2 and chapter 14), Mittal is quoted: "We are committed to partnering with the governments in these (African) countries in taking affordable telecom services to the remotest geographies and bridging the digital divide."

9. See Table A1, "Summary of World Output," in the IMF's 2013 World Economic Outlook, titled "Transitions and Tensions" (p. 153). More recent updates of the IMF's WEO available through October 2014 offer similar, though somewhat more modest growth forecasts among emerging and developed countries.

10. Jim O'Neil, *The Growth Map: Economic Opportunity in the BRICs and Beyond.*

11. O'Neil, *The Growth Map*, p. 36. Undoubtedly, the GES scores have continued to evolve over time not only in terms of the variables that are included in the indices, but also in the weights that they receive in the average index score. The most recent Global Economics Paper (Number 223, December 18, 2013) from the Goldman Sachs Economics Research team (coauthored by José Ursua and Julian Richers), titled *Our 2013 GES: Surprising the Markets*, lists six dimensions (what they call "buckets") to the scores: political conditions, macroeconomic stability, macroeconomic conditions, human capital, technology, and microeconomic environment. New variables that are added to these expanded scores include costs to starting a business, urbanization, patent applications, and expenditures on research and development, among others (see p. 4, "Box 1: Our GES—A Refresher on the Back of Better Data").

12. J. P. Morgan Securities Emerging Markets Research team publishes its *Local Markets Guide.* The 9th edition (September 2013) offers a detailed overview of the local markets in the emerging market universe, including their key market drivers. Their exhaustive country-by-country report, however, features background information on the country's monetary policy; market rules for their local bond, foreign exchange, and derivatives markets; and clearance and settlement issues. They discuss regulations, taxation policies, and capital controls. The key market rules address market size, liquidity, and transaction costs.

13. Other recent titles that feature discussion of elements of my very own risk indicator scores in emerging markets include *Opportunities in Emerging Markets: Investing in the Economies of Tomorrow* by Gordian Gaeta, *Investing in Emerging Markets: The BRIC Economies and Beyond* by Julian Marr and Cherry Reynard, and *The Little Book of Emerging Markets: How to Make Money in the World's Fastest Growth Markets* by Franklin Templeton's Mark Mobius. Franklin Templeton is a global investment management firm (www.franklintempleton.com).

14. "Normal" refers to the standard "bell-curved" distribution with a mean of zero and a standard deviation of one. It has the features that (a) half of the distribution lies above zero with the other half below it and (b) outcomes are symmetrically likely in the positive ranges as well as the negative ranges.

15. It is true that Israel was reclassified as a developed market from an emerging market in May 2010 by Morgan Stanley Capital International (MSCI). For details, see Shoshanna Solomon's article in *Bloomberg Businessweek*, "Israel Struggles with Upgrade from Emerging to Developed Market," August 22, 2013. FTSE International and Standard & Poor's (S&P) IFC index groups also upgraded Israel to developed-market status in 2010. South Korea has also been upgraded by S&P/IFC and FTSE International, but not yet by MSCI. More discussion will follow on which countries traditionally comprise the emerging market set and why in chapter 2. See http://www.businessweek.com/articles/2013-08-22/israel-struggles-with-upgrade-from-emerging-to-developed-market.

16. To be completely accurate, I perform the regression analysis with all emerging and developed markets, but to keep the figure simple, I exhibit only those for emerging markets.

Chapter 2

1. See page 4 of the introductory chapter of *The Emerging Markets Century: How a New Breed of World-Class Companies Is Overtaking the World.*

2. Van Agtmael, page 5. Van Agtmael states that "We had the goods. We had the data. We had the countries. What we did not have, however, was an elevator pitch that liberated

these developing economies from the stigma of being labeled as "Third World" basket cases, an image rife with negative associations of flimsy polyester, cheap toys, rampant corruption, Soviet-style tractors, and flooded rice paddies" (5).

3. The Emerging Markets Database (EMDB) covers emerging and "frontier" stock markets. It includes market performance, indicators, market capitalization, monthly value traded, local stock market price indices, prices in local currency and US dollars, etc. In addition, this database includes two series of indices, the IFC Global (IFCG) indices (which reflect restrictions on foreign ownership) and the IFC Investible (IFCI) index series (which reflects new opportunities for investment since the mid-1980s). These indices are calculated for prices and returns. Depending on the country, annual coverage starts as early as 1975, while monthly coverage starts in 1986. Since 1999, the International Finance Corporation no longer publishes this product. Instead, it is produced by Standard & Poor's Index Services. See www.spindices.com.

4. See Chapter 1 of the *Emerging Stock Markets Factbook 1999*.

5. See page 137 in the Statistical Appendix of the IMF's *World Economic Outlook: Transitions and Tensions*. In the WEO statistical appendix, detailed discussion follows on the challenge of classifying countries that are not included in the analysis (such as the Democratic People's Republic of Korea, Cuba) because they are not IMF members or because of data limitations (Somalia). The WEO also emphasizes how "country" and "economy" do not always refer to a territorial entity that is a state as understood by international law and practice (see footnote 4, page 137). These are important clarifications, but are not core elements for my analysis.

6. International Monetary Fund 2013, page 137.

7. The WFE is a trade association of 62 publicly regulated stock, futures, and options exchanges around the world. It conducts an annual survey of global markets which offers a rich source of data for scholars and market practitioners alike. See the statistical tab at http://www.world-exchanges.org/statistics/annual.

8. OTC Markets Group, Inc. (www.otcmarkets.com, headquartered in New York City, operates a financial marketplaces platform providing price and liquidity information for almost 10,000 over-the-counter (OTC) securities. OTC-traded securities are organized into three marketplaces to inform investors of opportunities and risks: OTCQX, OTCQB, and OTC Pink.

9. If one includes the Hong Kong exchanges from China's Special Administrative Region (SAR) together with the Shanghai and Shenzhen exchanges, China tops Japan's exchanges in terms of total market capitalization and by the number of stocks listed.

10. Bonds are any kind of fixed-income financial instrument issued by governments, local authorities, and state-owned or private organizations. They may be listed or traded in one or several exchanges, and ensure predetermined levels of returns in the form of interest rate. Interest rates may remain fixed throughout the bond's life or vary according to the bond's terms of listing. Data represent the number of bonds listed multiplied by their price at year-end. Some exchanges publish a bond market value at a notional value (signaled in a footnote); the other bourses use the real market value. The total number of bond issuers represents the number of organizations which issued the fixed-income instruments listed on the exchange. These issuers are broken down into *domestic private bonds*, which include corporate bonds, bonds issued by domestic banks and financial institutions; *domestic public bonds*, which include government state-owned organizations

bonds and bills, state-related institutions whose instruments are guaranteed by the state, and municipal bonds; and *foreign bonds*, which are listed on the exchange and are issued by nonresident institutions such as foreign governments, banks, financial institutions, and supranational organizations (e.g., European Investment Bank, European Bank for Reconstruction and Development, World Bank). They also include eurobonds (bonds issued under a law of a state different from the one of the issuer and placed in a foreign country inside the euro zone). An issuer may list bonds with different maturities, but the total number of issuers is unchanged.

11. In the June 2013 release of the first quarter of 2013 Federal Reserve Statistical Release, titled *Financial Accounts of the United States: Flow of Funds, Balance Sheets, and Integrated Macroeconomic Accounts*, the US bond market comprises $60.3 trillion in US Treasury notes and bonds; US Agency bonds; state and local government bonds; corporate, foreign, and financial company bonds; as well as consumer and trade credit, security credit, mortgages, mortgage-backed securities, and bank loans.

12. See the December 2011 monthly newsletter of the WFE *Focus* and the insightful article by Carl Johan Högbom and Henrik Wagenius, "Growing Need for Innovative SME Exchanges in Europe."

13. See a brief history of ChiNext at www.szse.cn/main/en/chinext.

14. The five main requirements for WFE members include: (1) be significant within its country of origin, defined by its size as well as the services to conduct market operations; (2) be regulated by a supervisory body within a statutory framework, with the capital market authority serving as a member of the International Organization of Securities Commissions (IOSCO); (3) facilitate capital raising and risk management; (4) be a public good, ensuring a fair, orderly market for all participants; and (5) maintain standards and pay requisite fees. See the member criteria tab at http://www.world-exchanges.org/member-exchanges/membership-criteria-0 for more details.

15. A reasonable question to ask is what the reader can do for those countries, like Qatar, that I exclude from my analysis for various reasons but for which they have an active interest. There are two options. First, the methodology can in principle be adapted to include such countries if the reader is willing to adopt the framework presented in the book and to build their own data. It is my own limitation to fail to provide a complete portrayal of Qatar, though the methodology could apply there. Second, one may infer that there is some unobservable characteristic about a country such that data are not readily available for their use in the construction of the risk indicators. The very lack of information about their clearance and settlement systems, the convertibility of the local currency, and the disclosure and governance practices of the public companies traded on their exchanges may represent, in and of itself, a note of caution for a prospective investor.

16. In fact, S&P/IFC has no such designation of "frontier." Rather, it is the S&P Broad Market Indices that feature it. I will treat them interchangeably for convenience, but recognize the important difference. More details are available in their publication *S&P Frontier Indices Methodology*. I also highly recommend the table of Appendix A of a second publication, *S&P Global BMI, S&P/IFCI Indices Methodology* (July 2013).

17. With regards to Slovenia and Slovakia, the distinction between the S&P Dow Jones Indices and the S&P/IFC Indices that I glossed over may be worth reprising. In fact, in the S&P Global BMI index, which I do not feature in Table 2.4, Slovenia was promoted to developed market status in July 2003. In October 2007 it was reassigned to emerging

market status, and in November 2008 it was further downgraded to frontier market status. The transitions in status are fascinating, but tracking them and the rationales behind them lie beyond the scope of this book.

18. See details in the June 2013 *Global Market Accessibility Review*, available at www. msci.com. See http://www.msci.com/resources/products/indexes/global_equity_indexes/ gimi/stdindex/MSCI_Global_Market_Accessibility_Review_June2013.pdf.

19. See FTSE International's *FTSE Frontier 50 Index Fact Sheet* (December 31, 2013) and their *FTSE Emerging Market Index* (also December 31, 2013) for a general discussion of their country classifications, their country breakdowns and some index characteristics. See http://www.ftse.com/analytics/factsheets/Home/Search and select either the Frontier 50 or Emerging Market Index as options.

20. Details are available in JP Morgan Securities' *Local Markets Guide: Emerging Markets Research* (9th edition, September 2013). Pages 38–42 detail the construction of the composite indices.

Chapter 3

1. See p. 559 of Pearson, "On Lines and Planes."

2. The title gives us this strong hint. See Harold Hotelling, "Analysis of a Complex of Statistical Variables into Principal Components," 417–41. He offers more details on construct in a follow-up study in 1936, titled "Relations Between Two Sets of Variates," 321–27.

3. The symbol denoted "·" in the equation means the sum of the cross-products of the elements of the two vectors, x and w. Think of it as $w_1 \times x_1 + w_2 \times x_2 + w_3 \times x_3 + \cdots + w_p \times x_p$.

4. Define X^* for the k-th principal component as having subtracted the first k principal components from X. Or, $X^*_{k-1} = X - \Sigma_{s=1}^{k-1} X \cdot w_{(s)} \cdot w_{(s)}'$ where the superscript denoted "'" in the equation means the vector has been transformed from a column to a row (i.e., transposed). I then search for the vector of loadings that maximizes the variance from this new data matrix. Mathematically, I write: $w_{(k)} = \arg\max_{\|w\|=1} \{ \Sigma_i (x^*_{k-1} \cdot w)^2 \}$.

5. The asymptotic distribution of eigenvalues and eigenvectors for a sample from a multivariate normal distribution was derived by Girshick in 1939 in his study "On the Sampling Theory of Roots of Determinantal Equations," 203–24. It is extended importantly by Anderson "Asymptotic Theory for Principal Components Analysis," 122–48.

6. See Stock and Watson, "Forecasting Using Principal Components from a Large Number of Predictors," 1167–79, and Engle and Watson, "Alternative Algorithms for the Estimation of Dynamic Factor, Mimic, and Varying Coefficient Regression Models," 385–400.

7. Consider the study of Doz, Giannone, and Reichlin, "A Quasi-Maximum Likelihood Approach for Large Approximate Dynamic Factor Models." They allow the EM algorithm to incorporate information along the time dimension using dynamic factor analysis. Bai and Li, in "Maximum Likelihood Estimation and Inference for Approximate Factor Models of High Dimension," allow errors in an approximate factor model, like a principal components structure, to be correlated and heteroskedastic (varying across time and over a cross-section) and in a way that is unknown. They refine the maximum likelihood estimation procedures to deal with this setting. A useful summary of the usefulness of the EM algorithm for PCA is by Sam Roweis, "EM Algorithms for

PCA and SPCA," 626–23. Scott Brave and Andrew Butters, in "Monitoring Financial Stability," 22–43, describe a number of challenges of operationalizing the EM algorithm in a time-series application.

8. The study is titled "What Determines Corporate Transparency?," 207–52.

9. Bushman et al., "What Determines Corporate Transparency?," see Section 3.

10. A well-cited study compares and contrasts the two methods and discusses the greater simplicity of PCA; see R. L. Gorsuch, "Common Factor Analysis versus Component Analysis: Some well and little known facts," 33–39.

11. See David Larcker, Scott Richardson, and Irem Tuna, "How Important Is Corporate Governance?," 963–1008.

12. See Paul Gompers, Joy Ishii, and Andrew Metrick, "Corporate Governance and Equity Prices," 107–55.

13. In later chapters, I will also discuss global corporate governance scores developed by Credit Lyonnais Securities Asia (CLSA) and Standard and Poor's (S&P) *Transparency and Disclosure* scores. These industry constructs predate the work of Gompers, Ishii, and Metrick ("Corporate Governance"), and they take on similar methodological approaches. CLSA's report in 2001 examined 494 companies in 24 countries, and the governance scores were based on responses from financial analysts to 57 questions that were used to construct scores on a 1 to 100 scale, where a higher number indicates better governance. Most of the questions had binary answers and based on objective information. The 57 questions were grouped into six categories related to managerial discipline, transparency, board accountability, management responsibility, protections for minority shareholders, and social responsibility. S&P's transparency scores were assembled from 91 possible items surveyed from objective, public data, such as financial statement information, for 573 companies in 16 emerging and 3 developed countries in 2000. The approach follows a similar summation scheme. Two studies, among many others, that have employed these data include Art Durnev and E. Han Kim's "To Steal or Not to Steal," 1461–93, and my own with Craig Doidge and René Stulz, "Why Do Countries Matter So Much for Corporate Governance?," 1–39.

14. See www.doingbusiness.org. Many attribute the origins of the Doing Business Indicators project at the World Bank to a study published in the *Quarterly Journal of Economics* by Simeon Djankov, a former Lead Economist in the Private Sector Group and former finance minister in Bulgaria, with Rafael La Porta, Florencio Lopez-de-Silanes and Andrei Shleifer. The study, titled "The Regulation of Entry," was published in 2002 by the *Quarterly Journal of Economics* (Volume 117, pages 1 to 37) and presented data on the regulation of entry of firms in 85 countries covering the number of procedures, official time, and official cost that a start-up must bear before it could operate legally. The main findings were that countries with heavier regulation were also less democratic with higher rates of corruption. I will feature this study's data in my risk indicator on limits to legal protections.

15. See references and links to www.soundcloud.com clip of Bin Han's remarks in "China Seeks to Water Down Key World Bank Report," *Financial Times*, May 6, 2013.

16. See also "The Wrangling Behind the World Bank Business Stats," *Financial Times*, October 30, 2013.

17. See http://www.dbrpanel.org/sites/dbrpanel/files/doing-business-review-panel-report.pdf.

18. See Bjørn Høyland, Karl Moene, and Fredrik Willumsen, "The Tyranny of International Index Rankings," University of Oslo working paper, 2010.

19. Other related studies from other disciplines include Tina Søreide, "Is it Wrong to Rank?," and Shawn Trier and Simon Jackman, "Democracy as a Latent Variable," 201–17.

Chapter 4

1. At the risk of shameless promotion of my own work, I offer to interested readers as background reading my edited three-volume collection *International Capital Markets*, with René Stulz. The first volume features seminal research papers on theories and empirical evidence on international portfolio choice and asset pricing. The second volume focuses on international portfolio diversification and the role of interest rates and exchange rates. And the third volume investigates theories of and empirical evidence on barriers to international investments, international capital flows, and anomalies in global capital markets. Our introduction to the three-volume set lays out the philosophy which is at the core of this book. Other useful references that support this vision of the importance of financial liberalization for emerging markets is found in a survey study I wrote with René Stulz titled "Are Assets Priced Locally or Globally?," and an excellent survey by Geert Bekaert and Campbell Harvey, "Emerging Markets Finance."

2. Thomas Piketty's influential 2014 book *Capital in the Twenty-First Century* proposes that inequality is a feature of capitalism, stemming from the excess rate of growth in profits, dividends, interest, rents, and other income from capital relative to income growth, and it can only be reversed with state intervention. He has argued that a number of developing Asian countries that have successfully emerged have not benefited from large foreign investments. For a useful summary of this view see Bernard Avishai's article in *The New Yorker*, "Thomas Piketty and the Foreign Investment Question," May 27, 2014.

3. See May 19, 2011 press conference of FF Group and Fosun International at IR releases for the FF Group, see http://www.ffgroup.com/files/Press%20conference%20 FOLLI%20FOLLIE%20GROUP.pdf. All of this discussion is based on the case study "Folli Follie Group and Fosun International: A Global Partnership," coauthored by Cheng Qiu, Andreas Skiadopoulos, Dong Yang, and Yina Shi under the supervision of Andrew Karolyi, and which is available upon request from the Emerging Market Institute at the Johnson Graduate School of Management at Cornell University.

4. See specific comments by Mr. Koutsoliousos in http://www.ffgroup.com/files/ Press%20conference%20FOLLI%20FOLLIE%20GROUP.pdf.

5. According to David Brophy, Page Ouimet and Clemens Sialm (2004, Table 4, "PIPE Dreams? The Performance of Companies Issuing Equity Privately," National Bureau of Economic Research Working Paper No. 11011, www.nber.org/papers/w11011) in their analysis of 5,260 PIPE deals in the United States over an eight-year period (1995-2002), companies issuing traditional PIPEs amounts experience, on average, a statistically significant and economically large 5.49% abnormal returns during a 10-day event window around the close. The cumulative abnormal return performance for up to 250 days following the announcement of a traditional PIPE deal is a statistically significant -4.73%.

6. See Folli Follie Group's 2010 Annual Report, IR releases for the FF Group, http:// www.ffgroup.com/default.asp?pid=36&la=1&cid=1.

7. See Thomas Louise and Nelson Schwartz, "Wall Street Helped to Mask Debt Fueling Europe's Crisis," *New York Times*, February 14, 2010. Also "Greek Deficit Revised to 13.6%; Moody's Cuts Rating," *Bloomberg*, May 2, 2010. See http://www.nytimes.com/2010/02/14/business/global/14debt.html?pagewanted=all&_r=0 and http://www.bloomberg.com/apps/news?pid=newsarchive&sid=aNEqq__19gRE.

8. See Eurobank EFG, Equity Research, Retail, April 13, 2011.

9. See the history of the company at http://www.fosun.com/en/about/about_1.html as of March 2, 2014.

10. See also http://www.fosun.com/en/about/about_1.html.

11. See *Meat Trade News Daily*, "China—Leaving the US Economy in the Dust," November 27, 2011. See http://www.meattradenewsdaily.co.uk/news/241111/china_leaving_the_us_economy_in_the_dust_.aspx.

12. *McKinsey Annual Retail and Consumer Goods Report*, 2010.

13. *McKinsey Annual Retail and Consumer Goods Report*, 2010.

14. See Reuters, "Chinese Private Equity Firms Set Sail Abroad," October 8, 2011. See http://www.reuters.com/article/2011/09/30/us-china-privateequity-idUSTRE78T09Z20110930.

15. See, among others, Eurobank EFG Equities, *Folli Follie Group: Eyes on the Cash Flow and Update on the Debt*, November 28, 2011.

16. See *Wall Street Journal*, "Fosun Is a Connoisseur of Brands: Chinese Firm's CEO, Liang Xinjun, Discusses Lure of Western Names and Maintaining Entrepreneurial Spirit," July 2, 2013.

17. See Gerard Debreu's *Theory of Value: An Axiomatic Analysis of Economic Equilibrium* and Kenneth Arrow's "The Role of Securities in the Optimal Allocation of Risk Bearing."

18. See Ross Levine, "Financial Development and Economic Growth," 688–726.

19. See Raymond Goldsmith, *Financial Structure and Development*. As Levine points out, Goldsmith understood many weaknesses of his approach, including the possible reverse-causality of the relationship between financial systems and growth. Levine writes (p. 48): "there is no possibility, however, of establishing with confidence the direction of the causal mechanisms, i.e., of deciding whether financial factors were responsible for the acceleration of economic development or whether financial development reflected economic growth whose mainsprings must be sought elsewhere."

20. King and Levine, "Finance and Growth"; Levine and Zervos, "Stock Markets, Banks, And Economic Growth"; Bekaert, Harvey, and Lundblad, "Emerging Equity Markets"; and Rajan and Zingales "Financial Dependence and Growth" and "The Great Reversals."

21. Goldsmith, *Financial Structure and Development*. See also King and Levine, "Finance and Growth," 717–37.

22. See Levine and Zervos, "Stock Markets, Banks, And Economic Growth"; Hargis, "Do Foreign Investors Stimulate or Inhibit"; Bekaert, Harvey, and Lundblad, "Emerging Equity Markets And Economic Development"; Bekaert, Harvey, and Lumsdaine, "Dating the Integration of World Equity Markets"; Rajan and Zingales "Financial Dependence and Growth," and "The Great Reversals"; and Karolyi, "ADRs and the Development of Emerging Equity Markets."

23. Bond market capitalization is an integral component to the measure of the depth of financial markets. Beck, Demirgüç-Kunt, and Levine describe the origination of the

data in "A New Database on the Structure and Development of the Financial Sector," 597–605. The same authors update their analysis in "Financial Institutions and Markets across Countries and Over Time," 77–92, and a thorough benchmarking analysis is found in Čihák, Demirgüc-Kunt, Feyen, and Levine, "Benchmarking Financial Systems around the World."

24. See Demirgüc-Kunt and Maksimovic, "Law, Finance and Firm Growth," 2107–37, and Demirgüc-Kunt and Maksimovic, "Institutions, Financial Markets, and Firm Debt Maturity," 295–336.

25. See La Porta, Lopez-de-Silanes, Shleifer, and Vishny, "Legal Determinants of External Finance"; Bekaert, Harvey, and Lundblad, "Emerging Equity Markets"; Rajan and Zingales, "Financial Dependence and Growth" and "The Great Reversals"; Karolyi, "ADRs and the Development of Emerging Equity Markets"; Djankov, La Porta, Lopez-de-Silanes, and Shleifer, 2008.

26. See La Porta, Lopez-de-Silanes, Shleifer, and Vishny, "Legal Determinants of External Finance," and Rajan and Zingales, "The Great Reversals."

27. See Doidge, Karolyi, and Stulz, "The U.S. Left Behind?," 546–73.

28. See Levine and Zervos, "Stock Markets, Banks"; Hargis, "Do Foreign Investors Stimulate"; Bekaert, Harvey, and Lundblad, "Emerging Equity Markets."

29. See Goldsmith, *Financial Structure and Development*, and subsequent King and Levine ("Finance and Growth") studies.

30. NT$ implies New Taiwan Dollars. See, for more details, the Central Bank of the Republic of China (Taiwan) website at www.cbc.gov.tw and the "Statistics" tab. The note, titled the "Conditions and Performance of Domestic Banks," for the fourth quarter of 2012 furnishes the relevant statistics. See http://www.cbc.gov.tw/lp.asp?ctNode=511&CtUnit=223&BaseDSD=7&mp=2.

Chapter 5

1. The term "transaction cost" is often attributed to Ronald Coase in his 1937 seminal article "The Nature of the Firm," in which he refers to the "costs of using the price mechanism," and in his 1960 article "The Problem of Social Cost," in which he discusses the "costs of market transactions." Oliver Williamson's 1981 work "The Economics of Organization" outlines a broader concept of not only "buying and selling, but also day-to-day emotional transactions, informal gift exchanges," among other examples.

2. See O'Hara, *Market Microstructure Theory*, 15.

3. See the working group mission statements at http://www.nber.org/workinggroups/mm/mm.html.

4. See Perold, "The Payment System and Derivative Instruments."

5. See the editorial survey by Saunders and Scholnik, "Introduction to Special Issue on Frontiers in Payment and Settlement Systems," on the challenges of gathering relevant data and information on securities settlement systems.

6. See www.elkinsmcsherry.com. This is one of the rare occasions in which I misled readers in the opening paragraphs. These data are not available for free, but on a subscription basis. I am grateful to Jim Bryson and Dick McSherry for early discussions about the data back in 2006 when I first contacted them. In 2011, Henry Marigliano was helpful in allowing me access to the historic quarterly country-level global equity universe data from 1996 to second quarter of 2011. I use the last set of observations for 2012.

7. Unfortunately, I was unable to secure permission of the firm to display the raw data in the book. As a result, I will only describe summary statistics in this chapter and will suppress the presentation in the actual tables.

8. See Gagnon and Karolyi, "Multimarket Trading and Arbitrage." Another earlier study that showcases the Elkins/McSherry data is by Domowitz, Glen, and Madhavan, "Liquidity, Volatility and Equity Trading Costs Across Countries and Over Time."

9. See, in particular, Table 6 of Gagnon and Karolyi, "Multimarket Trading and Arbitrage."

10. See Chapter 19 of Harris, *Trading and Exchanges*.

11. Harris, *Trading and Exchanges*, 399 and 400.

12. Karolyi, Lee, and Van Dijk, "Understanding Commonality in Liquidity around the World." The study's sample includes 27,447 stocks from 40 countries for the period January 1995 to December 2009. The daily turnover measure for individual stocks is the average of the ratio of the daily volume relative to the shares outstanding in a given month. This daily average across days is then averaged across stocks on a market-capitalization-weighted basis to compute the market turnover statistic. I report the latest observation for December 2009. The Karolyi et al. study seeks to measure the commonality, or common covariation, in daily innovations in turnover (and other proxies for liquidity) across stocks in a market and to predict those changes in commonality.

13. See Amihud, "Illiquidity and Stock Return."

14. Kyle, "Continuous Auctions and Insider Trading."

15. See Karolyi, Lee, and Van Dijk, "Understanding Commonality in Liquidity." Other useful work in which the Amihud proxy has been computed for a large cross-country sample includes Lang and Maffett, "Transparency and Liquidity Uncertainty in Crisis Periods," and Fong, Holden, and Trzcinka, "What Are the Best Liquidity Proxies for Global Research?" The Lang and Maffett sample includes 424,808 firm months across 35 countries from 1997 to 2008 (12 of which are emerging markets) and the Fong, Holden, and Trzcinka study covers 203,517 stock years across 42 countries (16 emerging) from 1996 to 2007.

16. See Lesmond, Ogden, and Trczinka, "A New Estimate of Transaction Costs."

17. See Lee, "The World Market Price of Liquidity Risk." I use the 2004 statistics, the last set he reports, though they are seriously out of phase with the 2012 analysis I seek. Chapter 1 laid out the caveats on timing and the problems are revealed starkly here.

18. See Lee, "The World Market Price of Liquidity Risk." Also, see Acharya and Pedersen (2005).

19. Effective spreads are measured as the absolute value of the difference between intra-day transaction prices relative to the prevailing midpoints. Fong, Holden, and Trzcinka ("What Are the Best Liquidity Proxies?") use the Thomson Reuters Tick History database of 8.5 billion trades and 13.6 billion quotes for 25,582 firms around the world over the 1996–2007 sample period for their cross-validation exercise.

20. Lee, "The World Market Price of Liquidity Risk," Column 1, first panel.

21. Cumming, Johan, and Li, "Exchange Trading Rules and Stock Market Liquidity," 652.

22. Cumming et al., "Exchange Trading Rules," 652.

23. See Bris, Goetzmann, and Zhu, "Efficiency and the Bear."

24. See Jain et al., "The Worldwide Reach of Short Selling Regulations."

25. Jain et al., "The Worldwide Reach of Short Selling Regulations," 180.

26. According to the classification of the Committee on Payment and Settlement Systems of the Bank for International Settlements (CPSS-BIS) (September 1992 report titled "Delivery versus Payment in Securities Settlement Systems," page 16, www.bis.org/cpss/), in DVP Model 1 securities and funds are settled on a trade-by-trade (gross) basis, with final transfer of securities from the seller to the buyer (delivery) occurring at the same time as final transfer of funds from the buyer to the seller (payment); in DVP Model 2, securities are settled on a gross basis with final delivery occurring throughout the processing cycle, but funds are settled on a net basis, with final payment occurring at the end of the processing cycle; in DVP Model 3, securities and funds are settled on a net basis, with final transfers of both securities and funds occurring at the end of the processing cycle.

27. Cumming et al., "Exchange Trading Rules"; Jain et al., "The Worldwide Reach"; Fong et al., "What Are the Best Liquidity Proxies."

28. Amihud, "Illiquidity and Stock Return"; Karolyi et al., "Understanding Commonality in Liquidity."

Chapter 6

1. The general topic of the benefits and costs of financial globalization is near and dear to my heart and has been the focus of my own research for the past 20 years. However, I am very grateful for the well-defined and instructive framework of Ayhan Kose, Eswar Prasad, Kenneth Rogoff, and Shang-Jin Wei, "Financial Globalization: A Reappraisal," which guides the logic in this chapter. Their survey paper complements well that of Geert Bekaert and Campbell Harvey, "Emerging Markets Finance," and of my own with René Stulz, "Are Assets Priced Locally or Globally?"

2. See, among others: Jagdish Bhagwati, "The Capital Myth," *Foreign Affairs* 7, pp. 7–12; Joseph Stiglitz, 2000, "Capital Market Liberalization, Economic Growth, and Instability," and his popular treatise from 2002, *Globalization and Its Discontents*; and Dani Rodrik, 1998, "Who Needs Capital-Account Convertibility?"

3. A cogent and well-articulated summary of the options various policymakers face today on reintroducing capital controls (as well as in which form) is found in Hélène Rey's working paper "Dilemma Not Trilemma."

4. See Kose et al., "Financial Globalization."

5. See the Bloomberg News report "Spreadtrum Says Muddy Waters Doubts on Results are 'Baseless,'" *Bloomberg News*, June 29, 2011, www.businessweek.com/news/2011-06-29/spreadtrum-says-muddy-waters-doubts-on-results-are-baseless-.html.

6. See "Open Letter to SPRD Chairman re Muddy Waters' Concerns," June 28, 2011, http://www.muddywatersresearch.com/research/sprd/mw-open-letter-to-chairman/.

7. "Open Letter to SPRD Chairman," 1–6.

8. See "Muddy Waters Initiating Coverage on TRE.TO, OTC:SNOFF—Strong Sell," June 2, 2011, www.muddywatersresearch.com. See for additional details the CNN Money Invest story by James O'Toole, "Sino-Forest Sues Muddy Waters for Defamation," April 3, 2012, http://money.cnn.com/2012/04/02/markets/sino-forest-muddy-waters/.

9. See "China Yurun Extends Slump as Muddy Waters Speculation Spurs Short Sellers," *Bloomberg News*, June 28, 2011, www.bloomberg.com/news/2011-06-27/yurun-isn-t-aware-of-a-short-seller-s-report.html.

10. See http://finance.sina.com.cn for a story titled "AMEX listed company Orient Paper Financial Mystery Investigation," by *21st Century Business Herald*, July 22, 2010, written by Wang Kang Yi Peng. A version of the story in Chinese is available at http://chinesecompanyanalyst.files.wordpress.com/2010/08/21cbh-onp-article-7-22-2010.pdf. A useful follow-up story is by *TheStreet.com*'s Robert Holmes, "Orient Paper Rally a Short Squeeze?," July 23, 2010, www.thestreet.com/story/10815854/1/orient-paper-rally-a-short-squeeze.html.

11. See Associated Press report on March 4, 2011, "Spreadtrum 4Q Results, Outlook Beat Analyst Views." http://news.yahoo.com/spreadtrum-4q-results-outlook-beat-analyst-views-20110303-195506-123.html.

12. Associated Press, "Spreadtrum 4Q Results," first paragraph.

13. All of this discussion is based on the case study "Spreadtrum Communications 2011: Spreading into Mobile Telecommunications in China," June 19, 2010, unpublished Cornell University working paper coauthored by Dominic Bow, Dingdin Feng, Winston Lin, Aloka Singh, and Elisabeth Cai, under the supervision of Andrew Karolyi, and which is available upon request from the Emerging Market Institute at the Johnson Graduate School of Management at Cornell University. Global Systems for Mobile Communication (GSM) describe the second-generation digital cellphone networks, and Time-Division Synchronous Code Division Multiple Access (TD-SCDMA) is a radio-based communication link between a mobile device and an active station used in Chinese networks. General Packet Radio Service (GPRS) is a mobile data service which charges fees based on the volume of data being transferred.

14. See Spreadtrum Communications, 2009 Annual Report, Securities and Exchange Commission Form 20-F (May 7, 2010). See http://www.sec.gov/Archives/edgar/data/128 7950/000119312510113017/0001193125-10-113017-index.htm. Additional data come from S&P Capital IQ.

15. Ibid., page 55.

16. See comprehensive report on China's telecommunications market in *China Telecommunications Panorama* (2005), http://chinese-school.netfirms.com/articles/Telecommunications-China.html. Also consult *China's Telecoms Industry: Reform and Prospects* (December, 2004), www.china-cic.org.cn/english/digital%20library/200412/5.pdf. The Spreadtrum Communications 2009 Annual Report, Form 20-F, stated that from 2005 to 2009, the growth rate of 3G sales has been steadily increasing from 3.5% to 25.7%. at www.asia.xorte.com.

17. See Bloomberg report in Exhibit 18 of Bow et al., "Spreadtrum Communications 2011," Chapter 16.

18. See Bow et al., "Spreadtrum Communications 2011," Exhibit 19. The short interest ratio can also be computed as the ratio of the total number of shares of a security that have been sold short to the average daily trading volume of the stock. Both versions are used as an indicator of market sentiment with respect to the stock; a high ratio indicates a transition to investor pessimism.

19. See comments from Chairman Leo Li in "Spreadtrum Says Muddy Waters Doubts on Results are 'Baseless." See also Doug Young, "Chinese Firms Finally Stand Up to Short Sellers' Barrage," *Global Times*, September 9, 2012.

20. See Associated Press report "Spreadtrum Shares Fall on Lower 2Q Net Income," August 10, 2012. See http://finance.yahoo.com/news/spreadtrum-shares-fall-lower-2q-net-income-180750618--finance.html. See also "Spreadtrum Comms Stock Rating Lowered

by Daiwa Capital Markets (SPRD)," September 25, 2012, by Patrick Bannon. See http://
www.benzinga.com/analyst-ratings/analyst-color/12/09/2938909/update-daiwa-capit
al-markets-downgrades-spreadtrum-commu.

21. See John Jannarone's piece in the *Wall Street Journal*, "Not All Chinese ADRs
Created Equal," July 28, 2011. See http://online.wsj.com/articles/SB100014240531119048883045764723607076166334. The *Wall Street Journal* article "U.S.-Chinese Progress on
Accounting Is Dealt Setback," October 4, 2011 describes the challenges faced by com-
missioners at the Public Company Accounting Oversight Board (PCAOB) in conducting
inspections of Chinese auditing firms which perform audits for US-listed and registered
Chinese firms. See http://online.wsj.com/articles/SB1000142405297020452460457660918357074455
2.

22. In July 2013, Spreadtrum agreed to be acquired by state-owned Tsinghua Unigroup
Holdings, a Chinese corporation funded by Tsinghua University, for $1.78 billion. The
takeover offer at $31 per American Depositary share represented a 9% upgrade on the
$28.75 bid in June. According to Sruthi Ramakrishnan's Reuters report "Chinese State
Company to Buy Chipmaker Spreadtrum," July 12, 2013, Tsinghua Unigroup Holdings
will offer Spreadtrum expertise in consumer products protection, support of a vast
intellectual-protection portfolio, and access to capital markets in China. See http://
www.reuters.com/article/2013/07/12/us-spreadtrum-takeover-tsinghua-idUSBRE-
96B0AX20130712. The deal was completed on December 23, 2013; see *Wall Street
Journal*, "Tsinghua Unigroup Completes Acquisition of Spreadtrum for US$31.00 per
ADS," December 23, 2013. Also, see http://www.spreadtrum.com/en/news/press-releases/
tsinghua-unigroup-completes-acquisition-of-spreadtrum-for-us31.00-per-ads.

23. See Kose et al., "Financial Globalization," 10.

24. Robert Lucas asks the hard question as to why this basic prediction does not hold in
his 1990 paper "Why Doesn't Capital Flow from Rich to Poor Countries."

25. A number of studies have shown how specialization of production through glo-
balization may lead to specialization activities that are not necessarily growth enhancing.
Useful contributions include the seminal study by Maurice Obstfeld "Risk-Taking, Global
Diversification, and Growth," and another by Sebnem Kalemli-Ozcan, Bent Sørensen, and
Oved Yosha, "Risk Sharing and Industrial Specialization."

26. Ayhan Kose, in "Explaining Business Cycles in Small-Open Economies," shows how
the limited diversification of emerging market exports and imports could make them sus-
ceptible to terms of trade and foreign demand shocks.

27. See Karen Lewis, "Trying to Explain Home Bias in Equities and Consumption,"
571-608. There is a useful section on the home-bias puzzle in G. Andrew Karolyi and René
Stulz, "Are Assets Priced Locally or Globally?" 995-1002.

28. The original study by Dennis Quinn, "The Correlates of Changes in International
Financial Regulation," was published in 1997, but its success if popularized by the sub-
sequent study with A. Maria Toyoda in 2008, "Does Capital Account Liberalization
Lead to Growth?" See also Chinn, Menzie, and Hiro Ito, "What Matters for Financial
Development?" The authors maintain the data through 2011 and make it available at http://
web.pdx.edu/~ito/Chinn-Ito_website.htm.

29. Kose et al., "Financial Globalization," 15.

30. The original study that launched an extensive research program by the team was
Geert Bekaert and Campbell R. Harvey, "Foreign Speculators and Emerging Equity

Markets." Using firm-level data, Anusha Chari and Peter Henry, in "Risk Sharing and Asset Prices," found that the reduction in the cost of equity capital and increased investment across their 11 emerging markets arose from a reduction in the systematic risk associated with holding stocks in emerging markets. Geert Bekaert, Campbell Harvey, and Robin Lumsdaine, in "Dating the Integration of World Equity Markets," take a novel approach to the problem of relying on just the official liberalization dates. They employ a multivariate structural-break time-series analysis technique for a host of relevant macroeconomic and capital market variables and allow the data to determine when a statistically significant departure point arises in the cross-section of time series. More often than not across the emerging markets in their sample, they found that the optimal breakpoint was well beyond the official liberalization date.

31. See Peter Henry, "Stock Market Liberalization, Economic Reform, and Emerging Market Equity Prices."

32. See Bekaert, Harvey, and Lundblad, "Does Financial Liberalization Spur Growth?"

33. See Karolyi and Stulz, "Are Assets Priced Locally or Globally?"

34. A sampling of recent studies that reveal the complexities of understanding integration versus segmentation of the pricing of risk across international markets include Bekaert, Hodrick, and Zhang, "International Stock Return Comovements"; Hou, Karolyi, and Kho, "What Factors Drive Global Stock Returns?"; Fama and French, "Size, Value, and Momentum in International Stock Returns"; Carrieri, Chaieb, and Errunza, "Do Implicit Barriers Matter for Globalization?"; and Karolyi and Wu, "Size, Value, and Momentum in International Stock Returns."

35. An intriguing returns-based approach using multifactor models is by Pukthuanthong and Roll, "Global Market Integration." Bekaert, Harvey, Lundblad, and Siegel, in their 2011 study "What Segments Equity Markets?," build a price-based measure of segmentation based on the deviations of a country's price-to-earnings ratio relative to its norm defined by the equivalent ratios of the global industries that are represented in that country's national markets. Louis Gagnon and I, in the 2010 study "Multimarket Trading and Arbitrage," do not test for market integration per se, but we measure the magnitude and persistence over days of deviations in prices of what are otherwise identical securities trading in different markets around the world. Namely, we focus on cross-listed stocks with ordinary shares trading in the home market and ADRs (like Spreadtrum Communications) on major US exchanges. The study shows how these price deviations can be quite substantial for cross-listed stocks from countries for which significant limits to arbitrage—direct ones like transaction costs, taxes and indirect ones, like differences in trading hours—exist.

36. See Kose et al., "Financial Globalization," 10.

37. The original study by Philip Lane and Gian Milesi-Ferretti, "The External Wealth of Nations," was published in 2001. Their follow-up study from 2007, "The External Wealth of Nations Mark II," extended the data to 2004. Philip Lane's website makes it available to researchers (www.philiplane.org/EWN.html), and they have updated the data now to 2011.

38. See Lane and Milesi-Ferretti, "The External Wealth of Nations Mark II."

39. See www.dits.deloitte.com. The Deloitte International Tax Source (DITS) site is updated regularly. My information was drawn as of January 2014. The site states that "All information in DITS is provided by Deloitte professionals in the jurisdictions concerned . . . and is intended as a general guide only. DITS does not provide the tax implications of a

particular investment nor does it explain how best to structure an investment. The relevant domestic law or tax treaty should always be consulted to determine the application of rates and/or rules in specific circumstances, and advisors should be consulted."

40. For example, in 1999 *The Salomon Smith Barney Guide to World Equity Markets 1999* was published by Euromoney Institutional Investor PLC and Salomon Smith Barney, edited by Jacqueline Grosch Lobo and Rob Irish (Euromoney Books, Nestor House, London). Earlier editions were published jointly with different firms, such as *The LGT Guide to World Equity Markets 1996* (Euromoney Books, Nestor House, London).

41. See the full report at http://iab.worldbank.org/~/media/FPDKM/IAB/Documents/IAB-report.pdf (as of March 2014), titled *Investing Across Borders 2010*. See Table 2.1 in particular, and the supplementary appendix on methodology, which outlines the survey approach by email, phone, or personal interviews and the team's composition, the survey instruments, and the survey respondents. Table 7.1 outlines each of the indicators and their type as to whether de jure or de facto.

42. See *Converting and Transferring Currency* (September 2013) by lead author John Anderson, of the Global Indicators and Analysis Department in Financial and Private Sector Development of the World Bank Group. See http://www-wds.worldbank.org/external/default/WDSContentServer/IW3P/IB/2013/09/24/000158349_20130924090028/Rendered/PDF/WPS6601.pdf.

43. The report is available at the Milken Institute publications website at http://www.milkeninstitute.org/publications/view/430.

44. See Edison and Warnock, "A Simple Measure of the Intensity of Capital Controls," and Bekaert, "Market Integration and Investment Barriers in Emerging Equity Markets."

45. See in particular the study by Bekaert, Harvey, and Lumsdaine, "Dating the Integration of World Equity Markets."

46. See Karolyi, "ADRs and the Development of Emerging Equity Markets."

47. I count US cross-listings as those by way of an ordinary share listing, a global or registered share listings, or an American depositary receipt (ADR) program on a major exchange, over-the-counter or SEC Rule 144a form as fraction of total count of all domestic listed companies (Doidge, Karolyi, and Stulz, "Has New York Become Less Competitive than London in Global Markets?").

48. From www.bis.org, please consult their consolidated banking statistics and Table 9A. See http://www.bis.org/statistics/r_qa1412_hanx9a.pdf. It reports total foreign claims on a contractual basis among BIS-reporting banks from OECD countries of $31.036 trillion as of the end of September 2013. The OECD includes all countries in Europe, five additional developed markets (Australia, Canada, Japan, New Zealand, and the United States), and a host of what BIS deems offshore financial centers (Bahamas, Cayman Islands, British Virgin Islands, and Guernsey, among others).

49. A useful reference on the sources for these data is Čihak, Demirgüc-Kunt, Feyen, and Levine, "Benchmarking Financial Systems around the World."

50. A recent paper by Houston, Lin, and Ma, "Regulatory Arbitrage and International Bank Flows," obtains the next level of detail on the BIS consolidated cross-border claims data on a bilateral country-pair basis. They show that differences in regulations are strongly positively linked to changes in the claims. That is, foreign claims are higher by banks from countries with tougher rules imposed on banks and in target markets with looser rules. The

authors interpret this as evidence in favor of a destructive form of regulatory arbitrage in cross-border bank flows.

51. Kose et al., "Financial Globalization," 40.

Chapter 7

1. My definition is precisely that which is most often cited among scholars by Andrei Shleifer and Robert Vishny. See their survey study "A Survey of Corporate Governance."

2. Much of my thinking on international corporate governance theory and practice is shaped by my extensive collaboration with Craig Doidge and René Stulz. The theory outlined in our coauthored paper "Why Do Countries Matter So Much for Corporate Governance?" lies at the core of the logic in this chapter.

3. See PR newswire report "Grupo Modelo Chairman, CEO Carlos Fernandez Resigns from Anheuser-Busch Board," posted by *St. Louis Business Journal*, June 20, 2008. See http://www.bizjournals.com/stlouis/stories/2008/06/16/daily70.html?page=all.

4. See *BBC News* story "Budweiser Brewer Rejects Takeover," June 27, 2008. See http://news.bbc.co.uk/2/hi/business/7476771.stm.

5. See *St. Louis Business Journal*, "Grupo Modelo Chairman." "Ann Gilpin, an analyst with Morningstar in Chicago, called the resignation confusing since she believes Fernandez is in favor of InBev acquiring A-B because he does not want to see Anheuser-Busch buy out the rest of Grupo Modelo. "It seems to me that (Fernandez) would want to stay on the board and vote yes (for the InBev acquisition)," Gilpin said. "I would think Grupo Modelo would be interested to have a say and vote on the ultimate fate of Anheuser-Busch and to some extent Grupo Modelo." The abrupt resignation is perhaps a public confirmation of a "strained relationship" between A-B and Grupo Modelo that was widely known in industry circles for years, Gilpin said.

6. See *St. Louis Business Journal*, "Grupo Modelo Chairman." All of this discussion is based on the case study "Grupo Modelo: Trouble Brewing in the Global Beer Industry," coauthored by Uma Kakde, Kristin O'Planick, Kevin Shuller, and Jennifer Walvoord, under the supervision of Andrew Karolyi, available upon request from the Emerging Market Institute at the Johnson Graduate School of Management at Cornell University.

7. See Grupo Modelo's 2007 Annual Report, www.grupomodelo.com. A useful history of the firm, its founders, products, services is also found at http://m.gmodelo.mx/quienes/historia_en.jsp.

8. Grupo Modelo 2007 Annual Report.

9. See "Constellation Brands CEO Sees No Bud Buyout Impact," Reuters News, May 29, 2008.

10. In fact, the six families owned 44.9% of the shares outstanding (A Series), A-B, 35.1% (B Series), and 20% floated freely (C Series). See "Modelo CEO Faces Limits of Family Firm," *Wall Street Journal*, June 27, 2008. See http://online.wsj.com/news/articles/SB121451572432208491?mod=_newsreel_5. Anheuser-Busch has a 35.12% ownership of Grupo Modelo and 23.25% holding in Diblo, while Grupo Modelo holds a 76.75% interest in Diblo. A-B's total direct and indirect holdings in Grupo Modelo and its subsidiaries is 50.2%. The Mexican families continued to have management control of Grupo Modelo and Diblo. See "Anheuser and Modelo Announce Resolution on Investment Price," *Modern Brewery Age*, September 21, 1998.

11. Ibid. See third paragraph in http://online.wsj.com/news/articles/SB12145157243 2208491?mod=_newsreel_5.

12. See "Anheuser CEO Fights for His Legacy," *Wall Street Journal*, May 27, 2008.

13. See "Modelo Defense May Be Out of Reach," *St. Louis Post-Dispatch*, June 14, 2008.

14. See Datamonitor *Industry Market Research*, December 15, 2007, and *Alcoholic Beverages and Tobacco*, Standard and Poor's Industry Survey, May 2008.

15. See story by Michael J. de la Merced, "InBev Raises Its Offer for Anheuser-Busch," *Wall Street Journal*, July 12, 2008. See also the corporate press release "InBev Completes Acquisition of Anheuser Busch," November 18, 2008, at http://www.ab-inbev.com/press_releases/20081118_1_e.pdf.

16. Ibid., see paragraph 6 in http://www.ab-inbev.com/press_releases/20081118_1_e.pdf.

17. See "Grupo Modelo Files Arbitration Notice against A-B," in *St. Louis Business Journal*, October 16, 2008. The filing claimed that "the investment agreement prohibits Anheuser-Busch from taking any actions that would result in a transfer or disposition of any portion of its investment in Group Modelo and Diblo without first giving the controlling shareholders of Group Modelo an opportunity to purchase the shares in Modelo and Diblo being transferred by Anheuser-Busch."

18. See "Anheuser Busch InBev to Buy Modelo This Year for $10.7B, Analyst Says," *St. Louis Post-Dispatch*, March 9, 2010. The analyst named is Evolution Securities analyst Andrew Holland.

19. "Anheuser Busch InBev to Buy Modelo."

20. See "Ruling in Modelo Case Favors Anheuser," *Wall Street Journal*, July 13, 2010; "AB InBev to Pay $20bn for Grupo Modelo," Louise Lucas and David Gelles, *Financial Times*, June 29, 2012. See http://online.wsj.com/articles/SB10001424052748704288204575363051277649806, and http://www.ft.com/intl/cms/s/0/1aada18a-c1da-11e1-8e7c-00144feabdc0.html.

21. Ibid. See eleventh paragraph in story, http://online.wsj.com/articles/SB10001424052 748704288204575363051277649806.

22. Ibid. See tenth paragraph in story, http://online.wsj.com/articles/SB1000142405274 8704288204575363051277649806.

23. See Department of Justice, Office of Public Affairs, "Justice Department Files Antitrust Lawsuit Challenging Anheuser-Busch InBev's Proposed Acquisition of Grupo Modelo," January 31, 2013, at http://www.justice.gov/opa/pr/justice-department-files-antitrust-lawsuit-challenging-anheuser-busch-inbev-s-proposed.

24. See Department of Justice, Office of Public Affairs, "Justice Department Reaches Settlement with Anheuser-Busch InBev and Grupo Modelo in Beer Case," April 19, 2013, at http://www.justice.gov/opa/pr/justice-department-reaches-settlement-anheuser-busch-in bev-and-grupo-modelo-beer-case.

25. See La Porta, Lopez-De-Silanes, and Shleifer, "Corporate Ownership around the World."

26. See Johnson, Boone, Breach, and Friedman, "Corporate Governance in the Asian Financial Crisis"; La Porta, Lopez-De-Silanes, Shleifer, and Vishny, "Investor Protection and Corporate Valuation"; Shleifer and Wolfenzon, "Investor Protection and Equity Markets"; Doidge, Karolyi, and Stulz, "Why Are Foreign Firms Listed in the US Worth

More?"; Durnev and Kim, "To Steal or Not to Steal"; Stulz, "The Limits of Financial Globalization."

27. Those of us who work in this area refer to this voluntary commitment to good governance using the term "bonding" (as in being joined securely to something else, in a physical sense, typically by means of an adhesive substance, heat, or pressure). Bonding to better governance systems can be accomplished by means of cross-border acquisitions or cross-border financing deals and is outlined in two concurrent studies by Jack Coffee, "The Future as History," and René Stulz, "Globalization, Corporate Finance, and the Cost of Capital."

28. See Allen and Gale, *Comparing Financial Systems*.

29. Two working papers by Kose John and Simi Kedia show theoretically that financial development and the quality of monitoring technologies of a country affect the choice of governance mechanisms. See "Institutions, Markets, and Growth" and "Design of Corporate Governance."

30. See Ball, "Infrastructure Requirements for an Economically Efficient System of Public Financial Reporting and Disclosure"; Black, "The Legal and Institutional Preconditions for strong Securities Markets."

31. See Bergman and Nicolaievsky, "Investor Protection and the Coasian View." A comprehensive study by Bushman, Piotroski, and Smith shows that characteristics of the political environment—like what I will feature in Chapter 9—are also important for some types of financial disclosures. I use their data among the measures of corporate transparency and governance. See their "What Determines Corporate Transparency?"

32. See Shleifer and Wolfenzon, "Investor Protection and Equity Markets."

33. This concept of borrowing better overseas institutions and standards is featured in the last section of Shleifer and Wolfenzon, "Investor Protection and Equity Markets." It is the core idea at the heart of the bonding literature started by Coffee, "The Future as History," and Stulz, "Globalization, Corporate Finance, and the Cost of Capital." And these are integral features of the models by Stulz, "The Limits of Financial Globalization," Stulz, "Securities Laws, Disclosure and National Capital Markets in the Age of Financial Globalization," and Doidge, Karolyi, and Stulz, "Why Do Countries Matter So Much for Corporate Governance?"

34. See Gill, *Credit Lyonnais Securities Asia*; and Patel, Balic, and Bwakira, "Measuring Transparency and Disclosure at Firm-level in Emerging Markets." A third popular index used for governance rankings is by Institutional Shareholder Services (ISS). It focuses on the United States and 23 developed countries, so it is of limited use here. Important papers that have used ISS rankings include: Doidge, Karolyi, and Stulz, "Why Do Countries Matter So Much?"; Aggarwal, Erel, Stulz, and Wiliamson, "Differences in Governance Practices between U.S. and Foreign Firms"; and Aggarwal, Erel, Ferreira, and Matos, "Does Governance Travel around the World?"

35. See Khanna, Kogan, and Palepu, "Globalization and Similarities in Corporate Governance: A Cross-country Analysis"; and Klapper and Love, "Corporate Governance, Investor Protection and Performance in Emerging Markets." See also Durnev and Kim, "To Steal or Not to Steal," and Doidge, Karolyi, and Stulz, "Why Do Countries Matter So Much."

36. See Table 1 of Doidge, Karolyi, and Stulz, "Why Do Countries Matter So Much?"

37. See Khanna, Palepu, and Srinivasan, "Disclosure Practices of Foreign Companies interacting with US Markets"; and Hugill and Siegel, "Which Does More to Determine the Quality of Corporate Governance in Emerging Economies, Firms or Countries?" See also Durnev and Kim, "To Steal or Not to Steal"; Patel, Balic, and Bwakira, "Measuring Transparency and Disclosure at Firm-level in Emerging Markets"; and Doidge, Karolyi, and Stulz, "Why Do Countries Matter So Much?"

38. Bushman, Piotroski, and Smith, "What Determines Corporate Transparency?"

39. See La Porta, Lopez-de-Silanes, Shleifer and Vishny, "Law and Finance"; Doidge, Karolyi, and Stulz, "Why Are Foreign Firms Listed"; and Bushman, Piotroski, and Smith, "What Determines Corporate Transparency?," among others.

40. The number of analysts following the largest 30 companies in each country in 1996, from Chang, Khanna, and Palepu, "Analyst Activity Around the World," and using data from Bailey, Karolyi, and Salva, "The Economic Consequences of Increased Disclosure." Bailey et al. track 7,389 firms around 45,000 earnings announcement events over a 10-year period. Almost 10,000 events arose for emerging market firms. Their main thesis relates to the functional convergence hypothesis discussed in the chapter. They show that the cumulative absolute abnormal returns and volume reactions around earnings announcement events are greater for developed market firms and for emerging market firms that pursue a secondary cross-listing in US markets. The more stringent disclosure requirements in US markets relative to what these firms face at home transform the capital market reactions to an important news event.

41. See Daske, Hail, Leuz, and Verdi, "Mandatory IFRS Reporting around the World." Two additional studies by the same research team examine how changes in the legal and regulatory systems in conjunction with the IFRS adoptions mattered especially among European Union firms. They also showed there were two kinds of voluntary IFRS adopters, those that were serious and those that did so in a perfunctory manner (what they call "label" adopters). All the gains accrued to the former set. See Daske, Hail, Leuz, and Verdi, "Adopting a Label," and Christensen, Hail, and Leuz, "Mandatory IFRS Reporting and Changes in Enforcement."

42. See PriceWaterhouseCoopers, *IFRS Adoption by Country*, April 2013.

43. See Bushman, Piotroski, and Smith, "What Determines Corporate Transparency?"

44. See La Porta, Lopez-de-Silanes, Shleifer, and Vishny, "Corporate Ownership around the World."

45. See Faccio and Lang, "The Ultimate Ownership of Western European Corporations."

46. See Claessens, Djankov, and Lang, "The Separation of Ownership and Control in East Asian Corporations."

47. See Lins, "Equity Ownership and Firm Value in Emerging Markets."

48. The variable is the fraction of shares controlled by the largest blockholder for the firms sampled by country. See Doidge, Karolyi, Lins, Miller, and Stulz, "Private Benefits of Control, Ownership and the Cross-Listing Decision."

49. See La Porta et al., "Corporate Ownership around the World."

50. This is Worldscope Data Item #05475, an annual item.

51. The sample is constructed in the 2014 working paper (and associated appendix) of Karolyi and Wu, "Size, Value, and Momentum in Global Stock Returns: A Partial Segmentation Approach." Its precursor is titled "The Role of Investability Restrictions

on Size, Value and Momentum in International Stocks Returns," SSRN Working Paper #2043156, April 2012. See http://papers.ssrn.com/sol3/papers.cfm?abstract_id=2043156.

52. See Morck, Yeung, and Yu, "The Information Content of Stock Markets." In fact, the argument about the information environment is closer to that in another study by Jin and Myers, "R^2 around the World."

53. See Karolyi, Lee, and Van Dijk, "Understanding Commonality in Liquidity around the World."

54. One example is Griffin, Kelly, and Nardari, "Do Market Efficiency Measures Yield Correct Inferences?" in which they compare several measures of weak- and semi-strong form informational efficiency (short-term reversal, variance ratios, price delay, post-earnings drift, momentum, and synchronicity) across developed and emerging equity markets. Counterintuitively, these measures suggest that, if anything, emerging markets are more efficient than developed markets. The authors argue that these common efficiency measures have "limitations that are featured in our international setting" (page 3276).

55. See Amihud, "Illiquidity and Stock Return."

56. An important part of the Karolyi et al. study "Understanding Commonality in Liquidity" is as much the time-series variation in the liquidity and returns commonality measures across countries as their values on average. In the study, we associate months in which the levels of commonality in illiquidity peak as potentially acute periods of dislocation. These are episodes in which liquidity dries up across lots of stocks all at the same time. Some have called these "liquidity black holes" or "liquidity spirals." We show that these episodes in countries are associated with periods of high market volatility (especially large market declines), intense trading activity, and large foreign portfolio inflows, and all of these occur more dramatically for emerging than developed countries.

57. See Bushman, Piotroski, and Smith, "What Determines Corporate Transparency?"

58. See Chang et al., "Analyst Activity around the World"; La Porta et al., "Corporate Ownership around the World."

59. See Karolyi et al., "Understanding Commonality in Liquidity around the World."

60. See Doidge, Karolyi, Lins, Miller, and Stulz, "Private Benefits of Control, Ownership, and the Cross-listing Decision," and La Porta et al., "Corporate Ownership around the World."

Chapter 8

1. Simeon Djankov, over the course of a 14-year run, rose to the position of chief economist of the finance and private sector vice-presidency of the World Bank. He left the bank in 2009 to serve as deputy prime minister and minister of finance of Bulgaria in the government of Prime Minister Boyko Borisov.

2. All of this discussion is based on the case study "Pulkovo Airport Expansion Project," March 14, 2011, unpublished Cornell University case study, coauthored by Ben Freeman, James Lewis, Vanida Wongdechsareekul, Ifat Wong, and Elisabeth Cai under the supervision of Andrew Karolyi, and available upon request from the Emerging Market Institute at the Johnson Graduate School of Management at Cornell University.

3. See "Russia's €1.1bn Pulkovo Airport PPP Reaches Financial Close," *Infrastructure Investor,* April 28, 2010. A public private partnership is often defined as a deal in which nongovernmental entities provide financing and services for an asset—often in the infrastructure sector—in cooperation with the government.

4. See Philip Alexander, "Russia Infrastructure Building Momentum: New State Funds and Laws Are Allowing Russia's Ailing Infrastructure to Catch Up with Its Fast-growing Economy," *The Banker*, October 1, 2008.

5. See Pulkovo Airport *2009 Annual Report*. Available at http://old.pulkovoairport.ru/files/File/AR-2009-eng.pdf.

6. "Pulkovo Vies to Become International Hub by 2025," *Airport Business*, March 2009.

7. These statistics are obtained from Rossiya Airlines. August 11, 2010. See http://siberianlight.net/russiaguide/rossiya-airline/.

8. See Cathy Bucyk, "Old Habits Are Hard to Break," *Air Transport World*, January 1, 2011.

9. See Gref's quote in "Putin Seeks Private Airport Investors," *Moscow Times*, July 8, 2010. Also see "Russia Fixed Asset Investment to Reach \$370 billion by 2010—Kudrin," *RIA Novosti*, September 21, 2007.

10. See Benjamin Esty and Irina Christov, "An Overview of Project Finance," Chapter 2, in Esty's *Modern Project Finance*. See also various postings at Harvard Business School Project Finance Portal at www.people.hbs.edu/besty/projfinportal/.

11. See Anatoli Temkin and Nadezhda Zaitzeva, "Pulkovo s aktzentom ["An Emphasis on Pulkovo"]," *Vedomosti* [*Statements*], February 9, 2011.

12. See "Pulkovo Airport Contract Awarded," *CAPA Centre for Aviation Report*, July 22, 2009. See http://centreforaviation.com/analysis/vtb-bank-led-group-wins-st-petersburg-pulkovo-airport-ppp-bid-8633.

13. See seventh paragraph in "Pulkovo Airport Contract Awarded."

14. See "Fraport AG Signs MOU for Airport Concession in St. Petersburg," *ETN Global Travel Industry News*, July 16, 2009.

15. "Fraport AG Signs MOU." See also VTB Bank Consolidated Financial Statements and Auditors' Report for the years ending December 31, 2008 and 2009, available at http://www.vtb.com/upload/iblock/fab/VTB_Annual_Report_2008.pdf; and Fraport AG company website (http://www.fraport.com/en/the-fraport-group/fraport-worldwide/our-airports/pulkovo-airport-st-petersburg.html).

16. See "IFC, EBRD and VEB Ready to Credit Upgrade of Pulkovo Airport," EBRD Press Release, August 8, 2008. See also the EBRD annual report's page 37 (http://www.ebrd.com/downloads/research/annual/ar10e.pdf).

17. The IFC regularly employs an A/B loan structure when it syndicates a loan that it lends for its own account at the same time. In such an arrangement, IFC is the sole contractual lender for itself and B loan (syndicate) participants. There typically is a single loan agreement between IFC and the borrower for the full financing amount encompassing both A and B loans. See http://www.ifc.org/wps/wcm/connect/Topics_Ext_Content/IFC_External_Corporate_Site/IFC+Syndications/Overview_Benefits_Structure/Syndications/B+Loan+Structure+And+Benefits/.

18. Step-in rights refer to the sponsor's right to step in and take over the asset if the concessionaire materially breaches its obligations under the agreement. See World Bank Report, entitled "Key Issues in Project Finance Transactions," available at http://ppp.worldbank.org/public-private-partnership/financing/issues-in-project-financed-transactions.

19. See "Pulkovo Airport Concession Finance and European Bank for Reconstruction and Development Transition/Environmental Impact Report for Project Number 39029," February 15, 2010, www.ebrd.com/pages/project/psd/2010/39029.shtml.

20. See "Russia Convicts Injured Editor as Fears for Media Grow," *BBC News*, November 10, 2010.

21. See "Commercial Close for Moscow-St. Petersburg Motorway," *Petroleum Economist*, July/August 2009.

22. See "IFC and EBRD Mobilize Financing for Expansion of Pulkovo Airport in Russia," *IFC Press Release*, July 19, 2010, http://ifcext.ifc.org/ifcext/pressroom/ifcpress-room.nsf/1f70cd9a07d692d685256ee1001cdd37/a8b4884c4438ee62852577650052d94f?OpenDocument.

23. "IFC and EBRD Mobilize Financing." More PPP project financing followed citing the Pulkovo deal as a catalyst. See "PPP Model to Fund Moscow—St. Petersburg High Speed Line," *Moscow Times*, October 20, 2011 and "Public-Private Partnerships Get Tactical," *Moscow Times*, October 13, 2011.

24. Ibid. See also "Foreigners Head Pulkovo Project," *Moscow Times*, February 15, 2011, in which Italy's Astaldi and Turkish developer Ictas Insaat were awarded the estimated $1.2 billion engineering, procurement and construction contract.

25. See Esty, "Modern Project Finance."

26. See extensive discussion by Shleifer and Vishny in their 1997 article "A Survey of Corporate Governance." Diversions of resources from firms to their controllers have been investigated in several contexts, including the Mexican and Asian financial crises.

Johnson, Boone, Breach, and Friedman, "Corporate Governance in the Asian Financial Crisis"; for legal disputes over tunneling see Johnson, La Porta, Lopez-de-Silanes, and Shleifer, "Tunneling"; for corporate governance during the transition from socialism see Glaeser, Johnson, and Shleifer, "Coase versus the Coasians." The extent of diversion has been measured by estimating the private benefits of control from the market pricing of shares with superior voting rights and from the treatment of controlling shareholders in takeovers (see Nenova, "The Value of Corporate Voting Rights and Control"; Dyck and Zingales, "Private Benefits of Control").

27. La Porta, Lopez-de-Silanes, Shleifer, and Vishny, "Law and Finance." The first published study was La Porta, Lopez-de-Silanes, Shleifer, and Vishny, "Legal Determinants of External Finance."

28. The most prominent of these challenges were by Pagano and Volpin, "The Political Economy of Corporate Governance," and Spamann, "The 'Anti-Director Rights Index' Revisited." Spamann furnishes corrections for 33 of the 46 countries analyzed in the original LLSV (1998) and reveals a low correlation of only 0.53 between the corrected and original values. He shows how the corrected values fail to show that shareholder protections are higher in common rather than civil law countries, that shareholder protection predicts stock market size or ownership dispersion, and that weak corporate governance explains the extent of exchange rate depreciation during the Asian financial crisis of 1997. Please note that I do not include among the critics the important contribution of Acemoglu and Johnson, "Unbundling Institutions," and Acemoglu, Johnson, and Robinson, "The Colonial Origins of Comparative Development." These author teams propose a distinction between property rights institutions that constrain government expropriation and contracting institutions that support private contract enforcement like those measured by LLSV. The research exploits exogenous variation in both types of institutions driven by colonial history (e.g., mortality rates of European settlers and population density before colonization, the identity of the colonizing power) and show

that property rights institutions are more important for growth, investment, and financial development than contracting institutions. Acemoglu and Robinson's 2012 tome *Why Nations Fail* outlines these arguments in a very enjoyable and engaging manner.

29. See Djankov et al., "Courts"; Djankov et al., "The Law and Economics of Self-Dealing"; and also La Porta, Lopez-de-Silanes, and Shleifer, "What Works in Securities Laws."

30. Many details about this important initiative within the World Bank on data, rankings across 189 countries, additional reports, methodology, and associated research is at http://www.doingbusiness.org/methodology.

31. La Porta et al., "Law and Finance."

32. See Djankov et al., "The Law and Economics of Self-Dealing."

33. See Subramanian and Tung, "Law and Project Finance."

34. La Porta et al., "Law and Finance." The *International Country Risk Guide* is produced by The PRS Group since 1980. It renders political, economic, and financial risk ratings for 140 countries. I will discuss this more extensively in Chapter 9. See https://www.prsgroup.com/about-us/our-two-methodologies/icrg for more details on the methodologies used to build the ratings.

35. See Djankov et al., "The Law and Economics of Self-Dealing."

36. See Rafael La Porta, Florencio Lopez-de-Silanes and Andrei Shleifer, 2008, "The Economic Consequences of Legal Origins," *Journal of Economic Literature* 46, 285–332.

37. See Djankov et al., "Courts."

38. See Djankov et al., "The Law and Economics of Self-Dealing."

39. See Djankov et al., "The Law and Economics of Self-Dealing."

40. See La Porta et al., "What Works in Securities Laws?"

41. The other seven World Bank Doing Business Indicators focus on starting a business, dealing with construction permits, getting electricity, registering property, paying taxes, trading across borders, and resolving insolvency. They introduced two additional measures in 2013 on employing workers and entrepreneurship. See www.doingbusiness.org/methodology.

42. The methodology is built in a separate study by Djankov, McLiesh, and Shleifer, "Private Credit in 129 Countries." See also "Getting Credit Methodology," www.doingbusiness.org/methodology/getting-credit.

43. See Han, Lee, and Park, "Legal Frameworks and Credit Information Systems in China, Korea, and Singapore." There is a nice discussion of the mechanisms the respective governments employ to build out the coverage of these public credit registries.

44. See "Protecting Investors Methodology," www.doingbusiness.org/methodology/protecting-investors. Much of this methodology is based on the study by Djankov et al., "The Law and Economics of Self-Dealing."

45. See www.doingbusiness.org/methodology/enforcing-contracts. Much of this work is based on the earlier study by Djankov et al., "Courts."

46. See La Porta et al., "Law and Finance."

Chapter 9

1. See, among many others, Henisz, "The Institutional Environment for Economic Growth," [2] Range of -10 (high autocracy) to +10 (high democracy), and Pagano and Volpin, "Political Economy of Corporate Governance."

2. See details in the report by Marshall and Cole, *Global Stability Report*. There are many reports of the team of scholars going back to the 1990s and up through to a most recent survey of the collective work of the project team in Goldstone, Bates, Epstein, Gurr, Lustik, Marshall, Ulfelder, and Woodward, "A Global Model for Forecasting Political Instability." The newly named Center for Global Policy at George Mason University, directed by Professor Robert Goldstone, is the home for the Polity IV project of regime characteristics. Their Political Instability Task Force lists a series of publications of use at http://globalpolicy.gmu.edu/political-instability-task-force-home/pitf-reports-and-replicant-data-sets/.

3. See Beck, Clarke, Groff, Keefer, and Walsh, "New Tools in Comparative Political Economy."

4. To understand their own methodology, consult the earliest reports of the World Bank team by Kaufmann, Kraay, and Mastruzzi, 1999a, 1999b, "Governance Matters III," and "Governance Matters IV."

5. See Jeremy Page, "India Faces Stand-Off With China on Sea Oil," *Wall Street Journal*. September 23, 2011. See http://online.wsj.com/articles/SB10001424053111904563 90457658662094841 1618.

6. See Red Herring Prospectus for 5% equity sale of ONGC at the website of the Stock Exchange Board of India (SEBI), www.sebi.gov.in/cms/sebi_data/attach-docs/1315392214565.pdf.

7. All of this discussion is based on the case study "Pulkovo Airport Expansion Project," August 29, 2012, unpublished Cornell University working paper coauthored by Gopal Bethmangalkar, Armina Hakobyan, Gokul Rajagopalan, and Jeff West under the supervision of Professor Andrew Karolyi, and is available upon request from the Emerging Market Institute at the Johnson Graduate School of Management at Cornell University.

8. See the company website for Oil & Natural Gas Company of India for company statistics in its profile and history. See, in particular, http://ongcindia.ongc.co.in/wps/wcm/connect/ongcindia/Home/Company/History/.

9. A useful history of India's Adjusted Pricing Mechanism is "Petroleum Pricing in India: Transition from APM to MDPM," by Kaushik Ranjan Bandyopadhyay of the Asian Institute of Transport Development, MPRA Working Paper No. 25905 (October 18, 2010, http://mpra.ub.uni-muenchen.de/25905/1/MPRA_paper_25905.pdf).

10. See Adit Mathai, "Oily Conundrum," *Outlook Business*, August 18, 2012, and Ramkrishna Kashelkar, "ONGC: Subsidy Burden, OVL Production Are Near-Term Concerns," *Economic Times*, February 9, 2012. See http://articles.economictimes.india-times.com/2012-02-09/news/31042025_1_subsidy-burden-ovl-oil-production.

11. Block 6.1 in Vietnam was the largest overseas production facility for ONGC with over 2.25 billion cubic meters (BCM) of gas produced and over 11.2 billion barrels of oil equivalent (BBOE). A block is an area of land or sea where exploration and production rights are granted. See ONGC Videsh Limited (OVL) website for historical references at http://www.ongcvidesh.com/Company.aspx?tab=0.

12. Ibid. See in particular the tab on specific corporate assets in the Asia Pacific region at http://www.ongcvidesh.com/Assets.aspx.

13. See a useful history of PetroVietnam and the development of the Phu Kanh Basin at http://english.pvn.vn/?portal=news&page=detail&category_id=7&id=1057.

14. See Peter Brown, "Calculated Ambiguity in the South China Sea," *Asia Times*, December 8, 2009. See http://www.atimes.com/atimes/Southeast_Asia/KL08Ae01.html.

15. See Jerry Esplanada, "PH Protests China's '9-Dash Line' Spratlys Claim," *Philippine Daily Inquirer*, April 14, 2011. See http://newsinfo.inquirer.net/inquirerheadlines/nation/view/20110415-331204/PH-runs-to-UN-to-protest-Chinas-9-dash-line-Spratlys-claim.

16. See Michael Wines, "Dispute Between Vietnam and China Escalates Over Competing Claims in South China Sea," *New York Times*, June 10, 2011. See http://www.nytimes.com/2011/06/11/world/asia/11vietnam.html?_r=0.

17. See "China Accuses Vietnam in South China Sea Row," *BBC News*, June 10, 2011. See http://www.bbc.co.uk/news/world-asia-pacific-13723443.

18. See Saibal Dasgupta, "China Warns India Against Exploring Oil in South China Sea Ahead of Krishna's Visit to Hanoi," *Times of India*, September 15, 2011. See http://timesofindia.indiatimes.com/india/China-warns-India-against-exploring-oil-in-South-China-Sea-ahead-of-Krishnas-visit-to-Hanoi/articleshow/9994277.cms.

19. See "India Freezes ONGC Share Sale; Fiscal Deficit Concerns Rise," Reuters, September 16, 2011. See http://uk.reuters.com/article/2011/09/16/ongc-sharesale-idUKL3E7KG0GT20110916.

20. See paragraph three in Reuters report, "India Freezes ONGC Share Sale."

21. See "Government Approves $2.5 billion ONGC Share Auction," Reuters, February 28, 2011. Also see "ONGC Surges to Nine-Month High as $2.5 Billion Stake Offered at Premium," Bloomberg News, February 29, 2011. See http://af.reuters.com/article/commoditiesNews/idAFI8E8DG00920120228 and http://www.bloomberg.com/news/2012-02-29/india-seeks-2-5-billion-auctioning-ongc-stake-to-close-budget-shortfall.html.

22. See Khushita Vasant and Romit Guha, "ONGC Share Auction Scrapes Through," *Wall Street Journal*, March 2, 2012. See http://online.wsj.com/news/articles/SB10001424052970203753704577254620773255922.

23. See "Rare Protest in Vietnam over China Claims to Offshore Oil Blocks," Reuters, July 1, 2012. See http://www.reuters.com/article/2012/07/01/us-vietnam-china-oil-idUSBRE86002V20120701.

24. See fifth paragraph in Reuters report, "Rare Protest in Vietnam."

25. See "CNOOC Says S. China Sea Blocks Tender Progressing Well," Reuters, July 17, 2012. See http://in.reuters.com/article/2012/07/17/china-cnooc-scs-idINL4E8IH1RD20120717.

26. See Keith Bradsher, "South China Sea Tensions a Backdrop to Kerry's Asia Visit," *New York Times*, February 14, 2014. In the article, Secretary of State John Kerry is quoted from a State Department release saying: "With respect to the South China Sea, it's important to resolve these differences in a peaceful, nonconfrontational way that honors the law of the sea and honors the rule of law itself." See http://sinosphere.blogs.nytimes.com/2014/02/14/south-china-sea-tensions-a-backdrop-to-kerrys-china-visit/. A useful review of the challenges in the region as of the time of the writing of this book can be found among the papers discussed at the June 5 and 6, 2013 Third Annual Center for Strategic and International Studies (CSIS) South China Sea Conference. Articles are available at https://csis.org/event/managing-tensions-south-china-sea.

27. Bekaert and Hodrick, *International Financial Management*, 509–510.

28. Consider as an example Chapter 3, "Estimation of Discount Rates," of Aswath Damodaran's *Damodaran on Valuation*.

29. See page 510, Bekaert and Hodrick, *International Financial Management*.

30. See, for example, the various lines of business at the credit and political risk division at Zurich's site at http://www.zurichna.com/zna/creditandpoliticalrisk/creditand politicalrisk.htm; the products page at Sovereign Risk Insurance Limited of Bermuda at http://www.sovereignbermuda.com/our_products/our_products.html; and Lloyds' service on risk location guidance for political risk insurance at http://www.lloyds.com/the-market/tools-and-resources/tools-e-services/risk-locator/risk-locator-class-of-business/political-risk. OPIC's site on political risk insurance is detailed at http://www.opic.gov/what-we-offer/political-risk-insurance.

31. The database created by the PRS Group has been used extensively in academic research on political risk. I will not use their data in this book, but this does not reflect in any way my judgment about their usefulness or lack thereof. See details on the company's services, the ICRG rating system, and their methodology at https://www.prsgroup.com/about-us/our-two-methodologies/prs. There are other country and political risk commercial services, such as by *Euromoney* magazine's country risk survey (http://www.euromoney.com/Poll/10683/PollsAndAwards/Country-Risk.html), *The Economist* magazine's Economist Intelligence Unit (EIU), a sister company of the magazine, and *Risk.net*, an online news and analysis service focusing on financial risk management (www.risk.net, Incisive Media Investments Limited).

32. See Bekaert, Harvey, and Lundblad, "Does Financial Liberalization Spur Growth?"

33. See, for example, the Salomon Smith Barney report titled *A Practical Approach to the International Valuation & Capital Allocation Puzzle*, July 26, 2002. The report describes a four-step methodology for estimating the unadjusted political risk premium using a sovereign yield spread over and above a global version of the Capital Asset Pricing Model. See also Chapter 14 of Bekaert and Hodrick, 2009, *International Financial Management*.

34. See Bekaert, Harvey, Lundblad, and Siegel, "Political Risk Spreads."

35. See Henisz, "The Institutional Environment for Economic Growth." He argues in his article that indices that measure the rule of law, the likelihood of government expropriation, or contract repudiation, like The PRS Group's ICRG, may very well be influenced by private sector perceptions of such economic outcomes, but it "does not, by itself, establish the inferred link between investment and political institutions." He calls his structural model of political interaction a "robust determinant of cross-national variation in economic growth."

36. The data is available, upon completion of a user survey, at http://mgmt5.wharton.upenn.edu/henisz/POLCON/ContactInfo.html.

37. See page 10 of Henisz, "The Institutional Environment for Economic Growth."

38. See numerous references to the earlier studies in the extended project in Goldstone, Bates, Epstein, Gurr, Lustik, Marshall, Ulfelder, and Woodward, "A Global Model for Forecasting Political Instability,

39. See methodology details at http://www.systemicpeace.org/polity/polity4.htm.

40. The two studies are Pagano and Volpin, "Political Economy of Corporate Governance," and Pagano and Volpin, "Shareholder Protection, Stock Market Development and Politics."

41. In the appendix to their paper, they define the proportionality index as PR minus PLURALTY—HOUSSYS + 2, in which each of the variables comes from the World Bank DPI. PR is a variable that equals one if there is any proportional representation in the electoral rules. PLURALTY equals one if the electoral system demands a plurality of votes.

HOUSSYS equals one if plurality governs the majority of the votes in the main legislative body and zero, if proportional representation does. There are three exceptions for Venezuela in 1989, for Japan in 1994, and Philippines in 1996 that lead them to override the computed scores. I follow the same guidelines. The appendix is available at http://www.csef.it/pagano/pv_aer_data_appendix.pdf.

42. The most relevant article is Beck et al., "New Tools in Comparative Political Economy: The Database of Political Institutions."

43. See details at http://econ.worldbank.org and the tab for Database for Political Institutions on the World Bank's extranet at http://econ.worldbank.org/WBSITE/EXTERNAL/EXTDEC/EXTRESEARCH/0,,contentMDK:20649465~pagePK:64214825~piPK:64214943~theSitePK:469382,00.html.

44. See page 3 of Beck et al., "New Tools in Comparative Political Economy: The Database of Political Institutions."

45. The main studies are Kaufmann, Kraay, and Zoido-Lobaton, "Aggregating Governance Indicators" and "Governance Matters"; Kaufmann, Kraay, and Mastruzzi, "Governance Matters III" and "The Worldwide Governance Indicators."

46. Kaufman et al., "The Worldwide Governance Indicators."

47. See Kaufmann et al., "The Worldwide Governance Indicators."

48. A useful survey is by my own Cornell colleague David Ng "The Impact of Corruption on Financial Markets." He draws on his own work with Ciocchini and Durbin, "Does Corruption Increase Emerging Market Bond Spreads?," and with Lee, "Corruption and International Valuation: Does Virtue Pay?"

49. See Ciocchini, Durbin, and Ng, "Does Corruption Increase Emerging Market Bond Spreads?"

50. See Ciocchini, Durbin, and Ng, "Does Corruption Increase Emerging Market Bond Spreads?"

51. See Lee and David Ng, "Corruption and International Valuation."

52. See http://www.transparency.org/whoweare/history for a history of Transparency International. Transparency International's International Secretariat is located at Alt-Moabit 96, 10559 Berlin, Germany. Their latest report on the indices can be downloaded at http://www.transparency.org/cpi2013. They have most recently adjusted the scale of their index to a 100-point range from the 10-point range of the data used up through 2012.

53. See www.heritage.org and the most recent reports on the Index of Economic Freedom are at http://www.heritage.org/index/.

54. See Henisz, "The Institutional Environment for Economic Growth."

Chapter 10

1. The seminal studies that scholars always cite are Grubel, "Internationally Diversified Portfolios," and Levy and Sarnat, "International Diversification of Investment Portfolios."

2. There are useful surveys of the rich literature on the home-bias puzzle with lots of data on how the phenomenon persists today. I will furnish some data to support this view as of 2012 later in the chapter. The most-cited surveys include two by Karen Lewis, "Trying to Explain Home Bias in Equities and Consumption" and "Global Asset Pricing"; one by René Stulz and me (especially Section 3 of Karolyi and Stulz, "Are Assets Priced Locally

or Globally?"; and the most recent comprehensive one by Ian Cooper, Piet Sercu, and Rosanne Vanpée, "The Equity Home Bias Puzzle; A Survey."

3. See Cooper et al., "The Equity Home Bias Puzzle," and, in particular, the authors' conclusions.

4. Section 2 of the Karolyi and Stulz 2003 survey paper, "Are Assets Priced Locally or Globally?" is, in fact, titled "the perfect financial markets model."

5. See Grauer, Litzenberger, and Stehle, "Sharing Rules and Equilibrium in an International Market under Uncertainty," and Solnik, "An Equilibrium Model of the International Capital Market."

6. See Adler and Dumas, "International Portfolio Choice and Corporation Finance: A Synthesis."

7. Cooper and Kaplanis, "Home Bias in Equity Portfolios, Inflation Hedging, and International Capital Market Equilibrium."

8. See Baxter and Jermann, "The International Diversification Puzzle Is Worse Than You Think"; Glassman and Riddick, "What Causes Home Asset Bias and How Should It Be Measured?"; and Jermann, "International Portfolio Diversification and Endogenous Labor Supply Choice."

9. See Errunza, Hogan, and Hung, "Can the Gains from International Diversification Be Achieved without Trading Abroad?"

10. See Gehrig, "An Information Based Explanation of the Domestic Bias in International Equity Investment." Van Nieuwenburgh and Veldkamp develop a model in which investors choose to become more informed about a set of assets. In their model they incorporate the costs of becoming informed in their expectations of future asset returns. They find that the investors will choose to do so in assets where they are likely to have less of a competitive disadvantage. See Van Nieuwerburgh and Veldkamp, "Information Immobility and the Home Bias Puzzle," and "Information Acquisition and Under-Diversification." A nice test of the van Nieuwenburgh and Veldkamp model in a global context is by Andrade and Chhaochharia, "Information Immobility and Foreign Portfolio Investment."

11. See Dahlquist, Pinkowitz, Stulz, and Williamson, "Corporate Governance and the Home Bias"; Stulz, "The Limits of Financial Globalization."

12. The idea was established in René Stulz's American Finance Association Presidential Address in 2007 ("The Limits of Financial Globalization"). A useful analysis is also by Kho, Stulz, and Warnock, "Financial Globalization, Governance, and the Evolution of the Home Bias."

13. See Ferreira and Matos, "The Color of Investors' Money."

14. See Grinblatt and Keloharju, "How Distance, Language, and Culture Influence Stock-Holdings and Trades." A related study by Shiller, Kon-Ya, and Tsutsui, "Why Did the Nikkei Crash?," provides direct survey evidence of the familiarity bias that domestic investors typically expect domestic stocks to earn more than foreign investors do.

15. See Chan, Covrig, and Ng, "What Determines the Domestic Bias and Foreign Bias?"

16. I offer no prescription with this statement. This is an objective analysis of describing the data, not a normative one advocating how Singapore or any other country can improve its risk indicator scores to improve its lot before global investors.

17. A valuable suggestion I obtained from Marc Lipson at the Darden School of the University of Virginia was to introduce a multivariate regression model that controls for foreign investability constraints first, and then *incrementally* evaluated whether one of the

other five risk indicators offered explanatory power. I conducted this test and verified that each of the findings for Models (2), (5), (6), and (7) for market capacity constraints, limits to legal protections, corporate opacity, and political instability reliably hold up as in Table 10.1.

18. See Koepke, "Quantifying the Fed's Impact on Capital Flows to EMs," *Institute of International Finance Research Note*, December 4, 2013. Available at http://www.iif.com/emr/resources+3219.php. See Koepke's Chart 2 with data from EPFR Global, a data provider on global fund flows and allocations.

Chapter 11

1. See Rob Minto's analysis in his report "2013 in Review: Currency Winners and Losers," *Financial Times*, December 30, 2013. His graphic lays out the large spot return declines (relative to the US dollar, as the Argentine peso, the Chilean peso, the Colombian peso, the Philippine peso, the Indonesian rupiah, the Turkish lira, and the South African rand). The five noteworthy appreciating currencies in Minto's report were the Bulgarian lev, Romanian leu, Chinese renminbi yuan, the Polish zloty, and Hungarian forint. See http://blogs.ft.com/beyond-brics/2013/12/30/2013-in-review-currency-winners-and-losers/.

2. See the BIS report by Tarashev and Von Peter, "International Banking and Financial Market Developments." See http://www.bis.org/publ/qtrpdf/r_qt1312.pdf. They obtain data on net portfolio flows from various sources, including EPFR (Emerging Portfolio Fund Research, www.epfr.com). See Graph 2, which includes only 13 of my emerging markets commingled with Hong Kong and Singapore. Another report by Robin Koepke of the Institute for International Finance, "Quantifying the Fed's Impact on Capital Flows to EMs," states that about $73 billion in emerging market stocks and bonds were withdrawn by investors in 2013. See Chart 2 in the study, page 2. The report is available at www.iif.com/emr/resources+3219.php.

3. See report by Ye Xie, "Emerging Market Funds Outflow Surpass Total 2013 Sales," Bloomberg News, February 14, 2014. See http://www.bloomberg.com/news/2014-02-14/emerging-market-funds-outflow-surpass-total-2013-sales.html.

4. Among many news stories, see "Bernanke's QE Dance: Fed Could Taper in Next Two Meetings, Tightening Would Collapse the Market," *Forbes*, May 22, 2013. See http://www.forbes.com/sites/afontevecchia/2013/05/22/bernankes-qe-dance-fed-could-taper-in-next-two-meetings-tightening-would-collapse-the-market/. The exchange arose in the Joint Economic Committee with Congressman Kevin Brady, who specifically asked if the Fed's asset purchases could end before Labor Day in September. The chairman said that the latest quantitative-easing program was not based on a "fixed quantity," as the first two rounds were, but based on a "flow rate," which could be modified up or down in response to incoming data. See story by Brian Solomon, "Banks Lead US Stock Rally after Fed Announces Tapering," *Forbes*, December 18, 2013. See http://www.forbes.com/sites/briansolomon/2013/12/18/banks-lead-us-stock-rally-after-fed-announces-tapering/.

5. See a study by Barry Eichengreen and Poonam Gupta, "Tapering Talk."

6. The comments were made at a meeting with Russian President Vladimir Putin at the St. Petersburg G20 summit in September, asserting that "the U.S. should work to contribute to the stability of the global financial markets, and the steady recovery of the global economy." See "Russia and China Warn of 'Spillover Effect' on Global Economy from U.S. Stimulus Tapering," Russia Today.com, September 5, 2013. See http://rt.com/business/brics-warn-us-stimulus-tapering-453/. Former Russian Finance Minister Aleksey Kudrin argued that "easy

money in the U.S. is going to fundamentally influence the global economy . . . now we are witnessing an attempt to win time to reform the economy, to consolidate budgets, to cut expenses, to increase taxes, to overhaul social welfare, to stimulate some of the industries . . . at a certain point this additional stimulus will have to be gone and the economy will have to function on its own . . . will the global economy be able to? Which countries won't cope with the situation. We still don't know. So, we'll have to adapt to this new kind of situation. This is going to be a challenge." In the final communiqué of the G20 Summit, there was language compelling an "orderly and clearly communicated" manner of exit from easy monetary policy and a call for the United States to "think beyond its borders." See a useful perspective on this dimension by Barry Eichengreen, "Does the Federal Reserve Care about the Rest of the World?"

7. See article by George Parker, Courtney Weaver, and Charles Clover, "G20 Leaders Grapple with Risks of Reduced U.S. Monetary Stimulus," *Financial Times*, September 5, 2013, which quotes Ben Rhodes, a White House official, responding to the criticism: "I think that what has been demonstrated is we've pursued a pro-growth policy, and we believe that that ultimately is good for the global economy, because when the US economy is growing it helps provide momentum more broadly." See http://www.ft.com/intl/cms/s/0/7 4ad09b0-1610-11e3-a57d-00144feabdc0.html#axzz3HOPLoSg1.

8. I am not exactly sure who coined the term "taper tantrum," but Tyler Durden, a writer at the time at ZeroHedge.com, a blog site appears to have even predicted it before Chairman Bernanke's testimony before Congress. See http://www.zerohedge.com/news/2013-05-10/previewing-markets-taper-tantrum.

9. See "Did the Fed Sink the Emerging Markets?" CNBC.com, January 26, 2014 (http://www.cnbc.com/id/101364562) and "India's Raghuram Rajan Hits Out at Uncoordinated Global Policy," *Financial Times*, January 30, 2014. See http://www.ft.com/intl/cms/s/0/cc1d1716-89ac-11e3-abc4-00144feab7de.html#axzz3HOPLoSg1.

10. See "Fed Tapering Good from Mexico," CNBC.com, January 27, 2014 (http://www.cnbc.com/id/101365356).

11. An eloquent articulation of the weak fundamentals in emerging markets that allows the United States and the US dollar to rise paradoxically to the top is a new book by my Cornell colleague Eswar Prasad, *The Dollar Trap*. Part III of the book focuses on the inadequate institutions in most countries around the world.

12. See Koepke, "Quantifying the Fed's Impact on Capital Flows to EMs."

13. See Eichengreen and Gupta, "Tapering Talk."

14. See public statements by China's Premier Li Keqiang in the May 30 State Council meeting and China Banking Regulatory Commission vice-chair, Wang Zhaoxing, both as reported by Bloomberg News ("China Regulator Plans to Expand Credit as Growth Slows," June 6, 2014). See http://www.bloomberg.com/news/2014-06-06/china-banks-regulator-pledges-to-expand-credit-as-economy-slows.html .

15. The actual standard deviation of each of the individual risk indicators is built to equal one, but that of the average across the six indicators is only 0.73 units. So to compute the economic significance, I need to multiply the coefficient of 0.77 times that standard deviation of 0.73 to get the 0.56% increase in net flows as a fraction of total equity holdings in 2012.

16. See Eichengreen and Gupta, "Tapering Talk."

{ BIBLIOGRAPHY }

Acemoglu, Daron, and James Robinson. 2012. *Why Nations Fail.* New York: Crown Books.

Acemoglu, Daron, and Simon Johnson. 2005. "Unbundling Institutions." *Journal of Political Economy* 113, no. 5, 949–995.

Acemoglu, Daron, Simon Johnson, and James Robinson. 2001. "The Colonial Origins of Comparative Development: An Empirical Investigation." *American Economic Review* 91, no. 5, 1369–1401.

Adler, Michael, and Bernard Dumas. 1983. "International Portfolio Choice and Corporation Finance: A Synthesis." *Journal of Finance* 38, no. 3, 925–984.

Aggarwal, Reena, Isil Erel, René Stulz, and Rohan Williamson. 2009. "Differences in Governance Practices between U.S. and Foreign Firms: Measurement, Causes, and Consequences." *Review of Financial Studies* 22, no. 8, 3131–3169.

Aggarwal, Reena, Isil Erel, Miguel Ferreira, and Pedro Matos. 2011. "Does Governance Travel around the World? Evidence from Institutional Investors." *Journal of Financial Economics* 100, no. 1, 154–182.

Allen, Franklin, and Douglas Gale. 2000. *Comparing Financial Systems*, Cambridge, MA: The MIT Press.

Amihud, Yakov. 2002. "Illiquidity and Stock Return: Cross-Section and Time-Series Effects." *Journal of Financial Markets* 5, no. 1, 31–56.

Anderson, T. W. 1963. "Asymptotic Theory for Principal Components Analysis." *Annals of Mathematical Statistics* 34, no. 1, 122–148.

Anderson, T. W. 1984. *An Introduction to Multivariate Statistical Analysis*, 2nd edition. New York: Wiley.

Andrade, Sandro, and Vidhi Chhaochharia. 2010. "Information Immobility and Foreign Portfolio Investment." *Review of Financial Studies* 23, no. 6, 2429–2463.

Arora, Saurabh, Chiropriya Dasgupta, Anuj Jain, and G. Andrew Karolyi. 2010. "India Dials Africa: Bharti Airtel Acquires Zain's African Assets." Unpublished Cornell University Case Study, Ithaca, NY: Cornell University.

Arrow, K. J. 1964. "The Role of Securities in the Optimal Allocation of Risk-bearing." *Review of Economic Studies* 31, no. 2, 91–96.

Bai, Jushan, and Kunpeng Li. 2012. "Maximum Likelihood Estimation and Inference for Approximate Factor Models of High Dimension." Working Paper, Department of Economics, Columbia University, New York.

Bailey, Warren, G. Andrew Karolyi, and Carolina Salva. 2006. "The Economic Consequences of Increased Disclosure: Evidence from International Cross-listings." *Journal of Financial Economics* 81, no. 1, 175–214.

Ball, Ray. 2001. "Infrastructure Requirements for an Economically Efficient System of Public Financial Reporting and Disclosure." Brookings Institution Press, 127–169.

Barth, James R., Tong Li, Wenling Lu, and Glenn Yago, eds. 2010. *Capital Access Index 2009: Best Markets for Business Access to Capital*. Santa Monica, CA: Milken Institute (http://www.milkeninstitute.org/publications/view/430).

Barth, James, Don McCarthy, Triphon Phumiwasana, Susanne Trimbath, and Glenn Yago. 2002. *Capital Access Index 2002: Missing Markets: Global Barriers to Financing the Future*. Milken Institute Report, Santa Monica, CA (http://www.milkeninstitute.org/publications/view/126).

Baxter, Marianne, and Urban Jermann. 1997. "The International Diversification Puzzle Is Worse Than You Think." *American Economic Review* 87, no. 1, 170–802.

Beck, Thorsten, George Clarke, Alberto Groff, Philip Keefer, and Patrick Walsh. 2001. "New Tools in Comparative Political Economy: The Database of Political Institutions." *World Bank Economic Review* 15, no. 1, 165–176.

Beck, Thorsten, Asli Demirgüc-Kunt, and Ross Levine. 2000. "A New Database on the Structure and Development of the Financial Sector." *World Bank Economic Review* 14, no. 3, 597–605.

Beck, Thorsten, Asli Demirgüc-Kunt, and Ross Levine. 2010. "Financial Institutions and Markets across Countries and Over Time." *World Bank Economic Review* 24, no. 1, 77–92.

Bekaert, Geert. 1995. "Market Integration and Investment Barriers in Emerging Equity Markets." *World Bank Economic Review* 9, no. 1, 75–107.

Bekaert, Geert, and Campbell R. Harvey. 1995. "Time-Varying World Market Integration." *Journal of Finance* 50, no. 2, 403–444.

Bekaert, Geert, and Campbell R. Harvey. 1997. "Emerging Equity Market Volatility." *Journal of Financial Economics* 43, no. 1, 29–77.

Bekaert, Geert, and Campbell R. Harvey. 2000. "Foreign Speculators and Emerging Equity Markets." *Journal of Finance* 55, no. 2, 565–613.

Bekaert, Geert, and Campbell R. Harvey. 2003. "Emerging Markets Finance." *Journal of Empirical Finance* 10, no. 1-2, 3–55.

Bekaert, Geert, Campbell R. Harvey, and Robin L. Lumsdaine. 2002. "Dating the Integration of World Equity Markets." *Journal of Financial Economics* 65, no. 2, 203–247.

Bekaert, Geert, Campbell R. Harvey, and Christian Lundblad. 2001. "Emerging Equity Markets and Economic Development." *Journal of Development Economics* 66, no. 2, 465–504.

Bekaert, Geert, Campbell R. Harvey, and Christian Lundblad. 2005. "Does Financial Liberalization Spur Growth?" *Journal of Financial Economics* 77, no. 1, 3–55.

Bekaert, Geert, Campbell Harvey, Christian Lundblad, and Stefan Siegel. 2011. "What Segments Equity Markets?" *Review of Financial Studies* 24, no. 12, 3841–3890.

Bekaert, Geert, Campbell Harvey, Christian Lundblad, and Stephan Siegel. 2014. "Political Risk Spreads." *Journal of International Business Studies* 45, no. 4, 471–493.

Bekaert, Geert, and Robert Hodrick. 2009. *International Financial Management*. New York: Pearson Prentice Hall.

Bekaert, Geert, Robert Hodrick, and Xiaoyan Zhang. 2011. "International Stock Return Comovements." *Journal of Finance* 64, no. 6, 2591–2626.

Bekaert, Geert, and Michael S. Urias. 1996. "Diversification, Integration and Emerging Market Closed-End Funds." *Journal of Finance* 51, no. 3, 835–869.

Bergman, Nittai, and Daniel Nicolaievsky. 2007. "Investor Protection and the Coasian View." *Journal of Financial Economics* 84, no. 3, 738–771.

Bethmangalkar, Gopal, Armina Hakobyan, G. Andrew Karolyi, Gokul Rajagopalan, and Jeff West. 2012. "Oil and Natural Gas Company of India: Trouble off the Vietnamese Coast in 2011." Unpublished Cornell University Case Study, Ithaca, NY: Cornell University.

Bhagwati, Jagdish. 1998. "The Capital Myth. The Difference between Trade in Widgets and Dollars." *Foreign Affairs* 77, no. 3, 7–12.

Bhagwati, Jagdish. 2000. "Capital Market Liberalization, Economic Growth, and Instability," *World Development* 28, no. 6, 1075–1086.

Bhagwati, Jagdish. 2002. *Globalization and Its Discontents*. New York: Norton.

Bhattacharya, Utpal, and Hazem Daouk. 2002. "The World Price of Insider Trading." *Journal of Finance* 57, no. 1, 75–108.

Bhattacharya, U., H. Daouk, and M. Welker. 2003. "The World Price of Earnings Opacity." *Accounting Review* 78, no. 3, 641–678.

Black, Bernard. 2001. "The Legal and Institutional Preconditions for Strong Securities Markets." *UCLA Law Review* 48, no. 4, 781–855.

Bow, Dominic, Dingding Feng, G. Andrew Karolyi, Winston Lin, Aloka Singh, and Elisabeth Cai. 2011. "Spreadtrum Communications, 2011: Spreading into Mobile Telecommunications in China." Unpublished Cornell University Case Study, Ithaca, NY: Cornell University.

Brave, Scott, and Andrew Butters. 2011. "Monitoring Financial Stability: A Financial Conditions Index Approach." *Federal Reserve Bank of Chicago Economic Perspectives* First Quarter, 22–43.

Bris, Arturo, Will Goetzmann, and Ning Zhu. 2007. "Efficiency and the Bear: Short Sales and Markets around the World." *Journal of Finance* 62, no. 3, 1029–1079.

Brophy, David, Page Ouimet, and Clemens Sialm. 2004. "PIPE Dreams? The Performance of Companies Issuing Equity Privately." National Bureau of Economic Research Working Paper No. 11011, www.nber.org/papers/w11011.

Bushman, Robert M., Joseph D. Piotroski, and Abbie J. Smith. 2004. "What Determines Corporate Transparency?" *Journal of Accounting Research* 42, no. 2, 207–252.

Carrieri, Francesca, Ines Chaieb, and Vihang Errunza. 2013. "Do Implicit Barriers Matter for Globalization?" *Review of Financial Studies* 26, no. 7, 1694–1739.

Center for International Financial Analysis & Research. 1995. *International Accounting and Auditing Trends*, 4th edition. Princeton, NJ: Center for International Financial Analysis & Research Publications.

Chan, Kalok, Vicentiu Covrig, and Lilian Ng. 2005. "What Determines the Domestic Bias and Foreign Bias? Evidence from Mutual Fund Allocations Worldwide." *Journal of Finance* 60, no. 3, 1495–1534.

Chang, James, Tarun Khanna, and Krishna Palepu. 2000. "Analyst Activity Around the World." Working Paper, Harvard Business School, Cambridge, MA.

Chari, Anusha, and Peter Henry. 2004. "Risk Sharing and Asset Prices: Evidence from a Natural Experiment." *Journal of Finance* 59, no. 3, 1295–1324.

Chinn, Menzie, and Hiro Ito. 2006. "What Matters for Financial Development? Capital Controls, Institutions and Interactions." *Journal of Development Economics* 81, no. 1, 163–192.

Christensen, Hans, Luzi Hail, and Christian Leuz. 2013. "Mandatory IFRS Reporting and Changes in Enforcement." *Journal of Accounting and Economics* 56, no. 2-3, 147–177.

Čihák, Martin, Asli Demirgüç-Kunt, Erik Feyen, and Ross Levine. 2012. "Benchmarking Financial Systems Around the World." World Bank Policy Research Working Paper No. 6175, Washington, DC.

Ciocchini, Francisco, Erik Durbin, and David Ng. 2003. "Does Corruption Increase Emerging Market Bond Spreads?" *Journal of Economics and Business* 55, no. 5-6, 503–528.

Claessens, Stijn, Simeon Djankov, and Larry H. P. Lang. 2000. "The Separation of Ownership and Control in East Asian Corporations." *Journal of Financial Economics* 58, no. 1-2, 81–112.

Coase, Ronald. 1937. "The Nature of the Firm." *Economica* 4, no. 16, 386–405.

Coase, Ronald. 1960. "The Problem of Social Cost." *Journal of Law and Economics* 3, 1–44.

Coffee, John. 1999. "The Future as History: The Prospects for Global Convergence in Corporate Governance and its Implications." *Northwestern University Law Review* 93, no. 3, 641–708.

Cooper, Ian, and Evi Kaplanis. 1994. "Home Bias in Equity Portfolios, Inflation Hedging, and International Capital Market Equilibrium." *Review of Financial Studies* 7, no. 1, 45–60.

Cooper, Ian, Piet Sercu, and Rosanne Vanpée. 2014. "The Equity Home Bias Puzzle; A Survey." *Foundations and Trends in Finance* 7, no. 4, 289–416.

Cumming, Douglas, Sofia Johan, and Dan Li. 2011. "Exchange Trading Rules and Stock Market Liquidity." *Journal of Financial Economics* 99, no. 3, 651–671.

Dahlquist, Magnus, Lee Pinkowitz, René M. Stulz, and Rohan Williamson. 2003. "Corporate Governance and the Home Bias." *Journal of Financial and Quantitative Analysis* 38, no. 1, 87–111.

Damodaran, Aswath. 1994. *Damodaran on Valuation: Security Analysis for Investment and Corporate Finance.* New York: Wiley.

Daske, Holger, Luzi Hail, Christian Leuz, and Rodrigo Verdi. 2008. "Mandatory IFRS Reporting Around the World: Early Evidence on the Economic Consequences." *Journal of Accounting Research* 46, no. 5, 1085–1142.

Daske, Holger, Luzi Hail, Christian Leuz, and Rodrigo Verdi. 2013. "Adopting a Label; Heterogeneity in the Economic Consequences around IAS/IFRS Adoptions." *Journal of Accounting Research* 51, no. 3, 495–547.

Debreu, Gerard. 1972. *Theory of Value: An Axiomatic Analysis of Economic Equilibrium.* New Haven, CT: Yale University Press.

De Roon, Frans A., Theo E. Nijman, and Bas J.M. Werker. 2001. "Testing for Mean-Variance Spanning with Short Sales Constraints and Transaction Costs: The Case of Emerging Markets." *Journal of Finance* 56, no. 2, 721–742.

De Santis, Giorgio. 1993. "Asset Pricing and Portfolio Diversification: Evidence from Emerging Financial Markets." International Economics Department, Debt and International Finance Division, World Bank.

Demirgüç-Kunt, Asli, and Vojislav Maksimovic. 1998. "Law, Finance and Firm Growth." *Journal of Finance* 53, no. 6, 2107–2137.

Demirgüç-Kunt, Asli, and Vojislav Maksimovic. 1999. "Institutions, Financial Markets, and Firm Debt Maturity." *Journal of Financial Economics* 54, no. 3, 295–336.

Divecha, Arjun B., Jaime Drach, and Dan Stefek. 1992. "Emerging Markets: A Quantitative Perspective." *Journal of Portfolio Management* 19, no. 1, 41–50.

Djankov, Simeon, Rafael La Porta, Florencio Lopez-de-Silanes, and Andrei Shleifer. 2002. "The Regulation of Entry." *Quarterly Journal of Economics* 117, no. 1, 1–37.

Djankov, Simeon, Rafael La Porta, Florencio Lopez-de-Silanes, and Andrei Shleifer. 2003. "Courts." *Quarterly Journal of Economics* 118, no. 2, 453–517.

Djankov, Simeon, Rafael La Porta, Florencio Lopez-de-Silanes, and Andrei Shleifer. 2008. "The Law and Economics of Self-Dealing." *Journal of Financial Economics* 88, no. 3, 430–463.

Djankov, Simeon, Caralee McLiesh, and Andrei Shleifer. 2007. "Private Credit in 129 Countries." *Journal of Financial Economics* 84, no. 2, 299–329.

Doidge, Craig, G. Andrew Karolyi, Karl L. Lins, Darius Miller, and Rene M. Stulz. 2006. "Private Benefits of Control, Ownership and the Cross-Listing Decision." *Journal of Finance* 64, no. 1, 425–466.

Doidge, Craig, G. Andrew Karolyi, and Rene M. Stulz. 2004. "Why Are Foreign Firms Listed in the U.S. Worth More?" *Journal of Financial Economics* 71, no. 2, 205–238.

Doidge, Craig, G. Andrew Karolyi, and Rene Stulz. 2007. "Why Do Countries Matter So Much for Corporate Governance?" *Journal of Financial Economics* 86, no. 1, 1–39.

Doidge, Craig, G. Andrew Karolyi, and René Stulz. 2009. "Has New York Become Less Competitive than London in Global Markets? Evaluating Foreign Listing Choices Over Time." *Journal of Financial Economics* 91, no. 3, 253–277.

Doidge, Craig, G. Andrew Karolyi, and René Stulz. 2013. "The U.S. Left Behind? Financial Globalization and the Rise of IPOs Outside the U.S." *Journal of Financial Economics* 110, no. 3, 546–573.

Domowitz, Ian, Jack Glen, and Ananth Madhavan. 2001. "Liquidity, Volatility and Equity Trading Costs Across Countries and Over Time." *International Finance* 4, no. 2, 221–255.

Doz, Catherine, Domenico Giannone, and Lucrezia Reichlin. 2006. "A Quasi-Maximum Likelihood Approach for Large Approximate Dynamic Factor Models." Working Paper, European Central Bank, No. 674, Frankfurt, Germany.

Durnev, Art, and E. Han Kim. 2005. "To Steal or Not to Steal: Firm Attributes, Legal Environment, and Valuation." *Journal of Finance* 60, no. 3, 1461–1493.

Dyck, Alexander, and Luigi Zingales. 2004. "Private Benefits of Control: An International Comparison." *Journal of Finance* 59, no. 2, 537–600.

Edison, H., and F. Warnock. 2003. "A Simple Measure of the Intensity of Capital Controls." *Journal of Empirical Finance* 10, no. 1, 81–103.

Eichengreen, Barry. 2013. "Does the Federal Reserve Care about the Rest of the World?" National Bureau of Economic Research Working Paper No. 19405, available at www.nber.org/papers/w19405.

Eichengreen, Barry, and Poonam Gupta. 2014. "Tapering Talk: The Impact of Expectations of Reduced Federal Reserve Security Purchases on Emerging Markets. Development Economics Vice Presidency, Operations and Strategy Unit, World Bank, Washington, DC.

Engerman, Stanley L., and Kenneth L. Sokoloff. 2002. "Factor Endowments, Inequality and Paths of Development among New World Economies." *Economica* 3, no. 1, 41–102.

Errunza, Vihang. 1977. "Gains from Portfolio Diversification into Less Developed Countries' Securities." *Journal of International Business Studies* 8, no. 2, 83–99.

Errunza, Vihang, Ked Hogan, and Mao-Wei Hung. 1999. "Can the Gains From International Diversification Be Achieved Without Trading Abroad?" *Journal of Finance* 54, no. 6, 2075–2107.

Esty, Benjamin. 2003. *Modern Project Finance: A Casebook*. New York: Wiley.

Faccio, Mara, and Larry H. P. Lang. 2002. "The Ultimate Ownership of Western European Corporations." *Journal of Financial Economics* 65, no. 3, 365–395.

Fama, Eugene, and Kenneth French. 2012. "Size, Value, and Momentum in International Stock Returns." *Journal of Financial Economics* 105, no. 3, 457–472.

Federal Reserve Board of Governors. 2013. Federal Reserve Statistical Release, Financial Accounts of the United States: Flow of Funds, Balance Sheets, and Integrated Macroeconomic Accounts, Board of Governors of the Federal Reserve. Washington, DC.

Ferreira, Miguel, and Pedro Matos. 2008. "The Color of Investors' Money: The Role of Institutional Investors around the World." *Journal of Financial Economics* 88, no. 3, 499–533.

Fong, Kingsley, Craig Holden, and Charles Trzcinka. 2014. "What Are the Best Liquidity Proxies for Global Research?" Social Science Research Network Working Paper No. 1558447, http://ssrn.com/abstract=1558447.

Freeman, Ben, G. Andrew Karolyi, James Lewis, Vanida Wongdechsareekul, Ifat Wong. and Elisabeth Cai, 2011. "Pulkovo Airport Expansion Project." Unpublished Cornell University Case Study, Ithaca, NY: Cornell University.

FTSE International. 2013. FTSE Frontier 50 Index Fact Sheet, December 31, FTSE International: London.

Gaeta, Gordian. 2013. *Opportunities in Emerging Markets: Investing in the Economies of Tomorrow*. New York: Wiley.

Gagnon, Louis, and G. Andrew Karolyi. 2010. "Multimarket Trading and Arbitrage." *Journal of Financial Economics* 97, no. 1, pages 53–80.

Gehrig, Thomas. 1993. "An Information Based Explanation of the Domestic Bias in International Equity Investment." *Scandinavian Journal of Economics* 95, no. 1, 97–109.

Gill, Amar. 2001. Corporate Governance in Emerging Markets: Saints and Sinners, Who's Got Religion? CLSA Emerging Markets Report, Credit Lyonnais Securities Asia, New York.

Girshick, M. Hermann. 1939. "On the Sampling Theory of Roots of Determinantal Equations." *Annals of Mathematical Statistics* 10, no. 3, 203–224.

Glaeser, Edward, Simon Johnson, and Andrei Shleifer. 2001. "Coase Versus the Coasians." *Quarterly Journal of Economics* 116, no. 3, 853–899.

Glassman, Debra, and Leigh A. Riddick. 2002. "What Causes Home Asset Bias and How Should It Be Measured?" *Journal of Empirical Finance* 8, no. 1, 35–54.

Goldsmith, Raymond. 1969. *Financial Structure and Development*. New Haven, CT: Yale University Press.

Goldestone, Jack A., Robert H. Bates, David L. Epstein, Ted Robert Gurr, Michael B. Lustik, Monty G. Marshall, Jay Ulfelder, and Mark Woodward. 2010. "A Global Model for Forecasting Political Instability." *American Journal of Political Science* 54, no. 1, 190–208.

Gompers, Paul, Joy Ishii, and Andrew Metrick. 2003. "Corporate Governance and Equity Prices." *Quarterly Journal of Economics* 118, no. 1, 107–155.

Gorsuch, R. L. 1990. "Common Factor Analysis Versus Component Analysis: Some Well and Little Known Facts." *Multivariate Behavioral Research* 25, no. 1, 33–39.

Grauer, Frederick, Robert Litzenberger, and Richard Stehle. 1976. "Sharing Rules and Equilibrium in an International Market under Uncertainty." *Journal of Financial Economics* 3, no. 3, 233–256.

Griffin, John, Patrick Kelley, and Federico Nardari, 2010. "Do Market Efficiency Measures Yield Correct Inferences? A Comparison of Developed and Emerging Markets," *Review of Financial Studies* 23, no. 11, 3225–3277.

Grinblatt, Mark, and Matti Keloharju. 2001. "How Distance, Language, and Culture Influence Stock-Holdings and Trades." *Journal of Finance* 56, no. 3, 1053–1073.

Grubel, Herbert. 1968. "Internationally Diversified Portfolios: Welfare Gains and Capital Flows." *American Economic Review* 58, no. 5, 1299–1314.

Han, Kwangsuk, Yeonho Lee, and Chanil Park. 2013. "Legal Frameworks and Credit Information Systems in China, Korea, and Singapore." *Asian-Pacific Economic Literature* 27, no. 1, 147–155.

Hargis, Kent. 1998. "Do Foreign Investors Stimulate or Inhibit Stock Market Development in Latin America?" *Quarterly Review of Economics and Finance* 38, no. 3, 303–318.

Harris, Larry. 2003. *Trading and Exchanges*. New York: Oxford University Press.

Henisz, Witold. 2000. "The Institutional Environment for Economic Growth." *Economics and Politics* 12, no. 1, 1–31.

Henry, Peter Blair. 2000a. "Do Stock Market Liberalizations Cause Investment Booms?" *Journal of Financial Economics* 58, no. 1-2, 301–334.

Henry, Peter Blair. 2000b. "Stock Market Liberalization, Economic Reform, and Emerging Market Equity Prices." *Journal of Finance* 55, no. 2, 529–564.

Högbom, Carl Johan, and Henrik Wagenius. 2011. "Growing Need for Innovative SME Exchanges in Europe." Focus Newsletter, December. Paris: World Federation of Stock Exchanges.

Hotelling, Harold. 1933. "Analysis of a Complex of Statistical Variables into Principal Components." *Journal of Educational Psychology* 24, no. 6, 417–441.

Hotelling, Harold. 1936. "Relations Between Two Sets of Variates." *Biometrika* 27, no. 3-4, 321–327.

Hou, Kewei, G. Andrew Karolyi, and Bong-Chan Kho. 2011. "What Factors Drive Global Stock Returns?" *Review of Financial Studies* 24, no. 8, 2527–2574.

Houston, Joel, Chen Lin, and Yue Ma. 2012. "Regulatory Arbitrage and International Bank Flows." *Journal of Finance* 67, no. 5, 1845–1895.

Hugill, Andrea, and Jordan Siegel. 2013. "Which Does More to Determine the Quality of Corporate Governance in Emerging Economies, Firms or Countries?" Working Paper, Harvard Business School, No. 13-055, Cambridge, MA.

International Finance Corporation. 1999. *Emerging Stock Markets Factbook 1999*. Washington, DC: International Finance Corporation.

International Monetary Fund. 2013. *World Economic Outlook: Transitions and Tensions (October 2013)*. Washington, DC: International Monetary Fund.

Jain, Anchara, Pankaj Jain, Thomas McInish, and Michael McKenzie. 2013. "The Worldwide Reach of Short Selling Regulations." *Journal of Financial Economics* 109, no. 1, 177–197.

Jermann, Urban. 2002. "International Portfolio Diversification and Endogenous Labor Supply Choice." *European Economic Review* 46, no. 3, 507–522.

Jin, Li, and Stewart Myers. 2006. "R2 Around the World: New Theory and New Tests." *Journal of Financial Economics* 79, no. 2, 257–292.

John, Kose, and Simi Kedia. 2003. "Institutions, Markets, and Growth: A Theory of Comparative Corporate Governance." Unpublished Working Paper, New York University, New York.

John, Kose, and Simi Kedia. 2004. "Design of Corporate Governance: Monitored Debt, Takeovers, and Ownership Structure." Unpublished Working Paper, New York University, New York.

Johnson, Simon, Peter Boone, A. Breach, and E. Friedman. 2000. "Corporate Governance in the Asian Financial Crisis." *Journal of Financial Economics* 58, no. 1-2, 141–186.

Johnson, Simon, Rafael La Porta, Florencio Lopez-de-Silanes, and Andrei Shleifer. 2000. "Tunneling." *American Economic Review Papers and Proceedings* 90, no. 2, 22–27.

JP Morgan Securities. 2013. *Local Markets Guide: Emerging Markets Research* (9th edition). New York: JP Morgan Securities.

Kakde, Uma, G. Andrew Karolyi, Kristin O'Planick, Kevin Shuller, and Jennifer Walvoord. 2010. "Grupo Modelo: Trouble Brewing in the Global Beer Industry." Unpublished Cornell University Case Study, Ithaca, NY: Cornell University.

Kalemli-Ozcan, Sebnem, Bent Sørensen, and Oved Yosha. 2003. "Risk Sharing and Industrial Specialization: Regional and International Evidence." *American Economic Review* 93, no. 3, 903–918.

Karolyi, G. Andrew. 2004. "ADRs and the Development of Emerging Equity Markets." *Review of Economics and Statistics* 86, no. 3, 670–690.

Karolyi, G. Andrew, Kuan-Hui Lee, and Mathijs van Dijk. 2012. "Understanding Commonality in Liquidity Around the World." *Journal of Financial Economics* 105, no. 1, 82–112.

Karolyi, G. Andrew, and Rene M. Stulz. 2003. "Are Assets Priced Locally or Globally?" In G. Constantinides, M. Harris, and R. Stulz, eds., *The Handbook of the Economics of Finance*. New York: North Holland Publishers, 975–1020.

Karolyi, G. Andrew, and Rene M. Stulz. 2003. *International Capital Markets*. Volume 12 of the International Library of Critical Writings in Financial Economics. London: Edward Elgar Publishers.

Karolyi, G. Andrew, and Ying Wu. 2012. "The Role of Investability Restrictions on Size, Value, and Momentum in International Stock Returns." Social Science Research Network Working Paper No.2043156, http://papers.ssrn.com/sol3/papers.cfm?abstract_id=2043156.

Karolyi, G. Andrew, and Ying Wu. 2014. "Size, Value, and Momentum in International Stock Returns: A New Partial-Segmentation Approach." Working Paper, Johnson Graduate School of Management, Cornell University, Ithaca, NY.

Kaufmann, Daniel, Aart Kraay, and Massimo Mastruzzi. 2003. "Governance Matters III: Governance Indicators for 1996, 1998, 2000, and 2002." *World Bank Economic Review* 18, no. 2, 253–287.

Kaufmann, Daniel, Aart Kraay, and Massimo Mastruzzi. 2005. "Governance Matters IV: Governance Indicators for 1996–2004." World Bank Policy Research Department Working Paper. Washington, DC: The World Bank.

Kaufmann, Daniel, Aart Kraay, and Massimo Mastruzzi. 2010. "The Worldwide Governance Indicators: Methodology and Analytical Issues." World Bank Policy Research Department Working Paper No. 5430 (September). Washington, DC: The World Bank.

Kaufmann, Daniel, Aart Kraay, and Pablo Zoido-Lobaton. 1999a. "Aggregating Governance Indicators." World Bank Policy Research Department Working Paper No. 2195. Washington, DC: The World Bank.

Kaufmann, Daniel, Aart Kraay, and Pablo Zoido-Lobaton. 1999b. "Governance Matters." World Bank Policy Research Department Working Paper No. 2196. Washington, DC: The World Bank.

Khanna, Tarun, Joseph Kogan, and Krishna Palepu. 2006. "Globalization and Similarities in Corporate Governance: A Cross-Country Analysis." *Review of Economics and Statistics* 88, no. 1, 69–90.

Khanna, Tarun, Krishna Palepu, and Suraj Srinivasan. 2004. "Disclosure Practices of Foreign Companies Interacting with US Markets." *Journal of Accounting Research* 42, no. 2, 475–508.

Kho, Bong-Chan, Rene Stulz, and Francis Warnock. 2009. "Financial Globalization, Governance and the Evolution of the Home Bias." *Journal of Accounting Research* 47, no. 2, 597–635.

Kim, E. Han, and Vijay Singal. 2000. "Stock Market Openings: Experience of Emerging Economies." *Journal of Business* 73, no. 1, 25–66.

King, Robert, and Ross Levine. 1993. "Finance and Growth: Schumpeter Might be Right." *Quarterly Journal of Economics* 108, no. 3, 717–737.

Klapper, Leora F., and Inessa Love. 2004. "Corporate Governance, Investor Protection, and Performance in Emerging Markets." *Journal of Corporate Finance* 10, no. 5, 703–728.

Koepke, Robin. 2013. "Quantifying the Fed's Impact on Capital Flows to Ems." Institute of International Finance Research Note, December 4, Washington, DC: The Institute of International Finance.

Kose, Ayhan. 2002. "Explaining Business Cycles in Small-Open Economies: How Much Do World Prices Matter?" *Journal of International Economics* 56, no. 2, 299–327.

Kose, Ayhan, Eswar Prasad, Kenneth Rogoff, and Shang-Jin Wei. 2009. "Financial Globalization: A Reappraisal." Washington, DC: IMF Staff Papers 56, no. 1, 8–62.

Kyle, Albert. 1985. "Continuous Auctions and Insider Trading." *Econometrica* 53, no. 6, 1315–1336.

La Porta, Rafael, Florencio Lopez-de-Silanes, and Andrei Shleifer. 1999. "Corporate Ownership around the World." *Journal of Finance* 54, no. 2, 471–518.

La Porta, Rafael, Florencio Lopez-de-Silanes, and Andrei Shleifer. 2006. "What Works in Securities Laws." *Journal of Finance* 61, no. 1, 1–32.

La Porta, Rafael, Florencio Lopez-de-Silanes, and Andrei Shleifer. 2008. "The Economic Consequences of Legal Origins." *Journal of Economic Literature* 46, no. 2, 285–332.

La Porta, Rafael, Florencio Lopez-de-Silanes, Andrei Shleifer, and Robert Vishny. 1997. "Legal Determinants of External Finance." *Journal of Finance* 52, no. 3, 1131–1150.

La Porta, Rafael, Florencio Lopez-de-Silanes, Andrei Shleifer, and Robert Vishny. 1998. "Law and Finance." *Journal of Political Economy* 106, no. 6, 1113–1155.

La Porta, Rafael, Florencio Lopez-De-Silanes, Andrei Shleifer, and Robert Vishny. 2002. "Investor Protection and Corporate Valuation." *Journal of Finance* 57, no. 3, 1147–1170.

Lane, Philip, and Gian Milesi-Ferretti. 2001. "The External Wealth of Nations: Measures of Foreign Assets and Liabilities for Industrial and Developing Nations." *Journal of International Economics* 55, no. 2, 263–294.

Lane, Philip, and Gian Milesi-Ferretti. 2007. "The External Wealth of Nations Mark II: Revised and Extended Estimates of Foreign Assets and Liabilities, 1970–2004." *Journal of International Economics* 73, no. 2, 223–250.

Lang, Mark, and Mark Maffett. 2011. "Transparency and Liquidity Uncertainty in Crisis Periods." *Journal of Accounting and Economics* 52, no. 2, 101–125.

Larcker, David, Scott Richardson, and Irem Tuna. 2005. "How Important Is Corporate Governance." Working Paper, Wharton School of Business, University of Pennsylvania, Philadelphia.

Larcker, David, Scott Richardson, and Irem Tuna. 2007. "How Important Is Corporate Governance?" *The Accounting Review* 83, no. 4, 963–1008.

Lee, Charles, and David Ng. 2009. "Corruption and International Valuation: Does Virtue Pay?" *Journal of Investing* 18, no. 4, 23–41.

Lee, Kuan-Hui. 2011. "The World Market Price of Liquidity Risk." *Journal of Financial Economics* 99, no. 1, 136–161.

Lesmond, David A. 2005. "Liquidity of Emerging Markets." *Journal of Financial Economics* 77, no. 2, 411–452.

Lesmond, D. A., J. P. Ogden, and C. A. Trzcinka. 1999. "A New Estimate of Transaction Costs." *Review of Financial Studies* 12, no. 5, 1113–1141.

Leuz, Christian, D. Nanda, and Peter Wysocki. 2003. "Earnings Management and Investor Protection." *Journal of Financial Economics* 69, no. 3, 505–527.

Levine, Ross. 1997. "Financial Development and Economic Growth: Views and Agenda." *Journal of Economic Literature* 35, no. 2, 688–726.

Levine, Ross. 2005. "Law, Endowments and Property Rights." *Journal of Economic Perspectives* 19, no. 3, 61–88.

Levine, Ross, and Sara Zervos. 1998. "Stock Markets, Banks, and Economic Growth." *American Economic Review* 88, no. 3, 537–558.

Levy, Haim, and Marshall Sarnat. 1970. "International Diversification of Investment Portfolios." *American Economic Review* 60, no. 4, 668–675.

Lewis, Karen. 1999. "Global Asset Pricing." *Annual Review of Financial Economics* 3, 435–466.

Lewis, Karen. 1999. "Trying to Explain Home Bias in Equities and Consumption." *Journal of Economic Literature* 37, no. 2, 571–608.

Lins, Karl V. 2003. "Equity Ownership and Firm Value in Emerging Markets." *Journal of Financial and Quantitative Analysis* 38, no. 1, 185–212.

Lucas, Robert. 1990. "Why Doesn't Capital Flow from Rich to Poor Countries?" *American Economic Review* 80, no. 2, 92–96.

Marr, Julian, and Cherry Reynard. 2013. *Investing in Emerging Markets: The BRIC Economies and Beyond.* New York: Wiley.

Marshall, Monty, and Benjamin Cole. 2011. *Global Stability Report: Conflict, Governance and State Fragility.* New York: Center for Systemic Peace.

McGaw, Ian W. T. 2004. *The World Clearing Houses: A Comprehensive Report and Analysis of Clearing for Exchange Traded and OTC Products.* Futures & Options World.

Mobius, Mark. 2012. *The Little Book of Emerging Markets: How to Make Money in the World's Fastest Growth Markets*. New York: Wiley.

Morck, Randall, Bernard Yeung, and Wayne Yu. 2000. "The Information Content of Stock Markets: Why Do Emerging Markets Have Synchronous Stock Price Movements?" *Journal of Financial Economics* 58, no. 1-2, 215–260.

Morgan Stanley Capital International. 2013. *Global Market Accessibility Review* (June). New York: Morgan Stanley Capital International.

Nenova, Tatiana. 2003. "The Value of Corporate Voting Rights and Control: A Cross-Country Analysis." *Journal of Financial Economics* 68, no. 3, 325–357.

Ng, David. 2006. "The Impact of Corruption on Financial Markets." *Managerial Finance* 32, no. 10, 822–836.

O'Hara, Maureen. 1995. *Market Microstructure Theory*. Oxford: Blackwell.

O'Neil, Jim. 2011. *The Growth Map: Economic Opportunity in the BRICs and Beyond*. London: Penguin.

Obstfeld, Maurice. 1994. "Risk-Taking, Global Diversification, and Growth." *American Economic Review* 84, no. 5, 1310–1329.

Pagano, Marco, and Paolo Volpin. 2005. "Political Economy of Corporate Governance." *American Economic Review* 95, no. 4, 1005–1030.

Pagano, Marco, and Paolo Volpin. 2006. "Shareholder Protection, Stock Market Development and Politics." *Journal of the European Economics Association* 4, no. 2-3, 315–341.

Patel, Sandeep, Amra Balic, and Liliane Bwakira. 2002. "Measuring Transparency and Disclosure at Firm-level in Emerging Markets." *Emerging Markets Review* 3, no. 3, 310–337.

Pearson, K. 1901. "On Lines and Planes of Closest Fit to Systems of Points in Space." *Philosophical Magazine* 6, no. 2, 559–572.

Perold, André. 1995. "The Payment System and Derivative Instruments." In D. Crane, K. Froot, S. Mason, André Perold, Robert Merton, Zvi Bodie, Erik Sirri and Peter Tufano, eds., *The Global Financial System: A Functional Perspective*. Cambridge, MA: Harvard Business School Press, 1–291.

Piketty, Thomas. 2014. *Capitalism in the Twenty-first Century*. Cambridge, MA: Harvard University Press.

Prasad, Prasad. 2014. *The Dollar Trap: How the U.S. Dollar Tightened its Grip on Global Finance*. Princeton, NJ: Princeton University Press.

Pukthuanthong, Kuntara, and Richard Roll. 2009. "Global Market Integration: A Better Way to Measure *t* and Its Application." *Journal of Financial Economics* 94, no. 2, 214–232.

Karolyi, G. Andrew, Cheng Qiu, Yina Shi, Andreas Skiadopoulos, and Dong Yang. 2011. "Folli Follie Group and Fosun International: A Global Partnership." Unpublished Cornell University Case Study, Ithaca, NY: Cornell University.

Quinn, Dennis. 1997. "The Correlates of Changes in International Financial Regulation." *American Political Science Review* 91, no. 3, 531–551.

Quinn, Dennis, and A. Maria Toyoda. 2008. "Does Capital Account Liberalization Lead to Growth?" *Review of Financial Studies* 21, no. 3, 1403–1449.

Rajan, Raghuram, and Luigi Zingales. 1998. "Financial Dependence and Growth." *American Economic Review* 88, no. 3, 559–586.

Rajan, Raghuram, and Luigi Zingales. 2003. "The Great Reversals: The Politics of Financial Development in the 20th Century." *Journal of Financial Economics* 69, no. 1, 5–49.

Rey, Helene. 2013. "Dilemma Not Trilemma: The Global Financial Cycle and Monetary Policy Independence." Working Paper, London Business School, Center for Economic Policy Research, and National Bureau for Economic Research, www.kc.frb.org/publicat/sympos/2013/2013Rey.pdf.

Rodrik, Dani. 1998. "Who Needs Capital-Account Convertibility?" In Fischer, Stanley, Richard N. Cooper, Rudiger Dornbusch, Peter M. Garber, Carlos Massad, Jacques J. Polak, Dani Rodrik, and Savak S. Tarapore, eds., *Essays in International Finance* No. 207. Princeton, NJ: Princeton University, 55–65.

Roll, Richard. 1984. "A Simple Implicit Measure of the Effective Bid-Ask Spread in an Efficient Market." *Journal of Finance* 39, no. 4, 1127–1139.

Roweis, Sam. 1998. "EM Algorithms for PCA and SPCA." *Neural Information Processing Systems* 10, 626–632.

Salomon Smith Barney. 2000. *Salomon Smith Barney Guide to World Equity Markets.* London: Euromoney Books, Euromoney Institutional Investor Publishers.

Saunders, A., and B. Scholnick. 2006. "Introduction to Special Issue on Frontiers in Payment and Settlement Systems." *Journal of Banking and Finance* 30, no. 6, 1605–1612.

Shiller, Robert, Fumiko Kon-Ya, and Yoshiro Tsutsui. 1996. "Why Did the Nikkei Crash? Expanding the Scope of Expectations Data Collection." *Review of Economics and Statistics* 78, no. 1, 156–164.

Shleifer, Andrei, and Robert Vishny. 1997. "A Survey of Corporate Governance." *Journal of Finance* 52, no. 2, 737–783.

Shleifer, Andrei, and Daniel Wolfenzon. 2002. "Investor Protection and Equity Markets." *Journal of Financial Economics* 66, no. 1, 3–27.

Solnik, Bruno. 1974. "An Equilibrium Model of the International Capital Market." *Journal of Economic Theory* 8, no. 4, 500–524.

Søreide, Tina. 2006. "Is it Wrong to Rank? A Critical Assessment of Corruption Indices." Working Paper, Chr. Michelsen Institute, Bergen, Norway.

Spamann, Holger. 2010. "The 'Anti-Director Rights Index' Revisited." *Review of Financial Studies* 23, no. 2, 467–486.

Standard and Poor's. 2013. *S&P Frontier Indices Methodology (July 2013).* New York: Standard and Poor's.

Stiglitz, Joseph. 2000. "Capital Market Liberalization, Economic Growth, and Instability." *World Development* 28, no. 6, 1075–1086.

Stiglitz, Joseph. 2002. *Globalization and Its Discontents.* New York: Norton.

Stock, James H., and Mark W. Watson. 2002. "Forecasting Using Principal Components from a Large Number of Predictors." *Journal of the American Statistical Association* 97, no. 460, 1167–1179.

Stulz, René. 1999. "Globalization, Corporate Finance, and the Cost of Capital." *Journal of Applied Corporate Finance* 12, no. 3, 8–25.

Stulz, René M. 2005. "The Limits of Financial Globalization." *Journal of Finance* 60, no. 4, 1595–1638.

Stulz, René. 2009. "Securities Laws, Disclosure and National Capital Markets in the Age of Financial Globalization." *Journal of Accounting Research* 47, no. 2, 349–390.

Subramanian, Krishnamurthy, and Frederick Tung. 2014. "Law and Project Finance." Social Science Research Network Working Paper No. 972415, forthcoming at the Journal of Financial Intermediation.

Tarashev, Nikola, and Goetz von Peter. 2013. "International Banking and Financial Market Developments." *BIS Quarterly Review* (December), 1–82.

Trier, Shawn, and Simon Jackman. 2008. "Democracy as a Latent Variable." *American Journal of Political Science* 52, no. 1, 201–217.

Van Agtmael, Antoine. 2007. *The Emerging Markets Century: How a New Breed of World-Class Companies Is Overtaking the World.* New York: Simon and Shuster.

Van Nieuwerburgh, Stijn, and Laura Veldkamp. 2009. "Information Immobility and the Home Bias Puzzle." *Journal of Finance* 64, no. 3, 1187–1215.

Van Nieuwerburgh, Stijn, and Laura Veldkamp. 2010. "Information Acquisition and Under-Diversifcation." *Review of Economic Studies* 77, no. 2, 779–805.

Watson, Mark W., and Robert F. Engle. 1983. "Alternative Algorithms for the Estimation of Dynamic Factor, Mimic and Varying Coefficient Regression Models." *Journal of Econometrics* 23, no. 3, 385–400.

Williamson, Oliver. 1981. "The Economics of Organization: The Transaction Cost Approach." *American Journal of Sociology* 87, no. 3, 548–577.

INDEX

The letter *f* following a page number denotes a figure, the letter *n* denotes a note, and the letter *t* denotes a table.